Prince FAQ

Prince FAQ

All That's Left to Know About the Purple Reign

Arthur Lizie

Backbeat
Books

Guilford, Connecticut

Backbeat Books
An imprint of The Rowman & Littlefield Publishing Group, Inc.
4501 Forbes Blvd., Ste. 200
Lanham, MD 20706
www.rowman.com

Distributed by NATIONAL BOOK NETWORK

The FAQ series was conceived by Robert Rodriguez and developed with Stuart Shea.

Book design by Snow Creative Services

British Library Cataloguing in Publication Information available

Library of Congress Cataloging-in-Publication Data available

ISBN 978-1-61713-670-2 (paperback)
ISBN 978-1-4930-5143-4 (e-book)

♾️™ The paper used in this publication meets the minimum requirements of American National Standard for Information Sciences—Permanence of Paper for Printed Library Materials, ANSI/NISO Z39.48-1992

Contents

Introduction

Welcome 2 the Dawn

Yeah, I'm a white guy.

I grew up in Manchester, New Hampshire, in the 1970s. As I remember it, there were no black people in Manchester in the 1970s. I saw black faces on trips to Boston, including visits to the still racially suspect Fenway Park. And my favorite baseball player was Red Sox left fielder Jim Rice. But these periodic sojourns and watching Rice on TV didn't instill a deep knowledge of African American culture.

I was into rock and punk when first acquainted with Prince in high school. I was introduced not by the one black person in my 2,000-student high school but by a neighbor who incorporated "1999" into his New Wave playlist. *Purple Rain* soon followed, and I was a fan. But in my world of U2, the Who, and the Smiths, Prince was still "The Other."

But I put in my time. I camped overnight at Ticketron that winter but didn't get tickets to either of Prince's March 1985 Worcester Centrum gigs (he didn't play an official Boston date from 1982 to 1997). But I have enjoyed the March 28 soundboard recording that leaked in 2016.

While in college, Prince ceased to be "The Other" and became "The One." He was "The One" in part because he was everything that I'm not: black, funky, erotic, and spiritual. It's not that I ever wanted to be black, not even in a sardonic, Lou Reed way, just that Prince opened windows on a fascinating culture I barely knew existed. A similar cultural awakening and obsession happened when I spent a month in Rome. Now people ask me if I'm Italian, but no one's ever asked me if I'm black.

The other thing Prince was that I'm not is obscenely talented musically. And it's that talent—writing, performing, producing—that really hooked me. And it's what this book is about.

The August 1988 Iron Horse show from The Hague finally sent me down the rabbit hole. The concept of an aftershow was unbelievable. Not only did Prince play a whole show after another show, but it was totally different and included unreleased songs! A band like U2 would play a handful of rarities during a yearlong tour, and Prince outdid them in one night. It was mind blowing. And that's without mentioning the guitar on "Rave Un2 the Joy Fantastic," still one of best things ever committed to tape. The whole thing was genius.

And that's also what this book is about—genius or, at least, amazing artistic creativity.

In his 1996 book *Creativity: The Work and Lives of 91 Eminent People*, Mihaly Csikszentmihalyi identified ten "antithetical traits" possessed by truly creative people. We know that Prince was creative, but it's shocking how integral some of these traits were to his persona. According to Csikszentmihalyi, creative people

- have a great deal of energy that's not ruled by the clock (often this energy is expressed sexually),
- are both extroverted and introverted,
- avoid strict gender categorizations, and
- are both rebellious and conservative.

While this book is not a psychological analysis of Prince, at times I do speculate on his thought process: Traces of these "antithetical traits" can be seen on almost every page.

The book is also not a critical analysis, although it makes clear what work I most value. Instead, it's a loose chronological history told through a look at Prince's audio and video output, his live performances, and his work with band members, associated artists, and protégés.

My work is deeply indebted to all sources in the selected bibliography, but Prince Vault (http://www.princevault.com) make me wanna holler extra loud. The site's fastidious research provides the online Prince community with an authoritative and reliable repository of Prince facts. It's an invaluable resource.

I would also like to acknowledge the support and feedback given to me by Ric Dube, Duane Tudahl, Alex Hahn, and many other correspondents over the years and editor Bernadette Malavarca.

The following sources have been kind enough to share their images for the book: Femke Niehof (unused-prince-tickets.com), Jeff Munson, Stéphane "Zed" Counil, Bob Poppo, and Ric Dube.

I'd also like to thank my alternative recording connections over the years, especially "My friend Dave" and Ron at Inner Light, the merchants who showed up at the University of New Hampshire's MUB every few months with cassettes, the unusually masculine telephone presence "Karen," and Dr. K.

Finally, I thank my family, Susan, Eloise, and Orson, for allowing me to mentally disappear for months of research and writing. I do it for you and couldn't do it without you.

Beginning Endlessly

7 Heck-a-Slammin' Ideas about Prince

Prince claimed that digital technology "can't be good for you" because it packed your head with numbers. But his head often seemed packed with numbers, from the apocalypse of "1999" to "the numbers" for his latest release to that "kickdrum pound on the 2 and 4." But it's folly to make those numbers mean too much. Musicology? Sure. Numerology? Not so much.

But one number seemed more important: 7. Prince was brought up a Seventh-day Adventist. He wrote the Time's "777-9311"—Dez Dickerson's phone number, which means he probably had the 777 telephone exchange as a kid. There are the songs "7" and "77 Beverly Park," the latter also his Beverly Hills address. And there are website fees: $77/year, $7.77/month, $1.77/video download. And he was born on the 7th. Prince missed 7/7/7 as *Planet Earth*'s release date by a week but performed a special Minneapolis concert that day.

Does it mean anything more than he liked the number 7? Probably not. But with this septenary tendency in mind, here are 7 thoughts about Prince that provide context for the tale that follows.

And once we have "The Truth," we can "all trade bank accounts and move to Neptune." Agreed?

1. O(+>

Even if Prince's music fades from memory, he'll be remembered for changing his name to an unpronounceable symbol. That a 2017 sports report calls the Buffalo Bills's football stadium the Stadium Formerly Known as Ralph Wilson points in this direction.

Pseudonym use in the entertainment industry is nothing outrageous or new. Everyone knows John Wayne. Few know Marion Morrison. Greta Gustafsson? Nope. Greta Garbo? Yup. But Prince's June 1993 name change was different for three reasons.

Before graphic designer Mitch Monson created the fused male/female icon that Prince adopted as his name in 1993, a simpler icon was frequently used, as on this CD single from summer 1990. *(Author's collection)*

First, Prince was his real name that he swapped after he was a star. This distinguishes him from artists who adopted a stage name before fame, such as Ringo Starr and David Bowie. It also separates him from those who swapped one stage name for another post-fame, such as Steven Georgiou, who hit as Cat Stevens and then changed his name to Yusuf Islam.

Second, he made the switch for political reasons. This puts him in some rarified air, with Muhammad Ali and Kareem Abdul-Jabbar, both of who changed their names for political and religious reasons

How is Prince's move political? It was a form of protest.

Prince changed his name because he wanted to benefit monetarily from his labor. He wanted to own his writing and music rather than allowing the benefits to flow to the record company, the capitalists who controlled the means of production. He professed that if he were no longer Prince, then he wouldn't have to abide by Prince's contract terms.

Does this method make Prince a Marxist? No. He was probably a libertarian, although actress/pal Rosario Dawson thought Prince's spirit was going to help elect Bernie Sanders president in 2016.

Does it make him crazy, as some would suggest? Again, no, although he wanted to go there. On the surface, the name change seems bizarre, and it's unlikely the reasoning would have withstood a legal challenge. But his label, Warner Bros., didn't challenge, deciding it wasn't worth the effort in the court of law or public opinion. Prince's move was more shrewd than crazy.

Finally, he changed his name to an unpronounceable symbol. As near as I can tell, no one had done that before. Prince left Alphabet Street and ventured down Symbol Alley. But even there, he could have chosen something pronounceable, such as $ or % or *. Instead, he changed his name to a symbol that didn't represent a sound; it just represented him.

And this is where he was subjected to public ridicule: he couldn't be called anything, so he could be called anything. People wrote O(+> and started calling him The Artist, The Artist Formerly Known as Prince, TAFKAP, Squiggle, Symbol, Symbolina, Glyph, and The Artist Who Formerly Had Hits. His employees called him "boss" until he told them they were thinking of Bruce Springsteen. Then they just called him "Hey."

And the jokes flew. "What's small, purple, and needs to see the doctor?" "Prince."

The name change is peculiar, but it's a purple herring, a flawed lens through which to view the whole Prince story. Rather than obsess about this one fact, this book looks at the bigger picture and focuses on Prince, his music, and those who made the music with him.

Whether this text calls him Prince or Symbol (or other names), it's nothing to get hung up on: it all points back to the same Purple Yoda.

2. Paisley Park

After Prince left his father's house in the early 1970s, he moved into Andre Cymone's basement. His bedroom doubled as his recording space and his band's rehearsal space. In 1987, he re-created this hybrid adolescent playground at Paisley Park Studios in Chanhassen, Minnesota.

Paisley Park was more than just Prince's home and recording studio; it was one of his Big Ideas, a primary lifestyle choice, along with the New Power Generation (NPG) concept. While the NPG was about "making love and music," Paisley Park was "a place in your heart" that "speaks of profound inner peace."

The main Paisley Park complex was Prince's go-to recording, rehearsal, and performance venue from 1987 onward, and hosted artists such as Neil Young, R.E.M., and The Muppets, but no one has figured out the intent of this unused outbuilding nicknamed "The Egg."
(Photo by Femke Niehof)

The Chanhassen studio was the most long-lasting of the Paisley Park creations. The name first applied to the Flying Cloud Drive Warehouse Studio in Minneapolis, where Prince recorded in 1984. It was then given to the *Around the World in a Day* song "Paisley Park" and then an unreleased instrumental on an early configuration of *The Family*. It also became the name for Prince's music label (Records), business (Enterprises), and movie production company (Films).

Paisley Park Studios officially opened September 11, 1987, but was christened on New Year's Eve with a charity concert featuring Miles Davis. The site included a soundstage, used for concerts and tour rehearsals and film and video productions. The location was open for outside business until 1996. Prince performed about 150 public concerts at Paisley Park.

Prince called Paisley Park home for most of the time from 1987 on, leaving for Los Angeles, Las Vegas, and other locations for about five years in the late 2000s. He also owned more than a dozen other properties around Minneapolis and at various times owned houses around the world, including Spain and Turks and Caicos.

Famously, Prince died at Paisley Park.

3. The Vault

Central to the Prince mythology is the Vault. Like Paisley Park, the Vault is both in your heart and an actual physical location. The physical Vault is the place in Paisley Park where Prince kept his recordings, his Grammys and Oscar, and his flying unicorn pictured on the back cover of *Prince*. Okay, that last part isn't true, but Prince raised such unrealistic hopes when he claimed his best material is still in the Vault.

The exact contents of the Vault are not known to the public. Prince claimed the Vault should be plural, so even if the main Paisley Park Vault is cataloged, who knows what else exists and where?

Sadly, the Vault was not maintained to archival standards. Associates report that Prince would record over tapes, add to older tracks, and leave materials on the floor or unprotected. After Prince's death, representatives of Prince's estate moved the contents of the Vault to a secure facility in the Los Angeles area, over the objections of Prince's heirs. Since Prince didn't leave a will, it's impossible to know which he would have valued more: keeping the recordings at Paisley Park or ensuring the existence of the recordings.

The Vault probably contains three types of recordings: studio, rehearsal, and live.

Studio recordings include alternate versions of released songs, including demos and guide-vocal songs for other artists, and unreleased songs. In the most extreme form, the Vault might include half a dozen versions of a song. For example, "We Can Funk" exists as 1983's "We Can Fuck," released in 2017, as an unreleased version from 1986, and as the *Graffiti Bridge* track featuring George Clinton.

Since Prince recorded most studio material himself, rehearsals are most often prep for live shows, either Prince teaching songs to band members or the band practicing the live set. Prince became fond of streaming rehearsals in the 2000s. Rehearsals are typically my favorite Prince recordings because they give some insight into how Prince thought about songs and how he interacted with other musicians. Prince recorded almost all live shows for training purposes, like a corporate telephone call. The fact that he did this holds out hope for future releases similar to Bob Dylan's thirty-six-CD *The 1966 Live Recordings*. For our purposes, "live" means concert performances, including Paisley Park shows, non–lip-synched TV appearances, and NPG Music Club sound checks.

All three types of recordings are referenced in this book as released or unreleased. Released recordings have been sold or shared by Prince in physical form or online, commercially or promotionally. Unreleased songs have not been legally available. Some are circulating among regular fans, some reside only with elite collectors, and others are known by name only, often through copyright research.

Due to Prince's legal wishes, this volume does not discuss bootleg releases, although multiple chapters could be dedicated to the subject.

4. The Revolution

It borders on heresy, but I'll say it: The Revolution is overrated. In Prince's four decades of live performances and recordings, The Revolution was around for just a bit over three years. The group appears on only about a dozen Prince recordings and never recorded an album independently. The main advantages The Revolution had over Prince's other pre-NPG bands is that he named the group and that *Purple Rain* gave the members face recognition. The Revolution is beloved more than critically considered—which is how nostalgia works.

This isn't to say that the music produced during The Revolution period isn't amazing—it is—or that the group wasn't competent as a backing rock band. But they weren't as strong a backing band as the nameless 1988 band, the NPG 1995 and 2002 configurations, or even 2013 3rdEyeGirl.

The Revolution is important, but, like the name change, it's not the end of the story.

5. Sex

When I told people I was writing this book, the first response was usually, "He must have had some life!" followed by a wink. They said this because they were too polite to say, "Wow! He must have had a lot of sex with beautiful women!" If the name change is Prince fact number 1, then sex is a close 1A. But I guess you make your bed and you lie in it. Or you do it in the kitchen on the floor, standing in the tub, in the bedroom on the dresser, in the pantry on the shelf, or on the pool table.

Yes, sex is a central theme in Prince's work. There's good ol' intercourse ("We Can Fuck"), cunnilingus ("Head"), incest ("Sister"), "making love with only words" ("Lovesexy"), and doing it with your mind and "blindfold, gagged and bound" ("Sexy M.F."). And this doesn't even get into "Come" or "Sex" or "Orgasm." Sex was explicit, it was implicit, and it was ever present—at least until Prince became a Jehovah's Witness in the late 1990s, when he toned it down. "Sexuality" became "Spirituality." The "Peach" line "the way her titties bounced" live became "the way her thingies bounce." Whether this is less offensive is a discussion for another book.

But Prince never abandoned sex. His final album includes one song about screwing ("Screwdriver") and another about "When She Comes"—it's like a "limoncello ballet" and Fourth of July fireworks. Tick tick bang, indeed.

6. Race

Prince wasn't multiracial, he wasn't half Italian, he wasn't Puerto Rican, and he wasn't just a-freakin'. He was a black African American. In the early years, he pushed back against his race, insisting he didn't want to be a black artist but wanted to be a popular artist. He also didn't hire only male, black musicians because he wanted to construct a diverse band to appeal to blacks and whites, men and women. To compensate, he created the Time as a black band and created "*The Black Album*" (but didn't release it).

In the mid-1990s, Prince began to engage race more directly but concluded in "Race" that he didn't want to know "why those before us hated each other." But it's around this time, at the time of the name change, that he starts to see racial issues as political issues. This appears most pointedly in his writing "slave" on his face but also comes through in social justice songs, such as "We March" and "Face Down." From this time forward, race becomes a common topic, from the extended narrative of *The Rainbow Children* to "free your mind and your ass will follow" tales such as "Dear. Mr. Man," "Dreamer," and "Colonized Mind," to the overt race and social justice song "Baltimore."

7. Religion

Prince was brought up a Seventh-day Adventist and drifted toward becoming a Jehovah's Witness in the late 1990s, a process he called less a conversion than a realization. Many associates—and fans—were put off by this change, but religion had always been an underlying component of Prince's career. Early on, Gayle Chapman and Dez Dickerson could not reconcile their religious beliefs with Prince's overt sexuality, so they quit. But by 1988, the tables turned, and other band members were concerned with the overt religious themes on the *Lovesexy* tour.

Prince complained about having to hide his religious side, but it's hard to reconcile this complaint with his music. While he may have felt pressure early on to not be as public spiritually as he was sexually, it's difficult to say religion wasn't always present when the first song on your first album is a benediction. To be fair, the faith was often buried, as in "1999" or "Let's Go Crazy," and didn't really become obvious until 1987's "The Cross."

Ultimately, Prince's God didn't want to hurt you; he only wanted to have some fun.

2

Born on a Blood-Stained Table

The Pre–Warner Bros. Years

Prince Rogers Nelson was born on June 7, 1958, to John L. and Mattie (Shaw) Nelson. Two days later, the number one US single was Sheb Wooley's "The Purple People Eater." Coincidence? Since "Purple Rain" stalled at number two, the only other purple number one was "Deep Purple" by the lightweight sibling act April Stevens and Nino Tempo. This song has the notoriety of being the top song when President John F. Kennedy was assassinated on November 22, 1963.

The year 1963 was also the one in which Prince began his path to stardom. In Prince's origin backstory, one discovered through the finely tuned skills of Prince's early public relations handler Harold Bloom, his mother brought him to a theater to see his father play piano. The younger Nelson loved the pretty women and the attention his father received, and that's when he decided to be a musician. Within two years, Prince was playing the theme from TV's *Batman* and writing his first song: "Funkmachine." He would return to the *Batman* theme on January 21, 2016, at Paisley Park.

John L. Nelson

John L. Nelson's was the leader of the jazz group the Prince Rogers Trio that gave Prince his name. John was born in Louisiana in 1916 and moved to Minnesota in the early 1950s. He was married with three kids and working at Honeywell when he met Mattie Shaw, an aspiring singer with a Billie Holiday–like voice, at a 1956 gig. The two were married in 1957, and Prince arrived the next year. John's music career was already in the rearview mirror when Tyka, Prince's sister, arrived in 1960. But John continued to try to pursue his dream, putting a strain on the family. John left the house in 1965, and in 1968 the couple divorced.

After his mother remarried in 1970, Prince moved in with his father. He enrolled at Bryant Junior High School in South Minneapolis and played on the basketball team. He took up saxophone but abandoned it to work on keyboards (allegedly, he didn't want to play an instrument on which he had to use his lips). Perhaps most important, he took a class, "The Business of Music," that influenced his professional decision-making process. He also hung around with Duane Nelson, mentioned in "Lady Cab Driver" and later head of Paisley Park security. Prince believed that Duane, who died in 2013, was his half brother, but it was revealed after Prince died that John L. Nelson wasn't Duane's father.

Prince and John had usual parent–teen squabbles that bubbled over in 1972 when the elder Nelson caught the younger in bed with a girl. He tossed him out of the house. Prince moved in with his Aunt Olivia and transferred to Central High School.

It's easy to view *Purple Rain* as Prince's attempt to come to terms with his parents, especially his father. And it's probably not far off the mark, as Prince used the early- to mid-1980s to try to make peace with his father. This resulted in seven writing or cowriting credits and a flow of gifts, including the Kiowa Trail "purple house." At some point, the relationship again crumbled. John wasn't invited to Prince's 1996 wedding, and Prince didn't attend John's 2001 funeral. In March 2003, Prince seemed to officially close their relationship by having the Kiowa house demolished, but he played "Unchain My Heart" on January 21, 2016, at Paisley Park in memory of playing the song with his father.

Mattie Shaw

Like Prince's father, his mother, Mattie Shaw, had been married, had a child, and was an aspiring musician. And, like his father, the arrival of two more children all but shut the door on her artistic dreams.

Perhaps the most important Prince fact about Mattie is that, like her husband, she was a black African American. Stories persist that Prince was of interracial ancestry, with his *New York Times* obituary calling him biracial. The story seems to have started in a *Rolling Stone* article from February 19, 1981. By June 6, his father was Italian Filipino, and his mother was black. This, in part, led Prince to write "Controversy" for his next album.

While Prince's childhood nickname "Skipper" didn't last, another gift from his mother did: a slightly unorthodox sexual education. There are conflicting reports about his mother's intent, but it's clear that the preteen Prince had access to pornography, most likely *Playboy* magazines. The "dirty mind" was primed at an early age.

Prince's life took a turn for the worse in 1968, at the age of ten, when Mattie married Hayward Baker. When it was good, it was really good, as Baker would give Prince and Tyka presents and brought Prince to a James Brown show and placed him onstage. When it was bad, it was really bad, as Prince claimed that

Baker would punish him by locking him in a room and making him pick dandelions for long periods of time. Outside observers saw Prince change from smiling and outgoing to introverted and guarded. It's assumed that the abusive title character in "Papa" is Baker. Prince moved out in 1970.

Prince helped his mother around the time of *Purple Rain*, and the two remained close despite his animosity toward Baker. She appeared publicly and privately at Paisley Park numerous times before her death on February 15, 2002.

Bernadette Anderson

When Prince left his father's house in 1972, he moved in with his strict Aunt Olivia Nelson. He was no happier there than at his father's—and without a piano. John let him use the piano on occasion and bought him a guitar that Prince quickly taught himself to play.

From Aunt Olivia's, Prince drifted to Bernadette Anderson's house in 1973. If there's any hero in the early Prince narrative, it's Bernadette, who added Prince to a house with six kids but without a recently departed husband. As Prince sang in "The Sacrifice of Victor," "Bernadette's a lady" who taught him that education's "more important than ripple and weed."

Prince's connection to Bernadette was through her son, Andre "Cymone" Anderson, who attended third grade and Seventh-day Adventist services with Prince. At first, Prince and Andre shared a room, but Prince grew tired of Andre's clutter and moved into the basement. Along with the burlesque hall and the *Playboy* magazines, the basement is mythically considered an essential element of Prince's erotic outlook. In reality, according to Prince's cousin Charles Smith, the basement flooded, and Prince couldn't wait to leave it.

At this time, Prince joined his first band, Soul Explosion, which was soon renamed Phoenix, after the 1972 Grand Funk Railroad album. Soon the band was re-renamed Grand Central, in part after the local high school. Grand Central rehearsed in the Anderson basement, the same place Prince slept—a proto–Paisley Park.

Grand Central was the brainchild of drummer Smith. The band featured Prince on guitar, Andre on bass, his sister Linda Anderson on keyboards, and later Terry Jackson on percussion. The group played out frequently, performing covers of bands like Kool & the Gang and Earth, Wind & Fire. They also performed originals, such as Smith's "Danger Lover" and Anderson's "Funk It Up," plus Prince's "Machine" (aka "Sex Machine") and the trio's "Do You Feel Like Dancing?"

In 1974, after winning a Battle of the Bands, the group entered Cookhouse Studios and recorded four tracks: Prince's "Whenever," Anderson's "You Remind Me of Me," and covers of Love Unlimited's "Love's Theme" and Carole King and Toni Stern's "It's Too Late." As Grand Central became better known, the band evolved. What was a democracy was becoming Prince's band. The other members wanted to add sax player David Eiland of rival group Flyte Tyme, but Prince nixed the idea. This panned out when, after attending a Sly and the Family Stone concert, Prince hit on the idea of having Linda play horn parts on her keyboards. A sound is born.

Around the same time, local drummer Morris Day was pestering Cymone about joining the band. Prince and Jackson, meanwhile, wanted to replace Smith with their own drummer: Keith King. But Prince and Jackson caught a bus to Day's house instead of King's, heard Day jamming on Tower of Power's "What Is Hip?," and hired Morris on the spot. Prince was either blamed for the firing or asserted responsibility for it, depending on who's telling the story. Either way, Prince was now the band leader.

LaVonne Daugherty

While the band had a musical leader, as teenagers they needed more guidance. That came in early 1974 in the form of LaVonne Daugherty, Day's mother. Daugherty viewed Grand Central as her stepping-stone to success and encouraged the group to become more professional, even having them wear matching suede jackets with zodiac signs on the back (Gemini for Prince, of course). The group, now augmented by percussionist William Doughty, signed a contract and changed their name to Grand Central Corporation.

In addition to an air of professionalism, Daugherty also brought Linster "Pepe" Willie into the mix. Willie was married to Prince's cousin Shauntel Manderville. He had returned to Minneapolis to form a band, 94 East, and had an air of exotic New York City about him when he caught Grand Central Corporation playing at a ski party. He observed the band's rehearsals, offering advice and being peppered with industry questions from Prince.

Willie was so impressed with the band, especially Prince, that he invited them to record as his band. The group recorded five tracks on December 4, 1975: "Games," "I'll Always Love You," "If We Don't," "Better Than You Think," and "If You See Me." All tracks feature Prince on guitar and mark the earliest recorded Prince music to be released. The tracks have been repackaged multiple times, most interestingly on 2011's *The Cookhouse Five*, remixed by Dr. Fink. "Do Yourself a Favor," Prince's 1982 recording of "If You See Me," was released on *1999 Super Deluxe*.

The three-piece Grand Central Corporation (Prince, Cymone, Day) soon entered Minneapolis's ASI Studios to demo six original compositions. They emerged with Prince's instrumental "Whenever" and "Machine" (again), Anderson's "39th St. Party," and the trio's "Lady Pleasure," "You're Such a Fox," and

"Grand Central." Daugherty shopped the songs to Isaac Hayes and his Hot But-tered Soul label. The feedback was so positive that Cymone quit high school. Prince refers to the impending release in his first interview in the February 13, 1976, *Central High Pioneer*. Even though he longed for stardom and hated school, as is clear in the article, Prince remained in school. Although it might not have mattered in the long run, he made the right decision in the short term, as Hayes went bankrupt.

After the Hayes disappointment, Daugherty and Pepe Willie began to fade into the background. Prince began to write his own songs and record them on cassette recorders borrowed from school. These 1976 home recordings produced eighteen tracks. Of these, six are complete songs ("Wouldn't You Love to Love Me?," released in 1987 by Taja Sevelle and 2019 by Prince; "Nightingale"; "I Spend My Time Loving You;"; "Rock Me, Lover"; "Don't You Wanna Ride?"; and "Leaving for New York"), one is a cover (Chaka Khan's "Sweet Thing"), and the balance are brief instrumentals or song ideas, such as "For You." Setting prece-dent, Prince played all the instruments on these tracks.

Chris Moon

In the spring of 1976, Grand Central Corporation became Shampagne. Sham-pagne put their gig money toward sessions at Chris Moon's Moonsound Stu-dios. As when Pepe Willie watched the band and saw something, Moon watched Shampagne and was impressed with Prince's demeanor and discipline. A lyricist in search of music, Moon approached Prince with an offer of open-door studio time in exchange for songwriting. Prince hesitated but relented. He jettisoned the band and, effectively, his friends. Shampagne evolved into Shampayne, and by early 1978, they were no more.

Although working alongside Moon and learning production and engineer-ing, Prince was now a solo studio musician (although no longer a live per-former). Moon and Prince have cowriting credit on six tracks recorded during America's Bicentennial summer: "Aces," "Don't Forget," "Don't Hold Back," "Fantasy," "Surprise," and "Soft and Wet." The latter was rerecorded on *For You*, as were the Prince-only compositions "Baby," "I'm Yours," "Love Is Forever" (renamed "My Love Is Forever"), and "Jelly Jam," which was the instrumental portion of "Just as Long as We're Together." "Since We've Been Together" and the rerecorded "Leaving for New York" were never released in any form, but "Make It through the Storm" was released on the B-side of protégé Sue Ann Carwell's 1981 single "Let Me Let You Rock Me" single.

Prince graduated from high school in 1976 on his birthday and contin-ued to be supported by Bernadette Anderson. But he wanted more. Prince and Moon assembled a four-song demo of "Soft and Wet," "Love Is Forever,"

Early collaborator Chris Moon recorded Prince and other local Minneapolis artists at his home-based Moonsound Recording Studios before moving to a dedicated studio space. In 2018 Moon attempted to sell his cowriting credit on "Soft and Wet" for around half a million dollars.   *(Photo by Femke Niehof)*

"Baby," and "Aces," and Prince headed to New York in the fall to sell his wares. He stayed with his half sister Sharon Nelson in New Jersey. His phone calls failed to interest music industry reps. Admitting defeat, he contacted the equally unqualified Moon, who got nowhere until he lied to Atlantic Records about representing Stevie Wonder. It got Prince a meeting but not a recording contract, although he received an offer to sell his song rights to Tiffany Entertainment.

Owen Husney

Moon viewed himself as a music creator, not a talent manager. He played the demo tape for acquaintances in the Minneapolis entertainment industry, attracting the interest of marketer Owen Husney. Moon sold Husney on Prince, who had his first solo manager when he signed with Husney's American Artists in December. He also had $50,000 to support his work, an apartment, new instruments, a weekly allowance, and his first handler, Bobby Rivkin (aka Bobby Z.), who helped Prince get his driver's license and find the apartment.

The same month, on December 29, 1976, Husney put Prince in his first real recording studio, Minneapolis's Sound 80. Bobby Z.'s brother, David Rivkin, Husney's former bandmate in a mid-1960s band High Spirits, was behind the mixing board, as he was at the earlier ASI sessions. The better-equipped studio gave Prince access to Polymoogs, further refining the Prince sound. These sessions lasted until the summer of 1977 and produced alternate versions of five earlier songs and new *For You* songs: "In Love" and "Just as Long as We're Together." Prince also recorded an untitled instrumental and the unreleased songs "Love in the Morning" and "You Really Get to Me."

In the spring, while Moon was assembling press kits for an assault on Los Angeles record labels, Prince took some session work. At Sound 80, he worked with Pepe Willie on 94 East's "Fortune Teller" and "10:15," both unreleased until 2002. He also played guitar and sang background vocals on "Got to Be Something Here," a Sonny T. composition recorded by The Lewis Connection. With Cymone and drummer Bobby Z., he recorded an eight-track instrumental session at Husney's Loring Park rehearsal studio. He also recorded solo songs at Loring Park, including "Neurotic Lover's Baby's Bedroom," "Hello, My Love," and "I Like What You're Doing," all of which remain unreleased.

Emboldened by a classy homemade press kit, Husney began calling labels, telling them that CBS was flying Prince to Los Angeles for a meeting. He got a "yes" from Russ Thyret at Warner Bros. and then told the story in reverse to CBS. Prince and Husney, accompanied by attorney Gary Levenson, set up April meetings with CBS, Warner Bros., A&M, RSO, and ABC-Dunhill. Without telling the labels, the trio left Minnesota with three nonnegotiable demands. First, they needed a three-record deal. Second, Prince had to play all the instruments. Third, Prince would produce himself. The trio eventually left Los Angeles with their first two demands met.

Prince went through a dog and pony show for the labels, although he kept his mouth shut. CBS doubted that he produced the music on the demo by himself, so executives watched as Prince assembled "Just as Long as We're Together" from scratch. ABC and RSO passed out of hand. This type of executive decision-making led to ABC closing in 1979 and RSO shutting its doors in 1983. A&M would give only a two-album deal, and CBS insisted that Verdine White of Earth, Wind & Fire produce. Both Warner's Thyret and A&R man Lenny Waronker urged Warner Bros. label head Mo Ostin to sign Prince. Prince signed a three-album, $180,000 contract on June 25, 1977. The one compromise was that Prince would coproduce the albums. To celebrate, Prince recorded "We Can Work It Out" at Sound 80 with Bobby Z. on drums. The sentiment would eventually prove overly optimistic.

Even though he had already signed a contract, in July, Warner Bros. put Prince through the same paces as CBS but this time without telling him. Although they were impressed with what they saw, the label still pushed for a big-name producer, such as Earth, Wind, & Fire leader Maurice White. Warner Bros. relented but installed Tommy Vicari as executive producer. It was, at best, a nominal title.

Prince rounded out 1977 by recording *For You* at the Record Plant in Sausalito, California, from October 1 to December 22 after an aborted start at Sound 80. During the sessions, he recorded six tracks with Cymone on bass and *For You* assistant engineer Steve Fontano on drums. The still-unreleased sessions include an untitled instrumental, plus full songs "Life Is So Neat," "E-Pluribus Funk," "Shine Your Light/Red Zone," "Bump This," and "Waiting for You." Fontano would go on to win two Grammys for engineering Santana's *Supernatural* LP in 1999.

By the time Prince was on to Owen Husney, he was all but done with Chris Moon beyond legal entanglements and financial settlements. By the end of the year, after a disagreement about a space heater and Husney being treated more like a gopher than a manager, Husney quit. He was reportedly followed by a settlement in the range of $50,000.

3

Remember When I Met U

First Four Albums, 1978–1982

For You (1978)

For You is the best debut album ever released by a horny but sentimental multi-instrumentalist on his twentieth birthday. After that, the superlatives are a bit tougher to muster, and the most surprising aspect of the disc is that it wasn't titled *4U*. While there's musical variety and some virtuosity, it's hard to believe that anyone but Prince believed this was the first step to music immortality.

Legend says that Prince did everything on *For You*. He's credited as producer, arranger, engineer, and cover designer and with playing more than 5,000 instruments. The last part is an exaggeration, but he lists twenty-seven instrument credits. Do three different synthesizers really count as three different instruments? And he did receive studio help, with keyboardist Patrice Rushen and her boyfriend Charles Veal contributing to "Baby" and Warner Bros. mole Tommy Vicari acting as executive producer. But it is true that Prince spent $170,000 of the $180,000 budget for his first three albums while learning to record an album.

For You is brief, nine tunes clocking in at just over half an hour. The songs are a mix of reworked 1976 Minneapolis songs and new songs, pulled together at plush California studios from late 1977 to early 1978. While a variety of musical styles and instruments are on offer, the album exhibits a tame similarity: it's nine love songs written by a writer who knows love through other love songs encased in generic disco-era production. Prince is in charge, but he's not yet in control.

But tea leaves are here to be read, as the two best songs hint at the major musical styles and risqué lyrical pathways Prince would soon reinvent. The first single, "Soft and Wet," is three minutes of naughty synthesizer-based funk-pop heaven (his stock-in-trade), and album closer "I'm Yours" cranks the guitars to eleven, presaging guitar-god status. The a cappella title song teases at future choral wonders. And while there are a few other memorable melodies, the second single, "Just as Long as We're Together," still sounds like it couldn't get past the velvet rope at Studio 54, and "Baby" probably shouldn't have made it out of the high school notebook, where it would feel comfortable among sketches of unicorns and rainbows.

The album was released on Prince's twentieth birthday, June 7, 1978. It barely dented the *Billboard* 200, hanging around five weeks and peaking at 163, but fared better on the R&B chart, hitting number twenty-one. The debut single "Soft and Wet" likewise broke the top 100 only at ninety-two but made it to number twelve on the R&B chart. The second single, an edit of "Just as Long as We're Together," hit number ninety-one on the R&B chart. No non-LP B-sides were offered, but promo mono and disco mixes of each song exist.

There was no *For You* tour. All songs, except "In Love" and "My Love Is Forever," were performed live, and those might have been performed at the January 1979 Warner Bros. executive showcases. Two songs have interesting live histories. Prince first played "I'm Yours" on March 28, 2009, at the Conga Room in Los Angeles, more than thirty-one years after its release. This release-to-performance lapse was bested by the thirty-seven-year delay of "Baby," performed for the only time on January 21, 2016, at Paisley Park, three months before his death.

Prince (1979)

Prince was released on October 19, 1979. It went platinum on the back of the R&B number one "I Wanna Be Your Lover," hitting twenty-two on the pop charts and the top five on the R&B charts. The LP also found Prince releasing his first video ("I Wanna Be Your Lover") and making his first national television appearances on *American Bandstand* and *Midnight Special*. *Prince* started the process of making Prince a household name.

As on *For You*, Prince plays everything, although Bobby Z. and Andre Cymone are listed as "heaven-sent helpers," and the latter contributed vocals to "Why You Wanna Treat Me So Bad?" Unlike the expensive and elongated first-LP process, *Prince* was recorded quickly from April to June 1979 at Alpha Studios in Burbank, with overdubs and remixes soon after. The goal this time wasn't learning a craft but rather crafting hits. To this end, the album was a success—to a degree.

While *Prince* had only one unqualified radio hit at the time, it produced three classics and doesn't have a weak song. However, it falls short of masterpiece status. The main issue is a lack of dynamics and subtlety both in song selection and in production. You've got five bright and bombastic songs that hit you over the head and four mellow ballads (strong on sentiment but often

Backed by his five-piece band, Prince performed his first concert as a solo artist on January 5, 1979. The show, and one the subsequent night, was designed for Warner Bros. executives to determine if Prince was ready to tour in support of *For You*.
(*Courtesy Thomas de Bruin, unused-prince-tickets.com*)

in search of a strong hook). For all the appraisals that claim the album is more varied than the first, there's no middle ground. If *Prince* were a dog (and it's not an uncommon canine name), it would be either humping your leg or trying to give you a big mushy kiss.

The three classics? The most enduring is lead single "I Wanna Be Your Lover." The latter half of the song is an instrumental groove that lays the groundwork for future funk experiments. "Sexy Dancer" pushes past pure disco and lays down the funk. The best-known song is "I Feel for You" because of Chaka Khan. Khan's version won Prince a Grammy, but Prince's version is three minutes and twenty-four seconds of pure pop funk and is better, and, in a more just world, it would have been a hit single. The newly surfaced, longer "I Feel for You (Acoustic Demo)" was released as a limited-edition purple vinyl single in 2020.

"Why You Wanna Treat Me So Bad?" is a catchy pop song with a hard rock edge, while "Bambi" is a hard rock song that is more memorable for its anti-lesbian lyrics than it is catchy. "It's Gonna Be Lonely" is the first trip into power ballad territory. Both "When We're Dancing Close and Slow" and "Still Waiting" find Prince in his finest chanteuse form, channeling his inner Billie Holiday, as on "So Blue." The weakest song is "With You," which sounds like a Lionel Richie outtake commissioned for a wedding photography commercial.

Prince spawned three US singles. "I Wanna Be Your Lover" had the most success, providing his first pop top twenty hit at number eleven and his first R&B number one. "Why You Wanna Treat Me So Bad" hit number thirteen on the R&B chart, and "Still Waiting" hit number sixty-five. All three songs were released in mono versions that have not appeared on CD or download, and the New Zealand version of "Still Waiting" contained the full-length version of the song that appeared only on initial vinyl versions of the LP. None of these releases contained non-LP songs, but the UK "Sexy Dancer" twelve-inch includes the uncollected "Long Version."

All of the songs appear to be written for this album except "With You" and "I Feel for You." These were the two Prince-penned of six songs recorded in New York City at Music Farm Studios on February 17, 1979, with Cymone on bass and mentor Willie Pepe leading the proceedings. The session demoed songs for Little Anthony and the Imperials, who released 94 East's "One Man Jam" as "Fast Freddie the Roller Disco King." The session also produced a version of "Do Me, Baby" and "Thrill You or Kill You" with Cymone on lead vocals and the 94 East instrumental "If You Feel Like Dancin'."

In late 1978, Prince assembled his first solo band, with Cymone on bass, Bobby Z. on drums, Dez Dickerson on guitar, and Matt Fink and Gayle Chapman on keyboards. This lineup lasted from the January 1979 Capri Theater debut gig until the May 1980 end of the Rick James Tour but never released a song as Prince's band. The group, including Prince, recorded nine unreleased songs in 1979 as The Rebels.

Prince leaned heavily on *Prince* songs through the *Dirty Mind* tour and then abandoned most of them until the late 2000s. Only "It's Gonna Be Lonely" was never performed live.

Dirty Mind (1980)

Dirty Mind is Prince's first masterpiece. It pairs a bare electro-funk pulse with stark, sexual lyrics and adorns them in the naked ambition of blossoming genius. It's aggressive, impish, oddly optimistic, and utterly irresistible. In other words, it's Prince. The only complaint is that there's not more of the eight-song, thirty-minute album.

On the surface, *Dirty Mind* appears to be a simple case of one-upmanship in a post-tour battle with Rick James. It's Prince jumping James's naughty funk-punk train. But whatever Prince hijacked musically, lyrically, and visually from James—and he seems to have borrowed more than a bit—Prince's determination, creativity, and superior talent transformed a potential shtick into a relevant and enduring artistic persona.

Dirty Mind's synthesizer-driven sound signals a sharp break from the previous albums' radio-friendly rounded edges. These songs, left in demo form, are angular and mechanical. This isn't pop music that politely invites you over to listen but rather raw funk that gets in your face, shakes your shoulders, and demands that you listen. And it's one of the few times that Prince the producer outpaces Prince the performer.

Lyrically, Prince extends the sexual sad sack persona on "When You Were Mine" and "Gotta Broken Heart Again," but the revelation here is the increasingly explicit sexual content, as last year's unspoken "sex-related fantasies" are now increasingly verbalized, especially in "Head" and "Sister." The gates of Erotic City have swung wide open.

There isn't a weak song on the album. Each track is catchy enough to warrant radio play, and any one would be the crowning achievement of most musical careers.

For all this, *Dirty Mind* was a commercial failure. Released on October 8, 1980, the album reached only number forty-five, the lowest pop ranking of an LP of strictly new material until 2001's *Rainbow Children* failed to crack the top 100.

The LP was recorded during May and June 1980 "somewhere in Uptown" (aka Prince's Home Studio in Wayzata), about thirteen miles west of Minneapolis. There was slightly more outside participation on these tracks, with Dr. Fink playing on and cowriting the title track and contributing synthesizer on "Head," which included vocal contributions from keyboardist Lisa Coleman. Uncredited, Andre Cymone cowrote "Uptown," and Morris Day cowrote "Partyup." Day relinquished official credit in exchange for Prince's production of the first Time LP. And, officially, The Time LP was coproduced by Jamie Starr, Prince's earliest alias and the credited engineer of *Dirty Mind*.

Dirty Mind saw the US release of two commercial and two promo singles and "Do It All Night" as a UK-only release. The first US single, "Uptown," was released on September 10, 1980. The edit hit number 101 on the *Billboard* "Bubbling Under" chart and number five on the R&B chart. Along with the US promo release single "Head," the non-charting single "Dirty Mind," and the LP track "Partyup," "Uptown" hit number five on the disco chart, which tracked club play. "When You Were Mine" was released exclusively for radio play.

The singles contain no non-LP songs but offer three non-collected variations, mono versions of the edited "Uptown" and "Dirty Mind" tracks, and an alternate, Philippines-only edit of "Dirty Mind." It's unclear if Imelda Marcos traded Prince designer shoes for exclusive rights to the track. "Head" circulates unofficially as a 1994 Kirky J remix.

The album sessions also produced the non-LP single "Gotta Stop (Messin' About)," released commercially in the United Kingdom on May 29, 1981. This was the same day as Prince's first non-US concert at the Paradiso in Amsterdam and four days prior to his first London concert at the Lyceum, a venue now best known for housing *The Lion King* since 1999. The "Dirty Mind" session track failed to chart in the United Kingdom. It was released in the United States as a "Let's Work" twelve-inch B-side and has appeared on hits collections.

The two-leg US *Dirty Mind* tour began December 4, 1980, in Buffalo, New York, and ended on April 6, 1981, in New Orleans, Louisiana. Prince used the same five-piece band as on the two *Prince* tours. Further promotional dates brought the group to Europe for three dates before a final show at Dez Dickerson's wedding on June 6, bassist Andre Cymone's last gig.

Prince played all the LP songs at most dates on the *Dirty Mind* tour and intermittently through the 2000s, except for "Sister." In addition to a few earlier songs, the tour also featured two unreleased songs: "Everybody Dance," a loose live-feel jam with few lyrics, and "Broken" (aka "Broken, Lonely, and Crying"), a "Jack U Off/Delirious" prototype. The latter also exists in a studio version.

Controversy (1981)

Controversy is an uneven, quirky album, but at that, it pales only in comparison to the masterpiece it followed. Like *Dirty Mind*, it's not quite a concept album, but the songs are thematically linked by the title and, in this case, the sleeve visuals. Musically, *Controversy* is a transition piece, with Prince shaping the dry synthesizer funk of its predecessor toward his more polished pop sound. The lyrics begin the move beyond a simple focus on love and sex, marking the first overt entry into Prince's "controversial" mixture of the carnal and the Christian.

Released on October 14, 1981, *Controversy* provided his highest-charting pop LP to date at number twenty-one; it equaled the number three position of *Prince* on the soul charts. Most recording took place at the Kiowa Trail Home Studio during the late spring and early summer of 1981. Overdubs, mixing, and the recording of the final song, "Private Joy," took place at Sunset Sound from August 14 to 23. It was the first song Prince recorded at the Hollywood studio, which he would use off and on through 2009's *Lotusflow3r*.

As usual, Prince "produced, arranged, composed and performed" the album but not totally. "Jack U Off," the first title using "Princebonics," is the closest thing yet to a true band recording as Bobby Z. sits in on drums, Dr. Fink plays keys, and Lisa provides background vocals. Lisa also contributes vocals to the title song and "Ronnie, Talk to Russia." The composition of "Do Me, Baby" is generally credited to Cymone.

The album saw the release of three US singles. An edited "Controversy" was released on September 2, 1981. It hit number three on the soul charts and stalled at number seventy on the pop charts but shared the top spot on the disco charts with its follow-up single "Let's Work." The "Let's Work" edit hit number nine on the soul chart but failed to crack the Hot 100. The "Do Me, Baby" edit didn't chart. These edits feature on hits collections, although each song's mono edit has appeared only on promo seven-inch releases. "Let's Work" was released as a twelve-inch "Dance Remix" featuring Morris Day on drums; this version is found on *Ultimate*.

The thirty-eight-minute album features two classics: "Controversy" and "Do Me, Baby." The title song consolidates the pulsating dance beat of *Dirty*

The first compact discs were released in Japan in November 1982, one month after the release of *1999*. The back covers for early Warner Bros. CDs typically featured promotional write-ups for the artists' catalog. *Purple Rain* was Prince's first simultaneous release on CD, vinyl, cassette, … and 8-track. *(Author's collection)*

Mind and previews the (real) horn-driven sound that would feature on later studio tracks. Lyrically, it's not "The Ballad of John and Yoko," but it's a clever look at the pressure of living in the public eye, with an unexpected interlude of "The Lord's Prayer." After some noncommittal ballads on the first two LPs, "Do Me, Baby" is Prince's first after-dark slow jam. The other songs talk about sex. This is sex.

"Sexuality," "Let's Work," and "Jack U Off" are all solid, superior to most tunes on the first two LPs, but, as with the ambitious but flawed "Annie Christian," they almost seem like warm-ups for similar and superior *1999* tracks. "Ronnie, Talk to Russia" is a brief novelty. The only misfire is "Private Joy." Save for the wailing guitars toward the end, the only rock music on the LP, the song sounds very much like the generic early 1980s pop it was on La Toya Jackson's 1983 cover.

The *Controversy* live period began with an October 5, 1981, appearance at Sam's in Minneapolis. This debut of new bassist Brown Mark was quickly followed by the disastrous Rolling Stones gigs in Los Angeles on October 9 and 11. The official fifty-five-show tour began on November 20, 1981, at the Stanley Theater in Pittsburgh, Pennsylvania, and wrapped on March 14 at the Riverfront

Coliseum in Cincinnati, Ohio. The disgruntled, seven-member Time served as opening act, often working to annoy the headliner much as Prince did on his 1980 Rick James tour.

The shows opened with a recording of "The Second Coming." Referenced in "Sexuality," the still unreleased song shares a title with an uncompleted film and live album. The sets generally featured about a dozen songs, equally split between hits from the first three albums and new songs. The most enduring songs from the tour/LP are "Controversy" and "Do Me, Baby," played periodically through 2016, and "Let's Work," which saw its last appearance in 2015. Two songs were strategically resurrected once, as "Jack U Off" was played alongside "Sister" in the "naughty" part of 1988's *Lovesexy* tour and "Sexuality" returned in the 2000s, primarily in 2006–2007 at Club 3121 in Las Vegas, as "Spirituality." "Private Joy" and "Annie Christian" were performed exclusively on the *Controversy* tour, while "Ronnie, Talk to Russia" was never performed live.

4

Some Ol' Skool Company

Early 1980s Band Members

Once Prince released his solo Warner Bros. albums, he needed a band. Manager Owen Husney tackled this problem in mid-1978 by renting audition/rehearsal space at Minneapolis's Del's Tire Mart—funk bass and tire rotations.

The first hire was easy: Prince tabbed Andre Cymone on bass. He next flirted with Grand Central's Terry Jackson on drums but chose Bobby Z. Prince offered Jackson a spot as percussionist, but this flamed out when Jackson arrived with timbales, which Prince proclaimed as not the future of R&B music.

Guitarist Dez Dickerson and keyboardists Gayle Chapman and Matt Fink soon followed.

The band rehearsed throughout the fall at the Tire Mart until band equipment was stolen in November, necessitating a move to Pepe Willie's cellar.

The group made their live debut on January 5, 1979, at the Capri Theater in Minneapolis. The event showcased the band for Warner Bros. to determine if it was ready for the road. It wasn't. After an August showcase, they got the okay, and the brief *Prince* tour opened in November.

This chapter covers original Prince band members who performed live through the *1999* tour.

Andre Cymone (1977–1981)

Bassist Andre "Cymone" Anderson first met Prince in third grade, and they started working together in 1973 when Prince moved into Cymone's house. The two played and recorded together over the next few years until Prince went solo in 1976.

After Prince signed with Warner Bros. in 1977, Prince and Cymone worked together off and on, with Cymone signing up on bass in the summer of 1978. Cymone played with Prince from the first January 1979 gigs through the 1981 *Dirty Mind* tour. He was also in the Rebels.

Whether Cymone left or was replaced is up for debate. The two had been drifting apart, with Cymone realizing that his Prince-like ambitions of leading his own band and producing other artists couldn't happen while he was with

Prince. According to Cymone, the final straw came when he didn't get credit for largely writing the music for "Controversy," this after not receiving credit for "Uptown." Cymone's final gig—and the last appearance of the first band—was at Dickerson's birthday party on June 6, 1981.

Cymone released two albums immediately after departing and in 1983 released *Girls Talk* by The Girls, his response to Vanity 6. In 1985, his record company convinced him to accept "The Dance Electric" as a gift from Prince, a choice Cymone regretted after Prince indulged in his own largess. The song became Cymone's biggest hit. Prince's version of the song was released in 2017.

Cymone continued producing until the mid-1990s, when he left the music industry.

For all the time that Cymone worked with Prince, the only released Prince studio track he appears on is harmony on "Why You Wanna Treat Me So Bad." Cymone performed with Prince in 1986 and 2012, singing "The Dance Electric."

Bobby Z. (1977–1986)

Drummer Bobby Z. (Rivkin) met Prince in the summer of 1976 when Chris Moon invited him to Moonsound. Bobby had been around the scene for a while, as his brother, David Rivkin, had engineered Grand Central Corporation's 1976 ASI demos. Bobby heard Prince on piano at Moonsound and decided he wanted to be part of the next big thing. In 1977, Bobby drummed on Prince's Warner Bros. signing song "We Can Work It Out."

Bobby Z.'s uncluttered style suited Prince's vision for his live band. He was hired in the summer of 1978 and continued behind the kit until he was unceremoniously fired from the Revolution by phone on October 7, 1986.

Bobby Z. appeared on fourteen Prince studio recordings, "Jack U Off," and the regular thirteen Revolution tracks (see chapter 19). He also drummed on the Loring Park and The Rebels sessions. Bobby wrote "Rivers Run Dry" on *The Family*, but he doesn't appear on the LP. After producing Boy George in 1988, he released a self-titled solo album in 1990 that included "Rivers Run Dry." Bobby joined Prince onstage in 2000 and 2013.

Dez Dickerson (1979–1983)

Desmond D'andrea "Dez" Dickerson answered an ad in the summer of 1979 in the *Twin Cities Reader* for a guitarist. Dickerson showed up for the audition, but Prince didn't until about two hours later. Dez had only fifteen minutes before he had to leave for a gig with his band Romeo. He played with Prince, highlighting his easy, New Wave rhythms without ever overshadowing Prince. Prince walked him out, asking deep, probing questions. He got the job.

Dickerson was in the live band from the January 1979 beginning until the April 10, 1983, end of the *1999* tour, his final gig the next month at the Minnesota Music Awards. After Dr. Fink's medical outfit, Dickerson's flashy New Wave style and kamikaze head wrap was probably the most recognizable visual element of Prince's early band.

After the *Dirty Mind* tour in December 1980, on December 22, at 11:30 p.m. precisely, Dickerson became a born-again Christian. This conversion conflicted with pansexual attitudes promoted by Prince's music, and Dickerson became increasingly uncomfortable in the band. According to sources, the feeling was mutual, as Dickerson's beliefs and the constant presence of his wife made life difficult for the rest of the group. The end came when Prince asked for a three-year *Purple Rain* commitment and Dickerson rejected the offer.

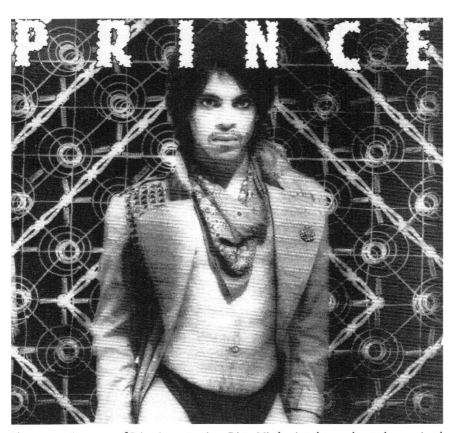

The provocative cover of Prince's masterpiece *Dirty Mind* pointed toward a stark new visual and musical approach, one aimed at generating a following with new wave/punk fans. It worked. The era's non-LP B-side "Gotta Stop (Messin' About)" was number five on progressive Boston radio station WBCN's best singles of 1981, nestled between the Stray Cats' "Rock This Town" and Adam and the Ants' "Stand and Deliver." *(Author's collection)*

Dickerson's most memorable moment in Prince's band occurred during the disastrous October 9 and 11, 1981, opening gigs for the Rolling Stones at the Memorial Coliseum in Los Angeles. Dickerson warned Prince that the Rolling Stones's traditional rock crowd might not be receptive to a funk–New Wave band led by a guy wearing lingerie. Prince ignored him. Dez kept the band together as Prince took off from the stage. He also persuaded him to return to Los Angeles for the second gig after he fled to Minneapolis, convincing him that it would be a racist victory if he let the white audience defeat him. Prince returned for the second show, but it went no better than the first.

Dickerson first recorded with Prince as The Rebels. In 1981, he contributed "After High School" and cowrote "Cool" with Prince for *The Time*. He also cowrote "Wild and Loose" with Prince for *What Time Is It?* For 1982's *Vanity 6* LP, he wrote, produced, and played drums and guitar on "He's So Dull" and played drums on "$3 \times 2 = 6$."

Dickerson's only contributions to Prince studio songs are co–lead vocals on "1999" and background vocals and lead guitar on "Little Red Corvette." But what wonderful guitar work it is.

Although Dickerson didn't commit to *Purple Rain*, he appeared on-screen with his band the Modernaires performing Prince's "Modernaire." Dickerson released the song, which featured Prince on everything but vocals, as "(I Want 2 B A) Modernaire" on his 2005 *A Retrospective*. Dickerson released a book in 2003 titled *My Time with Prince: Confessions of a Former Revolutionary*, last saw Prince in 2004, and talked to him two weeks before his death.

Matt Fink (1979–1990)

A friend of engineer David Rivkin, Matt Fink first met Prince in early 1977 after hearing the Sound 80 demos and being blown away. The next year, David's brother, drummer Bobby Z., recruited Fink into Prince's live band. Future Time member and producer Jimmy Jam (James Samuel Harris III) was considered for the position, but Prince, seeking to duplicate the race and gender diversity of Sly and the Family Stone, decided on the white Fink. Fink was the longest-lasting member of Prince's first band, surviving multiple purges before leaving in 1990.

Fink's bright, poppy keyboard riffs on early tunes stand out but not as much as his doctor's outfit. Fink wore a prisoner's outfit to start the 1980 Rick James tour. James appropriated Fink's outfit, and Prince didn't want him wearing it anymore. He went back to an old idea (medical scrubs) and soon became the much-loved Dr. Fink. Prince initially insisted on Fink wearing a medical mask for an air of mystery but relented when it interfered with Fink's breathing and playing.

Dr. Fink is the first band member other than Prince to get a musician credit on a Prince LP: synthesizer on "Dirty Mind" and "Head" (which was a huge Fink live number). He cowrote the former song. He also received cowriting credit, with Prince and Eric Leeds, on "It's Gonna Be a Beautiful Night." He appears on an additional fourteen tracks, stretching from 1981's "Jack U Off" to "Eye Know" from 1988's *Lovesexy*. He's also on all of Madhouse *8*, "Sixteen" from *16*, Jill Jones's "All Day, All Night," "Interesting" by Mavis Staples, and "Get It Up" and "The Stick" from *The Time*. And he drummed with The Rebels.

Fink played his last gig in Yokohama, Japan, on September 10, 1990. Prince asked him to play two gigs in South America in January 1991. When he couldn't commit because of production responsibilities, he was replaced by Tommy Barbarella, and the NPG was born.

After leaving Prince, Dr. Fink released one LP: 2001's jazz/funk collection *Ultrasound*. He also remixed the 2001 *Cookhouse Five* CD, a release of the December 1975 94 East songs.

Gayle Chapman (1978–1980)

Keyboardist Gayle Chapman was listening to *For You* when a voice told her that Prince would need a band to play live. She prepped for months before she got an audition. And then she waited another three months before she got a call from Prince asking her to come to a rehearsal. When she asked Prince why she got the gig, he said because "you have blond hair, blue eyes and you can sing." And because she was a funky white chick.

Chapman's keyboards filled the group's sound and fit in well with the band, but the same could not be said of Chapman herself. She was a member of The Way International, and her unorthodox Christian beliefs put her in conflict not only with the rock 'n' roll lifestyle but also, more specifically, with Prince's flaunting of sexual and social norms. Things came to a head on the Rick James tour as Chapman was getting hit on by James and had to wear increasingly risqué lingerie onstage to perform increasingly erotic acts with Prince. Chapman left, deciding to attend a retreat with The Way rather than some hastily called band rehearsals.

Chapman was with the band on the first two tours, through May 3, 1980, at the Capital Centre in Landover, Maryland. She doesn't appear on any released recordings but did sing "You," "If I Love You Tonight," and "Turn Me On" for The Rebels. After leaving Prince, she worked in different fields but continued singing. In 2013, she was singing The Rebel songs as part of a "One Night with Gayle" performance in Seattle, Washington.

Lisa Coleman (1980–1986)

Lisa Coleman, the second half of the breathless conjunction Wendy & Lisa, joined the early Prince band in May 1980 when original keyboardist Gayle Chapman decided she'd rather not simulate fellatio onstage every night during "Head."

Lisa is often credited with being the most important member of Prince's bands, the one with the most immersion in the creative process and the greatest impact on his musical outlook. At the very least, her involvement has probably been the best documented.

Coleman grew up in the Los Angeles music industry. Her father is legendary Wrecking Crew member Gary Coleman, who worked with scores of artists, from Aretha Franklin to the Monkees to Marvin Gaye. In 1973, the elder Coleman created the kid group Waldorf Salad, featuring Lisa and her siblings David and Debbie and Jonathan Melvoin, Wendy's brother. The group released one single, "Look at the Children/Doncha Know," on A&M Records. Not surprisingly, this slice of shrill un-funkiness did not feature as one of Grand Central's cover songs.

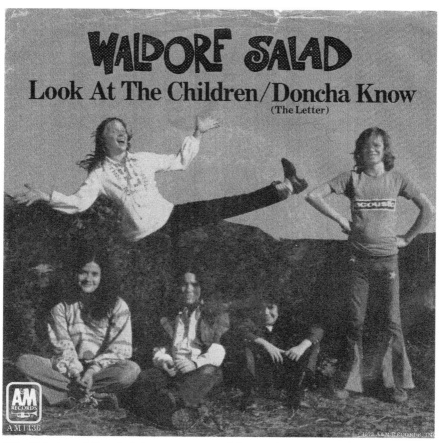

Mike Melvoin and Gary L. Coleman were part of The Wrecking Crew, the faceless LA session band that backed countless hits during the 1960s. In 1973 Melvoin created the kid group Waldorf Salad, featuring his son Jonathan, brother of Prince-realm twins Wendy and Susannah, and Coleman's kids Lisa, Debbie, and David, the latter of whom cowrote "Around the World in a Day."   *(Author's collection)*

Prince and Lisa met in May 1980. Lisa heard through friends at Prince's Los Angeles management group that he was looking for a new keyboardist. She made a demo tape and sent it to Prince, and he was waiting at the airport in Minneapolis when her plane arrived. He gave her an impromptu three-hour audition. He was smitten, and she was soon a member of the band. Prince took to wooing her on songs such as the unreleased "Lisa," but she is a lesbian, so that didn't work out.

During the summer of 1980, Lisa was around the home studio as Prince recorded *Dirty Mind* and at least another album's worth of still unreleased material. She is credited with singing background vocals on "Head," and it's believed that she and Matt Fink wrote the core of the song, uncredited. She first appeared with the band on October 24, 1980, at the live-audience Hollywood studio recording for the "Uptown" and "Dirty Mind" videos. Her first live show was the December 4 Buffalo start of the *Dirty Mind* tour. Her last gig was the September 9, 1986, Yokohama show.

In addition to bringing Wendy into the band, Lisa is credited with expanding Prince's cultural (LBGT) and musical (1960s rock and psychedelia) horizons. At times, such as the 1986 *Rolling Stone* cover interview, she and Wendy literally spoke for Prince. Much of this expansion happened during what many consider the Golden Age of Prince, the period from the May 1983 initial Revolution rehearsals through about June 1986, when the fun stopped being fun. This period includes the *Purple Rain* filming, movie release, album, and subsequent tour and the *Around the World in a Day*, *Parade*, and *Dream Factory* sessions.

Wendy's first studio work with Prince was in April 1981 on *The Time*. She cowrote "The Stick" with Prince and sang background on that tune and "Cool." She sang vocals on about fifteen released songs from *Controversy* through *Sign 'o' the Times*, most famously the first line of "1999," and the 2017 release "Our Destiny." She played keyboards on a like number of tunes from *Controversy* through *Sign 'o' the Times* plus non-LP tracks, including both versions of "4 the Tears in Your Eyes." She reappeared twenty years later on "The One U Wanna C" and "Resolution" from *Planet Earth* and gets cowriting credit on "Computer Blue," "17 Days," "Mountains," and "Power Fantastic."

Lisa, with Wendy, interacted with Prince a few times after the Revolution broke up, but they never really seemed to make up. In 1996, Prince sent "In This Bed Eye Scream" to the duo for suggestions, but the feedback wasn't figured into the apologetic *Emancipation* tune. The LP booklet dedicated the track to "Wendy and Lisa and Susannah" in backward text. In 1998, Prince announced the *Roadhouse Garden* project, a Revolution reunion based on 1986 tracks. This got unhinged when Prince supposedly said that Wendy and Lisa would need to renounce their sexuality before the project could proceed. They didn't, and it didn't. The duo joined him for four songs at the 2006 Brit Awards on February 15, 2006. The spectacle of the event seemed to overshadow the music, which was one of Wendy and Lisa's complaints with The Revolution's final performances.

Brown Mark (1981–1986)

Mark Brown was a bassist for the Minneapolis band Fantasy. The band played 7th St. Entry on a semi-regular basis, and Prince was a semi-regular audience member at these gigs. Prince auditioned Mark Brown and installed him as his new bass player in July 1981, renaming him Brown Mark.

Brown Mark's first gig was at the hometown-friendly Sam's in Minneapolis on October 5, 1981, in a show billed as the band *Controversy*. His next shows were at the less friendly Rolling Stones opening act gigs a few nights later. The crowd unnerved him, but Brown Mark stayed through the end of the Revolution in the fall of 1986.

Brown's tenure was one marked by slights perceived and otherwise, which came to a head during the *Purple Rain* period. According to Brown Mark, the *Purple Rain* tour made Prince a multimillionaire but made Brown only $2,200 a week plus a $15,000 bonus at the end of the tour. By the tour's end, he and other members were pushed to the back of stage to make room for additional members. When he was offered $3,500 per week by Stevie Nicks in the summer of 1986, the choice to defect seemed obvious, but Prince convinced him to stay through the *Parade* tour. In the studio, Brown feels that he didn't get credit for producing "Kiss."

Brown Mark produced the 1985 *Mazarati* LP with coproducer Rivkin and cowrote "Strawberry Lover" and "I Guess It's All Over" with Prince. For released Prince LP tracks, Brown Mark appeared on "D.M.S.R." on background vocals and hand claps and on bass on the standard thirteen tracks that include all Revolution members.

Brown Mark's second album, the Levi Seacer Jr.–produced *Good Feeling*, was released in 1989 on Paisley Park. Prince wrote and sings background on "Shall We Dance" and sings background on "Bang Bang."

Jill Jones (1982–1988)

Jill Jones was a background singer on the 1982–1983 Triple Threat tour and a Prince triple threat herself: band member, protégé, and girlfriend. She was the first Prince band member who didn't play an instrument, but she didn't have to, as she's probably best known for appearing in lingerie and a cap in the "1999" video.

Jones comes from an entertainment family. Her stepfather is Motown founder Berry Gordy, and her mother managed Teena Marie ("Ooo La La La"). Her uncle, Earl Jones, was Prince's hairdresser from 1983 to 1989. Jill was eighteen years old and singing for Teena Marie on the 1980 *Dirty Mind* tour winter leg when she first met Prince.

Jones sang background on "1999," "Automatic," "Free," and "Lady Cab Driver" as J.J., then joined the *1999* tour. On tour, she sang for Vanity 6 from behind a curtain. In addition to the *1999* material, Jones sang background on numerous Prince and associate recordings and lead on "Wednesday," which was cut from *Purple Rain*. She's in the movie as the scene-stealing waitress and shows up in *Graffiti Bridge*, typecast as the Kid's Girlfriend.

Jones released one Paisley Park album before leaving the Purple Realm in 1993.

5

Musicology

Musical Influences

P rince's work feels both familiar and different. As with other talented artists, it's like he joined an ongoing conversation, but he says things no one ever said before and says them in ways no one else imagined. This chapter is about the familiar that allowed Prince to be different, the other speakers in the ongoing conversation Prince joined with his music. Whom was he listening to? Whom was he responding to? On the shoulders of which giants was he standing in his custom-made, high-heel Andre No. 1 boots?

James Brown

Brown is a Prince influence, blueprint, and mirror. He battled record companies, founded labels, used aliases, and released instrumental jazz/soul/funk as a faceless group. He employed top-notch backing bands and a Svengali-like approach to cultivating acts. He was the top live performer of his generation and had an LP chart for more than a year (*Live at the Apollo* for sixty-six weeks). He had drug problems. He married multiple times. He was African American, which meant a lot to Prince but something different to Brown in the pre–civil rights American South. He played a concert to keep the peace after the senseless killing of a black man. He was a demanding bandleader. He employed Alan Leeds as his tour manager. He had a many-year victory lap playing his greatest hits live.

And then there's the music. James Brown invented funk, solidified soul, and maximized R&B. He blended gospel, blues, jazz, and, later, disco into his mix. And his beats made hip-hop and rap happen. What didn't he do that Prince did? He stayed away from rock and pop.

Like Prince, when James was onstage, it was impossible not to watch him and, watching him, impossible not to want to be him—ask Mick Jagger. When producer Rick Rubin visited Prince, there was an endless video loop of Brown performing. The live influence blossomed on the *Purple Rain* tour, Prince's first with dancers and real horns. On 1992's *Diamond and Pearls* tour, Prince's bigger horn section included trombone, a defining feature of Brown's early 1970s sound. Brown's horn section at that time included sax player Maceo Parker, who would later join Prince, and trombonist Fred Wesley. Wesley appears on one Prince track: George Clinton's unreleased early 1990s track "My Pony."

Brown and Prince shared a stage twice. In the mid-1960s, Prince's stepfather put him onstage at a Brown show. He danced and was dazzled by both Brown's command of his band and the pretty ladies. He went home and started practicing to be Brown. On August 20, 1983, bodyguard Chick Huntsberry piggybacked Prince to Brown's stage at the request of Michael Jackson, who had just moonwalked his way into the hearts of the crowd at the Beverly Theater in Los Angeles. Brown had no idea who Prince was, and that was just the beginning of the awkwardness. Prince flubbed around with a borrowed guitar, gave a weak try at dancing, and then left the stage, battering a prop on the way off. Brown would be riding Prince's coattails in just over a year, playing a September 10, 1984, gig at First Avenue.

Prince played bits of more than a dozen Brown songs live, with 1972's "Talkin' Loud and Sayin' Nothing" racking up around 150 performances. Prince never released a studio version of a Brown song but was reminded of something James used to say and sampled "Mother Popcorn" on "Gett Off."

Stevie Wonder

Stevie Wonder was a child prodigy, releasing his Little Stevie LP at age twelve and hitting number one with "Fingertips—Part 1" at age thirteen. Throughout his teens, he consistently manufactured top 100 pop singles and released more than a dozen successful albums. But by the 1970s, he felt like another cog in the Motown machine. Wonder all but wrote "slave" on his cheek in a protracted contract stare-down with Motown boss Berry Gordy. It wasn't until Wonder hit twenty-one and was free of his contract that Gordy blinked and relented to his demands.

On 1972's *Music of My Mind*, Wonder assumed total control of the recording process, including songwriting, innovative multilayered production, and most instrumentation. This began a string of albums from 1972 to 1976 that stands up to the greatest work of any recording artist over a five-year period. These albums, including *Innervisions* (1973) *and Talking Book* (1972), helped define and fine-tune funk and led to the left-turn *Stevie Wonder's Journey Through "The Secret Life of Plants"* (1979), a genre-defying LP that influenced Prince's thinking on *Around the World in a Day*.

In the fall of 1976, Prince went to New York, scoping a recording contract. Chris Moon got Prince a meeting by first claiming that he managed Stevie Wonder, then admitting he had the "new" Stevie Wonder. In the spring of 1977,

Moon-recruited manager Owen Husney hit Los Angeles, also peddling the "new" Stevie Wonder: a black crossover artist who could write, produce, and play everything. This trip resulted in Prince's first Warner Bros. contract.

Wonder's "Cold Chill (Prince Version)" was released on the UK promo CD *Polydor Brighton Conference 1995*, then surfaced commercially a decade later on the iTunes *Remixes* album as part of a thirty-nine-disc *The Complete Stevie Wonder* collection. Prince plays guitar on the track, as he does on Wonder's 2005 single "So What the Fuss" and its multiple remixes.

Stevie Wonder joined Prince onstage on June 26, 1994, at Glam Slam Los Angeles, singing "Maybe Your Baby," and multiple times over the next two decades. Prince first returned the favor during a 2005 Wonder show in Las Vegas on "Superstition" and "Maybe Your Baby." The two collaborated at the June 13, 2015, performance for Barack Obama at the White House to celebrate African American Music Appreciation Month.

Wonder's harmonica on Chaka Khan's million-selling version of "I Feel for You" most famously connects the duo. The most tangential connections are the 1977 Pepe Willie recordings "Fortune Teller" and "10:15," which feature Prince on guitar and background vocals, produced by Henry/Hank Crosby, the Motown producer of Wonder's early hits.

Prince didn't cover Wonder very much live, most frequently performing "Superstition" and "Another Star." The November 18, 2002, Tokyo sound check (which produced "Tokyo" on *C-Note*) features a tender Prince vocal on "Living for the City."

Sly and the Family Stone

Born Sylvester Stewart, Sly Stone could do it all and do it young—guitar, keyboard, vocals, bass, and drums before he was a teen. He listened to black and white radio growing up. He not only led his own band, the Family Stone, but also wrote for others and tried to cultivate a stable of artists on his own label: Stone Flower. He self-produced his debut album. His band was purposefully mixed by race and gender. He dressed to make a woman stare. Larry Graham was his bassist.

Musically, Sly helped not only to invent funk but also to wed it with catchy pop hooks, placing multiple singles in the top 100 and landing three at the top of the charts; a song like "Mountains" would fit in on any late 1960s Sly album. He mastered the art of blending multiple voices and harmonies on songs like "You Can Make It If You Try," a mixture that Prince used on many songs, such as "Daddy Pop." According to the *Crystal Ball* liner notes, Prince recorded "Make Your Mama Happy" after listening to *Fresh*. Further, Sly was a technological pioneer, with *There's a Riot Going On* the first major album and "Family Affair"

Like fellow Prince influencers Jimi Hendrix and Santana, Sly Stone indelibly stamped himself on the public consciousness with a jaw-dropping live performance at Woodstock. Equally adept in the studio, 1973's *Fresh*, often considered his greatest LP, found Stone playing most of the instruments and engaging in bend-but-don't-break aural experimentation. The cover of the classic "Qué Será, Será (Whatever Will Be, Will Be)" might be the slowest pop song ever.

(Author's collection)

the first number one single to feature Prince's early go-to studio instrument: the drum machine. Lyrically, Sly's early career was marked by an almost naive self-help optimism that, like Prince, turned later to a more race-aware resolve. And Larry Graham was his bassist.

Prince dug deeper and more often into the Sly and the Family Stone catalog than any other artist's, due in part to his friendship with Graham. Prince most frequently covered the number one hit "Everyday People." It appeared on 1998's New Power Soul tour and was played about 100 times over the next two decades, occasionally with Family Stone members Jerry Martini (saxophone) and Cynthia Robinson (trumpet). "If You Want Me to Stay" was released in a medley with "Just Friends (Sunny)" on the *One Nite Alone… The Aftershow* LP.

Carlos Santana

Carlos Santana is a solo artist and leader of the ever-enduring band Santana. The Mexican-born guitarist is best known for fusing rock music and Latin American rhythms in the late 1960s, typified by the FM classic "Black Magic Woman." He became a household name in 1969 with the release of the band's double-platinum self-titled debut LP and a star-making appearance at Woodstock. Featuring a revolving door of lead singers, most notably Journey founder Greg Rolie, Santana released thirteen consecutive top forty albums through 1982's *Shangó*. The band enjoyed a revival—seven straight top ten LPs—starting with 1999's *Supernatural*, which has outsold *Purple Rain* by a cool 2 million copies.

Santana is known for his sweet, soaring guitar solos, and that's his primary influence on Prince. His style is inviting and pleasant, challenging but never disrupting the listener. A line can be drawn from Santana to some of Prince's most anthemic solos, such as "Empty Room," "Gold," and, of course, "Purple Rain." The guitar-fueled *Lotusflow3r* is more Hendrix in sound but echoes the title of the 1974 live album *Lotus*. *Santana IV*, released less than a week before Prince's death, was one of six albums he purchased at Electric Fetus in Minneapolis on April 16, Record Store Day 2016.

Prince often played the "Santana Medley," known to Santana followers as "Santana Sandwich," a union of "Jungle Strut," "Batuka, "Soul Sacrifice," and "Toussaint L'Overture." On June 20, 1999, Prince and Larry Graham joined Santana onstage in Minneapolis on the number one smash "The Calling," and Santana repaid the favor on February 21, 2011, at the Oakland Coliseum in Oakland, California, Santana taking the lead on "Santana Medley."

Joni Mitchell

Joni Mitchell is a Canadian singer-songwriter with big US hits in 1974 with the number one LP *Court and Spark* and the Grammy Award–winning single "Help Me." Her influence on Prince's career and music is not readily apparent, and she often seems more of a muse or an unattainable high school crush. Mitchell almost says as much, recalling Prince as a doe-eyed fan at a mid-1970s Minneapolis show, one whose fan mail was deemed "lunatic fringe" by her management. She now claims him as the artist she's influenced whose work she most appreciates.

That being said, there are references and traces. *Controversy* includes her name as a star-bordered newspaper headline on the back cover; 1975's experimental *The Hissing of Summer Lawns* album is said to have inspired Prince's eclectic departures on *Around the World in a Day*." "Help Me" is name checked in "The Ballad of Dorothy Parker," and other lyrics and titles are influenced by

In 1986 Prince wrote and recorded "Emotional Pump" for Joni Mitchell, presumably for her 1988 *Chalk Mark in a Rain Storm* LP. She rejected the song, it's never been released, and she never worked with Prince, but Wendy and Lisa sing on "The Tea Leaf Prophecy (Lay Down Your Arms)" on the 1988 album.
(Author's collection)

Mitchell, such as "When We're Dancing Close and Slow" from a "Coyote" lyric and "Ice Cream Castles" from "Both Sides Now."

"A Case of You" is the first cover song Prince performed live, at the landmark August 3, 1983, First Avenue show. A studio version appears on *One Nite Alone…* as "A Case of U" and an edited version on 2007's *A Tribute to Joni Mitchell* LP, while 2018 saw the release of his piano rehearsal version on *Piano & a Microphone 1983*. He performed the song regularly, with the last performance at the Atlanta, Georgia, early show on April 14, 2016. He performed the Mitchell-associated song "Twisted" during a few 2002 shows and recorded an unreleased studio version; he also paraphrases the song's Annie Ross–written lyrics in the unreleased "Lust U Always." He covered Mitchell's "Blue Motel Room," with lead vocals by Elisa Fiorillo (Dease), at the epic July 23, 2010, Paris New Morning aftershow.

Jimi Hendrix

Jimi Hendrix was a charismatic stage performer, an effortless songwriter, and a distinctive singer. And the greatest guitarist of all time. Except Prince.

Comparing Prince to Hendrix was a knee-jerk reaction once Prince got popular and the media needed quick copy. And the comps are obvious. Early on, Hendrix wrote tight rock songs infused with blues and soul that had pop appeal. In person, he was shy with a good sense of humor but live was an extrovert. A wizard onstage, he was also at home in the studio creating deep sonic landscapes using the latest technology. In both places, he could do things that no one else had even dreamed about. And he oozed sexuality, a sexuality that made him exotic and dangerous.

Prince bristled at the comparisons, saying his guitar style was more Santana than Jimi. He was right, but the comparison wasn't musical, simply what clicked in a lot of heads when they saw a black guy in flamboyant clothes tearing up a guitar on "Let's Go Crazy." And maybe it's easy to confuse "Purple Haze" and "Purple Rain" if you're in a rush.

The closest Prince got to a Hendrix phase was in 2009 with *Lotusflow3r*'s turned-to-eleven guitar attack. Hendrix is most obvious on "Dreamer," which would be at home on *Are You Experienced*, and the 1960s cover "Crimson & Clover." The latter includes the classic garage-band riff from "Wild Thing," which Hendrix claimed as his own at 1967's Monterey International Pop Music Festival by scorching the song and then torching his guitar.

Prince covered about ten Hendrix songs. Among the highlights are "Who Knows," from *Band of Gypsys*, with a "Voodoo Child (Slight Return)" quote, from a 2002 Copenhagen aftershow, and multiple performances of "Villanova Junction," Hendrix's Woodstock set closer.

Prince released two studio Hendrix covers. The renamed "Red House" appeared as "Purple House" on the LP *Power of Soul: A Tribute to Jimi Hendrix*, and the reworked "Machine Gun" was an NPG Music Club Download in 2001 as "Habibi" (later edited to eliminate Hendrix references). Prince also recorded "Fire" with Margie Cox for the unfinished Flash/MC Flash album project in 1989. And some claim to hear the Experience's "Third Stone from the Sun" mixed in with "Take Me with U" on "Rocknroll Loveaffair."

Miles Davis

Miles Davis was a musical genius, endlessly creative on the trumpet and equally skilled as a bandleader, composer, and arranger. He helped create or perfect at least half a dozen jazz styles, including bebop, cool jazz, and fusion. Like Santana, his playing was lyrical, sweet, and reflexive but without cheap sentimentality or pandering. Like Hendrix, he could be nasty when he wanted to be, whipping up an electric brew of dissonance, often punctuated by resounding silence.

According to Wendy, Miles Davis influenced Prince by allowing him to be confident enough to break barriers, to play by jazz logic rather than pop rules. In many ways, the relationship was less one of influence than a mutual admiration society, as Davis was praising Prince as early as *1999*.

Prince and Davis never pulled together a full project. After Davis signed with Warner Bros. in 1985, he asked Prince for a song for his next LP: *Tutu*. In December 1985 during the *Parade* sessions, Prince created "Can I Play with U?" for Davis, who later overdubbed some trumpet. Neither was happy with the results, and the song remains unreleased (but widely available). At the same session, Prince recorded the tribute instrumental "A Couple of Miles" (also unreleased). Writing these songs motivated further December 1985 and January 1986 instrumental sessions that set the groundwork for future jazz projects, including Madhouse.

Prince continued to offer Davis songs until the latter's death in 1991, but none were recorded and released by Davis. These songs include unreleased Madhouse *24* songs "17 (Penetration)," "19 (Jailbait), "and "20 (A Girl and Her Puppy)," and 1989's instrumental "Funky"; Davis incorporated "Penetration" and "Movie Star" into his late 1980s/early 1990s live repertoire. Two days after Davis's death Prince recorded the unreleased tribute "Letter 4 Miles" (aka "Miles Is Not Dead").

Beyond all this and the copy of Davis's 1986 LP *You're Under Arrest* hanging around Christopher Tracy's room in the film *Under the Cherry Moon*, Prince dipped into Davis's songbooks at least half a dozen times live (more often playing songs associated with rather than composed by Davis). Most notable are the *Miles Smiles* classic "Footprints," which was frequently played in Las Vegas in early 2007, and "Freddie Freeloader" from a December 5, 1987, one-off gig at the Fine Line Café in Minneapolis. A few weeks later, Prince celebrated New Year's Eve at Paisley Park, closing with Davis playing on "It's Gonna Be a Beautiful Night" in a medley that included Davis's "So What." Prince's "Copenhagen" was originally released as an NPG Music Club download, including part of Davis's "Jean-Pierre," but the quote from the *We Want Miles* track was left off a subsequent download and the *C-Note* LP.

Parliament/Funkadelic

P-Funk is a half-century-long party united under one hellacious groove by ringleader George Clinton. Anchored by the (nominally) more vocally oriented Parliament and more instrumentally inclined Funkadelic, the P-Funk collective is at turns doo-wop, hard rock, stand-up comedy, pure funk, frat party, political activism, and circus act. And that's just during the first song of their three-plus-hour set.

Perhaps the biggest influence Clinton had on Prince is showing that it's okay to have fun and even be goofy, but that doesn't mean you shouldn't be taken seriously. For Parliament, that meant there's no shame starting an LP side with the tongue-in-cheek (and other places) "I Call My Baby Pussycat" and ending it with "Oh Lord, Why Lord/Prayer." And there's no shame if one of your members appears onstage in diapers.

Parliament taught Prince, everyone really, the importance of stagecraft. The well-staged storytelling of *Lovesexy* live and the mammoth (if flawed) ambition of the Endorphinmachine don't happen without P-Funk landing the Mothership onstage back in 1976. And it's in the *Lovesexy/Black Album* period that the P-Funk influence mainly shows up in the grooves. In terms of song titles, it's impossible not to see the influence of Parliament songs such as "Aqua Boogie (A Psychoalphadiscobetabioaquadoloop)" in "Superfunkycalifragisexy" and the unreleased "Soulpsychodelicide." And the same P-Funk song, among others, leads a direct path in terms of electronically altered vocals to tunes such as "Lovesexy" and "Bob George," not to mention 2007's "F.U.N.K.," which was originally streamed with the title "PFUnk."

Prince played more than a dozen Parliament and Funkadelic songs live but often just played snippets or grooves interpolated into other songs or as parts of medleys. "Flash Light" from 1977's *Funkentelechy vs. the Placebo Syndrome* was played most often and given the most care. A live version from Amsterdam on July 26, 2011, was streamed the same day on Andy Allo's Facebook page. In addition, Prince occasionally performed "Bootzilla" and "PsychoticBumpSchool" from P-Funk bassist extraordinaire Bootsy Collins, who also played with James Brown. Prince recorded, but left unreleased, "Cookie Jar," originally written and recorded by early Parliament vocalist Fuzzy Haskins and also released by P-Funk's girl-group blueprint for Vanity 6: Parlet.

The Rolling Stones

In a genre almost defined by white appropriation of black music and culture, the Rolling Stones stand out as the rock act that has benefited the most by repackaging black music for white audiences (Elvis Presley included). This is not to belie their accomplishments or to attribute malicious intent but rather to give some context for Dez Dickerson's claim that Prince wanted to be the "black version" of the Rolling Stones, with Dez's Keith Richards to Prince's Mick Jagger. What exactly is the black version of a white band that wants to be a black band? Maybe that's the explanation of Prince that makes the most sense.

What about the Rolling Stones inspired Prince? Musically, they're cut from the same cloth: their best songs are R&B-based pop songs with a rock edge, danceable, but more than just dance music. Lyrically, especially in the 1970s,

Jagger pushed the boundaries of innuendo and appropriate language (e.g., "Star Star" aka "Star Fucker" and "Short and Curlies"), boundaries that Prince would push even further. Onstage, Prince copped many of Jagger's moves (moves Jagger had copped from James Brown and others) and embraced the role of the hypersexualized singing/dancing front man. There's also the sustained financial success helped in part by astute business acumen, from the genius branding of the tongue logo to pioneering sponsorship deals to the creation of the money-generating Mobile Studio. And the anger with management and record labels played out in song in ways that Prince could only dream about, on both the filthy unreleased "Andrew's Blues," about their manager Andrew Loog Oldham, and "Schoolboy Blues" (aka "Cocksucker Blues"), a barely released bit of obscenity created as a middle finger to Decca Records, which required one more single to fulfill the band's 1970s contract.

The Stones were early Prince fans, inviting him to open two ill-fated Los Angeles shows in October 1981. Jagger learned "Little Red Corvette" on guitar for the band's October 2016 appearances at Coachella's Desert Trip (aka Oldchella), but the band didn't follow suit and instead debuted a frequent Prince cover: The Beatles's "Come Together."

Prince played a few Rolling Stones songs live. "Miss You" debuted at an August 13, 1986, aftershow at Busby's in London, accompanied by Stones guitarist Ron Wood. "Honky Tonk Women" made numerous aftershow appearances and was recorded live in studio on June 14, 1993, for *The Undertaker* video.

The Beatles

The Beatles are the most important popular band ever—so important that they have two books in this series. Among their many influential achievements, they insisted on performing their own material, were as comfortable on the screen as onstage, established the LP as a work of art rather than a few singles with some added filler, made studio creation as valuable as live performance, and started their own (still successful) record company. These successes (and many more) had both direct and indirect effects on Prince (and everyone else in the music industry).

There's debate about Prince's early feelings about The Beatles. Wendy claims he hated them or at least what they seemed to stand for in his mind. Matt Fink, a big Beatles fan, never heard Prince disparage them. This minor controversy arose from the media reception for *Around the World in a Day*, which compared the LP to the 1967–1968 Beatles for its trippy cover, diverse musicality, and psychedelic feel. The fact that Prince's LP, like *Sgt. Pepper's Lonely Hearts Club Band*, was intended as a stand-alone release with no singles did nothing to discourage the comparisons. Prince bristled at the association and said the album wasn't influenced by The Beatles and further questioned if they could "hang" in 1985.

It can be difficult to hear a direct Beatles musical influence on Prince. There are always "Beatlesesque" references to "When You Were Mine," but I hear more of The Beatles's love of Motown in the song. Mitch Ryder gave a Detroit spin to the song in 1983, but the tune was tailor-made for late-period Supremes. Alternately, it's hard not to hear The Beatles directly in "Raspberry Beret" or especially "Take Me with U," and I'd love to have heard John and Yoko record the latter.

Prince's earliest live work with a Beatles song was the 2004 solo on "While My Guitar Gently Weeps" at the Rock and Roll Hall of Fame. He started playing a handful of Fab Four tunes in 2006. "Come Together" was played most often through 2011, typically as a medley with "7." In 1989, Prince recorded a dance version of "Day Tripper" with Margie Cox on lead vocals for the unreleased Flash album. The same session included a cover of Hendrix's "Fire," which leads one to believe that Prince was listening to the 1988 Hendrix release *Radio One*, which included both songs.

Ain't Nobody Bad Like Me

The Time

In addition to the right to coproduce his own music, Prince's early agreement with Warner Bros. included a provision for producing other artists. It's likely that Warner Bros. saw this as a way to stroke Prince's ego. It's unlikely that they saw it as leading the way to dozens of non-Prince albums, including a literal Vanity project.

Prince first tried to create another band in the summer of 1979, recording his touring band as The Rebels. This studio project was never released, but Prince seemed to learn that he preferred hiring people and telling them what to do rather than working with other people or helping artists find their own voices. He would need to make his own groups if he wanted his extracurricular visions realized.

According to manager Alan Leeds, Prince's impresario inspiration got a jump start with the 1980 film *The Idolmaker*. It's the story of Bob Marcucci, the Philadelphia label owner who discovered and molded stars such as Fabian and Frankie Avalon. And as a child of the 1970s, Prince undoubtedly saw the "Johnny Bravo" *Brady Bunch* episode in which Greg is set to be a rock star because he "fit the suit."

The Time never quite fit the suit, at least not in the same way as Vanity or Apollonia, but they were Prince's first and greatest alter-ego creation.

Flyte Tyme

Prince was adamant that he didn't want to be pigeonholed as a black artist: He wanted to be a popular artist. But that didn't mean he didn't want to make "black" music. To do that without damaging the Prince brand, he created The Time.

The Time project brought together drummer Morris Day with members of Prince high school rivals Flyte Tyme. In the late 1970s, Flyte Tyme featured vocalist Cynthia Johnson, but she left to sing for Lipps Inc. ("Funkytown"). Replaced by Alexander O'Neal, the Prince-recruited Flyte Tyme in 1980 included keyboardists Monte Moir and Jimmy Jam, Terry Lewis on bass, and drummer Garry "Jellybean" Johnson. All but Johnson were asked to join Prince's new band then called The Nerve. For drums, Prince turned to Morris Day, who was in another local band: Enterprise (aka Enterprise Band of Pleasure).

Day's participation was the result of a choice Prince offered Day. Day wrote the music for *Dirty Mind*'s "Partyup." Prince said he'd pay Day $10,000 for the song or get him a record deal. Day chose the latter. Day brought along guitarist Jesse Johnson. Johnson had moved to Minneapolis in 1981 and auditioned as bassist Andre Cymone's replacement. Prince preferred him on guitar rather than bass and asked him to join The Nerve.

O'Neal recorded a few songs with Prince in early 1981, including "Rough," but the two fell out, as O'Neal wanted more money and didn't appreciate that Jellybean had been left behind. O'Neal was booted, Day became the singer, and Jellybean was hired as drummer. Problem solved, as The Nerve became The Time. O'Neal went on to enjoy a 1987 number one R&B single, "Fake," written and performed by Jam and Lewis.

For all these machinations, when it came time to record the band's first LP in April 1981, only Day appeared on the album.

The Time (1981)

Prince recorded The Time's debut album in April 1981. The sessions took place at his Kiowa Trail Home Studio, although credits claim "Time Studio." The studio fiction is extended to production and songwriting, both credited to Prince pseudonym Jamie Starr. The album contains no songwriting credits, part of the marketing fiction that The Time is a real band and not just Prince.

Prince plays almost everything on the six-track LP. Day sings and plays drums on "Girl," "Cool," "Oh, Baby," and "The Stick." Dr. Fink plays keys on "Get It Up" and "The Stick," and Lisa Coleman sings background on "The Stick" and "Cool." Otherwise, it's Prince.

All but one song is written by Prince: Dez Dickerson's "After Hi School." "Get It Up," "Girl" (unrelated to his 1985 B-side), and "Oh, Baby" are Prince solo songs. The latter is left over from the *Prince* sessions. "Cool" was cowritten with Dickerson, and "The Stick" was cowritten with Coleman, who was living with Prince at the time.

The songs here are looser and longer than anything Prince would release until *1999*, with half of the tracks over eight minutes. But they're also more generic soul/funk, simpler lyrically and musically than just about anything in the official Prince catalog. The highlights are the two cowritten tunes, both rising above standard funk workouts.

The Time was released on July 29, 1981. It hit number fifty on the top 200 and number seven on the soul chart and spawned three singles. "Get It Up" reached number six on the soul chart, "Cool" reached number seven, and "Girl" hit number forty-nine. Collectively, the singles outperformed soul chart singles from Prince's first three LPs. The Time remains unanthologized, and the A-side and B-side edits remain unavailable on CD.

The Time made their live debut on October 7, 1981, at Sam's (later First Avenue) before embarking as the *Controversy* opening act on November 20 at the Stanley Theater in Pittsburgh. They added Jerome Benton, Lewis's cousin, as Day's valet/mirror holder for the live act. The average set was about thirty minutes, including all songs except "Girl." Prince would often aid the band from offstage.

Just as Prince did with Rick James, The Time was intent on upstaging Prince, upset at their lack of creative input and low wages. This resulted in Jesse Johnson getting pulled offstage and getting handcuffed to a coatrack, a major food fight, and Morris Day paying for hotel damages.

Prince first played "Cool" live at Paisley Park on November 4, 1998, before going on to play it more than 100 times, mainly from 2010 on. He also played "The Stick" live four times between 2002 and 2011.

What Time Is It? (1982)

What Time Is It? was released on August 25, 1982. Recorded between January and June 1982 at the home studio and Sunset Sound, it's once again mostly Prince, although songwriting is credited to The Time (four songs) and Morris Day (two songs) and production to Day and the Starr* Company, another Prince pseudonym.

Most of the music is Prince. Morris Day plays drums on "Wild and Loose," "The Walk," and "Gigolos Get Lonely Too" (which Prince released on *Originals* in 2019). Jesse Johnson contributes a guitar solo to the latter song and Vanity a spoken part on "The Walk." Prince wrote five of the six songs and cowrote "Wild and Loose" with Dez Dickerson.

The album refines the funk/dance grooves of the first outing and focuses on Day's predator/prankster character. It's mainly silly, stretched-out fun on "Wild and Loose," "777-9311" (Dickerson's phone number), and "The Walk" until the last two ballads turn a bit more introspective. The sessions also produced "Bold Generation" and "Colleen," both of which show up on *1999 Super Deluxe*.

What Time Is It? hit number two on the black charts and number twenty-six on the pop charts and included three singles. The single "777-9311" hit number two on the black charts, "The Walk" number twenty-four, and "Gigolos Get Lonely Too" number seventy-seven. A-side and B-side edits are unavailable, as is the Prince-written B-side "Grace," lyrically reminiscent of the Vanessa Bartholomew material on *Symbol*.

The Time played two headlining gigs before joining the *1999* Triple Threat tour on November 11, 1982, in Chattanooga, Tennessee. Joined by Jill Jones, they backed Vanity 6 from behind a curtain, for $250 each per gig, before performing their own set.

There was again discord between Prince and The Time. It reached a climax on March 24, 1983, when Jam and Lewis, picking up production work to supplement Prince's meager wages, missed a gig. Benton mimed the bass while Prince played offstage, and Lisa Coleman played Jam's parts offstage. This led to a fine and a firing on April 18. Jam and Lewis became prodigious producers, producing sixteen pop and twenty-six R&B number one singles, including a slew by Janet Jackson. They played on many of these hits, joined often by Monte Moir, who followed them out of loyalty. In October 1983, the trio was replaced by Paul "St. Paul" Peterson and Mark Cardenas on keyboards and Rocky Harris on bass, although Harris was replaced by Jerry Hubbard after he showed up late for the first day of *Purple Rain*'s filming.

On the Triple Threat Tour The Time played a standard forty-minute, seven-song set of the debut's "Get It Up," "Cool," and "Girl, joined by "Wild and Loose," "Gigolos Get Lonely Too," "777-9311," and "The Walk."

"777-9311" got the most love from Prince, performed about forty times from June 19, 1994, at Glam Slam LA through the March 5, 2016, San Francisco sampler set. "Wild and Loose" and "The Walk" were interpolated live a few times.

Ice Cream Castle (1984)

Prince started working with Day and Jesse Johnson on *Ice Cream Castle* at Sunset Sound on March 26–27, 1983, two days after the Jam/Lewis incident. The session produced the Time's "Jungle Love" and *Crystal Ball*'s "Cloreen Bacon Skin," featuring Day on drums. Recordings continued in April and wrapped in January 1984. In between these last two sessions, the group recorded "The Bird" live at First Avenue on October 4, the only complete band song on the first three records, and filmed *Purple Rain*.

Purple Rain proved a triumph for The Time and a star turn for Day, but it also signaled the end of the band's first phase. Day had grown tired of aping Prince's guide vocals in the studio, although it was also clear that Prince had grown tired of Day's growing cocaine habit. After Day's solo career floundered, he was back in the fold by 1989 for the *Graffiti Bridge* and *Pandemonium* projects.

Jesse Johnson also left in 1984, taking along Cardenas and Hubbard. Aided by Prince's former manager Owen Husney, he signed a deal with A&M Records and released three moderately successful albums.

By June 1984, The Time ceased to exist. Prince salvaged Peterson, Benton, and Jellybean Johnson as half of The Family.

EXECUTIVE PRODUCER:
PETER MACDONALD

GRAFFITI BRIDGE INC.

NOTE: ALL CREW CALLS ARE "HAVING HAD" MEALS BEFORE REPORT TIME

NO FORCED CALLS WITHOUT PRODUCTION MANAGER APPROVAL

CALL SHEET

"GRAFFITI BRIDGE"

CREW CALL: 7A
SHOOTING CALL: 8A
PRODUCER: STIEFEL/PHILLIPS   PROD. # _____
CO-PRODUCER: CRAIG RICE

DAY 24 OF 36 DAYS
DATE: THURSDAY 3/15/90
DIRECTOR: PRINCE

SET	SCENES	CAST #	D/N	PAGES	LOCATION
					PAISLEY PARK
EXT. MELODY COOL'S	104	1,2,3,4,5,9,11,13,14, 19,12,22	N	1/8	STUDIO
EXT. CLINTON'S HOUSE	105	1,2,3,4,5,21,13,14,19	N	1/8	(612) 474-4827
EXT. CLINTON'S HOUSE	106	1,3,4,5,6,13,14,19	N	1/8	
EXT. CLINTON'S HOUSE	107	10,14,32,21,14	N	1/8	
EXT. CLINTON'S HOUSE	108	4,5,6,21,13,14	N	1/8	
EXT. GLAM SLAM	109	1,20,14,22,13,14	N	1/8	
EXT. GLAM SLAM	110	2,14,31,56,31,11,13	N	1/8	
EXT. CLINTON'S HOUSE	111	1,3,4,5,20,11,13,14	N	1/8	
EXT. GLAM SLAM	112	14,19,20,21,22,31	N	1/8	
EXT. CLINTON'S HOUSE	113	1,3,4,5,6,11,13,14, 19,20,21,22,27	N	1/8	TOTAL PGS. 1 2/8

CAST#	CAST & DAY PLAYER	PART OF	LEAVE	REPORT	SET CALL	REMARKS
1	PRINCE	KID		7:00A	8:00A	
2	MORRIS DAY	MORRIS		9:00A	10:30A	
3	INGRID CHAVEZ	AURA	6:00A	6:30A	8:00A	
4	JEROME BENTON	JEROME		9:00A	10:00A	
5	MAVIS STAPLES	MELODY COOL	6:00A	6:30A	8:00A	
6	JILL JONES	JILL	6:00A	6:30A	8:00A	
7	LEVI SEACER	LEVI	———			HOLD
8	ROBIN HERRON	ROBIN	8:30A	9:00A	10:30A	
9	DAVID ELLIS	T.C.	———			HOLD
10	MIKO WEAVER	MIKO				HOLD
11	GEORGE CLINTON	GEORGE	7:00A	7:30A	8:00A	
13	TERRY LEWIS	TERRY		7:00A	8:00A	
14	JIMMY HARRIS	JIMMY		7:00A	8:00A	
19	GARY JOHNSON	JELLYBEAN		7:00A	8:00A	
20	JESSE JOHNSON	JESSE		9:00A	10:00A	
21	MONTE MOIR	MONTE		9:00A	10:00A	
22	JOPHERY BROWN	GEORGE'S GUARD	7:00A	7:30A	8:00A	
25	MICHAEL BLAND	MICHAEL	———			HOLD
30	TRACY BASS	COUP DANCER	———			
31	JONATHAN WEBB		———			
32	DAVID ROBERTSON		———			
33	MONIQUE MANNEN		———			
46	ROSIE GAINES	ROSIE				
47	KIRK JOHNSON	KIRK				
48	DAMON DICKSON	K.B. DANCER				
49	TONY MOSLEY					
50	PHIL CARREON	PHILLIP				
52	KIMBERLY DIONNE	COUP DANCER	———			
53	BARBERA KOVAL					
54	ROCKY SANTO					
27	JANET BRADY	AURA ST. DBL.	7:30A	8:00A	10:00A	

#'s	ATMOSPHERE & STANDINS RPT TO LOC@		SPECIAL INSTRUCTIONS
1,2,3,4,5,6,8 STAND INS	7:00A		ART DEPT/ PROPS: LEASE, PEN, AMBULANCE
			PROPS
5	STREET/ BAG PEOPLE	7:00A	SFX: JEEP ON FIRE (SC. 110,111,112,113)
10	CLINTON CLUB ATMOS.		VEH: JEEP, AMBULANCE, MOTORCYCLE
			STUNTS: GUARD SHOVES MORRIS' MEN. DRIVES JEEP + HITS

Morris Day had a lead role and other members of the reformed The Time played Seven Corners musicians in Prince's 1990 film *Graffiti Bridge*.   *(Courtesy Jeff Munson)*

Splitting initially during the *Purple Rain* and *Ice Cream Castle* era, The Time broke up a second time after fulfilling *Graffiti Bridge* and *Pandemonium* contractual obligations in early 1991. Morris Day pulled the group back together in late 1995 and some version of the band has been performing off-and-on ever since.
(Courtesy Thomas de Bruin, unused-prince-tickets.com)

Ice Cream Castle sticks to the same formula as the first two LPs—three long grooves paired with three shorter songs. While not pop, the music here is brighter and more accessible than the first two albums, especially the group's trademark "The Bird."

Prince composed "Chili Sauce," "My Drawers," and "If the Kid Can't Make You Come" on his own; "Ice Cream Castles" with Day; and "Jungle Love" and "The Bird" with Day and Johnson, although the songs are credited to Day or Day and Johnson. Day sings lead on all songs and drums on "My Drawers." Johnson is on guitar for much of the LP, solos on "My Drawers, and drums on "If the Kid Can't Make You Come." The live band performs "The Bird" without Prince.

Ice Cream Castle was released on July 2, 1984. It reached number twenty-four on the top 200 and number three on the soul LP charts and went gold. As with the first two LPs, there were three singles: the title song, which hit number eleven on the black charts; "Jungle Love," which hit number twenty; and "The Bird," which hit number thirty-three. Two singles featured the non-LP "Tricky," with the drums and bass from "Cloreen Bacon Skin," and a US twelve-inch offers "The Bird (Remix)."

Since the band dissolved, there was no tour, but a stripped-down version of the group, led by Jesse Johnson, performed at the third annual Minnesota Black Music Awards at the Prom Center in St. Paul on June 8, 1984. Accompanied by Prince, they performed "Jungle Love." Prince performed that song and "The Bird" about fifty times each and the title song a few times but didn't perform the other three songs. His version of "Jungle Love" was released on *Originals* in 2019.

Pandemonium (1990)

From June to August 1989, Prince worked with Morris Day and Jerome Benton on The Time reunion album *Corporate World*. An eleven-track album was submitted to Warner Bros. with a November 14, 1989, release date. Warner Bros. had second thoughts and instead wanted a full band reunion in exchange for financially supporting the *Graffiti Bridge* movie. Prince met with Jesse Johnson, Monte Moir, Terry Lewis, and Jimmy Jam and told them that the movie would tell The Time's side of the story. They agreed to participate and began working independently on their own material. How did that all work out? Not so well for The Time, who again ended up controlled by Prince in the studio and marginalized in the film. As some recompense, the resulting album, *Pandemonium*, hit the top twenty on both the pop and the R&B charts and went gold.

All the Prince tracks on the LP are strong, although the songs get a bit lost in the slick production of the era. Three Day vocals/Prince instrumentation *Corporate World* songs were brought over wholesale to *Pandemonium*: "Data Bank," "Donald Trump (Black Version)," and "My Summertime Thang," with the latter two featuring Candy Dulfer on sax. As with much of the *Graffiti Bridge* material, Prince dug into the Vault for some of this material as the tracking for "My Summertime Thang" comes from the same 1983 session as "Cloreen Bacon Skin," and "Data Bank" had been kicking around since 1986. The fourth full Prince song, "Chocolate," comes from an April 1983 *Ice Cream Castle* session and includes Wendy, Lisa, and Jill Jones on background vocals and a Wendy guitar solo. Prince wrote those four songs and four segues—"Dreamland," "Sexy Socialites," "Yount," and "Cooking Class"—although only The Time appear on the latter four Jam/Lewis-produced songs.

The Prince-produced "Jerk Out" is a Prince, Jam, Lewis, and Day song updated from the second Time album sessions that features all members of the Time plus Prince. Mazarati recorded and rejected it for their Paisley Park LP. The title track is written by Jam, Lewis, Jesse Johnson, and Prince but otherwise had no Prince involvement. The album's final five songs include no Prince involvement.

The three *Graffiti Bridge* songs—"The Latest Fashion," "Shake!," and "Release It"—were recorded during the *Corporate World* sessions, although the first was originally recorded by Prince in 1987. The songs include no Time member input other than Morris Day's vocals.

Of the original eleven-track *Corporate World*, only the title song remains totally unreleased. "Murph Drag," also featuring Dulfer, was released in an edited form through NPG Music Club in 2001. "Rollerskate" was partially incorporated into "My Summertime Thang" and "The Latest Fashion (Remix)."

Pandemonium was released on July 10, 1990. It has the ugliest cover of any Prince-associated album. It hit number nine on the R&B charts and number eighteen on the pop charts, going gold as The Time's best-selling album. "Jerk Out" was The Time's biggest single, hitting number one on the R&B charts and number nine on the Hot 100. The seven-inch single is an edit backed with "Mo' Jerk Out," and the twelve-inch and CD single offer five remixes. The second single, an edit of "Chocolate," reached number forty-four on the R&B charts. The twelve-inch and CD single offered five remixes plus the single B-side: the album version of "My Drawers."

The year 1991 saw the release of The Time's "Shake!" from *Graffiti Bridge*. Prince and Day wrote and performed the song. There was no seven-inch release, and the single failed to chart. The twelve-inch and CD include the album version and four remixes plus a remix of "The Latest Fashion."

The *Graffiti Bridge* album was released on August 21, 1990, and the movie on November 2. All Time members are in the movie. The six-piece Time, augmented by keyboardist Keith Lewis, played two London promo gigs on August 31 and September 1, then a Warner Bros. Convention in San Francisco. The shows lasted thirteen songs (forty-five minutes), adding the title track and the two singles to the previous song mix. A ferociously tame version of "The Walk" from the Warner Bros. gig is available online.

On September 18, 1990, the Time played *The Tonight Show* and on October 20 played *Saturday Night Live*. While in New York, Jesse Johnson was voted out of the band. Jimmy Jam and Terry Lewis soon followed. The trio was replaced by guitarist Bobby G., bassist Derek "DOA" Allen, and future NPG keyboardist Morris Hayes. This lineup played two contractually obligated shows in Japan in February 1991. These were the last shows by The Time until 1995. Day and Benton would team up live with Prince on occasion in the new millennium.

Prince performed "Jerk Out" once, on September 2, 1990, in Nishinomiya, Japan. "Chocolate" was referenced a few times from 1982 on but performed in toto only three times in 2011.

Various permutations of The Time have played live from 2008 on. In 2011, the group changed their name to the Original 7ven since Prince owned the name of The Time, although Day tours as Morris Day & The Time.

7

We Need a Purple High

The Purple Rain Era, 1983–1986

1999 (1982)

Prince later said *1999* wasn't as varied as it should be because he did all the computer work himself. But he failed to properly value his own work. *1999* is a masterpiece not only because each song is a marvel but also because all eleven meld sonically, technically, and emotionally. This is a symphony in eleven movements. Needle-drop anywhere, and you know it's the sound of peak Prince.

What's that sound? It's an expansive synthesizer sound accompanied by Prince's new best friend, the Linn LM-1 drum machine. It's multilayered funk with grooves simultaneously driving and loose, not afraid of stretching out songs for seven, eight, or nine minutes. It's letting it all hang out and not caring who's watching.

1999 sessions stretched from January to August 1982, with recording completed in August with "Little Red Corvette" and the title song. *1999* is almost all Prince, with Jill Jones, Wendy, and Dez Dickerson contributing co-lead on the title song, Dez sizzling on the "Little Red Corvette" guitar solos, and various background singers.

1999 was released on October 27, 1982, in the United States as a double vinyl LP. The United Kingdom saw a seven-song, one-disc LP released on March 4, 1983 (rereleased on vinyl April 21, 2018, with an alternate cover), with the full set released only on November 9, 1984. The initial CD release left off "D.M.S.R." due to space limitations. The cover features a no-question-about-it penis as the number "1," the first inkling of The Revolution (in backward writing), the reappearance of *Controversy*'s "Rude Boy" button, and a resplendent purple background.

1999 Deluxe and *1999 Super Deluxe* were released on Black Friday, November 29, 2019. The two-CD *1999 Deluxe* features a 2019 remaster of the original LP and an eighteen-track non-LP singles/B-sides collection. *1999 Super Deluxe* adds two CDs with twenty-four tracks of unreleased material from the Vault, a *Live in Detroit* CD (November 30, 1982), and the *Live in Houston* DVD (December 29, 1982).

The original album was Prince's commercial breakthrough, reaching number nine on the pop charts and number four on the black charts. The LP went gold and achieved 4x platinum status.

The album spawned four commercial singles in the United States, a UK promo single, and an Australian release. A "1999" edit was released September 24, 1982. It reached number four on the black charts and number forty-four on the pop charts; the album-length twelve-inch version reached number one on the dance charts. The edited "Little Red Corvette" was the major hit, fueled by constant rotation on MTV, hitting number six on the Hot 100 and number fifteen on the black charts. The uninspired "Dance Remix" hit only number sixty-one on the dance charts. Finally, a "Delirious" edit reached numbers eight and eighteen, while the "Let's Pretend We're Married" edit reached the fifties.

The edit versions of the first three singles appear on hits collections, while *1999 Deluxe* gathers almost all available single edits, promo only, mono, remix, and video releases, offering different versions of all but "Something in the Water (Does Not Compute)" and "International Lover." The non-LP sides "How Come U Don't Call Me Anymore," "Horny Toad," and "Irresistible Bitch" are available on multiple collections.

As with *Dirty Mind*, there's no filler. The album starts off with the dance anthem "1999" and the soulful pop of "Little Red Corvette," both quintessentially Prince and now simply part of the fabric of pop music. "Delirious" is almost a novelty rockabilly song that seems almost too easy. "Let's Pretend We're Married," "D.M.S.R.," and "Automatic" form a twenty-five-minute suite that pushes the erotic bounds of electronic dance music—Kraftwerk as sex-obsessed cyborgs rather than robots. Both "Something in the Water (Does Not Compute)" and "All the Critics Love U in New York" flip the equation, with the soul and experimental balance now tipping toward the latter. The album is rounded out by the two ballads, the uplifting anthem "Free" and the up-in-a-jet-screwing slow jam "International Lover," and the nasty down-in-a-cab-screwing "Lady Cab Driver."

1999 Super Deluxe offers twenty-four tracks from the Vault. "Moonbeam Levels" appeared on *4Ever*, and ten tracks are alternate versions of previously released songs. Nine of the remaining songs were attached to contemporaneous projects, such as the Hookers, Vanity 6, and the Time, while "Money Don't Grow on Trees," "Rearrange," "You're All I Want," and "Don't Let Him Fool Ya" appear to be free agents. More on *1999 Super Deluxe* in chapter 35.

The *1999* Triple Threat tour covered eighty-seven US dates from November 1982 to April 1983. Jill Jones joined the *Controversy* tour band, while The Time hit the stage before Prince and served as the offstage backing band for opener Vanity 6. All the *1999* material got a live airing on the tour except "All the Critics

Love U in New York," which debuted on *Controversy* and then hit its stride on the *One Nite Alone* tour.

The B-side "How Come You Don't Call Me Anymore" was played throughout the tour, and session outtake and *4Ever/1999 Super Deluxe* track "Moonbeam Levels" appeared on March 28 in Universal City, California.

Purple Rain (1984)

With *1999*, Prince became a music superstar. With *Purple Rain,* he became a household name.

Much ink and many bytes have been consumed on *Purple Rain*, as is common when trying to come to terms with a masterpiece. So what makes it tick? Succinctly, on *Purple Rain*, Prince channeled the diverse influences and tendencies of his first five albums and synthesized them into individual and unique songs. Well, duh, isn't that what everyone is trying to do? But he did all that not only with a memorable hook for each song but also with a memorable gimmick. There's the bored Wendy and Lisa song and the Hendrix solo song and the dirty masturbation song and the one where he screams at the end. It's all catchy and clever and all memorable. And when the LP was released, the fact that you could not only hear all these songs on the radio or on your Walkman but also watch some of them on TV and all of them at the movie theater made the deal that much sweeter.

Purple Rain is accused of rocking rather than funking, and it's guilty as charged. How can you tell? When you're standing up and listening to the song, do you just move your body above or below the shoulders? The former is rock, the latter is funk. And there's a lot more head banging here than ever before. Whether this change was a cynical appeal to gather white rock fans doesn't matter because it's so great.

For all that, the LP has only one all-out rocker: the opener "Let's Go Crazy." "Computer Blue" and "Darling Nikki" have some hard guitar, but both have backbeats that get your butt moving albeit in very different ways. "Take Me with U," "I Would Die 4 U," and "Baby I'm a Star" are pop songs. "The Beautiful Ones" might be his best straightforward ballad, and "Purple Rain" is, well, "Purple Rain"—eternally anthemic without being cheesy. That leaves the top highlight, "When Doves Cry," a bass-free organic-mechanical cry of pain, its own genre.

Purple Rain started on the *1999* tour, as Prince was often seen scribbling ideas for a movie into notebooks on the bus. The tour ended in April 1983, and during the late spring and early summer, Prince developed songs for this movie. In June, he began rehearsals for the new songs with his band, which now included Wendy Melvoin on guitar, at a warehouse in St. Louis Park, Minnesota. On August 3, 1983, this band, now The Revolution, debuted at First Avenue.

Prince and the Revolution
Purple Rain
Music From The Movie

1984 was the year of the blockbuster LP, with only five albums holding down the pop number one spot: *Purple Rain*, Michael Jackson's *Thriller*, the Footloose sound track, Bruce Springsteen's *Born in the USA*, and Huey Lewis and the News's *Sports*, the latter for one week. Most record stores typically used handmade dividers to separate all of one artist's vinyl catalog from another artist's, but with the popularity of *Purple Rain* and the marketability of Prince's iconic look, Warner Bros. distributed album-specific promotional dividers.   *(Author's collection)*

They played a dozen songs, six of which were new and three of which would end up on *Purple Rain*. The rest of the album and B-sides and outtakes were recorded between then and April 1984 at the Warehouse, Prince's Kiowa Trail Home Studio, and Sunset Sound.

Purple Rain was released on June 25, 1984, a month before the film. It's the first of three albums credited to Prince and the Revolution. It hit number one on the US pop charts for twenty-four weeks, preceded and followed by Bruce Springsteen's *Born in the USA*. It reached number one on the black charts, chasing out Tina Turner's *Tiny Dancer* and replaced by another sound track: Stevie Wonder's *The Woman in Red*. It reentered the top 200 at number two on May 7, 2016, and stayed in the top ten for four weeks It is the twenty-sixth-best-selling album of all time with sales of more than 13 million. It chalked up three Grammys.

Purple Rain featured five singles. Both "When Doves Cry" and "Let's Go Crazy" hit number one and are featured in chapter 12.

Released on September 26, 1984, in the United States, "Purple Rain" was the third single, reaching number two in the United States. The seven-inch edit was first collected in 2017 on the four-disc *Deluxe Purple Rain*. The twelve-inch featured the album version, but three versions are still uncollected on CD: the German twelve-inch "Long Version," the UK seven-inch promo "Radio Edit," and "Long Radio Edit." We can hold our breath for *Purple Rain Deluxe Deluxe*.

The fourth single, "I Would Die 4 U," was released on November 28. The single version hit number eight in the United States and has appeared on multiple collections. "I Would Die 4 U (Extended Version)" was available on a German "Erotic City" CD in 1989 and finally hit the United States in 2017 on *Deluxe*.

"Take Me with U" was the final single, released on January 25, 1985, reaching number twenty-five. The edit and the B-side edit for "Baby I'm a Star" appear on *Deluxe*.

B-sides "Erotic City," "Erotic City ('Make Love Not War Erotic City Come Alive')," "God," "God (Love Theme from *Purple Rain*)," "Another Lonely Christmas," and "Another Lonely Christmas (Extended Version)" all appear on *Deluxe*. "17 Days" appears as "B-Side Edit," but the full version has not been released and wasn't circulating until December 2017.

The *Purple Rain* tour started on November 4, 1984, with seven nights at Detroit's Joe Louis Arena. It encompassed ninety-eight shows, ending on April 7, 1985, at Miami's Orange Bowl. All nine album tracks were performed at most shows, and seven were performed regularly until 2016, "Computer Blue" and "Darling Nikki" less favored. Non-LP songs "God," "How Come You Don't Call Me Anymore," "Irresistible Bitch," "Father's Song," and "Possessed" were played on a semi-regular basis. The tour is documented on the *Prince and the Revolution: Live* home video, available in the *Purple Rain Deluxe* package.

Around the World in a Day (1985)

As Tag Team sang, "Whoop! There it is!" That pretty much describes Prince dropping *Around the World in a Day (ATWIAD)* just ten months after *Purple Rain*. But Prince was on top of the world, and Warner Bros. let him have his way, but the relative underperformance of *ATWIAD*, which was decidedly not *Purple Rain* volume 2, would portend future release battles.

ATWIAD is the second LP credited to Prince and the Revolution, but the full band is on only three songs: "Pop Life," "America," and "The Ladder." Unlike many Prince LPs where the first hit is a late addition, "Raspberry Beret" is the earliest existing song, given a run-through in April 1982. The balance of the LP was written and recorded prior to and during the *Purple Rain* tour, with the final tracks recorded on December 23 ("The Ladder") and December 24 ("Temptation") 1984 in and around the St. Paul Civic Center.

The songs are easy to like, but the album is hard to love, the disjointed recording schedule reflected in the mishmash of styles. Like his best tracks, "Raspberry Beret" is both nothing-but-Prince and a song pulled from our collective consciousness, easy, breezy, and portable. This might be the song that people remember Prince for 100 years from now. The other highlights are the brash "Temptation," a first foray into a blues style that would reappear with the mid-1990s NPG, the manic "America," and the deceptively aggressive "Paisley Park," which is the emotional heart of the LP.

Of the second-tier songs, "Pop Life" is likable fluff, the brief "Tamborine" sounds like a template for the Time's "Release It," and the title track, adapted from an original song by Lisa's brother David Coleman, is jerky and Middle Eastern trippy, a sound Prince would revisit. There are two clunkers here. On "Condition of the Heart," Prince noodles around on the keys for three minutes before entering histrionic diva mode, while "The Ladder" attempts to replicate the grandeur of "Purple Rain" but with annoying sax riffs that sound lifted from mid-1970s Paul Simon albums.

On the strength of *Purple Rain*, the un-funky *ATWIAD* reached number one on the pop charts but only number four on the black charts. The intent was to release no singles, but as the LP floundered, that changed, and "Raspberry Beret," "Pop Life," and "America" were released in the United States and "Paisley Park" in other territories. The first two songs hit the US top ten on both charts.

Each single had non-LP material. "Raspberry Beret (New Mix)," "She's Always in My Hair," "She's Always in My Hair (New Mix)," "Pop Life (Fresh Dance Mix)," and "Hello" have all appeared on collections. "Pop Life (Extended Version)," "Hello (Fresh Dance Mix)," "Girl (Extended Version)," and the luscious twenty-one-minute, forty-six second, version of "America" remain uncollected, as do a mono French promo version and a UK twelve-inch "Remix" of "Paisley Park." All await a deluxe *ATWIAD* release.

There was no tour for this album, time being consumed filming *Under the Cherry Moon* and recording *Parade*. All songs were played during the *Parade* tour except "Tamborine," which was only ever played twice, and "Temptation," which was never played at a concert. However, it was rehearsed (for what?) at the video shoot for "America" on October 27, 1985, in a scorching version that makes you sorry it wasn't a tour regular.

Parade (*Music from the Motion Picture* Under the Cherry Moon) (1986)

At this point, one must ask, when did Prince sleep in the mid-1980s? In February 1985, still on the *Purple Rain* tour, he finished *Sheila E in Romance 1600*. Ten days after the April 7 tour ended, he began recording *Parade (Music from the Motion Picture* Under the Cherry Moon), which bled into *Mazarati*, which bled into *Jill Jones*. Back and forth from Los Angeles to Minneapolis, he completed *Parade*, recording "Anotherloverholenyohead" at Sunset Sound during a December 16–26 session, and then developed his jazz sound at four- and seven-hour jam sessions before completing the unreleased *The Flesh* EP on January 22, 1986. And he starred in and directed a major motion picture that fall. And he was juggling about five girlfriends. And that's before he really cranked into high gear on his next project.

Parade was released on March 31, 1986, less than a year after *ATWIAD*, reaching only number three. The stark black-and-white cover is the first since *Controversy* with a close-up of Prince. The album is the last credited to Prince

By the fall 1986 European *Parade* tour The Revolution was a tight, almost flawless band, but with Wendy, Lisa, and Brown Mark previously expressing a desire to leave the band, there is a rote, anti-climactic element to most of the performances. The exception is the one-off gig at Paris's New Morning Club on August 24, notable for the debut of a handful of songs and the only performance of the brief jam "Susannah's Blues."   *(Courtesy Thomas de Bruin, unused-prince-tickets.com)*

and The Revolution, but the full band features on only four tracks. *Parade* also offers the first Clare Fischer appearance on a Prince album. His orchestration expands nine tunes, so the LP might better be credited to Prince and the Clare Fischer Orchestra.

Parade is a solid album, if a bit underdeveloped in its thought process and hesitant in its experimentation. The album features one unqualified classic, "Kiss," and one of Prince's best-loved songs, the gentle piano ballad "Sometimes It Snows in April," often quoted after Prince's death. "Girls & Boys," "Mountains," and "Anotherloverholenyohead" are all concise slices of pop funk à la Sly and the Family Stone. The other songs feel like clever rhythms and orchestration in search of fleshed-out songs, as six of the tracks clock in at under three minutes, with the cluttered "Life Can Be So Nice" stretching out to three minutes, fourteen seconds. Prince seemed to recognize this issue as he incorporated movements into songs on the subsequent *Dream Factory* and *Crystal Ball* projects. Maybe the opening "Christopher's Tracy's Parade," "New Position," and "I Wonder U" (total time six minutes, twelve seconds) should be considered a suite.

The LP produced four international singles, led by the first single "Kiss" (see chapter 12). The LP version of "Mountains" was released on May 7, 1986, and reached number twenty-three on the pop charts and number fifteen on the black charts. An "Anotherloverholenyohead" edit also did well on the black charts, hitting number eighteen. An edit of "Girls & Boys" reached number eleven in the United Kingdom.

All single non-LP versions have been collected on CD except "Mountains (Extended Version)," "Alexa de Paris," and edited and extended versions of "Anotherloverholenyohead." "Alexa de Paris (Extended Version)" appeared on the UK "Letitgo" single but not on any CD collection.

The *Parade* live era started with ten US Hit N Run shows from March until the official tour started on August 12, 1986, at London's Wembley Arena. It comprised nineteen shows in Europe and Japan, ending on September 9, 1986, at Yokohama Stadium. The shows focused on a mixture of *ATWIAD* and *Parade* material with a smattering of earlier hits. All the songs were played during the tour, except "Do U Lie," which debuted in 1988. B-sides "Love or Money" and "Alexa de Paris" were each played a handful of times.

The Yokohama show marked the last group appearance for Wendy, Lisa, Bobby Z., and Brown Mark and the end of Prince and The Revolution.

8

At Least U Got Friends

The Revolution and Late 1980s Band

Prince's band at the April 1983 end of the 1999 tour included original members Bobby Z., Matt Fink, and Dez Dickerson plus recent enlistees Brown Mark, Lisa Coleman, and Jill Jones. Jones drifted away, and Dickerson quit after deciding not to sign up for the three-year *Purple Rain* commitment. He was replaced by guitarist Wendy Melvoin, creating The Revolution. The band debuted on August 3, 1983, at First Avenue in Minneapolis and closed shop with a September 9, 1986, show in Yokohama. Except for Fink, who would last until 1990, and occasional member Eric Leeds, member turnover would be complete by the end of the 1980s.

Wendy Melvoin (1982–1986)

Prince noticed Wendy Melvoin during 1982's *Controversy* tour when she was hanging around the bus with her girlfriend Lisa Coleman. She was soon in the studio adding background vocals to "Free," and in May 1983, she assumed guitar duties when Dez Dickerson left the band.

Melvoin's addition not only pushed Prince more toward rock and increased the bands' diversity but also upped the internecine drama, as her twin sister Susannah became engaged to Prince. If *Lifetime* ever makes a Prince movie, this drama gets my vote.

Wendy made her debut on August 3, 1983, at First Avenue, the first Revolution show. She was onstage until the September 9, 1986, Yokohama show. She is the only musician who was only a member of The Revolution.

After "Free," Wendy added background vocals on "Irresistible Bitch" and half a dozen other songs and lead vocals on *Parade*'s "I Wonder U." She's a member of the Revolution on the standard baker's dozen of band studio tracks and adds tambourine and congas on "Strange Relationship." She cowrote "Computer Blue" and "Mountains" and is on "Power Fantastic" and both versions of "4 the Tears in Your Eyes." She also has the uncredited guitar solo on The Time's "Chocolate." Like Lisa, Wendy had a large stake in *Dream Factory*, although both claim that the album never existed as anything more than a loose collection of songs.

Wendy & Lisa released three major label albums after leaving Prince and placed one single on the US Hot 100: 1987's "Waterfall." They've scored a number of TV shows and received a Title Theme Emmy in 2010 for *Nurse Jackie*.

Wendy had worked with Prince a few times without Lisa. She appeared on February 12, 2004, on the *Tavis Smiley* show performing "Reflection." On July 2, 2004, she appeared in New Orleans at the Superdome on nine songs, mostly from *Purple Rain*. The two duetted on guitar for seven songs on June 25, 2007, at the Roosevelt Hotel in Hollywood and she appeared at a few smaller shows around this time, occasionally with Susannah.

Sheila E. (1984–2010)

Prince first saw Sheila E. (Escovedo) backstage at an Al Jarreau concert in 1978. When they met a year later at a Prince concert, he asked her how much she'd charge to play drums for him. She told him, and he said, "I'll never be able to afford that." Cut to: Prince and Sheila started recording together in early 1984, working on drum tracks for an unreleased version of "A Million Miles (I Love You)" and "Pop Life" and vocal overdubs for "Erotic City" before finishing *Sheila E. in the Glamorous Life* (April 1–4).

Sheila E. opened the July 27, 1984, *Purple Rain* premiere party and the subsequent tour. Her band jumped onstage almost every night for an extended "Baby I'm a Star." Her band also opened the September 1986 Japan leg of the *Parade* tour. She was the full-time Prince drummer from March 21, 1987, at First Avenue through February 13, 1989, at the final Osaka *Lovesexy* show. They guested with each other's bands numerous times from 2000 through 2011.

Sheila drums on about ten Prince album tracks, including "Pop Life," "U Got the Look," and "2 Nigs United 4 West Compton," but appears on only two associated artist tracks. Her most significant Prince-associated studio work was on Madhouse *16*. She cowrote "Ten," "Eleven," and "Fifteen" and plays drums on those tracks. She cowrote three songs and plays on Eric Leeds's *Times Squared*. She's also the drummer on the never-released late 1985/early 1986 instrumental jazz/funk sessions.

Although there were relationship issues, Sheila left the band in 1989 because she wasn't happy about the direction the music was going, especially the lyrics. After leaving Prince, she was thrice a part of Ringo Starr and His All-Starr Band, playing a humorous drum duet with Ringo, and in 2006, she formed the group C.O.E.D. (Chronicles of Every Diva) with Prince alum Rhonda Smith and Kat Dyson.

ERIC LEEDS
MADHOUSE

WARNER BROS

Eric Leeds worked with Prince for almost two decades, from 1984's *The Family* project to 2004's *C-Note*. The two Madhouse LPs were mostly Leeds and Prince collaboration projects and Leeds's image appeared in Paisley Park/Warner Bros. promotional materials as the group leader. *(Author's collection)*

Eric Leeds (1984–2003)

In 1984, Prince was looking for a saxophonist for his new band The Family. Tour manager Alan Leeds encouraged his younger brother Eric to take a stab. Eric wasn't into Prince's music but was convinced to demo with and eventually join the group. Prince quickly took to Leeds's more jazz-oriented sound, crediting him as "the expert" on *Purple Rain*. Leeds believes Prince was influenced to use a horn in his band after watching Clarence Clemons perform with Bruce Springsteen and the E Street Band. Prince soon not only incorporated Leeds into The Revolution, to the chagrin of other members, but also used him as a springboard to a sideline jazz career.

Leeds appears on seven of eight *The Family* tracks (not on "The Screams of Passion") and cowrote the instrumentals "Yes" and "Susannah's Pajamas" with Prince. He was part of the original band's one performance, on August 13, 1985, at First Avenue.

Leeds joined the *Purple Rain* tour full time in February 1985. He remained Prince's sax/flute player through the February 13, 1989, end of the *Lovesexy* tour. He returned for appearances in 1995–1997 and in 2002 for portions of the *One Nite Alone* tour.

Leeds didn't appear on a Prince album until *Parade*, on "Girls & Boys" and "Mountains," around the same time he recorded "Sexual Suicide." From there, he appeared on about twenty-five tracks, most notably sax on "Slow Love" and "Eye Know," flute on "Gett Off" and "Letitgo," all of *N.E.W.S.*, and all of *C-Note* except "Empty Room." He also cowrote "It's Gonna Be a Beautiful Night" with Prince and Dr. Fink and "Rockhard in a Funky Place" with Prince.

Leeds's most well-known side work with Prince is Madhouse. January 1987's Madhouse *8* is a two-person collaboration, while December's *16* includes Sheila E., Levi Seacer Jr., and Dr. Fink on a few tracks. Madhouse opened some *Sign 'o' the Times* dates with Leeds, Seacer, Fink, and 94 East drummer Dale Alexander. Initial efforts to produce a third LP resulted in Leeds's first solo album: *Times Squared*.

Leeds appears on more than twenty songs from about a dozen Prince associates and protégés, mostly on songs he wrote or cowrote. He released two solo albums after leaving Prince. Prince received cowriting credit on 1993's "Aguadilla" from *Things Left Unsaid*, as it used a melody from The Family's "Desire," but he was not involved in the LP. Leeds re-formed The Family as Fdeluxe in 2007.

Atlanta Bliss (1986–1991)

Trumpeter Matthew Blistan is a Duquesne University classmate of Eric Leeds who joined the extended Revolution in 1985. Prince spontaneously gave Blistan the name Atlanta Bliss in the studio, perhaps remembering that Leeds lived in Atlanta when he joined Prince.

Bliss played live with Prince from the March 3, 1986, First Avenue show until the February 1989 final *Lovesexy* show in Yokohama. His time in the Revolution was marked by a backhanded compliment from Wendy, who appreciated that at least he was a musician while other new members were merely part of a circus.

Bliss appeared on fifteen Prince-released studio tracks, including "Mountains," "Eye Know," and "Trust." He's also on *Dream Factory*'s "In a Large Room with No Light" and "Train" as well as some of the best Vault material, including the studio version of "Rebirth of the Flesh," "The Ball," and the abridged version of "Wally." Bliss plays on Prince-associated tracks from Chaka Khan, Mavis Staples, George Clinton, Tevin Campbell, and Carmen Electra.

Jerome Benton (1985–1986)

In this long story of Prince band members, Jerome Benton is the most fortunate. Variously described as the brother or cousin of the Time bassist Terry Lewis, Benton joined Prince's side project as Morris Day's valet on 1981's *Controversy* opening slot. He quickly rode his mirror-holding skills to a position in the top backing band in the world: The Revolution (with apologies to the E Street Band).

Benton costarred in *Purple Rain*. His group, The Time, broke up, but he joined Prince's new band, The Family, before jumping on the *Purple Rain* tour as a dancer. He starred in *Under the Cherry Moon*, but The Family dissolved, and Benton joined The Revolution. The Revolution broke up in late 1986, but he showed up again in *Graffiti Bridge*—three dead bands, Benton left standing. We'd all be so lucky to get a gig like this.

Benton is credited on one Prince track: background vocals on "It's Gonna Be a Beautiful Night." He's mentioned for background vocals, noise, and hollers on four Time tracks plus all of *Pandemonium*.

Greg Brooks (1984–1987) and Wally Safford (1984–1987)

Speaking of lucky. Gregory Allen Brooks and Wally Safford worked security on the *Purple Rain* tour. The duo often joined the Revolution onstage, dancing and eventually singing. Like fellow dancer Benton, they became full-fledged members of The Revolution with the March 3, 1986, First Avenue show. Unlike Benton, they continued on the *Sign 'o' the Times* tour, ending their run at the December 31, 1987, Paisley Park show featuring Miles Davis, with Prince dissing

Greg Brooks from the stage. Not bad for a duo that Matt Fink considered "not even good dancers."

Brooks and Safford appear on two Prince songs—"It's Gonna Be a Beautiful Night" and "Eye Know"—and in the *Sign 'o' the Times* movie. Brooks has a larger role in the film as Prince's competition for Cat, resplendent in an enormous coonskin hat.

It's likely that Brooks is the "Gregory" in "Anna Stesia," who looks like a ghost.

Safford figures in two Prince songs. He was Prince's second bodyguard on January 28, 1985, the night Prince snubbed the "We Are the World" recording. A photographer tried to snap a photo and tangled with Safford, getting hurt. This incident is rendered in "Hello," in which Prince calls Safford a friend, not a bodyguard. Safford is also the title character in the unreleased Susannah Melvoin breakup song "Wally." He's the cat with the craziest sunglasses.

Video from a 2017 Detroit appearance shows that Brooks can still rock the coonskin hat albeit more slowly.

Miko Weaver (1984–1991)

Michael "Miko" Weaver was Sheila E.'s guitarist for the *Purple Rain* tour. He was a frequent onstage guest with The Revolution and fully joined The Revolution on March 3, 1986. He continued as a Prince band member through the September 10, 1990, Nude tour finale in Yokohama.

Weaver doesn't loom large in Prince lore but does figure in one story. During rehearsals for the Nude tour, Prince kept turning down Weaver's amp. They argued about it to the point that Prince asked Weaver to step outside to settle the matter. Weaver wisely declined, factoring in the presence and size of Prince's bodyguards.

Although a member of Shelia E.'s band, Weaver doesn't appear on her debut and only sings background on Prince's "Toy Box" from *Romance 1600*. He is credited as a member of The Family but doesn't perform on the LP. Weaver joined the Revolution when The Family folded.

Weaver gets credit on four released Prince tracks: "Mountains," "It's Gonna Be a Beautiful Night," "Eye Know," and "I Would Die 4 U (Extended Version)." The latter is an essential half-hour rehearsal jam with Sheila E.'s band that was edited to a ten-minute, fifteen-second, twelve-inch version.

Levi Seacer Jr. (1985–1994)

Levi Seacer Jr. did a little bit of everything for Prince—guitarist, bassist, songwriter, producer, and finally president of NPG Records. Like other mid-1980s band members, Seacer joined Prince through Sheila E.'s band, where he was a guitarist before joining Prince on bass. For reasons unclear, Prince trusted Levi as a "Mini-Me," a role he hadn't been willing to cede to Andre Cymone, Dez Dickerson, or Brown Mark, whom Seacer replaced on bass.

Seacer and keyboardist/vocalist Boni Boyer were in Sheila E.'s band on the September 1986 Japanese *Parade* tour and transitioned to full-time Prince status for the March 21, 1987, First Avenue show. Seacer remained on bass through the Nude tour, swapping to guitar in the first version of the NPG. He stayed on through the European Act II tour, ending his live run at the September 8, 1993, Bagley's Warehouse gig. During this time, he also played live bass for Madhouse and guitar for Carmen Electra during her ill-fated 1992 London opening shows.

Seacer began his Prince studio career during the Flash sessions. He appears on bass on eight released Prince album tracks, including "Daddy Pop" and "Eye Know," and guitar on at least fifteen tracks, including "Cream" and "Sexy M.F." He cowrote "Sex" with Prince and "Willing and Able" and "Sexy M.F." with Prince and Tony M. On *Graffiti Bridge*, he coproduced "Release It" and "Love Machine" and cowrote the former with Prince and the latter with Prince and Morris Day.

For associated bands, Seacer is credited on the first Madhouse album and *Sheila E.* but doesn't play on either. On Madhouse *16*, he cowrote and plays bass on "Ten," "Eleven," and "Fifteen." He cowrote four songs and appears on five from Leeds's 1991 Paisley Park LP. He also plays guitar on six 1993 unreleased New Power Madhouse songs. From 1989 through 1993, Seacer worked on at least thirteen Prince side projects. He was everywhere Prince couldn't be.

Seacer plays guitar and cowrote nine songs on NPG's *Gold Nigga*. At the end of Act II, Prince assumed NPG guitar duties and asked Seacer to head NPG Records. Seacer quit as NPG Records president in November 1994, unwilling to endlessly herd cats.

Seacer and Tony M. sued Prince for $800,000 in 1998 for royalties on songs they cowrote, such as "Sexy M.F." They won the suit but collected only $40,000 each.

Cat Glover (1986–1989)

Cat (Glover) debuted as a dancer and backing vocalist at the March 21, 1987, Fine Line show, a few weeks after she mysteriously appeared on the "Sign 'o' the Times" single sleeve. She was featured on the *Sign 'o' the Times* tour and was on the *Lovesexy* tour through the end. She was replaced, in part, by the Game Boyz. In the studio, Cat was needed to rap on "Alphabet St." and contributed vocals to "Anna Stesia," "Le Grind," "Cindy C.," and "2 Nigs United 4 West Compton." Prince removed her rap from "Positivity" when he found out it was lifted from J. M. Silk's "Music Is the Key." Cat recorded at least four unreleased songs in late 1988/early 1989 for an aborted solo album ("Cat Attack," "A Man Called Jesus,"

Cat Glover doesn't perform on a Prince recording until 1988's *Lovesexy*, but her appearance on the February 1987 "Sign 'o' the Times" single sleeve confused a lot of people about what seemed at first glance to be Prince's latest look.   *(Author's collection)*

"Cat and Mouse," and "Nine Lives"). She appeared in five promo videos, from "U Got the Look" through "I Wish U Heaven." She left the purple entourage to work with producer Tim Simenon (Bomb the Bass).

Boni Boyer (1987–1989)

Boni Boyer played keys and sang for Sheila E.'s opening band during the September 1986 Revolution shows in Japan. She graduated to the unnamed A Team at the March 21, 1987, Fine Line show. Like Rosie Gaines who followed her, Boyer provided a rich female presence to the stage sound. She was with Prince on the *Sign 'o' the Times* tour and ended her run on *Lovesexy*. Boyer appeared on keyboards on "Eye Know," vocals on "Anna Stesia" and "Positivity," and on "Graffiti Bridge." She also appears on *Sheila E.* and Mavis Staples's *Time Waits for No One*. Boyer died of a brain aneurysm on December 4, 1996.

The *Lovesexy* tour is considered by many to be Prince's most complete live experience. This ticket is from the first of three 1988 Rotterdam shows attended by Dutch native Candy Dulfer, who jammed on "Blues in C (If I Had a Harem)" on the third night after Prince nixed her band Funky Stuff's opening slot.

(Courtesy Thomas de Bruin, unused-prince-tickets.com)

Candy Dulfer (1989; 2002–2004)

Dutch saxophonist Candy Dulfer started her band Funky Stuff when she was fourteen and within three years was opening shows for Madonna. She would go on to multiple gold records and Grammy nominations. She was scheduled to open three Rotterdam *Lovesexy* shows, but Prince canceled the supporting slot. She sent him a note that said he lost an opportunity to "see a girl play her ass off on the saxophone." He let her guest the third night, August 19, 1988, on "Blues in C (If I Had a Harem)."

Dulfer worked with Prince in the studio during the summer of 1989 and appeared on the September *Saturday Night Live* broadcast of "Electric Chair." She also appeared in the "Partyman" video, released in the fall of 1989. She played live with the NPG from 1998 through 2007, on some of the *One Nite Alone* tour, and on all of *Musicology*.

In her late 1980s studio stint, Prince hooked Dulfer up with The Time for the failed *Corporate World*. She appears on six Time tracks from the period plus Mavis Staples's 1993 release "A Man Called Jesus" and the unreleased Jill Jones tracks "My Baby Knows" and "Flesh and Blood."

In her return engagement, Dulfer plays sax on all three *One Nite Alone* live LPs, all *Xpectation* tracks except "Xhalation," and eight tracks from *Musicology* and *3121*.

Michael Bland (1989–1996; 2006–2015)

Rock/pop drummer Michael B. (Bland) joined Minneapolis mainstay Dr. Mambo's Combo in 1987 and was behind the kit when Prince played with the band on September 28, 1988, at the Fine Line. He debuted with Prince on the September 24, 1989, *Saturday Night Live* "Electric Chair" performance and was the regular drummer from the Nude tour through the first incarnation of the NPG until the February 1996 Hawaii Honeymoon shows. He returned live briefly in 2009: for "Dreamer" on March 26 on the *Tonight Show* and the second Nokia show on March 28 (the "rock" show). Away from Prince, he backed multiple performers, including Paul Westerberg and Nick Jonas, auditioned for Guns N' Roses, and is a full-time member of Soul Asylum.

Michael B. is a stalwart, playing on more than fifty LP tracks from *Diamonds and Pearls* through *The Vault* compilation plus the non-LP "Rock 'N' Roll Is Alive! (And It Lives in Minneapolis)," the video LP *The Undertaker*, and the unreleased mid-1990s Madhouse *24*. He reappeared on "Baby Knows," "3121," "Planet Earth," "Guitar," "Groovy Potential," and five *Lotusflow3r* tracks. He was behind the kit for the first two NPG albums and at least nine Prince-associated LPs. He was also part of the Margie Cox–led Flash and drummed on the unreleased Prince track "Good Body Every Evening."

9

U Don't Have 2 Watch *Dynasty*

TV Appearances

Prince made around 100 televised appearances. Some were nothing more than lip-synching, while others stretched the better part of an hour and included in-depth interviews and essential live performances. This chapter focuses on the dozen most noteworthy TV appearances.

American Bandstand

America Bandstand host and music industry mogul Dick Clark was a gatekeeper of American televisual pop success from the show's 1957 national debut through the early 1980s when MTV happened. The January 26, 1980, show is remembered less for the two mimed *Prince* cuts than for Prince's interview behavior.

According to Dez Dickerson, Prince was put off by Clark's condescension in the green room and told the band not respond to Clark's questions. Clark steps directly into the green room hole by starting his on-camera banter with bemusement that "this kind of music" comes from Minneapolis. Then it goes downhill. Prince introduces the band, then throws off Clark by responding to a question about how long the band's been playing by holding up four fingers. He then alternates between a 1,000-yard stare and a penetrating glare into Clark's eyes. Uncomfortable.

The *Bandstand* oddness helped solidify Prince as a mysterious and controversial figure. It also allowed him to show his fans that he was in the game but not playing the game. More pointedly, he was working with old white men, but he wasn't working for old white men.

Bandstand is actually Prince's second American TV slot. His debut occurred January 12 on NBC's *The Midnight Special*. The lip-synched "I Wanna Be Your Lover" appearance is uneventful save for a glimpse into the substance-fueled music industry of the early 1980s with an introduction by two members of Dr. Hook's Medicine Show.

Saturday Night Live

Playing *Saturday Night Live* (*SNL*) early career is confirmation of buzz, while playing later is an indication of continued relevancy. Prince played *SNL* four times, the first on February 21, 1981, and the last on November 1, 2014. These shows, thirty-three years apart, bookend Prince's live TV career.

The 1981 gig occurred when Prince was breaking through with white, New Wave audiences and *SNL* was begging for street cred. It was mutually benefi-cial. Prince, regaled in *Dirty Mind* finery, tore the roof off with a performance of "Uptown." Unfortunately, he got only one song, as he shared the musical spotlight with Todd Rundgren. In 2017, *Rolling Stone* claimed this as the twenty-first-best *SNL* musical performance.

Prince wouldn't find his way back to NBC's Studio 8H until September 24, 1989. Prince again got only one song. But it was a scorching rendition of "Electric Chair," the song's only live performance.

The 1995 *SNL* season opener was supposed to feature Symbol, but he reneged, not wanting to promote Warner Bros.'s *The Gold Experience*, released just prior to the intended air date. Blues Traveler replaced Prince and the world was a sadder place.

Prince next appeared on *SNL* February 4, 2006, performing the weak "Fury." He also duetted with Tamar on "Beautiful, Loved, and Blessed." The energy is there, but the song isn't strong—a disappointing go around.

Prince performed on *SNL* for the final time during his life on November 1, 2014, appearing with 3rdEyeGirl plus Lianne La Havas and Josh Welton. This four-song set promoting *Art Official Age* and *Plectrumelectrum* was played as an unprecedented, continuous mini-concert lasting seven minutes, thirty seconds. The performance captured all the strengths of the two discs, opening with a third-eye glasses–wearing Prince at the keyboards fluttering on "Clouds" before taking the gloves off, picking up the guitar, and blistering through "Plectrumelectrum," "Marz," and "Anotherlove" (for the latter's only full run-through)—an astounding performance.

Prince attended *SNL*'s fortieth-anniversary celebration on February 15, 2015, but didn't perform until a set-burning aftershow that featured "Let's Go Crazy (Reloaded)" interpolated with Edgar Winter's "Frankenstein." This perfor-mance was featured as part of *SNL*'s April 23, 2016, broadcast "Goodnight Sweet Prince," an episode celebrating Prince's life.

American Music Awards

Purple Rain's big wins at 1985's *American Music Awards* (*AMA*) began Prince's victory lap and the inevitable backlash against his success. Prince won three awards and delivered his first of too many "Purple Rain" spots in a performance that was startling in its grandeur. This was the moment he became a household name in the United States, the first time a middle-aged TV crowd not prone to watching MTV welcomed Prince into their living rooms.

After the show, Prince refused to join other *AMA*-attending musicians at the Los Angeles recording of "We Are the World," knowing that the song is horrible and that he didn't want to be a part of it. Prince appeared at an additional four *AMA* shows. At the 1995 show, he sucked on a lollipop while aggressively not joining a "We Are the World" group finale. His November 22, 2015, appearance, presenting an award to The Weeknd, marked his last time on TV.

MTV Video Music Awards

In a career marked by outrageousness, this performance might be the pinnacle. Prince was anxious to recapture the public's attention after the relative failure of the *Graffiti Bridge* LP and the abject failure of the movie—and what better way than to appear at the current place-to-be-seen event amid a flaming, triple-decker, pansexual orgy in assless pants. And this description doesn't do the act justice.

The September 5, 1991, "Gett Off" performance marked the American TV debut of the NPG, resplendent in the most garish early 1990s colors, and the jump start that Prince's career needed. Although the music is clearly secondary to the visuals, it marked Prince's US public foray into rap, Tony M. stalking a garish stage cluttered with other Game Boyz, Diamond and Pearl, and multiple orgy participants. It all worked. *Diamonds and Pearls* was Prince's biggest non–sound track album since *Around the World in a Day*.

It was later revealed that the bodysuit was not, in fact, assless, merely gauzy, but that in no way diminishes the overall effect.

Aresnio Hall Show

Prince first appeared on the *Arsenio Hall Show* on September 9, 1991, promoting the *Diamonds and Pearls* LP. The program featured Hall chatting with Patti Labelle between Prince and the NPG performances. Prince opened with a nod toward "Diamond and Pearls" before a dance medley of "Let's Go Crazy" and "Kiss." In a show heavy with costume changes, he changed to black for "Cream," then purple for "Purple Rain," and then burning yellow for an energetic "Daddy Pop." Tony M. closed the show with "Call the Law." The show was slick but satisfying.

Prince and the NPG also took over Arsenio's show on February 25, 1993, and Prince and 3rdEyeGirl joined Arsenio Hall on his briefly revived hour-long syndicated show on March 5, 2014.

In May 2016, Sinead O'Connor accused Arsenio on Facebook of providing Prince with illegal drugs that contributed to Prince's death. Arsenio filed a defamation suit for $5 million, to which Sinead responded, "Suck my dick." Arsenio dropped the suit in February 2017 after O'Connor apologized. In August 2017, the "Nothing Compares 2 U" singer posted a gripping Facebook video announcing her problems with mental illness and depression.

NBC's *The Today Show*

NBC's *The Today Show* is another US TV institution that Prince embraced. The New York City–based show is the first and longest-running American morning news and entertainment program. Prince performed on the show four times and was interviewed an additional six times, including his final (brief) interview.

The July 9, 1996, outdoor performance is the best *Today* appearance. "Dinner with Delores" offers an honest, essential version of the song in its only live performance. It features a slave-face Symbol on keys and Eric Leeds on a very central flute plus Sonny T.'s last official performance (on guitar rather than bass). "Zannalee" is smooth and sultry with Symbol on guitar and Leeds taking over on sax. This unique set was supported by the same-day release of *Chaos and Disorder*, an album that Symbol ostensibly rejected.

On December 19, 1996, Prince and Mayte, surrounded by poinsettias, were interviewed by longtime host Bryant Gumbel. The interview deftly avoided the recent death of their newborn son, focusing instead on whether Prince would wear Gumbel's shoes. The response was a disdainful "no." This interchange set up one of Prince's biggest pranks, a return appearance on January 3, 1997, in which he dressed as the staid Gumbel. He also performed a crowd-pleasing set of "Take Me with U," "Raspberry Beret," and "Talkin' Loud and Sayin' Nothing."

Oprah

The November 21, 1996, *Oprah* appearance is uncomfortable to watch. Prince looks like he'd rather be elsewhere as Oprah explores how he's "different" and "weird" and takes a dig at Minnesota (Prince says the cold keeps the bad people away). But more disturbing is a segment with Prince and Mayte.

Oprah's interview was recorded at Paisley Park on November 4. Unbeknownst to the public, this was only about ten days after the couple's newborn boy died of complications from Pfeiffer syndrome. According to Mayte, Prince forced her out of bed to conduct the interview (in which Prince said that "our family exists" in response to baby questions) and gave Oprah a tour of the now-not-needed nursery that Mayte knew nothing about. The music, recorded November 20 at Oprah's Harpo Studios in Chicago, was pedestrian. The Oprah Winfrey Network rebroadcast the episode on April 23, 2016.

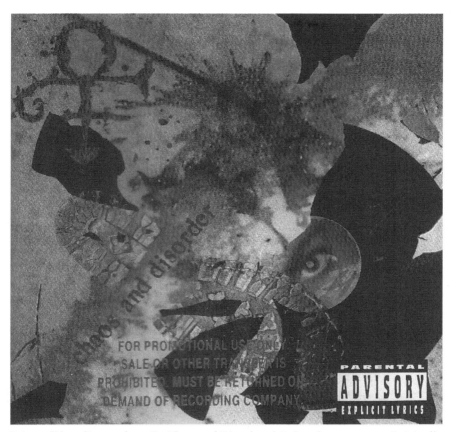

Prince all but disowned 1996's *Chaos and Disorder*, claiming the songs were "originally intended 4 private use only," but promoted the LP with July TV performances of "Dinner with Delores" on *The Late Show* with David Letterman and *The Today Show*, plus "Zannalee" on the latter.   *(Author's collection)*

Muppets Tonight

Ten months after his *Oprah* appearance, Prince was amid his first US greatest-hits tour, still making the rounds to update and personalize the kinder, gentler Symbol brand. As part of this process, he appeared on the premier episode of the second and final season of *Muppets Tonight* on September 13, 1997.

The show's conceit is that the Muppets bring in a star every week to join their Vaudeville-like review. Prince appears on the show as Symbol, which generates much of the humor. How to read the fact that Prince states that "I'm normal, just like the next guy" in a room full of mostly unidentifiable creatures? (Take that, Oprah!) The best laugh of the episode is probably when he tells Gonzo, he of unknown species, that he is "definitely working these pumps and fishnets." Or maybe it's when, dressed as a hillbilly, Symbol sings a country tune, "Bear Tracks," then skedaddles away from an alligator, or when he starts singing the food-inspired "Raspberry Sorbet." Prince does manage to fit in two songs: a magical, reconceived "Starfish and Coffee" that takes place in Muppet Prince's grammar school, and a bit-too-serious "She Gave Her Angels," the *Crystal Ball* song from the ill-fated Prince/Mayte children's album. All in all, this appearance is unlike anything else Prince ever did.

While Prince hadn't worked with the Muppets before, he had worked near them. On September 15, 1988, they were prepping their touring stage show at Paisley Park. Prince wanted to host a party during a *Lovesexy* tour break but was forced to set up in the parking lot. At 2:20 a.m., Prince hit the stage pledging to "wake up the farmers across the street." He did. He was shut down and hit with a noise violation citation. With Prince on the outside and Miss Piggy on the inside, there must be some (diamonds and) "Pearls b4 the Swine" joke here, but I can't find it.

The Tonight Show with Jay Leno

Prince conquered another US TV institution on July 24, 1998, with his first of ten appearances on *The Tonight Show*, on the air since 1954. Prince and host Jay Leno seemingly had nothing in common except for homes in Los Angeles, the need for an audience, and a love of vintage cars, but the relationship worked. Some of Prince's best TV appearances took place on the American late-night staple.

The NPG appeared on the July 24, 1998, plugging *Newpower Soul*. They performed "Come On" twice—regular and remix. Symbol, sporting an era-worthy sticking-up Coolio-do, shines on keys.

Prince performed on back-to-back nights on May 3 and 4, 2001. Both are must-sees. The first night's interview is one of the most satisfying of Prince's career. He's funny, loose, and in control, talking pranks, Bill Maher's TV show, and the economics of the recording industry. "The Work Part 1" is unremarkable. The second night opened with a prank in which Leno posed as the NBC lot security guard and gave Prince a hard time getting his limo past the gate. The jazz performance of "The Ballad of Dorothy Parker" and "Four" was a stirring preview of the *One Nite Alone* tour.

The December 13, 2002, appearance features a breathtaking version of "The Everlasting Now." It swings, then hits a Latin gear with Sheila E.'s drum solo and Prince's Santana-inspired guitar solo. Too good for broadcast TV!

Prince showed up on February 26, 2004, to promote the *Musicology* album and tour. The title-song performance is not that far off from the similar "The Work Part 1" gig three years earlier, and the interview is standard "last time I'm doing the hits" fare.

As a run-up to his Coachella show, Prince played *The Tonight Show* on April 25, 2008. It marked one of the few performances of "Turn Me Loose," a stunning dance number that sounds like, well, "Musicology" and "The Work Part 1." Renato Neto on keyboards is the star here.

In March 2009, Prince used *The Tonight Show* to promote both his unprecedented March 28 three shows in one night at the Nokia Theater in Los Angeles and the March 29 *Lotusflow3r* collection release. He appeared on three consecutive shows from March 25 to 27. The first ("Ol' Skool Company") and third ("Feel Better, Feel Good, Feel Wonderful") were funk/pop nights, while the middle featured the psychedelic rocker "Dreamer."

Prince's last appearance on *The Tonight Show* was on May 28, 2009, Leno's first penultimate night (he returned from 2011 to 2014). Again, in a jazzy mood, Prince performed a tender version of *Planet Earth*'s "Somewhere Here on Earth."

2004 Rock and Roll Hall of Fame Induction Ceremony

Prince was inducted into the Rock and Roll Hall of Fame on March 15, 2004, by musician/fan Alicia Keys. He'd use the clip to open *Musicology* shows. Prince accepted the award and followed with a respectable three-song set that included "Let's Go Crazy," an out-of-kilter "Sign 'o' the Times," and a "Soul Man/Kiss" medley.

But the highlight of the show, perhaps of Prince's guitar career, came during the all-star tribute to fellow inductee George Harrison. Prince joined Tom Petty and his band The Heartbreakers, ELO's Jeff Lynne, Traffic's Steve Winwood, and Dhani Harrison (George Harrison's guitar-playing son) on a run-through of The Beatles's "While My Guitar Gently Weeps." The song chugs through the first three minutes, thirty seconds, with Petty and Lynne trading vocals before Prince steps forward and owns Eric Clapton's original solo for the next two and a half minutes, draining every bit of sound possible out of his guitar. Dhani can't contain his joy, and Petty finally cracks a smile as Prince leans backward off the stage, propped up to continue by a stagehand. Prince's throwing his guitar at the end of the song caused controversy among those who like to find controversy in nothing. This is how the guitar is played.

Super Bowl XLI Halftime Show

The first twenty-four Super Bowl halftime shows were a mishmash of university marching bands, creepy-clean performers Up with People, and lamentable acts, such as the magician Elvis Presto. It wasn't until the 1991 appearance of New Kids on the Block that the National Football League got serious about halftime entertainment. NKOTB was followed by a who's who of music royalty, including the Rolling Stones, Katy Perry, and, of course, Janet Jackson and her wardrobe malfunction. But the all-time halftime performance goes to Prince (with U2's post-9/11 show in its own category).

Prince's performance began February 1, 2007, at the pre-game press conference. He marched onstage with a ten-piece band and announced that "contrary to rumor, I'd like to take a few questions right now." And then he opened fire with a six-minute lesson in rock history, performing blistering versions of "Johnny B. Goode" and "Anotherloverholenyohead," which ended with a ninety-second solo. He closed the unique "press conference" with a Miami-tinged "Get on the Boat."

The February 4 halftime show topped the press conference. Performing in a driving rain, the show opened with a resounding "We Will Rock You," which led into a pyrotechnics explosion from the centrally located Prince symbol. This flowed into a guitar-mad "Let's Go Crazy," which flowed into a brief "1999" and into a medley of "Baby I'm a Star" and "Proud Mary," accompanied by the Florida A&M University Marching 100. An unexpected medley of Dylan's "All Along the Watchtower" and Foo Fighters's "Best of You" came next, capped by an expected, triumphant, and meteorologically accurate closer "Purple Rain." It's hard to believe that one performer could pack so many thrills, both expected and unexpected, into a dozen minutes.

New Girl

How did Prince end up on Fox's *New Girl*? He liked the show, and he wanted to be on it. And he's Prince, so it happened.

New Girl is an amusing sitcom about Jess, a female schoolteacher who lives with three guys: hilarity ensues. Jess is played by Zooey Deschanel, one-half of indie folk darlings She & Him.

In the episode, Jess and her friend are invited to a Prince party. As the two women leave for the party, Jess responds to an "I love you" from her boyfriend with finger guns. The boyfriend and his three wingmen must sneak into the party and resolve the "love" issue. At the party, Prince operates as Spike Lee's "Magical Negro," effortlessly commanding a butterfly and fixing problems for white folks. It's funny but disappointing in its reliance on such a tired trope. The episode ends with a Prince/Deschanel duet on "Fallinlove2nite," which was released as a single six weeks later.

The episode highlights are a lack of the Kardashians, as Prince expressly forbid even the hint that he'd have them at his house, and Prince's megaphone use on "Fallinlove2nite." It's Prince's second most famous appearance with the sound projection device, just after his March 29, 1980, arrest along with Dr. Fink in Jackson, Mississippi, for stealing a megaphone from an airplane.

Revolutionary winners: "Lisa?" "Yes, Wendy." Two Studebaker Living Legends: Alice Willis, Pee We[...]

We are family: Mr. & Mrs. W., Mrs. & Mr. O, Russ Titelman [...]

Although it's one of the biggest nights for popular music on TV, Prince only appeared on the Grammys twice, in 1985 ("Baby I'm a Star") and 2004. He did not attend the 1987 Awards at which "Kiss" won Best R&B Performance by a Duo or Group with Vocals, but Wendy and Lisa did. Also in attendance was "Mr. O," Mo Ostin, who signed Prince to Warner Bros. and oversaw the company during Prince's name change. *(Author's collection)*

10

Be My Mirror, Be Like Me

Protégés, Part 1

Prince created side projects from scratch to feature his own work under a different name: the Time, Vanity 6, Madhouse, and so on. He also mentored protégés—another group of side projects featuring new or reclaimed artists, such as Sheila E., Mavis Staples, and Ingrid Chavez. The distinction appears subtle and might be arbitrary. However, gender issues aside, I could see Prince fronting the first group of side projects, but I have more difficulty envisioning him as, say, Jill Jones.

This chapter is the first of two covering protégé projects.

Sheila E. in the Glamorous Life (1984)

Sheila E. and Prince started working together in early 1984 while Prince was finishing *Purple Rain* and The Time's *Ice Cream Castle* and aggressively taking a disinterest in *Apollonia 6*. She first played on the unreleased Apollonia 6's "A Million Miles (I Love You)" in late January, contributed drums on "Pop Life" in February, and in the spring added vocals to "Erotic City." From April 1 to 4 at Sunset Sound in Los Angeles, she added percussion and vocal overdubs for the six tracks on her debut LP: *Sheila E. in the Glamorous Life*.

The Glamorous Life benefits from Sheila receiving all the good female songs of the period. Of the six tracks here, only "Noon Rendezvous," which sounds like a *Purple Rain* B-side, wasn't earmarked for Apollonia 6. Although the writing is credited to Sheila E., with Apollonia 6's Brenda Bennett on "Next Time Wipe the Lipstick Off Your Collar" and The Time's Jesse Johnson on "Shortberry Strawcake," all the tracks were written by Prince except "Noon Rendezvous," cowritten with Sheila. Prince produced all the tracks, credited to Sheila E. and the Starr* Company. He plays all the basic instruments. Sheila E. sings lead, except on "Shortberry Strawcake," which is Prince, and Jill Jones sings some background.

The album is conceived as a movie called *The Glamorous Life*. The highlights are the expansive title track, a nearly nine-minute dance workout, and "Noon

Rendezvous," a complex ballad. Prince released his versions of these two songs on 2019's *Originals*.

The album was released on June 4, 1984. It hit number twenty-eight on the Hot 200 and number seven on the soul LP charts and went gold. There were three singles. "The Glamorous Life" edit was released May 2, 1984, backed by "Part II." It reached number seven on the pop charts and number nine on the R&B charts. The twelve-inch "Club Edit" went to number one on the dance airplay chart. "The Belle of St. Mark" was released as an edit, reaching numbers thirty-four and sixty-eight. The UK twelve-inch featured a "Dance Remix." The final single, edits of "Noon Rendezvous" and "Oliver's House," failed to chart.

Sheila E. and her band, including guitarist Miko Weaver, opened the *Purple Rain* tour. All six songs were played live, and the set often featured "Erotic City" with Prince singing offstage.

As with most songs written for female performers, Prince didn't embrace this material live. From 1988 on, Prince referenced "The Glamorous Life" musically and lyrically about 150 times but often with Sheila on lead vocals. "Noon Rendezvous" made its debut at the 1984 First Avenue birthday show, then was performed four more times. He performed "Shortberry Strawcake" as part of "Hot Thing" in the sampler set twice in 2011 and once in 2014. He never performed the other three songs.

Sheila E. in Romance 1600 (1985)

While the first album tried to hide Prince's involvement, *Sheila E. in Romance 1600* features the title character on the cover pretty much dressed as Prince and goes from there. The conceit of the album is sexuality wrapped up in the colorful garb of the early 1980s New Romantics, echoing the original romantics of the turn of the eighteenth century. It's the technicolor response to sophisticated black-and-white haberdashery of the Family, whose album was released one week prior.

Prince and Sheila E. recorded most of *Romance 1600* during *Purple Rain* tour stops in Atlanta in December 1984 and January 1985, completing the album in early February at Sunset Sound. Prince wrote six of the album's eight songs, cowriting "A Love Bizarre" with Sheila, and was uninvolved with the track "Merci for the Speed of a Mad Clown in Summer," an extended drum jam. Sheila E.'s band was credited with playing on the album, but most of the instrumentation is likely Prince, with Sheila E. on drums and percussion, and her sax player, Eddie M., on most tracks. The album has one bona fide classic, "A Love Bizarre," and other tunes bridge the gap between the frantic percussion of *Purple Rain Deluxe*'s "Love and Sex" and *Sign 'o' the Times*'s "It's Gonna Be a Beautiful Night."

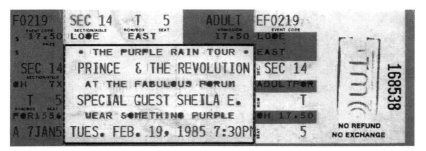

The *Purple Rain* live jaunt was supposed to feature The Time and Apollonia 6 as openers, but both groups disintegrated before the tour could start in November 1984. New protégé Sheila E. opened the tour and joined The Revolution onstage most nights during an extended "Baby I'm A Star." Sheila became Prince's full-time drummer on the *Sign 'o' The Times* tour.   *(Courtesy Thomas de Bruin, unused-prince-tickets.com)*

Romance 1600 was released on August 26, 1985, the second Paisley Park Records LP. It reached number twelve on both the Top 200 and the soul charts. The first single, "Sister Fate," was released on July 26, 1985. The seven-inch included an edit backed by an instrumental version. It reached number fifty on the black singles chart. The twelve-inch included an "Extended Version." The second single featured album versions of "Bedtime Story" backed with "Dear Michaelangelo"; it failed to chart. The third time was the charm with the "A Love Bizarre" edit backed by "Part II" reaching number eleven on the Hot 100 and number two on the black charts. A German twelve-inch featured a seven-minute, thirteen-second edit of the twelve-minute, eighteen-second original called "A Love Bizarre (Parts I & II)."

On April 24, 1985, Prince and Sheila E. recorded "Holly Rock." Although Prince was adamantly against rap music, this Prince-written and -performed song was part of the sound track of *Krush Groove*, a rap movie starring Sheila E. and Run-DMC. Released as an edited single on July 4, 1986, it failed to chart. A US promo twelve-inch included an "Extended Version."

Prince's versions of "Dear Michaelangelo" and "Holly Rock" found the light of day on *Originals* in 2019.

Shelia E. toured Japan as a headliner in the early fall of 1985, then joined Prince on occasion during the early 1986 Hit N Run shows before joining the *Parade* tour as an opener. Prince played only one *Romance 1600* song live, but he played it a lot. "A Love Bizarre" is among Prince's top twenty-five most played songs, although often just the main riff was featured. It debuted at the 1985 Prom Center birthday show, was played at the *Around the World in a Day* masquerade ball, and was last played March 26, 2016, in Toronto as part of a brief sampler set. "Holly Rock" also debuted at the Prom Center show and was played a handful of times after that, usually as a chant.

Sheila E. (1987)

Recording for Prince's five tracks on Sheila E.'s third and final Paisley Park album stretched from December 1985 to September 1986. The LP suffers from a lack of coherence and from lesser songs, as Prince was dedicating his best female material of this time to Jill Jones and his own persona: Camille. The fact that Prince wasn't giving his full attention to the project is revealed in David Z.'s coproduction credit on the five Prince tracks—this was work for hire for the label.

Prince and Sheila E. cowrote "Love on a Blue Train," "Boy's Club," "Pride and the Passion," "One Day (I'm Gonna Make You Mine)," and "Koo Koo." Sheila E.'s band is credited with instrumentation, but it's her and Prince, joined occasionally by Eric Leeds and Atlanta Bliss.

Sheila E. was released on February 19, 1987. It hit number fifty-six on the Top 200 and number twenty-four on the black chart, the last non-Prince Paisley Park album that can remotely be called a hit until The Time's *Pandemonium*. An edited "Love on a Blue Train" was released as a single in Japan. Japan also saw the release of *The Glamorous Club Dance EP* on March 25, 1986. This included the only released complete version of the title song. The album version "Koo Koo" single reached number thirty-five on the black charts, with a twelve-inch featuring a "Remix" by Bobby Z. Sheila E. played a few songs from this LP during her *Parade* opening dates. Prince never sang any of the songs live.

Sheila E. worked with Prince on a fourth album from January 1987 to November 1988 and was the *Lovesexy* drummer from July 1988 to the end of the tour on February 13, 1989. Sheila had a health issue and left the band and was soon dropped from Paisley Park Records. The album wasn't finished and remains unreleased.

Three of the album's ten tracks had no Prince input, while a cover of Donnie Hathaway's "The Ghetto" only featured Prince on instruments and production. Of the six remaining tracks, five remain unreleased. The instrumental "3 Nigs Watchin' a Kung Fu Movie," "Knucklehead," "Soul Company," and "Girl Power" were untouched, but "Latino Barbie Doll" was reworked and rejected in 1993 as the title track of a Mayte album. "Scarlett Pussy" ended up as the "I Wish U Heaven" B-side.

In 2010, Sheila released Prince's "The Leader of the Band" on an EP. An alternate version of the song, featuring Prince on keys and background vocals, was released on her 2013 LP *Icon*.

Jill Jones (1987)

Jill Jones had to endure more than four years of recording, from July 1982 to October 1986, to complete her self-titled LP. On release, the collection was greeting with profound indifference, although it's in the top tier of protégé work. Former Paisley Park Records head Alan Leeds blamed Prince for the commercial failure of this and other late 1980s albums, claiming he spread himself too thin to put in the work to make "competitive" records. At the very least, consumers were tired, with the fourteen months prior to *Jill Jones* seeing the release of *Mazarati*, *Parade*, *Madhouse 8*, *Sheila E.*, and *Sign 'o' the Times*. Counting the two-LP *Sign 'o' the Times*, that's a new album every other month.

As with the *Sheila E.*, Prince farmed out production to David Z., who worked with Jones on all tracks except the Prince/Jones-produced "Mia Bocca," "All Day, All Night," and "For Love." Prince wrote all the songs (as Joey Coco) and plays the basic tracks on all but "All Day, All Night," which is a live Revolution number; "For Love," which features the Family's Jellybean Johnson on drums and St. Paul Peterson on bass; and the rerecording of "For You" with studio musicians. He released his guide-vocal version of "Baby, You're a Trip" in 2019.

The highlights are the surprisingly sweet-sounding "G-Spot," originally a Vanity 6 tune, and the driving "All Day, All Night." There isn't a weak song except "My Man," which sounds like Prince had been listening to a bit too much *Born in the USA*.

Over four years, the sessions produced a wealth of unreleased and repurposed material including "Come Elektra Tuesday," "Married Man," "Killin' at the Soda Shop," "Living Doll," "My Sex," and "Euphoria Highway." "G-Spot" was originally considered for inclusion in *Purple Rain*, as were "Our Destiny," released in 2017 with Lisa Coleman on vocals, and "Wednesday," released in 2018 with Prince on piano.

The album was released on May 26, 1987. It failed to chart but managed to spawn three singles, all of which also failed to chart. An edited "Mia Bocca" was released on April 6, 1987. The B-side, Jill Jones–composed "77 Bleeker St." features Prince on guitar. A twelve-inch included a dub version of the A-side and extended versions of both sides. "G-Spot" was released as an edit and an "Extended Version." "For Love" was released as a "Remix Edit and on twelve-inch as "4-Play Remix" and "Bonus Beats." That Prince would wait four years to assemble this album and then spend the money on this many singles and twelve-inches defies logic.

Jones toured briefly in 1987, opening for Jody Watley, Andre Cymone's hugely successful protégé. Discounting his own "For You," Prince played two songs live: "For Love" and "All Day, All Night."

Prince and Jones recorded in the fall of 1988 and the summer of 1989, recording more than a dozen songs. The duo went so far as to record a video for "Boom, Boom (Can't U Feel the Beat of My Heart)." But Prince wanted to keep Jones under his thumb, and she wanted to graduate to more mature material. Her contract expired in April 1993, and she sat out the balance of her contract in the Paisley Park penalty box.

Mavis Staples's *Time Waits for No One* (1989)

Mavis Staples joined her family's gospel group the Staples Singers in 1950 at the age of eleven. The group hit it big nationally in 1956 with "Uncloudy Day" and had two US number one singles in the 1970s ("I'll Take You There" and "Let's Do It Again"). Prince was a longtime fan. He signed Staples to Paisley Park in 1987, his first reclamation project.

Prince created six of *Time Waits for No One*'s eight songs but didn't work directly with Staples. Prince recorded the tracks and then shipped them to Memphis's Ardent Studios, where house producers added Staples's vocals. The result is solid songs that suffer from some pedestrian production. There's a warmth and dignity to Staples's voice not done justice here.

Prince wrote five songs and cowrote the title song with Staples. The highlight is the *Dream Factory* outtake "Train," a blues-based song better handled by Staples than Prince. Intended for Jermaine Jackson, "Interesting" is, well, interesting. "Jaguar" was written for Sheena Easton, while "Come Home" was meant for Meli'sa Morgan, who had covered "Do Me Baby." "I Guess I'm Crazy" rounds out the Prince involvement. Prince never played these songs live.

Time Waits for No One was released on May 24, 1989, about a month before *Batman*. It was barely promoted and didn't chart but did see the release of three singles, two with Prince involvement. "Jaguar" was released as an edited single and on twelve-inch in four unique remixes and edits. It failed to chart. The edited title track hit number sixty-three on the R&B charts. The album version showed up on the twelve-inch, which also features the terrifying "Christmas Vacation" from *National Lampoon's Christmas Vacation*. Ho ho ho!

Staples joined Prince a few times on the *Lovesexy* tour, singing "I'll Take You There." She opened the UK/Irish leg of 1990's Nude tour. Her band featured Michael B. on drums and future NPGers Sonny T. on bass and Tommy "Barbarella" Elm on keys.

In July 1988, Staples went into the studio for the first time with Prince. The duo recorded the unreleased "God Is Alive," performed often on the *Lovesexy* tour. The winter of 1989 saw the recording of "My Tree," which was on an early configuration of the "New Power Generation" maxi-single, and a try at *Graffiti Bridge*'s "Melody Cool." Prince cast Staples as Melody Cool in *Graffiti Bridge*, and she performed the too-busy song in the film. The single edit, released on December 4, 1990, in the United States, reached number thirty-six on the R&B charts. A US twelve-inch added four remixes and edits.

Mavis Staples's *The Voice* (1993)

The Voice features five classic Prince songs and is among the top albums released by a Prince-produced artist. Unfortunately, it was released during the

Prince tried to jumpstart Mavis Staples's career through a role in the *Graffiti Bridge* project and the production of two LPs, but his multiple musical concerns and the demise of Paisley Park Records ultimately undermined Staples's career advancement. Prince released the Staples Singers's "When Will We B Paid?" as a duet with Angie Stone in 2000 and is referenced in the biographical film *Mavis!*   *(Courtesy Ric Dube)*

height of Prince's battles with Warner Bros., leaving the LP with no prospects for success. It probably also didn't help that even though Staples considered herself Prince's second mom, he was apprehensive about talking with the legend, and she wrote letters to communicate with him.

Prince had a hand in writing eight of the twelve tracks on the original Paisley Park release. A 1995 NPG Records reissue added the previously released "Come Home." Prince wrote "House in Order," "Blood Is Thicker Than Time," "You Will Be Moved," "A Man Called Jesus," and the retreads "Melody Cool" and "Positivity." He cowrote "The Undertaker" and the title song.

Prince handed most production chores to Ricky Peterson, brother of the Family's Paul Peterson. Prince produced "The Voice," as Paisley Park, featuring instrumentation by Prince, Levi Seacer Jr., and Gaines, and coproduced "Melody Cool," "A Man Called Jesus," and "Positivity" with Peterson. The other Prince-written, Peterson-produced songs are played by a mixture of NPG members.

Unlike *Time Waits for No One*, pulled together largely from leftover songs, Prince wrote *The Voice* for Staples. And she says that he wrote her life. "The Undertaker," loosely based on Staples's mortician ex-husband, is on the Prince A-list. It's a slinky blues number, almost matched by the expectant "You Will Be Moved." "House in Order," its roots in *Batman*'s "200 Balloons," is a fast-paced dance number, and both "Blood Is Thicker Than Time" and "A Man Called Jesus" allow Staples to show us what she's got.

The Voice was released on August 24, 1993, and rapidly disappeared from collective memory. "The Voice," available as a promo remix, and "Blood Is Thicker Than Time" were released as singles, but neither charted.

With no label support and eventually no label, Staples didn't tour *The Voice*, but she joined Prince a few times live in 1993, typically on "I'll Take You There." She performed that classic, "The Undertaker," and "House in Order" at the September 8 Begley's Warehouse show captured on *The Sacrifice of Victor* video. Prince performed "House in Order" and "The Undertaker" live a few times. Aside from his own "Positivity" performances, he played none of the other tunes live.

"You Will Be Moved" showed up on 1994's NPG sampler *1-800-NEW-FUNK*, and Staples showed up at Prince shows on occasion through 2007 to sing "I'll Take You There." Prince released a cover of Staples's "When Will We B Paid?" as the B-side of "U Make My Sun Shine" in December 1990. The 2015 documentary *Mavis!* is worth viewing.

11

Dance with the Devil

Late 1980s LPs

Sign 'o' the Times (1987)

S *ign 'o' the Times* was released in the United States one year to the day after *Parade* on March 31, 1987. It was Prince's fourth album in less than three years and his first solo adventure since *1999*. The double LP contains sixteen songs and almost eighty minutes of music. But those eighty minutes are both the best music Prince ever assembled and only a fraction of his 1986 production.

Sign 'o' the Times is so strong because it's essentially a greatest-hits collection culled from three albums. It includes versions of fifteen of the forty tracks spread across different 1986 configurations of *Dream Factory*, *Camille*, and *Crystal Ball* (rejected by Warner Bros., which didn't want to release a triple album). The sole dedicated track is "U Got the Look," recorded in December 1986. Of the twenty-five tracks that don't show up on *Sign 'o' the Times*, a dozen remain unreleased by Prince.

Sign 'o' the Times reached number six on the Top 200 and number four on the black charts. The cover features an out-of-focus Prince, presumably dressed as alter ego Camille, in front of a cluttered stage set cum Bourbon Street party. The album finds a return to fully developed songs that mostly explore the fine line between romantic and erotic love but that also point toward a future with more political (the title track) and spiritual concerns ("The Cross"). Except for "It's Gonna Be a Beautiful Night," which is based on a live Revolution recording, Prince performs the entire album (except Eric Leeds and Atlanta Bliss horn parts), some background vocals, and contributions from Sheena Easton, Sheila E., and Wendy and Lisa on "Strange Relationship" and "Slow Love."

The highlight here is everything. At one time or another, every track on this album has been my favorite Prince track. For most performers, any song here would be the highlight of his or her career. Perhaps what's most striking is Prince's voice. It's sweet, it's rough, it's high, it's low, it's tweaked, and it's layered, but mostly it is beautiful.

The album leads off with the title track. Most noted for its socially conscious lyrics, the music's the real deal: sparse and funky, a bass-forward inverse of "When Doves Cry." Prince's guitar solo here ties in with "I Could Never Take the Place of Your Man," which stretches out with a thrilling call-and-response guitar break. The second disc opens with "U Got the Look," a duet with Sheena Easton. The song's simple and catchy and shows off an appealing, self-deprecating sense of humor. It's dumb fun.

Sign 'o' the Times features four of Prince's most enduring ballads. "The Cross" gives "Purple Rain" competition for its top anthem spot; "Forever in My Life" rethinks the spiritual through a jaw-dropping vocal layer of Prince vocals; "Adore" is pure 1970s soul, providing everything but the mint on the pillow; and "Slow Love," an adaptation of a Carole Davis lyric, is "so much better" because it takes its time.

Four songs show up in Camille's distorted, high-pitched voice. "U Got the Look," which wasn't on *Camille*; the beat-heavy "Housequake"; the tender, gender-bending-and-back-again confessional "If I Was Your Girlfriend"; and the bouncy, heartbreaking "Strange Relationship."

"Starfish and Coffee" is a short, quirky sing-along, while "Play in the Sunshine" is a short, quirky call-and-response that seems a bit out of place. The obtuse "The Ballad of Dorothy Parker" recalls Sly Stone's more freewheeling moments at the keyboard, and "Hot Thing" nods toward James Brown at his nastiest. "It's Gonna Be a Beautiful Night" closes the book on The Revolution and highlights how the band could jam. "It" is a Fairlight anthem that's about "it."

Sign 'o' the Times had four commercial singles and one promo single. The first single and title track was released on February 18, 1987. It reached number three on the pop charts and number one on the black charts. The second single, "If I Was Your Girlfriend," was released in an edit that's on hits collections; the twelve-inch featured the album version. On the B-side, the *Camille* tune "Shockadelica" featured in a three-minute, thirty-second, single version and an "Extended Version" on the twelve-inch. The A-side hit number twelve on the black charts but only number sixty-seven on the pop charts.

"U Got the Look" hit number two on the Hot 100 and number eleven on the black charts. The single featured the album version backed with a "Housequake" edit on the B-side that remains unavailable. The twelve-inch featured "U Got the Look (Long Look)" and "Housequake (7 Minutes MoQuake)," the former on *Ultimate*, the latter uncollected.

The final commercial single was the top-ten "I Could Never Take the Place of Your Man," released on November 3, 1987. The single edit is on hits collections. The US twelve-inch features three otherwise unavailable versions of "Hot

Thing": "Edit," "Extended Remix," and "Dub Version." The promo-only edit of "Hot Thing" remains uncollected.

The live band featured new members Sheila E. (drums), Levi Seacer Jr. (bass), Boni Boyer (keyboards/vocals), and dancer/vocalist Cat (Glover) in addition to Revolution carryovers Miko Weaver (guitar), Dr. Fink (keyboards), and horn players Eric Leeds and Atlanta Bliss. It debuted on March 21, 1987, at First Avenue. The *Sign 'o' the Times* tour played thirty-four scheduled dates and many aftershows in Europe, starting on May 8, 1987, in Stockholm and ending on June 29 in Antwerp. Most of the songs were played live frequently, although "It" never enjoyed a complete performance.

Lovesexy (1988)

"*The Black Album*" was Prince's follow-up LP to masterpiece *Sign 'o' the Times*. It was scheduled for release on December 8, 1987, but was pulled from the Warner Bros. schedule a week before the date when Prince had second thoughts about the album's dark nature. It was replaced by *Lovesexy*, released in the United States on May 10, 1988.

Except for "*The Black Album*" carryover "When 2 R in Love," *Lovesexy*'s nine tracks were new compositions, recorded by Prince between December 1987 and early 1988. And save for a few instruments and the song "(Eye) Know," which features the *Lovesexy* touring band, the album was a Prince solo project.

There isn't a weak track on the LP—any song on *Lovesexy* could be a viable single. Despite the individual strength of songs, there's coherence among the tracks, although it's not, strictly speaking, a concept album. This is probably due to the condensed recording time frame and the fact that Prince didn't dig into the vault to mix and match old tracks. The unity is reflected in the fact that original version of the CD ran as one continuous forty-five-minute, seven-second track, frustrating consumers who just got their first CD players, players with the amazing ability to jump from track to track instantaneously. Grrrrr.

But, while all the songs are strong, apart from "Alphabet St." (the angular, deconstructed first single), the album contains nothing groundbreaking or, if you'll pardon the pun, revolutionary. Instead, what we get is Prince at his most Prince, doing a bit of everything he does well and doing it very well. We've got some metaphysical screwing ("Glam Slam"), good versus evil ("Positivity"), and partying in the face of the apocalypse ("Dance On"). It's got Prince's mom's favorite song: "Anna Stesia." It's consolidation and muscle flexing. It's a great LP.

Beyond "Alphabet St.," which reached a disappointing number eight on the US charts, *Lovesexy* featured two additional singles: "Glam Slam" and "I Wish U Heaven." Both singles failed to chart on the US Top 100 but performed modestly on the black charts.

Perhaps the most remarkable aspect of the album is its cover. Let's face it: it's a photo of Prince lying on a bed of flowers with a flower penis—not really any wiggle room on this. At least this was probably less painful than the other cover featuring Prince and flowers, *Lotusflow3r*, on which he has flames and a ray of light coming out the top of his head.

The controversial album cover led to major US retailers refusing to carry the album, which hurt sales. The album reached number eleven, the first Prince album to fail to crack the top ten since *Controversy*. It also achieved only gold status, the first to not go platinum since *Dirty Mind*. By Prince's lofty standards, the LP wasn't a success.

What was a critical and popular success was the *Lovesexy* tour, which began in Paris on July 8, 1988; spent the fall in the United States for thirty-eight arena dates and the winter for eight days in Japan; and closed in Osaka on February 13, 1989. But the tour failed to make money due to the high production costs, which included a functioning car, a basketball court, and a rising piano on the well-decorated in-the-round stage.

The first part of the show featured "nasty," secular tunes and interplay between Prince and female band members—Cat, Sheila E., and Boni Boyer—typically kicking off with "Erotic City" and including the two best *Black Album* songs: "Bob George" and "Superfunkycalifragisexy." After an intermission following the transitional soul cleansing of "Anna Stesia," Prince ran through more "uplifting" songs, such as "The Cross" and "I Wish U Heaven," along with the expected hits. All the *Lovesexy* songs were played on the tour, although "Dance On" was performed only as an instrumental. "Alphabet St." was played live frequently through 2016, and "Anna Stesia" was performed off and on. The year 1989 was the end of the line for the rest of the songs.

While an artistic success, the *Lovesexy* period was not a lucrative one for Prince, with diminished record sales and tour losses not keeping up with an expensive lifestyle that included the open-24/7 Paisley Park Studios. Prince was looking for someone to blame for this change in fortune. July 1988 saw the sacking of his longtime publicist Howard Bloom, and December saw the firing of his longtime management team of Cavallo, Ruffalo, and Fargnoli. Prince needed cash. He found *Batman*.

Batman (1989)

It's difficult not to see *Batman* as an opportunistic money grab. There was little in Prince's history that suggested any connection with Batman. But the money wasn't rolling in like it had in the recent past, so now there was a connection with Batman. Prince hired Warner Bros. publicists Bob Merlis and Liz Rosenberg to replace Harold Bloom ("Prince, baby, we've got a really hot property in house you should look at!"). He signed the publishing rights to the songs over to Warner Bros. (which probably meant cash up front or at least debt relief). It seemed like Prince was more than willing to line up on the streets of Gotham City, hands out, ready to collect his share of the Joker's $20 million giveaway.

But *Batman* is more than just a money grab, and it works, once again, as a complete album—just not one of his best.

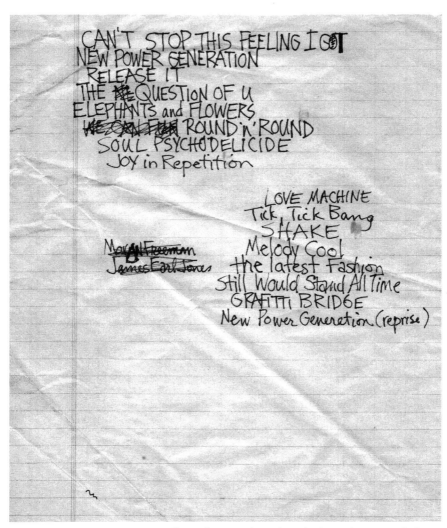

As with most Prince projects, *Graffiti Bridge* went through multiple configurations before a final release. This song list, in Prince's handwriting, is from an early 1990 version and includes the never released "Soul Psychodelicide." *(Courtesy Jeff Munson)*

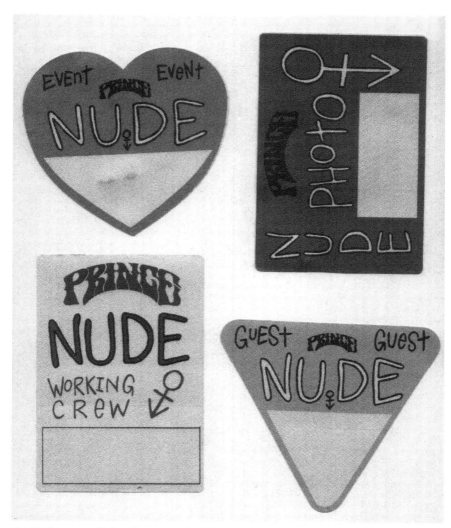

The Nude tour took place from June through September 1990 in Europe and Japan. Although the *Graffiti Bridge* album was released during the tour, the perfunctory greatest hits outing was meant more to line the purple coffers than to highlight the album.   *(Courtesy Jeff Munson)*

Batman director Tim Burton met Prince in January 1989 to recruit him for the sound track. Burton already had a rough cut of the film that included "1999" and "Baby I'm a Star." Prince accepted the challenge, dropping ongoing work on *Rave Unto the Joy Fantastic* and *Graffiti Bridge*.

While we can't know for certain how Burton approached Prince, it's apparent that the concept of Batman and the Joker as two sides of the same coin appealed to Prince's belief in his own dual nature (and later belief that he had another person living inside him). He also seemed drawn to the opportunity to explicitly tell a story from multiple points of view, as the voices on the songs are credited to the film characters (Bruce Wayne, Batman, the Joker, and Vicki Vale) in addition to Prince and his star-sign alter ego Gemini.

Prince recorded most of the nine songs in the spring of 1989; the exceptions are "Electric Chair," "Vicki Waiting," and "Scandalous" from 1988. These three tunes, along with "The Future" and "Partyman," are the album's strongest tunes. Three other songs are forgettable pop ("Trust," "Lemon Crush," and "The Arms of Orion," a duet with Sheena Easton) designed not to offend a large cinematic audience. And "not offend" is probably too nice since the Easton duet is less forgettable than memorable in its languorous delivery. The LP's final track is the non-song aural collage "Batdance," which is a fun rocker but a slight entry in the overall Prince catalog.

There are strong B-sides and one outtake that's among Prince's most experimental tunes. "200 Balloons" ("Batdance"), "Feel U Up" ("Partyman"), and "I Love U in Me" ("The Arms of Orion") are all found on the B-sides collection, while "Sex" can be located on *The Scandalous Sex Suite* CD. The outtake is the seven-plus-minute "Dance with the Devil," an odd suite based on a Joker phrase featured in the movie and "Batdance."

The *Batman* album, like the film, was wildly successful, hitting number one on the US charts for six weeks and going double platinum (the biggest seller since *Around the World in a Day*). In spite of this success, Prince didn't tour for *Batman*, instead focusing on business affairs and the *Graffiti Bridge* project until the summer of 1990 Nude tour of Europe and Asia. "The Future," "Partyman," and "Batdance" were part of most Nude tour set lists. "Lemon Crush" and "Trust" never found their way to the stage.

Graffiti Bridge (1990)

Graffiti Bridge is a mess. It's brilliant in places, was well reviewed when released, but ultimately a mishmash of unfortunate spotlight sharing, repurposed songs, and overproduction. It's the weakest album of Prince's first two decades, the one least likely to find its way into my headphones.

The single CD/double vinyl *Graffiti Bridge* was released on August 21, 1990, in the United States, about two months before the accompanying film. Prince wanted a blockbuster sequel to *Purple Rain* and felt that his longtime management team of Cavallo, Ruffalo, and Fargnoli wasn't working hard enough to make it happen, so he fired them in late 1988. He replaced them with *Purple Rain* director Albert Magnoli, trying to catch lightning in a bottle twice. Magnoli leveraged his contacts to secure Prince the lucrative *Batman* gig but was also gone within a year, replaced by Arnold Stiefel and Randy Phillips. That *Graffiti Bridge* is the product of an artist who won't hear "no" from people paid to say "yes" is evident.

Although all seventeen songs are written or cowritten by Prince and the music is almost totally played by Prince, fewer than half the songs feature Prince lead vocals. As such, it often feels like a Paisley Park Records sampler—three songs by The Time, one each by newcomer Tevin Campbell (the fourteen-year-old protégé-for-a-moment, one of the few males in the stable) and veteran Mavis Staples, and four songs with Prince on co-vocals.

Most songs were at least two years old when released (the project began in late 1987, *Batman* intervening), and most were recycled from aborted projects, such as *Dream Factory* and The Time's *Corporate World* (which morphed into *Pandemonium*), and earlier configurations of *Crystal Ball*, *Rave Un2 the Joy Fantastic*, and *Sign 'o' the Times*. Individual songs date back to the early 1980s, and these are the strongest on the LP. "Tick Tick Bang" is from 1981 (same session as "Controversy"), "Can't Stop This Feeling I Got" dates from 1982 (released in 2019 on *1999 Super Deluxe*), and the George Clinton duet, "We Can Funk," was recorded in 1983 as "We Can Fuck" (released in 2017 on *Purple Rain Deluxe*). Most of the songs for the other vocalists were newer songs from 1989.

But the main issue isn't that the earlier songs are superior to the more recent songs (although it's true); rather, it's that all the songs are bathed in a generic, painfully dated, New Jack production style that's cynical in its attempt not to offend the ears. It's especially difficult to take since most of the older songs are available in superior alternate versions. Part of Prince's early genius was being able to make cold instruments like the synthesizer sound human, even erotic, but a lot of the sounds on *Graffiti Bridge* are as intimate as HAL's version of "Daisy Bell (Bicycle Built for Two)" in Kubrick's *2001*. This album makes you wish the unplugged craze had hit a few years earlier—and that Babyface had never been born.

When Prince was done with the album, he was done with most of the music on it. There was no *Graffiti Bridge* tour, and most songs were never played live or were played only in snippets or medleys. "Thieves in the Temple," the last song recorded for the LP and one of two classics, was played in full for only a couple of years. The other classic, "Joy in Repetition," was performed regularly from 2001 on and was a set piece on the *One Nite Alone* live collection. The title song is a contender for Prince's worst song. It's a sappy mid-tempo aspirational song featuring co-vocals by Staples and Campbell. Yuck.

The album reached number six on the *Billboard* LP charts and went gold. It reached number one in England. It included five singles: two from Prince ("Thieves in the Temple" and "New Power Generation") and one each from Campbell ("Round and Round"), Staples ("Melody Cool"), and The Time ("Shake!").

The one thing the album did do right was point toward a New Power future.

12

Don't Wanna Stop 'til I Reach the Top

Number One Singles

Prince didn't want to stop until he reached the top. He enjoyed the luxury of stopping nine times on the US singles charts, five times on the pop chart, and eight times on the hot soul, black, and R&B charts. Four songs topped both charts. This chapter looks at these nine US number one hits.

Prince released fifty-eight singles that charted on the pop or R&B 100 charts. "Soft and Wet," Prince's first single, was released in the United States on March 7, 1978. The "naughty" lyrics were banned on many radio stations, in part contributing to the single's low pop showing (number ninety-two but not hurting his R&B credibility at number twelve).

From 1979 to 1995, Prince placed nineteen songs in the top ten of the pop charts and twenty-two on the R&B top ten. "I Wanna Be Your Lover" was his first R&B top ten, and 1983's "Little Red Corvette" was his first pop top ten. Prince's last trip to the R&B top ten was 1995's "I Hate U," and his last pop top ten appearance was 1994's "The Most Beautiful Girl in the World." Prince's final Top 100 single was "Black Sweat," the second single from *3121*. It reached number sixty on the Hot 100 and number eighty-three on the R&B chart in early 2006.

"I Wanna Be Your Lover"

Concerned about the middling success of his initial singles, Prince was determined to create a hit. "I Wanna Be Your Lover," released on August 24, 1979, accomplished that goal. It reached number one on the US R&B charts for two weeks and rose to number eleven for two weeks on the pop charts. The edited single version appears on hits compilations.

The song rides a fine line between self-deprecation and bravado. It's a more straightforward come-on than Michael Jackson's "Rock with You," which was number one on the Hot 100. And Prince doesn't confuse matters by encouraging his partner to ride on the boogie. Musically, the song is a compact statement of his unique evolving sound—jaunty synthesizer and drums as the backbeat for sweet falsetto and a mix-central guitar.

The song enjoyed perhaps the longest shelf life of any song in the Prince live repertoire, debuting in the fall of 1979 and appearing regularly up through 2016's *Piano and a Microphone* tour.

"I Wanna Be Your Lover" completed its three-month climb to the top of the hot soul charts on December 1, 1979. It bumped off "Still" by the Commodores. "Do You Love What You Feel" by Rufus and Chaka Khan unseated Prince's tune.

"When Doves Cry"

The May 16, 1984, release of "When Doves Cry" returned Prince to the top of the black charts, gave him his first pop number one, and propelled him from "popular musician" to "musical icon." If he had done nothing else, he'd be remembered for this.

Why did "When Doves Cry" strike such a loud and resounding chord? For what's there and what's not there. Lyrically, there's not much difference between this and his first number one: it's meant to get someone into bed. But how do you get someone into bed? Self-deprecation worked in the past, but soul-searching and vulnerability work even better.

So what's not there? The most remarkable instrument on the song is the one he doesn't play: the bass. The heart of soul, the soul of rock 'n' roll, isn't there. But the synthesizers are. And the guitar. Lots of it.

The single edit is on hits collections and the four-disc *Purple Rain Deluxe Edition*. The non-LP "17 Days" appears on *The B-Sides* and *Deluxe*.

The song was 1984's top-selling single. It hit number one on the US Hot 100 on July 7, 1984, and spent five weeks atop the charts. It replaced Duran Duran's first US number one, "The Reflex," at the top of the charts (their other was "A View to a Kill"). It was replaced by another sound track single, "Ghostbusters," by Ray Parker Jr. (who sported a very Prince-like moustache, unlike the excessively clean-shaven Duran Duran).

The song hit the top of the black charts on June 30, 1984, replacing O'Bryan's "Lovelite," his only number one. The black chart likewise saw "When Doves Cry" replaced by "Ghostbusters." Ray Parker's only number one, "Ghostbusters," sounds like a half-baked Huey Lewis and the News song, so much so that he was forced to pay Lewis out of court for "borrowing" from "I Want a New Drug."

"Let's Go Crazy"

If "When Doves Cry" was Prince soul-searching, "Let's Go Crazy" is Prince searching for souls. While the sex is still there (at least for his "old lady"), this song is about salvation—about how to defeat de-elevator (the devil) by avoiding bad earthly solutions (doctors and pills) and concentrating on friends, the afterworld, and going nuts. And looking for purple bananas.

But "Let's Go Crazy" isn't all about what's being said; it's also about what's being heard. The point of this song is the guitar. It's got one of Prince's most recognizable guitar riffs (a mimic of the song title vocal melody) and one of his most blistering solos, a musical apotheosis that coincides with the song's apocalyptic second-coming ending. Take me away!

"Let's Go Crazy" was a live battle horse, and at times its performance was more perfunctory than perfection, a bathroom break for hard-core fans. Prince seemed to admit this with his burning slower reworking "Let's Go Crazy (Reloaded)," rerecorded with 3rdEyeGirl and released in 2013.

The single featured an edit of the LP version and the twelve-inch a "Special Dance Mix." "Let's Go Crazy" featured one of Prince's most popular B-sides, "Erotic City," with the seven-inch featuring an edited version and the twelve-inch featuring the full-length version: "Erotic City (Make Love Not War Erotic City Come Alive)." Both edits and longer versions are on *Deluxe*.

"Let's Go Crazy" hit number one on the Hot 100 on September 29, 1984 (two weeks), following "Missing You" by John Waite, the former Babys front man's only number one. It hit the top of the black charts on October 6, 1984, staying for one week, replacing Billy Ocean's "Caribbean Queen (No More Love on the Run)." This was one of four US chart toppers for the laid-back Islander. On both charts, "Let's Go Crazy" was replaced by yet another sound track song: Stevie Wonder's "I Just Called to Say I Love You" from *The Woman in Red*. Stevie is beyond reproach—except for this song, which makes Disney's "It's a Small World" a welcome ear worm. Wonder's song would be replaced on the black charts by Chaka Khan's "I Feel for You."

"Kiss"

"Kiss" is close to perfect. The lyrics are sassy and memorable but never mean. The music is light, danceable R&B, just dangerous enough to get you really moving— Bryan Ferry with a funkier tux and, again, the guitar. This time it's not the histrionics of "Let's Go Crazy" but a tribute to both unsung R&B rhythm guitarists, like Jimmy Nolen of James Brown's 1960s bands, and understated soloists, like Freddie Stone of Sly and the Family Stone. And, like "When Doves Cry," there's no bass.

The single version of "Kiss" has a slightly different ending than the version on *Parade*, which segues into "Anotherloverholenyohead." The twelve-inch "Extended Version" is among the least compelling of the 1980s remixes. The single version is on hits collections, and the extended version is on the *Ultimate* bonus disc. The song also appears as an instrumental on the *Interactive* CD-ROM.

"Kiss" hit the pop top for two weeks on April 19, 1986. It was preceded by Falco's "Rock Me Amadeus," which would have been the nadir of pop music in the 1980s if Milli Vanilli hadn't snuck in under the wire in 1989. It was followed by "Addicted to Love" by Robert Palmer. But for Prince, Palmer's synthesizer-driven R&B-tinged rocker doesn't happen, nor does his next hit: the Jimmy Jam and Terry Lewis–written "I Didn't Mean to Turn You On." And that's double for the sartorial androgyny of the still-popular video. It's almost surprising that Prince never covered "Addicted to Love." Almost. But he often quoted live the number one black chart song prior to "Kiss": Janet Jackson's "What Have You Done for Me Lately." "Kiss" hit the top on April 5, 1986, and stayed for four weeks, replaced by Stephanie Mills's "I Have Learned to Respect the Power of Love," her first of five R&B number ones.

"Sign 'o' the Times"

Released on February 18, 1987, "Sign 'o' the Times" is a surprising hit. The vocal's not really catchy but rather more monotone than melodious. It's hard to sing. The lyrics are about disease, disaster, and devastation. The chorus? A single repeated word: "time(s)." Try humming that in the shower. The guitar and bass are more in conversation than in unison. There's martial drumming. The song continually sounds like it's going to fall apart. Not a recipe for a successful pop song.

But it works. Beautifully.

The single edit appears on the hits albums. The seven-inch B-side is a "La, La, La, He, He, Hee" edit, while the cassette and twelve-inch contain the full ten-minute, thirty-two-second "La, La, La, He, He, Hee (Highly Explosive)." Legend has it that Sheena Easton, who cowrote the B-side, challenged Prince to write a song with such mundane lyrics.

"Sign 'o' the Times" hit number one on the black chart April 11, 1987 (three weeks). It was preceded by Janet Jackson wannabe Jody Watley's "Looking for a New Love," which was produced by Andre Cymone and David Z. It was followed by the forgettable "Don't Disturb This Groove" (what groove?) by The System. The tune reached number three on the Top 100 on April 25, 1987. The number one song on the charts was the Aretha Franklin and George Michael duet "I Knew You Were Waiting for Me."

"Batdance"

Synergy. There's no other word to describe both the success and composition of "Batdance." Like four previous number ones, this is a movie tie-in, this time for Tm Burton's *Batman*, another Warner Bros. product and the top-grossing film of 1989. The single's June 6, 1989, release came two weeks before the sound track album and film release.

Unlike "Sign 'o' the Times," which holds together in spite of itself, "Batdance" uses Prince's production skills to tightly bind disparate pieces into a compelling sonic statement. On the song level, there's not really a song, at least not in the traditional verse/chorus format. There are samples from other songs ("The Future," "Electric Chair," "200 Balloons," and "Rave Un2 the Joy Fantastic"), quotes and sound bites from the movie (the movie's stars are credited with "special guest presence"), drastic time changes, and aural punctuations—less a song than a very popular commercial.

The single edit appeared on *4Ever*. The US twelve-inch and CD maxi contained two mixes—"The Batmix" and "The Vicki Vale Mix"—in addition to "200 Balloons," a non-LP track that appeared across all formats and on *The B-Sides*. "Batdance" was performed live only in 1990 on the perfunctory Nude tour and a few one-off shows in Minnesota.

"Batdance" spent one week, August 5, 1989, at the top of the pop charts. It was preceded by Martika's only US number one: "Toy Soldiers." Two years later would see Martika's only other US top ten hit, "Love . . . Thy Will Be Done," written and produced by Prince. "Batdance" was followed on the charts by "Right Here Waiting," Richard Marx's third of three number ones. A week later, "Batdance" topped the black charts for one week. Former Whitney Houston husband and perpetual late-night punch line Bobby Brown was replaced by Prince. Prince was again nudged from the top spot by Stephanie Mills, this time with "Something in the Way (You Make Me Feel)."

"Thieves in the Temple"

For the fifth and final time, Prince hit the top of a US singles charts with a track from a sound track album. "Thieves in the Temple" was released on July 17, 1990, about six weeks prior to the *Graffiti Bridge* sound track LP and three and a half months before the painful release of the Prince-directed/starring movie. Unlike the other products that supported one another, "Thieves in the Temple" benefited from the distance and had to stand on its merit, with the movie cracking the box office top ten in its first week before disappearing from theaters two weeks later.

"Thieves in the Temple" is an understated, tight R&B number with a Middle Eastern flavor. It's a standout track on an album that marks a low point in

Prince's career, the end of genius that's followed by a period of chasing rather than setting trends.

Prince handles all instruments, joined by the Steeles on background vocals. The song was added to the sound track at the last minute, to the benefit of the LP, and in many ways feels divorced from Prince's other work at this time both in sound and in texture. The song has more affinity with later Eastern tendencies, although the Middle Eastern feel here inspired a young belly dancer, Mayte Garcia, to get in touch with Prince.

The vinyl and cassette single releases feature the full-length LP version, backed by the brief non-LP "Thieves in the Temple (Part II)." The twelve-inch, cassette maxi-single, and CD-single all contain exclusive versions (but not the original song): "Thieves in the Temple (Remix)," the Junior Vasquez remix "Thieves in the House Mix," and "Temple House Dub." The single version appears on hits collections, while "Remix" appears on *Ultimate*. The song was performed regularly in the early 1990s before making a medley reappearance in 2016.

"Thieves in the Temple" hit the number one spot on the black charts on September 29, 1990, and stuck around one week. It replaced "Crazy" by The Boys, a group with the light New Jack sound that Prince started chasing around this time, especially with *Graffiti Bridge* protégé Tevin Campbell. It was followed by Pebbles and her third of four black number ones: "Giving You the Benefit." If you ever need to explain how late 1980s/early 1990s pop music allowed glossy production to overwhelm performers and songs, use this song as an example. "Thieves in the Temple" reached number six on the Hot 100 on September 26, 1990. The chart topper that week was "Release Me," the second of three number ones from 1960s pop progeny Wilson Phillips.

"Cream

Like "Kiss," "Cream" is the kind of easy, unfussy pop song that feels familiar after the first listen but not so much so that you'll quickly tire of it. While it seems to lyrically mine erotic innuendoes and double entendres, taken at face value it's just an extended pep talk with a lot of well-meaning nonsense thrown in. It's all style, little substance, but all the better for it.

"Cream" was released on September 9, 1991. The single edit appears on the hits collection, and an "N.P.G. Mix" edit is included on the *Ultimate* remix disc. The maxi-single is discussed in chapter 31. The B-side, "Horny Pony," was a 2001 NPG Music Club download. "Cream" was performed live on a regular basis until the final show but was never a show highlight.

"Cream" reached the Hot 100 top position on September 9, 1991 (two weeks), replacing "Romantic" by Karyn White. It was replaced by "When a Man Loves a

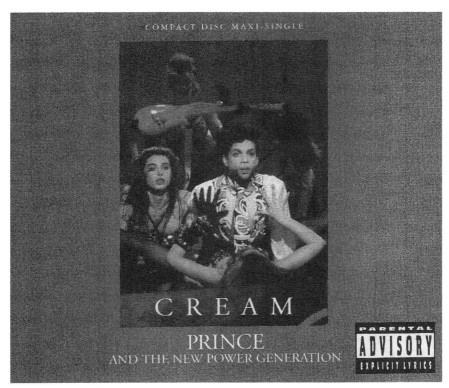

The ascent of "Cream" to number one on the US Billboard Hot 100 in November 1991 marked the beginning of Prince's first commercial renaissance. The accompanying *Diamonds and Pearls* album reached US double platinum status, Prince's first non-sound track LP to reach that level since 1986's *Around the World in a Day*.   *(Author's collection)*

Woman" by one of the most divisive pop singers of all time: Michael Bolton (not the character from *Office Space*). Tellingly, "Cream" failed to reach the R&B chart.

"Diamonds and Pearls"

If "Gett Off" was somewhat nasty and "Cream" somewhat silly, then "Diamonds and Pearls" was somewhat mushy. Released November 21, 1991, "Diamonds and Pearls" was the fourth single from the album of the same name, following the steamy ballad "Insatiable," which reached number three on the R&B charts.

Lyrically, "Diamonds and Pearls" is Prince's only US number one that's simply a love song from the heart and head, not the groin. It's something you can play for the kids with no worries, seemingly addressed to an innocent "boy or a girl" (most likely an unborn child). Musically, the song is a mid-tempo ballad, marred in part by some "triumphant" horn-like synthesizer sounds but redeemed by the central position accorded NPG co–lead vocalist Rosie Gaines.

The single edit appears on the hits collections. The vinyl B-side was the compilation "X-cerpts from the Songs: Thunder, Daddy Pop, Strollin', Jughead, Money Don't Matter 2 Night, Push, Live 4 Love," which is unavailable on CD except in Japan. There was no US twelve-inch or CD single/maxi. The song was played live on a regular basis through 2016.

"Diamonds and Pearls" hit number one on the R&B chart on March 21, 1992, for one week. It is the last Prince single to reach number one in the United States. It followed Michael Jackson's "Remember the Time" (one of his thirteen R&B chart toppers) and preceded "Save the Best for Last" by Vanessa Williams, one of three R&B number ones for the dethroned Miss America. The song reached number three on the pop charts on February 15, 1992. Sitting atop the charts that week was one of the greatest all-time novelty songs, at one time thought to be a sign of an impending apocalypse: "I'm Too Sexy" by Right Said Fred.

13

Produced by the Starr* Company

Vanity 6, Apollonia 6, the Family, and Madhouse

In addition to The Time, Prince manufactured four groups in the 1980s to expand his market share without flooding the market with Prince product and to corral his extra creative energy. This chapter looks at those four projects.

Vanity 6 (1982)

Sometime in 1981, Jamie Starr (ah, Prince) decided that his musical stable needed some balance for The Time's aggressive masculinity. Naturally, that balance meant women in lingerie. Jamie Shoop, who worked for his management team, and Prince's girlfriend, Susan Moonsie, were recruited for The Hookers.

The Hookers recorded eight songs over two 1981 sessions. "Make-Up," "Wet Dream," and "Drive Me Wild" made their way to *Vanity 6*; Prince released "Vagina" in 2019 on *1999 Super Deluxe*, while the rest—"Jealous Girl," "I Need a Man," "Pizza," and "Moral Majority"—remain unreleased.

The Hookers went on hiatus when the *Controversy* tour opened in November 1981. On the road, Prince recruited a third member, Brenda Bennett, who worked wardrobe alongside her husband Roy, a lighting guy. Unlike the other two members, Bennett could sing, having been a member of the Tombstone Blues Band.

On January 25, 1982, Prince spied Denise Matthews at the American Music Awards and arranged a backstage meeting. The two exchanged jackets, found they were the same size, and instantly hit it off. In quick succession, Matthews joined the tour, was recruited to The Hookers, and moved to Minneapolis as Prince's girlfriend.

Prince wanted Matthews to change her name to Vagina, but she objected. Prince instead named her Vanity, feeling that she was a mirror of him. Shoop

The Prince-curated sound track to Spike Lee's *Girl 6* featured three new songs, eight old Prince tunes, and The Family's "Screams of Passion" and Vanity 6's "Nasty Girl." This marks one of the few times that material from Prince protégé acts was re-purposed and marketed, a disappointing but not surprising realization for those awaiting proper treatment for protégé catalogs, such as a Vanity collection that includes a remastered LP and hard-to-find single mixes.

(Author's collection)

returned to her day job, and Vanity 6 was born. Subtly, six is the number of breasts among the three women. It's unknown if Prince ever considered 6 Dicks as a name for The Time.

Vanity added vocals in the spring of 1982, and the thirty-one-minute *Vanity 6* was released on August 11, 1982. Production is credited to the Starr* Company and Vanity 6, although it's Prince aside from Dez Dickerson on "Bite the Beat." The album was controversial for its revealing cover, racy videos, and explicit lyrics, all of which helped propel it to number six on the black charts and number forty-five on the pop charts.

Vanity gets four lead vocals ("Nasty Girl," "Wet Dream," "He's So Dull," and "$3 \times 2 = 6$"), Moonsie two ("Drive Me Wild" and "Make-Up"), and Bennett one

("Bite the Beat"), with Vanity and Bennett sharing "If a Girl Answers (Don't Hang Up)." Prince plays everything as The Time except the Dez Dickerson and Jesses Johnson parts on "He's So Dull," "3 x 2 = 6," and "Bite the Beat." Prince's version of "Make-Up" was released in 2019.

Prince had a part in writing all songs except Dickerson's "He's So Dull." He cowrote "If a Girl Answers" with Time bassist Terry Lewis and "Bite the Beat" with Johnson.

The album produced four singles, with a "Nasty Girl" edit reaching number seven on the black chart and the twelve-inch album version hitting number one on the dance charts.

Vanity 6 opened the *1999* Triple Threat tour, backed by The Time plus Jill Jones, who all appeared offstage. To call the performances underwhelming might give them too much credit. Vanity can barely sing, and Moonsie didn't— she lip-synched. Only Bennett, adopting a tough-girl persona, fares well. But people weren't watching them for their singing.

After the tour, the *Purple Rain* project swung into high gear. Late spring/ early summer sessions for the second album produced six songs, including the still-unreleased "Promise to Be True," "Vibrator," and the instrumental "Wet Dream Cousin." In mid-May, rehearsals started, and by August, Vanity was gone from the film and the group. One story says she was fired after an affair with *Purple Rain* director Albert Magnoli and another that she quit over a chance at a role as Mary Magdalene in Martin Scorsese's *The Last Temptation of Christ*. Somewhere in the middle, she left because of addiction problems.

Vanity 6 was back down to Vanity 4.

Apollonia 6 (1984)

With Vanity gone, Prince's live lingerie act needed another leader. Prince and Magnoli ran through almost 1,000 possible replacements before settling on actress Patricia Kotero. Kotero got the part because she looked like Vanity/Matthews and she said she believed in God and was hungry. Prince renamed her Apollonia after Michael Corleone's first wife, who's blown up by a car bomb in *The Godfather*.

And a bomb is probably appropriate. Prince soon realized that Kotero can't really sing and decided not to waste decent material on Apollonia 6. And what she possessed in singing talent she equaled in acting talent. Byron Hechter, Prince's body double, was fired after telling a Minnesota journalist that she "can't act to save her life." For her part, Kotero found Prince to be a controlling "tyrant," forcing her to hide her marriage and controlling her food intake.

Album sessions began late 1983. Of the six session songs, only "In a Spanish Villa" ended up on the LP, with four songs willed to upcoming protégé Sheila E.

and "Moral Majority" still unreleased. Sessions continued through the spring, ending in June. The group recorded "Take Me with U" and "Manic Monday," but these songs were replaced by the lesser "Blue Limousine" and "Happy Birthday, Mr. Christian" when Prince grew tired of the project. "17 Days" and "Shortberry Strawcake" were also pulled from consideration.

Production credit went to The Starr* Company and Apollonia 6, but it was all Prince. Group members and Revolution members were given writing credits, but Prince wrote four of the seven songs on his own plus "A Million Miles (I Love You)" with Lisa Coleman, "Blue Limousine" with Sheila E., and "Some Kind of Lover" with Brenda Bennett. Bennet sings lead on her song and "Blue Limousine" and Moonsie on "Ooo She She Wa Wa," with Apollonia on the other four tunes. Prince plays all the instruments except on "A Million Miles (I Love You)," which features Sheila E., Wendy, and Lisa.

Apollonia 6 was released on October 1, 1984. It hit number twenty-four on the black charts and number sixty-two on the Top 200, grossly underperforming *Vanity 6* in spite of nonstop promotion at Strawberries record chain where I worked at the time. The album produced two singles. An edit of "Sex Shooter" reached number fourteen on the black charts and number eighty-five on the Hot 100, but "Blue Limousine" tanked. Prince's version of "Sex Shooter" was released in 2019.

Apollonia 6 didn't tour, although they purportedly lip-synched on a promotional European jaunt in the fall of 1984. The group was slated to open the *Purple Rain* tour, but the slot was given to Sheila E.

Their obligations done, all three women left Prince's orbit. Jill Jones says that before Moonsie and Bennett's departures, Prince thought about recruiting a new leader for Pandora 6, but he wisely left that (toy) box closed.

The Family (1985)

After seeing saxophonist Clarence "The Big Man" Clemons perform with Bruce Springsteen in 1984, Prince wanted a sax player. He turned to his tour manager Alan Leeds. Leeds hooked him up with his brother Eric Leeds. Simultaneously, Prince wanted the remaining members of The Time—keyboardist/vocalist St. Paul Peterson, drummer Jellybean Johnson, and man-about-town Jerome Benton—to earn their paychecks. And he needed a project for a current girlfriend, Susannah Melvoin, an occasional vocalist. The Family was born.

Basic tracking for *The Family* encompassed two 1984 sessions at the Eden Prairie Warehouse. These sessions produced the album's eight songs plus the still-unreleased tracks "Feline" and "Miss Understood." Peterson's vocals were added later.

Although album credit is spread around, Prince wrote or cowrote all tracks except Revolution drummer Bobby Z.'s "River Run Dry." "High Fashion,"

"Mutiny" (about The Times's defections), "Nothing Compares 2 U," "The Screams of Passion," and "Desire" are all solo efforts. The two instrumentals, "Yes" and "Susannah's Pajamas," are cowritten with Leeds, dry runs for Madhouse. Engineer David Z. Rivkin and The Family receive credit for Prince's production work.

The album credits Leeds, Jellybean Johnson, and guitarist Miko Weaver, but only Leeds appears, and Prince plays everything save some Wendy guitar on "Yes." Peterson sings lead on everything except "The Screams of Passion," which he shares with Susannah. According to David Rivkin, Peterson had a challenging time following Prince's guide vocals, and by the time they were completed, he began to sour on the project.

Aside from "Nothing Compares 2 U," the most enduring aspect of The Family is Prince's strange relationship with Clare Fischer. Fischer was a longtime orchestrator, familiar to Prince from Chaka Khan's "Sweet Thing." Either engineer Rivkin or Susannah put Prince in contact with Fischer. Not wanting to tinker with his own song, he sent Bobby Z.'s "River Run Dry" to Fischer for orchestration. Fisher sent it back and Prince liked what he heard, so he sent four of his Family songs to Los Angeles for the string treatment, along with Rivkin, Susannah, and Benton for guidance. Prince liked those results so much that he asked Fischer to add strings to Parade and scores of other songs through 2009. Not wanting to jinx the initial success the two enjoyed without a face-to-face meeting, Prince purposefully avoided contact with Fischer, and the two never met.

With The Family, Prince created a gender-diverse and musically and physically less "black" version of the Time, hoping to grab some of "that Duran Duran money." The strong, pop-heading-toward-jazz music and black-and-white New Romantic aesthetic reflect that vision, creating what many consider Prince's best puppet master LP. But economically, the results weren't worthy of a Simon LeBon weekly paycheck in 1985.

The Family was released in the United States on August 19, 1985, reaching number seventeen on the black charts and number sixty-two on the pop chart. The album produced two singles: "The Screams of Passion," number nine on the black chart and number sixty-three on the Hot 100, and "High Fashion," number thirty-four on the black charts.

From May on, The Family rehearsed for a tour with Sheila E. and Mazarati. The band eventually performed their only show on August 13, 1985, at First Avenue. Playing the entire LP, the music is tight and fluid, less funk and more jazz/pop than The Time. The singers are pretty and well coiffed, but Peterson is a most uncharismatic front man, and at times one feels uncomfortable watching him. The main band was joined by six additional members, half of whom would go on to join The Revolution.

By the week of the release/performance, the core band was disgruntled with the lack of promotion and live gigs and already disintegrating. On August 16, Prince took up residency in France to shoot Under the Cherry Moon, Susannah and Jerome in tow, all but abandoning the band. As "The Screams of Passion" generated some buzz, a bee got into Peterson's ear that he could be a solo star. While Prince wanted him to sign a contract for seven years, Peterson would agree to only one to keep his options open. Sick of being poorly paid and simultaneously neglected and bossed around by Prince, who told him what and how to sing and what to wear, in early November he called Prince in France and quit. The band was no more.

After the band evaporated, Leeds, Benton, Weaver, Brooks, and Safford joined The Revolution, while Johnson joined former Time bandmates Jimmy Jam and Terry Lewis's Flyte Tyme productions before heading out on a successful production/drumming career. Susannah remained with Prince through December 1986 before leaving show business. Peterson went on to a brief, unsuccessful solo turn, followed by a successful career as a session man. He re-formed The Family in 2011 as fDeluxe and, after Prince's death, recorded an album with Eric Leeds.

Prince performed three songs live. "Nothing Compares 2 U" was a show mainstay from April 1990 through the last show, featured on sixteen tours. It's in his top dozen most performed songs. "Mutiny" was performed more than sixty times, often in medley with "Controversy." "The Screams of Passion" showed up in sampler sets.

Madhouse *8* (1987)

Prince's nascent jazz ambitions were put on hold for much of 1986 while he worked through the *Dream Factory*, *Camille*, and *Crystal Ball* projects. He returned to instrumental jazz during home sessions from September 28 to October 1, producing and recording all eight tracks for Madhouse's *8*, joined by Eric Leeds the final day.

Eric Leeds pulled double duty during 1987's *Sign 'o' The Times* tour, fronting Madhouse during opening sets before backing Prince on sax and flute for the main performance.   *(Courtesy Thomas de Bruin, unused-prince-tickets.com)*

Much of the music is of a piece with contemporaneous material, especially The Family instrumentals and the horn-driven tracks on *Camille*. But Prince was apprehensive about how the work would be perceived and didn't want it to reach only Prince fans, so he created an elaborate fiction to mask his involvement. In press releases, the band was led and produced by Atlanta keyboardist Austra Chanel, joined by drummer John Lewis, bassist Bill Lewis, and Leeds. Only Leeds existed. On the LP, Dr. Fink, Levi Seacer Jr., and John Lewis are credited with recording at the fictional Madhouse Studios in Pittsburgh. The album's other conceits are that all the songs are spelled-out numbers and that the cover features the incongruous image of well-endowed model Meneca Lightner on the beach.

8 was released on January 21, 1987. It reached number twenty-five on the black charts. A "Six" edit reached number five on the black charts. The US twelve-inch included two non-LP tracks: "6 (End of the World Mix)" and "Six and ½." The latter is a unique track written by Eric Leeds, the only Madhouse track to feature trumpeter Atlanta Bliss.

Madhouse opened the May 8–June 29 *Sign 'o' the Times* tour, with Leeds joined by Seacer on bass, Fink on keys, and drummer Dale Alexander. Prince would occasionally sit in on drums. The standard set included The Family's "Mutiny," "Two," "Three," and "Six." They also performed "One" and "Seven" at headlining club gigs that occasionally turned into Prince aftershows, such as the stellar May 21, 1987, Munich Park Café show. Madhouse never performed "Four," "Five," or "Eight."

Prince performed "Six" and "Four" somewhat regularly.

Madhouse *16* (1987)

16's conceits are the same as on the first LP—same fake production and writing credits, same spelled-out numbering, and same cover model, this time posed as a gangster. The songs themselves also continue in a similar vein, although they are a bit more varied, both for the good (funky "Ten") and the bad (snoozer "Fourteen"). In terms of musicians, Prince and Leeds are joined by Sheila E. and Seacer on "Ten," "Eleven," and "Fifteen," and Dr. Fink plays keys on "Sixteen." Prince wrote four of the songs on his own: "Ten"; "Eleven" and "Fifteen" with Leeds, Seacer, and Sheila E.; and "Sixteen" with Leeds.

16 was released on November 18, 1987, ten months after the first album. Unlike the first LP, it failed to chart. There were two singles, and these also failed to chart. The US seven-inch featured the edit "(The Perfect) 10" backed with the non-LP "Ten and ½," while the twelve-inch also includes "10 (The Perfect Mix)" and the LP version of "Two." The "Thirteen" twelve-inch included the non-LP "Thirteen (The Paisley Park Mix)" and the unrelated "Thirteen and ¼."

Madhouse didn't tour for *16* but played "Nine" and "Sixteen" during a few 1987 European shows.

Prince took multiple tries at follow-up Madhouse albums, but none panned out.

On June 26, 1988, Leeds and Sheila E. joined Prince at Paisley Park to record the unreleased instrumentals "Uno," "Dos," and "Tres," but it's unclear if this was intended for a Madhouse album.

In December 1988, Prince worked with Leeds on *24*. While these Prince-written songs were still numbered, they used Hindu-Arabic numerals and included qualifying titles. "17 (Penetration)," "19 (Jailbait)," and "20 (A Girl and Her Puppy)" were all offered to Miles Davis. Davis recorded them with no Prince input. They weren't released, but Davis performed them live in 1991. The eighteen-plus-minute "21–24 (The Dopamine Rush Suite)," which includes "21 (The Dopamine Rush)," "22 (Amsterdam)," "23 (Spanish Eros)," and "24 (Orgasm)," was the continuation of a song Prince developed in July in London. "The Dopamine Rush" ended up on *Times Squared* as an edit of "21" and "24." "18 (R U Legal Yet?)" is the only song that wasn't put to some other use.

Leeds didn't like the mix on *24* and told Prince. Prince responded by giving him three dozen tracks to mix. These tracks failed to coalesce as *26* but did evolve into Leeds's solo album.

Prince returned to a Madhouse-style concept in September 1991 during the "Cream" remix sessions. He and Leeds recorded the instrumental "Boom Box" on September 28, the only track recorded for a project called Brass Monkey. Later in the year, Prince had the NPG Hornz rehearsing Madhouse material. It's unknown if this was in preparation for a Madhouse LP or tour.

Madhouse *24* took another leap forward on July 7, 1993, at Paisley Park, as Prince on keyboards, Leeds and the NPG, Seacer, Sonny T., and Michael B. recorded six tracks. "17," originally "Carnac," the only track with a number name, was released in 1994 on *1-800-NEW-FUNK*. "Asswhuppin' in a Trunk" (aka "Asswoop" or "Edward") was released through NPG Music Club in 2001. Both songs were performed by Prince with Leeds at the March 23, 1995, "New Power Madhouse" London Emporium show. *Come*'s "Space" shows up as a jazzy instrumental, while an edit of "Rootie Kazootie" commercially surfaced on the 2019 release *The Versace Experience (Prelude 2 Gold)*. Marvin Gaye's "Got to Give It Up" appears as "(Got 2) Give It Up" with daughter Nona Gaye on vocals. Neither this song nor "Parlor Games" has been commercially released, although the latter appeared in truncated version on 1995's promotional cassette *NPG Records Sampler Experience*.

Prince submitted *24* to Warner Bros. for a 1994 release as a ten-track LP, including four segues (one of which oxymoronically closed the album). It was rejected. He revised the LP in 1995 with slightly different segues, overture pieces that would show up on NPG Orchestra's *Kamasutra*, and an unreleased version of "18 & Over" that included Tommy Barbarella on keyboards. It's likely that this updated version was intended for an NPG records release, perhaps as a giveaway sampler. In 1999, Prince mentioned plans for a Madhouse greatest-hits collection, but nothing materialized.

Prince eventually dropped the Madhouse conceit and used his own name on jazz releases.

14

In a Word or 2

Early 1990s LPs

Diamonds and Pearls (1991)

*D*iamonds and Pearls, released on October 1, 1991, with a snazzy holo-gram cover, is the first of two studio albums credited to Prince and the New Power Generation. Working with a mostly new band seems to have stoked Prince's creative juices (almost literally with "Cream"), as, unlike its predecessor, all thirteen songs were written and recorded for this project. Prince was rewarded for this newfound focus with a number Three album, double-platinum sales in the United States, and half a dozen successful singles, including the number one "Cream." Prince was back on top. Sh-boogie bop.

Diamonds and Pearls finds Prince focusing more on songwriting—hooks and melodies—than on production gimmicks or histrionic playing. It's his most diverse album musically to date, featuring everything from jazz ("Strollin'") to Sly Stone funk ("Daddy Pop") to an old-school slow jam ("Insatiable"). Aside from the single "Gett Off" and the closing "Live 4 Love," it mostly avoids rock.

The album is a collaborative effort. Four songs were cowritten with NPG members, and all but two songs are performed with some configuration of the band. This is mainly a good thing (think Rosie Gaines's going-to-church vocals), but it does open the space for one of the most loathed Prince songs ever: rapper Tony M.'s inane "Jughead." The two Prince solo tracks are the respectable ballad "Insatiable" and the opening dance number "Thunder," which was augmented and turned into "The Thunder Ballet" for Joffrey Ballet's *Billboards* production.

The LP underwent numerous configurations, and most songs, except the late-addition "Gett Off," were circulating in some form prior to the album release. Two of those songs remain unreleased: "Something Funky (This House Comes)," which saw a few one-off live performances in 1991, and the creepy teen sex tune "Schoolyard." "Horny Pony" ended up on both the "Gett Off" and "Cream" singles, while "Call the Law," shades of James Brown's "Funky

Drummer," ended up on the B-side of "Money Don't Matter 2 Night" and the NPG *Gold Nigga* LP in 1993.

The album hit number three on the pop charts and number one on the R&B charts. It produced five US singles, including the pop chart–topping "Cream," the R&B chart–topping title song, plus US and UK promo-only releases. Non-LP tracks, edits of "Insatiable," "Money Don't Matter 2 Night," the US promo "Willing and Able," and the UK promo "Thunder," plus the commercial "X-cerpts from the Songs: Thunder, Daddy Pop, Strollin', Jughead, Money Don't Matter 2 Night, Push, Live 4 Love," remain uncollected.

Prince once again skipped the United States, the *Diamonds and Pearls* tour running from April to July 1992 with fifty dates covering Asia, Australia, and Europe. The tour featured the *Diamonds and Pearls* album (although "Walk Don't Walk" and "Money Don't Matter 2 Night" weren't performed) with a few of the expected hits thrown in. Four live tracks were included on the *Diamonds and Pearls Video Collection*, including the otherwise unreleased Aretha Franklin cover "Dr. Feelgood" featuring Rosie Gaines.

Symbol (1992)

Released on October 13, 1992, as the second Prince and the NPG album, what's initially striking about the LP is, of course, the title, the unpronounceable glyph that would become Prince's new name. Because of the flexibility of symbols (we won't get into a discussion of semiotics here), while Prince-as-glyph was called "The Artist Formerly Known as Prince" or the acronym "TAFKAP" or "The Artist" (and often simply "Crazy"), the LP has most typically been called *Symbol* or *Love Symbol* or the *Prince Symbol Album*. Also notable is that it was originally released with a symbol etched on the CD case and was available in a special limited-edition golden box. Unfortunately, the only special part of the box was that it didn't fit on the shelf alongside regular CDs, and it was limited only in its inability to convince people to pay twice as much for a shiny gold box featuring a disc with no bonus tracks.

While Prince had previously woven narratives throughout stage shows and LPs, *Symbol* is the first album that reaches the level of a formal story—it's Prince's *Tommy*. However, as with many rock operas, the story itself is a bit unclear. In part, this is because the album's original nine explanatory segues (including an introduction and "Arrogance") were whittled down to three on the final album to make space for the late inclusion of "I Wanna Melt with U." Cutting to the chase, the story is about an Arabian princess who needs help to get away from some bad guys. Digging any deeper is asking for needless frustration.

At fifteen real songs, *Symbol* is packed with tracks. All the songs, save for "The Flow," were written with this album in mind—no recycling. The album swings toward funk ("Sexy M.F."), soul ("Sweet Baby"), and dance ("The Continental" and "The Max"). It includes the first major rewrite of "Purple Rain" ("Morning Papers"), a sweet ballad ("Damn U"), and the most self-absorbed excesses of rock opera ("3 Chains O' Gold"). And "7" is a fist-pumping anthem. There's only one clunker: the meandering, slight "And God Created Woman."

The standout tracks bookend the album and are both among the highlights of Prince's career. The opening track, "My Name Is Prince," a bold declaration of something that soon wouldn't be true, is Prince's hardest, most direct tune, spoken/sung with an aggressiveness rarely heard from Prince. The closing number, "The Sacrifice of Victor," is one of Prince's most autobiographical songs and is an uplifting, horn-infused reminder of what you find if you make it over *Graffiti Bridge*.

Despite Prince's first US tour in nearly five years and an extensive promotional blitz, including this flat for the second single, 1992's *Symbol* album failed to sell as well as its predecessor. This, in part, led to ill will between Prince and Warner Bros., which culminated in Prince's name change and a multi-year power struggle between the two.   *(Courtesy Stéphane "Zed" Counil)*

Symbol also includes my Prince guilty pleasure (although Prince encourages pleasure without guilt), "Blue Light." It's a humorous humblebrag set to a slight reggae/island melody that could feature on some erotic-world screen that no one has ever reached on Super Mario Bros.

Half the tunes are performed by Prince solo, and half are with the NPG. Rosie Gaines, a major part of the previous album, is gone, the sidekick role filled by Tony M.

Symbol reached number five in the United States and went platinum. It featured five singles, with only "7" reaching the top ten (number seven, coincidently). Prince was stingy with non-LP tracks, offering only the self-promoting "2 Whom It May Concern." The edited "Damn U" single remains uncollected. The "My Name Is Prince" and "7" maxi-singles were replete with remixes.

The *Symbol* promotion included Prince's first full-fledged US tour since 1988's *Lovesexy*. The US Act I tour ran from March 8 through April 14. The show's first half was a semi-theatrical rendering of the *Symbol* Princess story starring Mayte, minus a few tracks but adding the new track "Peach" and NPG's "Johnny." The second half was a greatest-hits show that typically included B-sides "Irresistible Bitch" and "She's Always in My Hair."

Two weeks after the end of the tour, Prince announced his retirement from music and declared that Warner Bros. would no longer receive new music. On his birthday, June 7, he let the world know he would no longer be known as Prince. Nevertheless, Prince and the NPG played the Act II tour in Europe, a greatest-hits show rather than a performance of the album. The tour began on July 26, 1993, in Birmingham and closed in London on September 7, followed the next day by *The Sacrifice of Victor* video Bagley's Warehouse recording.

The Hits 1 (1993)
The Hits 2 (1993)
The Hits/The B-Sides (1993)

On August 31, 1992, Prince signed what was touted as a blockbuster contract—$100 million for six albums. This exciting development came just two months after Prince finished recording what he knew would be the blockbuster follow-up to his soon-to-be-released *Symbol* album: NPG's *Gold Nigga*. Warner Bros. thought otherwise and decided that it was finally time to unleash a long-planned greatest-hits collection. Prince thought that "best of" albums were for washed-up, non–glam-slam grannies. And thus it began. On April 27, 1993, Prince retired from music and said that Warner Bros. could have only music from the Vault. And on June 7, he confirmed that he had changed his name to Symbol. Things got worse for the relationship in August when Prince's longtime Warner Bros. champion, Mo Ostin, resigned.

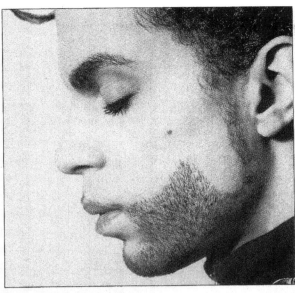

3 CD'S OF PRINCE'S
GREATEST HITS AND
RAREST SONGS. 56
TRACKS INCLUDING
6 NEVER BEFORE
RELEASED SONGS,
AND 18 RARE B-SIDES.
INCLUDES: **NOTHING
COMPARES 2 U,
PEACH** AND
PINK CASHMERE
**3 CD BOX SET (INCL.
28 PAGE BOOKLET)
9362-45440-2**

In 1993 Prince relented to Warner Bros.'s repeated requests and released his first retrospective, the three-CD *The Hits / The B-Sides*. The collection yielded three commercial singles worldwide, the new ballad "Pink Cashmere" and the new rocker "Peach," plus a UK-only release of "Controversy." The double-CD releases of the latter two songs included previously uncollected single edits of past hits. This image comes from part 2 of the UK "Peach" single.   *(Author's collection)*

The one-disc *The Hits 1* and *The Hits 2* and the three-disc *The Hits/The B-Sides* (the two albums packaged with an exclusive B-sides disc) were released in the United States on September 14, 1993. The collection includes singles and album tracks from 1978 to 1992, except *Batman* material, and six previously unavailable songs. The first disc focuses on almost family-friendly materials (though it includes "Soft and Wet"), while the second tends toward the erotic, except the set closer: "Purple Rain." The set was curated by former tour manager Alan Leeds, and, reportedly, Prince was paid to stay away from the project. He nevertheless contributed three recent recordings.

The thirty-two old songs on *The Hits* discs are a mix of single edits, album versions of singles, and LP favorites. Thirteen American A-sides are not represented. Of those, nine are edits that appear on later collections or songs in which the album and single version are the same. From "Soft and Wet" through

```
RC0326E 2 MEZZ    D 709        ADULT
    35.00  2ND MEZZ LEFT          35.00
      5.00   HBLS 107.5-FM WELCOMES
   2 MEZZ    PRINCE AND THE N.P.G.
   AC  46*     NOBODY BEATS THE WIZ
   D 709     RADIO CITY MUSIC HALL
  2U4427*   RESALE INVALIDATES TICKET
  9MAR93    FRI MAR 26, 1993 8:00PM
```

Prince's return to US stages found him playing smaller venues than in the past, including three nights at New York City's Radio City Music Hall, home of the Rockettes. Disappointingly, Mayte and the Game Boyz did not close the evening with a precision, eye-high "Baby I'm a Star" kick line.   *(Author's collection)*

"Damn U," the single edits of "Anotherloverholenyohead," "Insatiable," and "Damn U" remain uncollected.

While one could quibble about favorites left off, there is nothing to complain about. *The Hits/The B-Sides* is essential for any pop music fan. And that includes the third disc, which can compete with most artists' greatest-hits albums.

The six previously unreleased songs were recorded from 1985 to 1993. The two *The B-Sides* songs are the earliest of these tracks and were already a part of many cassette and VHS collections. The earliest is the Wendy and Lisa video version of "4 the Tears in Your Eyes," recorded in April 1985 for the July 13 Live Aid TV broadcast. "Power Fantastic" was recorded on March 19, 1986, for possible inclusion on *Dream Factory*. It was heavily bootlegged. An instrumental introduction, titled "Miles Ahead" on many unauthorized recordings, was left off here.

The Hits 1 features "Pink Cashmere," one of Prince's finest ballads, featuring a lush Clare Fischer arrangement, and "Nothing Compares 2 U." The latter is an NPG version recorded live at Paisley Park on January 27, 1992, featuring Rosie Gaines on co–lead vocals.

The Hits 2 includes the two newest songs. "Peach" was recorded in London in June 1992 during *Gold Nigga* sessions. While fun, the hard blues number is one of Prince's dumbest songs. "Pope" was recorded in May 1993 and debuted in August at *Glam Slam Ulysses*. It's a forgettable tune that recalls a Jamaican dance hall toast.

While subsequent hits collections and *Deluxe* editions have diminished this collection's exclusivity, there are still a few edits collected only here. *Hits 1* offers "Adore," while *Hits 2* features "Dirty Mind" and "Do Me, Baby" plus "Pope." *The B-Sides* offers access to thirteen B-sides plus the rerecorded "4 the Tear in Your

Eyes" and "Power Fantastic." Four era-appropriate songs also appear on *Purple Rain Deluxe*, while "How Come You Don't Call Me Anymore" was also on *Girl 6*.

Two US and two UK singles were released from the collection in addition to three promo discs. "Pink Cashmere" reached number fifty on the pop charts and number fourteen on the R&B charts in the United States, while "Peach" didn't hit the top 100. "Pink Cashmere (Vocal Version)," "Guitar Version," and "Remix" plus "Pope (Remix)" all remain uncollected.

There was no tour associated with this collection. In fact, due to the dispute with Warner Bros., Prince "untoured" (or he would have if such a word existed). Between the release of this collection in September 1993 and the March 3, 1995, opening of the *Ultimate Live Experience*, Symbol played only about a dozen shows outside of the Minneapolis area, a move designed expressly to not support the Warner Bros. Prince product. When he did play, such as three shows on July 14, 1994, at New York's Palladium (now a Trader Joe's), he played no Prince material.

All the new material on the collection got some live airing, with "Nothing Compares 2 U" one of Prince/Symbol's dozen most played songs. The song would be rereleased in original form on 2019's *Originals*.

Come (1994)

I come not to bury *Come* but to praise it. Like the child of a messy divorce who is nothing but a pawn between two conniving parents, *Come* has grown up respectably despite its early misfortunes.

Come was released on August 16, 1994, by Warner Bros. Although credited to Prince, the cover art, a black-and-white photo of Prince in front of a graveyard, reminds us that Prince is no longer with us, having lived from 1958 to 1993. And the former Prince did what he could to bury this record in the graveyard, including withholding the single "The Most Beautiful Girl in the World" and releasing the NPG Records compilation *1-800-NEW-FUNK*, featuring Symbol's new single "Love Sign," only four days before *Come*.

Although *Come* was the last album of newly recorded Prince material released by Warner Bros. in the 1990s, it wasn't without controversy and mostly wasn't new to anyone paying attention to Prince's career (admittedly, there were fewer of us than there had been). Seven of the ten tracks were recorded in early 1993 and used in some form in the unintentionally humorous stage show *Glam Slam Ulysses* in August 1993. And most had been performed live in 1993 and 1994.

Prince presented *Come* to Warner Bros. on March 11, 1994, in a configuration that included "Interactive," "Endorphinmachine," and "Strays of the World" (all from *Glam Slam Ulysses*). Warner Bros. rejected it, saying it wasn't strong enough. They wanted "Come" and "TMBGITW." Prince came back with a May

19 version that removed the Ulysses songs, didn't include "TMBGITW," but included a new "Come" and the newly recorded "Letitgo." Prince delivered *The Gold Experience* to Warner Bros. a week later. Prince wanted the two albums released simultaneously. Warner Bros. refused, and Prince, seemingly in turn, refused any changes to *Come*, which was released in its May 19 form. Imagine how this would have played out in the age of Twitter.

The songs are often lost in the all the fighting, and it didn't help that they were initially rejected by Warner Bros. But they aren't bad songs, although there's no apparent single (which probably most annoyed Warner Bros.), and the last-minute add-on "Letitgo" is little more than a trifle. The worst you can say about most of the songs is that they feel underdeveloped, often more ideas and riffs that work live rather than whole songs. But the riffs are memorable, with single-word titles that instantly evoke the choruses ("Space," "Loose!," "Papa," and "Dark"). "Race" is the most developed song narratively, although its abrupt, illogical ending undercuts the rest of the song. "Solo" doesn't cut it but can be forgiven as an experimental pairing with David Henry Hwang of *M. Butterfly* fame. "Orgasm" is just silly and ends the album with a "fuck you" to Warner Bros.

"Loose!" would appear in a thirty-three-second alternate form as "(Lemme See Your Body) Get Loose!," credited to Tora Tora, on the 1995 promo cassette release *NPG Records Sampler Experience*. Prince used the Tora Tora pseudonym on NPG's *Exodus* LP.

Come spawned two singles: "Letitgo" and "Space." The first hit number thirty-one, while the latter failed to chart. Both received extensive remixing on CD maxi-singles, but neither single included non-LP tracks.

In spite of all these issues, *Come* reached number fifteen on the US LP charts and achieved gold status. Even with this moderate success, Prince had no affection for *Come*, obscuring the album cover with a "Contractual Obligation" stamp on his website. There was no tour, although most songs were performed live during one-off shows in 1994. Most songs were orphaned live within a few years as Prince returned to playing old tunes.

"The Black Album" (1994)

The agreement to release the "*The Black Album*" came about during the height of the Prince–Warner Bros. war and reportedly happened only due to a $1 million payout to Prince. Over the seven years between its initial non-release and its official release, it became the most bootlegged album ever and thus was not really a mystery to any real fan when put on sale. Why Warner Bros. would pay that much money to release something everyone owned is a mystery, although I did buy a copy, and a collector paid $27,500 in 2018 for an original vinyl pressing.

"*The Black Album*" does *Symbol* one better: it has no name. There are no markings on the sleeve or disc, although the title "The Legendary Black Album" did appear on a sticker on the CD shrink-wrap. It's not called but is simply known as "*The Black Album*." It was finally released on November 22, 1994. The album reached number forty-seven and received no sales certifications, the first Prince LP since the debut not to sell at least half a million copies.

For all this, the music is great. There's not a weak track, and it's by far his funkiest album from stem to stern. The highlights are "Bob George" and "Super-funkycalifragisexy," the two songs used in the *Lovesexy* stage show (along with "When 2 R in Love," which appears here in the same form as on *Lovesexy*). While Prince reportedly didn't want to release the album because it was "dark," it's difficult to take the album's posturing seriously—it's all role playing, especially on the voice-altered "Bob George." In comparison with *Lovesexy*, which often deals with more lofty matters than rapper braggadocio, it almost feels lighthearted. Of course, the real "dark" might be that the album was the result of an alleged Ecstasy trip.

Except for horn parts and background vocals, the whole album is Prince. There were no singles and no outtakes. And there was no tour. "Le Grind" and "Cindy C." were never performed live, and, aside from previously mentioned *Lovesexy* tour songs, most of the other songs were played infrequently. "2 Nigs United 4 West Compton" was first played live on the *One Nite Alone* tour in 2002 and found its way onto the live album.

15

We're Gettin' Busy Y'All

The New Power Generation

The "New Power" concept began in 1988 on *Lovesexy*'s "Eye Know" and "Lovesexy." It developed on 1990's "New Power Generation," the first appearance of the New Power Generation (NPG). The concept turned into a full band on January 6, 1991, when the NPG backed Prince at Glam Slam Minneapolis.

The original NPG featured continuing Prince band members drummer Michael B., singer/keyboardist Rosie Gaines, guitarist Levi Seacer Jr. and the Game Boyz, Tony M., Damon Dickson, and Kirk Johnson, joined by newcomers bassist Sonny T. and keyboardist Tommy Barbarella. This lineup debuted on record on July 29, 1991, with the "Gett Off" single.

Five albums are credited to Prince and NPG: *Diamonds and Pearls*, *Love Symbol*, *One Nite Alone… Live!*, *One Nite Alone… The Aftershow: It Ain't Over*, and *C-Note*. Fourteen singles were attributed to Prince and the NPG, eleven from the two Prince studio albums plus "Nothing Compares 2 U" from *The Hits 1* and the stand-alone live "Days of Wild" (2002) and "Controversy (Live in Hawaii)" (2004).

The NPG also recorded three "solo" albums and eleven singles, and one album remains unreleased. This chapter covers the NPG's "solo" career, which stretches from 1993 to 2001. Although the line between Prince and the NPG exists at the beginning of this period, at least as much as it did with The Time, by about 1998 there is little distinction between the two artists.

Gold Nigga (1993)

Prince spent early 1992 touring *Diamonds and Pearls* and finishing *Symbol* and the *I'll Do Anything* sound track. He also started work on the NPG's *Gold Nigga*, recording in Melbourne, Sydney, and Paisley Park through the late spring of 1993. During this time, Morris Hayes replaced Gaines, starting with a February 18, 1993, show at Glam Slam Minneapolis.

During the Sydney sessions, Alan Leeds resigned as vice president of Paisley Park Records. And then the wheels really started to come off "Daddy's

Thunderbird." On August 31, 1992, Prince signed a six-album contract with Warner Bros. According to Leeds, part of this deal was that Paisley Park Records was a joint venture. This meant that Warner Bros. footed the bill for a label that had success with Prince records, but abject failure with artists such as Eric Leeds, T. C. Ellis, and Ingrid Chavez.

Warner Bros. reluctantly released *Carmen Electra* on February 9, 1993. It bombed. On April 27, Prince announced his retirement from music and Warner Bros.' future dependence on the Vault. On his birthday, June 7, Prince changed his name to Symbol. Soon after, Warner Bros. rejected *Gold Nigga*. On August 31, 1993, the newly formed, independent label NPG Records started selling *Gold Nigga* and the "2gether" single at concerts. On February 1, 1994, Warner Bros. closed Paisley Park Records. It all went downhill from there.

Back to the music.

Although much more free-form than anything by The Time, *Gold Nigga* is a return to the "black" aspects of The Time as an antidote to the more pop-friendly work of Prince's name-branded material, with "My Name Is Prince" and "Sexy M.F." bridging the gap between the two worlds. The major difference is that Prince cedes some creative space to this band, especially rapper/singer Tony M., space he didn't allow The Time in their heyday. If The Time was sitting in the backseat while Prince taught them how to drive, NPG is Tony M. at the wheel and Prince sitting in the driving instructor's seat, high-heeled foot perched above the second brake.

The original version of the LP features sixteen tracks. Of these, five are brief segues/skits, and the instrumental "Oil Can" clocks in at forty-three seconds. The labeled production and writing credits acknowledge the NPG, but, as usual, the actual story is different, although it's believed that only the segues were composed solely by Prince. "Oil Can" was cowritten by NPG horn player Michael Nelson. "2gether" was written with Tony M. "Call the Law," recycled from the "Money Don't Matter 2 Night" B-side, was written by Prince and the entire band with Gaines but not Hayes, while the other eight tracks include Hayes but not Gaines. "Guess Who's Knockin'" also credits Paul and Linda McCartney, who wrote Wings's "Let 'Em In," referenced liberally in the song. Reissue pressings of *Gold Nigga* do not include this song.

Unlike just about any other Prince album to this point, *Gold Nigga* is a real band recording from beginning to end, aided on many tracks by the NPG Hornz. Tony M. plays ringmaster, although Prince overpowers him on the clear highlights "Black M.F. in the House" and "Johnny." "2gether" is a nice slice of laid-back rap, and the rest of the full-length songs are solid if undistinguished. *Gold Nigga* gets a bad rap in some critical circles, but, segues edited, I'd reach for it before half of Prince's primary work.

Gold Nigga never got an official or widespread release. It was first sold on August 31, 1993, at the Palais Omnisports de Paris-Bercy. It was later available by phone and in person from the NPG Stores. It never charted and is now difficult to procure, especially the sixteen-track original album. "2gether" was the only single. It was available as a six-track CD and cassette, the album mix accompanied by five remixes.

The NPG opened eight 1993 European Act II shows between August 13 in Cadiz, Spain, and September 7 at London's Wembley Stadium. The group had no fixed set list, playing a few *Gold Nigga* songs, including the three-part title song condensed into one shorter tune, throwing in associated songs such as Mavis Staples's "House in Order," Madhouse's "Six," and the Hornheads' "Intermission."

"Johnny" was played at Prince's first Act I show on March 8, 1993, in Sunrise, Florida. It proved a Prince favorite, performed 112 times, about the same as "Bambi," through an instrumental Paris Bataclan performance on October 29, 2002. "Call the Law" was the earliest played, was featured at the inaugural NPG show in 1991, and was played about twenty times through the September 8, 1993, London Begley's Warehouse show. "Deuce & a Quarter" showed up a couple of times, also ending at Begley's Warehouse. Prince played "Goldnigga" throughout Act I and ended its run at a Berlin show on November 25, 1994, as an instrumental. "Black M.F. in the House" was played about a dozen times, mainly at Act I and Act II aftershows, although it was worked into the main set during encores in Detroit and Chicago in April 1993. "2gether" was played once, on July 26, 1993, in Birmingham's National Indoor Arena in the United Kingdom.

Sandwiched around the spring of 1993 "2gether" recording, the Prince offshoot band the NPG received its own offshoot, called the New Power Trio or Paisley Park Power Trio. Prince, Sonny T., and Michael B. recorded six songs on January 3, 1993, including the still-unreleased "Laurianne" and "Dream." They recorded again on June 14, 1993, resulting in *The Undertaker* video.

Exodus (1995)

Prince and the NPG began recording *Gold Nigga*'s follow-up *Exodus* in mid-May 1994, with an early version of the album compiled June 19. The group went back into the studio in the latter half of the year, completing a second configuration of the album on December 2. This happened in a year in which Prince, as Symbol, played about twenty-five one-off shows, simultaneously playing songs from and not promoting *Come* (released August 15) while actively pushing *Exodus* and songs from *The Gold Experience*, which wouldn't be released until September 1995. And to make things more confusing, Prince as Symbol began appearing with his face covered in chains or a see-through mask as Tora Tora during NPG performances. The cliché is that you can't tell the players without a scorecard, but even a scorecard made this period confusing. *Exodus* was finished in February 1995.

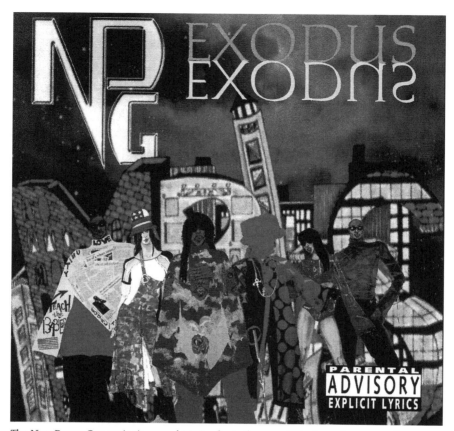

The New Power Generation's second LP *Exodus* is the most P-Funk-tacular groove that Prince (as Tora Tora) ever engaged. The P-Funk musical direction is mirrored in the comic-fantasy artwork and the album's loose, fanciful storyline.   *(Author's collection)*

When Act II ends in September 1993, the Game Boyz disappear, and Seacer leaves the band to step in as head of NPG Records, a post he quits in November 1994. With Tony M. gone, Sonny T. is promoted to lead singer, a post he shares with Prince/Tora Tora, who assumes guitar duties. Mayte participates as a background singer and dancer, the distaff Jerome Benton.

Exodus is a group effort; the band was backed by the NPG Hornz on three songs, Eric Leeds on a different three, and future guitarist Mike Scott on "Cherry, Cherry." Prince wrote all the tunes except "Get Wild" and "New Power Soul," cowritten by Sonny T. At twenty-one tracks, it's bogged down by twelve segues and skits. Despite the clutter, it's a great album with nothing weak among the nine actual songs. The best songs are the anthemic "Get Wild," the Funkadelic trips "Return of the Bump Squad" and "The Exodus Has Begun," and the mellow "Count the Days" and "The Good Life," both Sonny T. vocal highlights.

Exodus was released in Europe on NPG Records on March 27, 1995. It was never released in the United States. The album garnered three singles. "Get Wild" was released in Europe on March 20, 1995. The CD single and twelve-inch included the album version, called "Single Version" here; the LP's "Hallucination Rain"; and the otherwise unavailable Symbol and Eric Leeds's "Beautiful Girl," an instrumental version of "TMBGITW." This version was called "Single Version" to avoid confusion with the version that had been released in December 1994 as a US promo CD and on the *Prêt-A-Porter (Ready to Wear)* sound track. The CD maxi-single included the "Single Version" plus five remixes. A German promo CD featured the exclusive "Money Maker Radio Edit."

"The Good Life" was released on June 13, 1995, in the United States in its complete edited form, failing to chart, and on August 7 in the United Kingdom, hitting number twenty-nine. It was rereleased in the United Kingdom on June 23, 1997, and hit number fifteen. Six remix and edits are spread out over US and European CD maxi-singles, with "The Big City Remix" differing substantially, including a new rap by Prince. The US maxi-single includes a one-minute, forty-seven-second version of the *Exodus* medley "Free the Music," featuring Mayte, while a promo cassette, *The Good Life—Exodus Sampler Experience*, includes a longer version of the same song. The shorter version shows up on *The Versace*

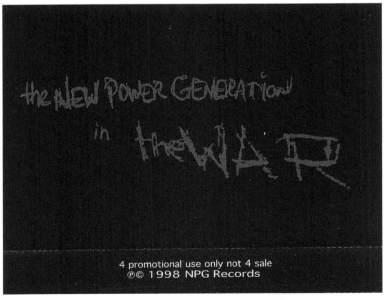

At twenty-six minutes, "The War" is Prince's longest track. Credited to the New Power Generation, the single materialized as a Love4OneAnother.com download about a month after the June 1998 final NPG album *Newpower Soul* before showing up in random mailboxes as a cassette in August.   *(Author's collection)*

Experience (Prelude 2 Gold), as does an edit of the "Get Wild" remix "Get Wild in the House."

This version of the NPG, without Mayte, also recorded Prince's Earth, Wind & Fire song "Super Hero" in the late spring of 1994. It was released by the NPG, featuring The Steeles on the *Blankman* sound track, on August 9, 1994. LP outtakes "Mad" and "Funky Design" were distributed through the NPG Music Club, but "It Takes 3" remains unreleased.

The NPG didn't tour *Exodus*. Aside from "Get Wild," which Prince played about fifty times from 1994 to 2012, the songs weren't performed frequently and not often after 1994–1995.

On March 8, Prince disbanded the NPG, only to re-form it with a new lineup three months later. At this point, the NPG as a functional unit autonomous from Prince ceases to exist.

The last hurrah for this NPG is the March 19, 1996, *Girl 6* sound track, featuring the original version of "Count the Days" and the new song "Girl 6." Recorded in December 1995, the title track is Tommy Barbarella music with Prince lyrics. Prince sings co-lead with Nona Gaye, and Kirk Johnson programs the drums, but there's not an original NPG member to be found.

Newpower Soul (1998)

After disbanding the NPG in early March 1996, Prince/Symbol brings Michael B., Sonny T., and Rosie Gaines back for *Chaos and Disorder* sessions in late March, then regroups the New Power Trio for Miami Beach sessions in late March to early April, recording the released version of "Dinner with Delores."

In June, rehearsals begin for NPG II, Morris Hayes providing continuity on keys, Kirk Johnson moving to drums, and newcomers Kat Dyson on guitar and Rhonda Smith on bass. This lineup makes its TV debut on *Late Show with David Letterman* on July 2, 1996, playing "Dinner with Delores," accompanied by Eric Leeds. Although this core group played live with Prince until April 1998, it appears they may have appeared together on only one Prince song, the "Somebody's Somebody (Livestudio Mix)," and, maybe, one NPG song, "Come On."

Prince began sessions for a third NPG "solo" album in the summer of 1997 and returned to the project at sessions from November 1997 to February 1998. In November and December, he worked simultaneously on Chaka Khan's *Come 2 My House* and Graham Central Station's *GCS 2000*.

As with many Prince projects involving Kirky J. and drum programming, the critical consensus on *Newpower Soul* is not kind, focusing on the clichéd beats and lack of innovation. That considered, the LP isn't bad, just forgettable. It's the type of music you put on and then tell yourself ten minutes later that you need to put on some music.

But the attempts at creativity here are more on the business side. As with *Crystal Ball/The Truth*, released five months earlier, this is another attempt at an end run around the music industry middlemen. Prince sold the album directly to US stores, pocketing more of the money, although BMG distributed it around the globe. And this is the first album of new material that props up touring rather than the other way around. It's perfunctory advertising, more about the bottom line than the bass line. And it gave him an excuse to open the European leg of the Newpower Soul tour in his new hometown of Marbella, Spain.

Only the NPG name upholds the pretense that *Newpower Soul* is a group effort. Prince/Symbol is alone on the cover, and it's unclear if any NPG member other than Kirky J. appears on the disc. For that, the Hornheadz are on three songs ("Newpower Soul," "Mad Sex," and "Freaks on This Side"), and Kat Dyson is on one: "Come On." The writing is credited to the NPG, but Prince wrote it all solo except "Mad Sex," one of many songs that actively or implicitly encourages head bopping, with Kirk Johnson, "(Eye Like) Funky Music" with Doug E. Fresh, and "Push It Up" with Fresh and Larry Graham.

Newpower Soul was released on June 30, 1998. It hit number twenty-two on the US album charts and number nine on the R&B charts. There were two US singles. "The One" was released as a promo edit on April 13, 1998, hitting number forty-four on the R&B airplay charts. "Come On" was released in the fall of 1998 as a European CD single, maxi-single, and twelve-inch. It was available only by mail order in the United States as a seven-track CD and a twelve-inch with six "Come On" remixes and edits and a remix of "The One."

The NPG didn't tour the album but did back Prince/Symbol on two tours. Kat Dyson was dropped on guitar in the winter of 1998 and replaced by Mike Scott on the April–December 1998 tours.

Only "The One" had longevity beyond these tours. It was played around 150 times, about the same as "Days of Wild," beginning on August 8, 1998, at Marbella and until the New Year's Day 2016 St. Barts show. "Come On" hit the stage about seventy-five times from March 1998 through the 2000–2001 Hit N Run tour, ending on June 27, 2001, at an Omaha, Nebraska, A Celebration gig. The rest of the songs were played on occasion, except "When U Love Somebody" and "Shoo-Bed-Ooh," which were never played live.

Peace

In addition to the three full albums, the NPG released three singles and had a 2001 album scrapped.

"The War" single was released three weeks after *Newpower Soul*. The song was available as a Love4OneAnother.com download on July 21, 1998, and in August as a free cassette to online *Crystal Ball* purchasers. At twenty-six minutes, it's Prince's longest commercially released song. The original forty-five-minute jam was the culmination of a June 20 Paisley Park "The One" show, featuring "The One," "One of Us," Shania Twain's "You're Still the One," and "The Christ." Although not exactly jazz, the loose jam feel, the song's apocalyptic "The Revolution Will Not Be Televised" themes, and "The One" set structure all feel like a dry run for the fanciful visions of *The Rainbow Children*. Not surprisingly, the song, the same length as NASA's perfect nap, failed to chart.

The NPG with Prince on vocals returned with two singles in 2001. Both "Peace," backed with "2045: Radical Man," and "The Daisy Chain," backed with "Gamillah," were sold at Atlanta shows starting on April 14, 2001, the same day as Prince's "Supercute" backed with "Underneath the Cream."

The NPG songs, basically Prince and Mr. Hayes, were intended as part of the aborted fourth NPG album: *Peace*. From these hints, it seems that the album was going to be a long-form meditation on race but was superseded by similar themes on *The Rainbow Children*. As with the later NPG material, it's unclear how these NPG songs were distinct from Prince's songs of the period. The Prince songs and "Gamillah" ended up on 2004's *The Chocolate Invasion*, while the other three songs are on the companion *The Slaughterhouse*.

At this point, the NPG was once again nothing more than a backing band.

16

I See Myself on a Silver Screen

Prince on Film

P rince released four theatrical films. Three were fiction films, while the fourth mixed concert footage with staged scenes. The theatrical films provide visual confirmation that Prince was at once sexy, serious, sullen, and occasionally silly.

Purple Rain

In early 1983, Prince told his management team, Cavallo, Ruffalo, and Fargnoli, that he'd re-up if they secured a movie deal. The task seemed impossible. Prince had never acted, and he didn't even have a top-ten single. Warner Bros. Pictures said no, but the trio secured $4 million from Mo Ostin at Warner Bros. Music. Ostin was sticking his neck out for Prince, as the artist-friendly CEO had recently taken a hit on Paul Simon's *One Trick Pony* vanity film/LP flop.

First on board was TV writer William Blinn, known for the weepy *Brian's Song*, the gritty *Starsky and Hutch*, and the historical adaptation *Roots*. *Purple Rain* pulls from all these. Blinn and Prince met over dinner in Los Angeles, Prince sharing his film ideas while ordering spaghetti marinara and orange juice. Blinn was confused about the project and Prince's meal but flew to Minneapolis on February 15 anyway. In May, he moved to Minneapolis but soon left, telling Fargnoli that Prince was a "rock and roll crazy." Prince apologized, and Blinn returned.

Simultaneously, Prince and his band, plus Vanity 6 and The Time, rehearsed and took acting classes. On August 3, 1983, Prince and his new band, The Revolution, played at Minneapolis's First Avenue. The show captured the basic tracks for "I Would Die 4 U," "Baby I'm a Star," and "Purple Rain," the film's last twenty minutes. Vanity soon left, and after an extensive search, Patricia "Apollonia" Kotero replaced her in the film and Vanity 6, redubbed Apollonia 6.

Prince's managers homed in on director James Foley ("Reckless"). Foley declined, but his editor, Albert Magnoli, agreed to talk. He went to Minneapolis,

Very Special Guest was Prince featuring the debut of his new band The Revolution. The twelve-song set included Prince's first live performance of Joni Mitchell's "A Case of You" and six new songs. Among the latter, the backing tracks for the *Purple Rain* version of the title song, "I Would Die 4 U," and "Baby I'm A Star" were recorded.
(Courtesy Thomas de Bruin, unused-prince-tickets.com)

where he told Prince that Blinn's work was horrible and then described what needed to happen. Prince was stunned and said to Magnoli, "You told me my life story." Soon after, Prince played Magnoli about 100 songs and instructed him to pick twelve for the movie. Magnoli rewrote the script, and shooting began on November 1 in Minneapolis. Shooting wrapped December 22 and brought good news: Prince's management team secured a distribution deal with Warner Bros. Pictures.

Purple Rain is a traditional backstage drama. Kid meets girl, kid loses girl, kid gets girl in the end. The powers that be doubt his talents, but he shows them. And what really counts is family.

But who watches *Purple Rain* for the story? *Purple Rain* is about Prince as a sensitive badass. And it's about Morris Day as an insensitive badass. It's about Magnoli and editor Ken Robinson's pitch-perfect refinement of *Footloose*'s feature-film-as-music-video aesthetic. It's about Apollonia barely (pun intended) being able to act. It's about a different era in the treatment of women. But mainly it's about the music, thirteen pieces of genius (plus Dez Dickerson's "Modernaire" and Apollonia 6's "Sex Shooter").

The film premiered on July 26, 1984, at Mann's Chinese Theater in Hollywood. Buzz was loud. According to public relations legend Dick Guttman, hype for the event included planting ads in local papers offering to trade two premiere tickets for two tickets to the August 12 Los Angeles Olympics Closing Ceremony.

Purple Rain received wide release on July 27. It was the number one film in the United States for one week, disrupting *Ghostbusters*'s run at the top. It cost $7 million to make and made it back that first week. It earned $63 million in the United States during a thirteen-week run. It finished as 1984's number eleven earner, just behind *Splash* and well ahead of Oscar winner *Amadeus*, another film about a nonconformist musician.

Purple Rain won four major awards. The big wins were a 1985 Oscar for Best Original Score and a 1985 Grammy for a long-titled version of the same award. It also won a Brit Award and an NAACP Image Award. The movie also received two Razzie Award nominations: for Worst Original Song, "Sex Shooter," losing (winning?) out to Dolly Parton's abominable "Drinkenstein" from *Rhinestone*, and Worst New Star, Apollonia, ceding the trophy to Olivia d'Abo for both *Bolero* and *Conan the Destroyer*.

The movie was released on VHS in the United States on November 19, 1984, and shot to number one on *Billboard*'s sales charts and number two on its rental charts; it remained on the sales charts for almost a year. Part of its sell-through success was its $29.95 price at a time when most films carried a $79.95 retail price. The lower price also allowed it to move beyond video stores to record retailers and even bookstores.

Purple Rain saw its first DVD release on June 25, 1997, in a no-frills package. On August 24, 1984, it was released in a *20th Anniversary Two-Disc Special Edition*, digitally remastered and restored to its theatrical 1.85:1 aspect ratio. There were several appealing extras. Magnoli, Cavallo, and cinematographer Donald E. Thorin added a commentary track. Original vignettes discuss First Avenue, the making of the film, and the film's legacy, while a twenty-seven-minute MTV Premiere clip gives a glimpse of both the start of Purplemania and 1980s low-tech production values. Finally, we get videos of the five *Purple Rain* singles, a thirteen-minute, two-second live take of "Baby I'm a Star," The Time videos "Jungle Love" and "The Bird," and Apollonia 6's "Sex Shooter." Three trailers round out the collection.

The film and extras had their Blu-ray debut on July 24, 2007. This disc was reissued and packed with *Under the Cherry Moon* and *Graffiti Bridge* for the *Prince Movie Collection*, released on October 4, 2016.

Under the Cherry Moon

Under the Cherry Moon (*UTCM*) is a beautiful film horribly directed, written, and acted. The film was shot by Michael Ballhaus, Martin Scorsese's cinematographer. Prince approached Scorsese about directing *UTCM* and was steered toward Ballhaus. Ballhaus's previous job as director of photography was Madonna's "Papa Don't Preach," directed by *Purple Rain* rejecter James Foley.

In early 1985, Cavallo got Prince a three-picture deal with up-front money and creative control. Prince exerted creative control by insisting that the film take place in the south of France and be shot in black and white. The first demand costs money on the front end and the second on the back end, unless you're Steven Spielberg. In addition, the movie wouldn't focus on music but would be a serious film that included some music. Bad signs.

Prince hired newcomer Becky Johnston (*The Prince of Tides*) in April to write a romantic comedy that evoked Roaring Twenties high society. On June 18, he flew to France to scout locations, settling on Nice. When he got back, he hired director Mary Lambert, another Madonna associate. Then he tried to hire Madonna for the female lead: Mary Sharon. She met with Prince and manager Fargnoli and, demonstrating her shrewd artistic and business sense, Madonna turned down the role. Prince gave the role to girlfriend Susannah Melvoin, who made Apollonia look like Katherine Hepburn. Susannah was sent home, and Kristin Scott Thomas received her first feature-length role. He also hired English legend Terrance Stamp as Mary's father.

The *UTCM* script was completed on September 7, and shooting began on September 16. Three days later, the "difficult" Mary Lambert was fired, and Prince took over. Stamp abandoned the sinking ship and was replaced by Steven Berkoff. Whatever grand ambitions were in Johnston's original script were undercut as Prince rushed to make up lost time, often shooting scenes in one take. Shooting wrapped on November 21. The wrap party included Prince inviting the remaining members of the now defunct The Family to join The Revolution.

UTCM originally ended with Prince's Christopher Tracy dying, but Warner Bros. had Prince change the ending. A test screening with this new ending went so badly that studio executives were "not really sure if this is a picture." A few weeks, later Prince restored the original ending with Tracy's death. This made more sense narratively but didn't improve the film or audience feedback.

Hype for the film began with MTV's "*Under the Cherry Moon* with Prince Contest." The setup: on Saturday, June 21, 1986, MTV would play "Kiss" and "Mountains" back to back, and the 10,000th caller would win the *UTCM* premiere party. Lisa Barber of Sheridan, Wyoming, won the contest. Sheridan in 1985 was 800 miles and about a century removed from urban Minneapolis. And it was even farther from Nice and Prince's new 1920s sophisticate look. But the costly $250,000 party worked, getting stars such as Ray Parker Jr. and Rosanna Arquette to the July 1 premiere at the Centennial. The Sheridan video, hosted by MTV's veejay Martha Quinn and Jerome Benton and featuring a four-song set by Prince and the Revolution, is more enjoyable than *UTCM*.

The movie opened Friday, July 4, on a meager 976 screens, somewhat banking on failure. It was the tenth earner that week and the thirteenth the next, and then it dropped from sight. It eventually made back only $10.1 million theatrically of its $12 million budget. It shared the bottom of the charts these weeks with the now beloved *Labyrinth* starting David Bowie. Most reviewers were about as receptive to the film as audiences, with the harshest criticism coming from *USA Today*: "Don't even turn up on the same continent where this is playing."

Unless one likes to watch Prince preening, which many people do, the film is a disaster offset by two moments of inspiration. Not surprisingly, both moments pull music to the forefront. "Girls and Boys" is essentially a video plopped down in the narrative, and "Mountains" is an incongruous Revolution video running over end credits.

UTCM cleaned up with five wins at the 1987 Razzie Awards. Prince won for Worst Director and Actor, Jerome Benton won Worst Supporting Actor, "Love or Money" won Worst Song (not true!), and the film tied George Lucas's legendary *Howard the Duck* for Worst Film. Also nominated were Thomas for Worst Supporting Actress and New Star and Johnston for Worst Screenplay. It was nominated for the 1986 Stinkers Bad Movie Award but lost to Lucas's costly Marvel movie flop.

UTCM was released on home video in November 1986. Its $79.95 price kept it off the sales chart, but it managed to peak at number thirty-one on the rental charts. The DVD was released on August 24, 2004, and added a theatrical trailer and videos for "Girls & Boys," "Anotherloverholenyohead," "Kiss," and "Mountains." *UTCM* was released on Blu-ray individually and in the three-CD set on October 4, 2016, without the videos.

In 2009, Prince dedicated "Better with Time" to Kristin Scott Thomas, in part an apology for her experiences working on this film.

Sign 'o' the Times

The *Sign 'o' the Times* tour started on May 8, 1987, in Stockholm. The tour was to continue to the United States, but Prince canceled in mid-June, opting instead for a concert movie. Eric Leeds thought this was a mistake because the LP needed a chart boost. Others were concerned about Prince turning his back on black American audiences in favor of white Europeans.

Prince filmed three June shows in Rotterdam and one in Antwerp, Belgium, but most of the footage was unusable. Working at Paisley Park in July, Prince remedied the problem by having the band lip-synching to the filmed audio, bringing in a live audience on July 23. He also filmed love-triangle vignettes with band members to add some drama.

Prince finished the film in August and wanted it out immediately. After losing big on *UTCM*, Warner Bros. said no. Prince's management team produced the film as Purple Music and Paisley Park Films and coproduced with Canada's Cineplex Odeon Films, which distributed the film theatrically in the United States.

Sign 'o' the Times premiered at a press screening on October 29, 1987, at Detroit's American Theater. MTV wasn't there, and Prince didn't perform. The movie opened on November 20 in 234 theaters. It finished the week in sixteenth place behind the painful Dudley Moore–Kirk Cameron body-switch comedy *Like Father, Like Son*. It failed to chart again but grossed more than $3 million.

Critics were kind—and rightfully so: it's a joy to watch. With acting held to a minimum, *Sign 'o' the Times* is Prince's best theatrical film, better than *Purple Rain*. It's also in the running as the best concert film of all time, neck and neck with the Rolling Stones's *Gimme Shelter* and the Talking Heads's *Stop Making Sense*.

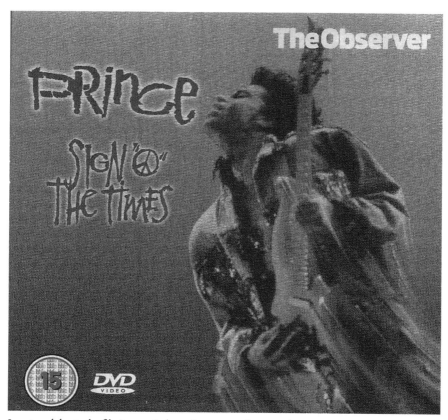

Less to celebrate the film's twentieth anniversary and more to boost sagging circulation, United Kingdom's *The Observer* distributed free *Sign 'o' The Times* DVDs in fall 2007. The film has never been released on DVD or Blu-ray in the United States, but received a thirtieth anniversary revival on cable network Showtime in fall 2017 and a German release in 2019.

(Author's collection)

The film was released on VHS at $29.95 on May 5, 1988, and ended up competing with the *Lovesexy* LP released five days later. The movie has never been available on US DVD but was released on DVD in January 2005 and on Blu-ray in 2012 in Canada, Japan, and other non-US locations. It was distributed free with the September 30, 2007, edition of the UK paper *The Observer*, which concurrently distributed the Talking Heads movie. A 2019 deluxe four-disc German Blu-ray/DVD edition included multiple audio options and mixes and a feature-length interview documentary.

Graffiti Bridge

Prince finished the first version of the *Graffiti Bridge* script in September 1987. This draft features Prince as Camille Blue, a performer looking for the magical

Graphic designer Jeff Munson was on the set of *Graffiti Bridge* showing Prince an unrelated project when the Purple One asked him if he wanted to work on the movie. After a quick "Yes!," Prince gave Munson "Graffiti Bridge" lyrics and assigned him the task of writing the words on wall. Looks like Munson found the Ladder.   *(Courtesy Jeff Munson)*

"Grand Progression" chord, at one corner of a love triangle, with Cat as Vienna and Madonna as Ruthie Washington in the other corners. Prince believed Madonna could give Ruthie "the inner strength and outer-bite" the character required. Other characters included a half-black/half-white character Almost, played by Dr. Fink and, according to Ronin Ro, "weird hobo characters" who were dealing with "angry cops and social problems." Wow.

Madonna arrived in Minneapolis in October, read the script, and told Prince it was "a piece of shit." She soon left. He met with his managers. They said they'd help find someone to finish the thirty-page script, but he insisted it was finished. They said it could be worked into a Broadway play. Prince gave his managers the bum's rush and hired *Purple Rain* director Albert Magnoli as his manager.

In January 1989, Prince met Kim Basinger on the *Batman* set. By July, she had moved into Paisley Park, and the duo were working on another draft with Basinger in the lead. But unlike many other Prince girlfriends, Basinger had a successful career. She got bored with hanging out and returned to Hollywood. Prince finished a new draft on December 19, with Basinger and Jill Jones in lead roles. As Prince and Basinger split as a couple in January, he finished another version of the script, combining Basinger and Jones's parts into one, Aura, played by Ingrid Chavez. The shooting script was completed on February 7, 1990.

Prince didn't secure the financing for *Graffiti Bridge* until November 1989. He had a falling-out with Magnoli, who couldn't find the money and didn't want to produce a cheap, thrown-together film shot at Paisley Park. Imagine that. Magnoli was out, and Prince hired Arnold Stiefel and Randy Phillips, who secured Warner Bros. financing when the script was reimagined as a *Purple Rain* sequel.

Prince, directing again, shot *Graffiti Bridge* from February 12 to March 23, 1990. Stiefel showed up at the first day and saw Prince dressed in an outfit that reminded him of *Flashdance*. Stiefel questioned the costuming choice. Prince asked, "What's wrong with it?" Stiefel responded, "Everything." Stiefel was asked to leave the set and Minneapolis. He and Phillips left Prince's employ on December 20, replaced by Gilbert Davidson, Prince's head of security.

The by-the-number greatest-hits Nude tour was scheduled to start on April 27, 1990, but was postponed as Prince was forced to edit the film after poor test screenings. At some point, Peter MacDonald, a second unit director on *The Empire Strikes Back*, was brought in to help the project. Further editing took place in May and July, and additional scenes were shot in Los Angeles in September. MacDonald received an executive producer credit but was unable to make sense of the project that did in Madonna, Kim Basinger, and three management teams.

Without press screenings, the film premiered on November 1 at the Ziegfeld Theater in New York City. The cast was in tow, but Prince a no-show at the party. The film was released the following day, the earlier 1,400 screens whittled to 688. The film finished ninth in earnings its inaugural week and sixteenth on 670 screens the next week, less than $100,000 ahead of future Oscar winner *Dances with Wolves* on fourteen screens. The film ended up grossing $4.5 million, well shy of the estimated $10 million budget.

As noted in a *Washington Post* review, *Under the Cherry Moon* is like *Citizen Kane* compared with this film. The story recycles Prince and Morris Day's feud over a nightclub. But the tired story isn't the worst part: the sets and costumes are ugly, the cinematography and editing are clumsy, and the acting is nonexistent. And for whatever faults Prince's earlier dramatic films have, at least they have quality music. This has too much non-Prince filler, and the very presence of the title song spirals the proceedings downward. While some reviews, such as those in the *Los Angeles Times*, don't totally bash the film, the *New York Times*'s appraisal that "Prince's direction is on a par with his acting, roughly equivalent to his aptitude for Presidential politics," is more indicative of the general outlook.

Graffiti Bridge was nominated for five Razzies. Prince lost for Worst Actor, Director, and Screenplay, and Chavez lost Worst New Star to now Oscar darling Sophia Coppola. Donald Trump picked up the Worst Supporting Actor Award for Bo Derek's *Ghosts Can't Do It*.

The film was released on VHS on April 15, 1992; DVD on February 8, 2005; and Blu-ray on October 4, 2016.

During shooting, someone asked Prince about the pressure of making a multi-million-dollar film. He bragged that it was no worry because it was someone else's money. *Graffiti Bridge* was the last time Prince didn't have to worry about wasting someone else's money to make a theatrical film.

17

Just a No-Name Reporter

Mid-1990s LPs

The Gold Experience (1995)

*T*he *Gold Experience* (*TGE*) is the first of seven Symbol LPs and the first bearing the NPG Records imprint. By its September 25, 1995, release, the songs had been in the can for more than a year, and most tracks were known to Prince fans through unauthorized videos of *Glam Slam Ulysses* and bootleg CDs of the spring of 1995 *Ultimate Live Experience* tour. Despite fan disappointment at scant "new" material, *TGE* became a fan favorite and endures as one of Prince's strongest works.

TGE was offered to Warner Bros. in May 1994 around the same time as Prince's *Come*. Prince wanted them released simultaneously to see which person the public liked more: Symbol or Prince. Warner Bros. wanted to release one album to see if the public liked either person and ended up with the inferior *Come*.

Reflecting the fact that the album's twelve songs (of eighteen tracks, including segues) were culled from a few different projects, *TGE*'s greatest strength is its diversity. On the flip side, its biggest weakness is over-polished and derivative production that successfully unifies the disparate tracks but not to their individual benefit. Many of the tracks are circulating in superior form that don't lose the songs in the mix.

The biggest offender is the title track, Prince's latest attempt to capture the "Purple Rain" anthem magic. There's a decent song (and a sizzling guitar solo) under the Disney veneer, but you must dig. Same thing with the civil rights blast "We March"—too many silly noises and canned vocals undo a decent groove. The other songs that were coproduced, arranged, and augmented with keyboards by Ricky Peterson ("The Most Beautiful Girl in the World," "319," and "Eye Hate U") suffer the same gauzy fate. This doesn't incapacitate these tracks, but it certainly dates them.

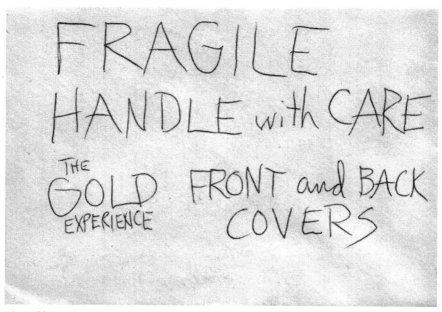

The Gold Experience was Prince's first album release as Symbol. This envelope, feature Symbol's handwriting, contained the back and front cover transparencies for the 1995 LP.

(Courtesy Jeff Munson)

The rocker "Endorphinmachine" showcases some of Prince's most driving guitar, while the moody "Dolphin" has a more fluid approach. "Shhh," first done by Tevin Campbell, is a slow jam that takes it down in the other direction. The two dance tracks here, "P Control" and "Billy Jack Bitch," sort of balance off one another in the gender-equity department, one oddly empowering women and the other insecurely attacking a particular woman. "Now" is watered-down reggae, and the strange-fitting gangsta saga "Shy" rounds out the album.

TGE reached number six on the pop charts and number two on the R&B charts. It spawned three commercial and three promo singles. Both "The Most Beautiful Girl in the World," which preceded the LP by nineteen months, and "Eye Hate U," which preceded it by two weeks, are covered in chapter 31.

The edited "Gold" was released on November 30, 1995, and barely cracked the top 100. Three promo mixes and the roaring B-side "Rock 'N' Roll Is Alive! (And It Lives in Minneapolis)" remain uncollected, although the B-side got a vinyl single release on April 5, 2019, at a Minnesota Timberwolves National Basketball Association game, backed by "Calhoun Square." Promo edits of "Dolphin," "We March," "Endorphinmachine," "319," "P. Control (House Mix)," and "Club Mix" also haven't been anthologized.

Thirty European, Hawaiian, and Japanese dates from March 1995 to February 1996 effectively served as the *TGE* tour and the end of the first incarnation

The March 30, 1995, Dublin Point Theater show closed out the twenty-date Ultimate Live Experience Tour, which relied heavily on then-unreleased material. An aftershow at The Pod included a confused contribution on "the Cross" from U2's lead vocalist Bono, a Dublin native.

(Courtesy Thomas de Bruin, unused-prince-tickets.com)

of the NPG. A core of nine *TGE* songs were typically played during these 1995–1996 shows (and some had been previewed earlier), with "Dolphin," "Shy," and "We March" played only a few times ever. Surprisingly, "Shhh" ended up in Prince's top thirty most performed songs.

The highlight of the 1994–1995 shows was "Days of Wild," which should have been on *TGE* but wasn't released until *Crystal Ball*. Other non-LP songs were played on a regular basis, including Graham Central Station's "The Jam," James Brown's "Sex Machine," and NPG's "Get Wild" and "Johnny." "Vicki Waiting," "I Love U in Me," and "Pink Cashmere" were also played often.

Girl 6 (1996)

Girl 6 is the sound track to Spike Lee's ninth feature film. Lee previously directed the "Money Don't Matter 2 Night" video. The thirteen-track LP contains three new songs, one from NPG and two credited to Prince, although he had been Symbol for two years. Confusingly, "She Spoke to Me," edited from the later *The Vault* version, is a full-blown NPG track, while the title track, cowritten by Tommy Barbarella and credited to the NPG, is mostly a Prince solo track. The other new track, the *I'll Say Anything* reject "Don't Talk 2 Strangers," is a track from early 1992 when Prince was still Prince. The balance of the tracks are previously released Prince/Revolution/NPG tracks plus The Family's "Screams of Passion" and Vanity 6's "Nasty Girl."

The album, which reached number seventy-five on the top 200 and number fifteen on the R&B charts, spawned one single, "Girl 6," with no non-LP tracks. Prince never performed "Girl 6" live and sang "She Spoke 2 Me" only four times in 2009 during jazz shows.

Chaos and Disorder (1996)

Prince re-upped with Warner Bros. in 1992 for six albums and $100 million, although both numbers were more in the realm of ego and publicity than reality because the money included non-LP deals (such as publishing) and unrealistic triggers (5 million album sales to guarantee advances). *Symbol*, *Come*, and *TGE* were the first LPs on the deal, at which point Prince said he'd give Warner Bros. only old material. Neither *The Black Album* nor *Girl 6* counted toward contract obligations.

In an April 26, 1996, agreement, Warner Bros. lowered the number of albums owed to two in exchange for two compilations (2001's *The Very Best of Prince* and 2006's *Ultimate*), ownership of the back catalog, and lower royalty fees (the 1992 contract gave Prince three times his old fee). Looking back, this agreement is odd. All that Prince really gets out of this is out of his contract. That makes sense since *Emancipation* and his new business model depend on artistic and economic freedom. But he fails to regain control of his back catalog—a huge loss. One must wonder if his April 21 trip to Fairview Southdale Hospital due to wine and "aspirin"–induced "chest palpitations" (exactly twenty years to the day before his overdose death) encouraged him to complete a deal.

Chaos and Disorder (*C&O*) was the second Symbol album, released on July 9, 1996, less than ten months after *TGE* and three months after *Girl 6* and only four months before *Emancipation*. Six discs in fourteen months—it was a great time to be a fan.

While Prince did give Warner Bros. some older material for *C&O* (some from 1993), much was recorded or rerecorded in early 1996. Although credited to Symbol, the album is mostly an NPG effort, with a returning Rosie Gaines on five tracks.

The eleven-track, thirty-nine-minute *C&O* is the most underrated album of Prince's first two decades and the closest Prince came to a straight rock record until 3rdEyeGirl's *Plectrumelectrum* in 2014. This is apparent in the one-two opening volley of the title song and "I Like It There," both full-tilt rockers. *The Undertaker*'s "Zannalee" returns in studio form as a harder-rocking cousin of the funky "Hide the Bone," and "The Same December" rocks for Jesus. "I Rock, Therefore I Am," featuring Rosie Gaines and the NPG Hornz, doesn't rock as much as invoke an island rhythm, while "Right the Wrong," a divisive track among fans, sort of hits a hoedown rhythm while tipping the cap to the mistreatment of Native Americans.

The Gaines pairing of "Into the Light" and "I Will" are both gentle, slight, and spiritual. The balance of the album, the nasty single "Dinner with Delores," and the final one-two closing slam of the left-hand one-finger salute to Warner Bros. on "Dig U Better Dead," followed by the right-hand one-finger salute "Had U," are anything but gentle and spiritual.

Mostly ignored by Prince, *C&O* reached number twenty-six on the pop charts for four weeks and failed to make the R&B chart. It's the first LP to fail at gold status since *For You* (except *The Black Album*, which would have if people had actually paid for it). The single "Dinner with Delores" wasn't released commercially in the United States. It was the first commercial single in the United States or the United Kingdom without a seven-inch vinyl version and the first Prince track initially released online: at a dedicated *C&O* site on Prince's birthday, June 7, five days before the promo single release.

There was no *Chaos and Disorder* tour. After the February Hawaii shows, Prince played only nine shows in 1996, all after October 1996 when he was on to *Emancipation* material.

Four songs were performed live: "Chaos and Disorder," "Zannalee," "Dinner with Delores," and "I Like It There." Only the latter featured on a complete tour: 2013's pounding Live Out Loud. Ultimately, *Chaos and Disorder* was a bang that turned into a whisper.

Emancipation (1996)

The triple-album *Emancipation*, the third Symbol album, was released on November 19, 1996. It came on the heels of a year of continual upheaval both personally and professionally for Prince (with the two often mixed).

Prince and Mayte married on February 14, 1996. Three weeks later, on March 6, he disbanded the NPG, firing everyone but Morris Hayes. Two weeks after that, Mayte's pregnancy was announced. Another three weeks later, on April 21, Prince was found passed out at Paisley Park and brought to the hospital. Sometime in May, he brought in bassist Rhonda Smith and recorded the bulk of *Emancipation* during the summer. On July 9, *Chaos and Disorder* was released to the opposite of fanfare. On October 13, he signed an *Emancipation* production and distribution deal with EMI-Capitol. Three days later, Mayte gave birth to a son, who died a week later of a genetic defect. Three days after that, on October 26, Prince unveiled the new NPG lineup—Hayes, Smith, Kirk Johnson, and guitarist Kat Dyson—at an *Emancipation* kickoff gig at Paisley Park. On November 21, he appeared on *Oprah* without a care in the world.

Based on all this, it's not surprising that Prince needed some guidance when he started hanging out with Larry Graham the following year.

In high-profile interviews in the fall of 1996, Prince touted *Emancipation* as his shot to make the album he always wanted to make, free of label restraint. At the very least, it was all the album that he wanted to release, with thirty-six tracks spread over three CDs, each CD with twelve songs and exactly sixty minutes of music, clocking in at 180 minutes, one of the longest albums of new studio material ever released.

While it's easy to make fun of the name change and shake your head at the label battles, *Emancipation* does feel like a rebirth or at least a return to a happier, more confident place that Prince inhabited in the past. It sounds like he cares. It has the most in common with *Diamonds and Pearls*, the first Prince and NPG album, his previous "rebirth." Both albums are R&B, not rock, and they sound contemporary without totally pandering (more so *Emancipation* than *Diamonds and Pearls*). They're also confidently mellow, mostly avoiding lyrical bitterness and bragging, with "Face Down" the exception that proves the generalizations. Less generously, it has much in common with *Parade* and its underdeveloped songs.

Emancipation is primarily a solo album, with both the old NPG, Morris Hayes, Sonny T., Michael B., and Tommy Barbarella and the new NPG, Hayes, Rhonda Smith, Kat Dyson, and Kirk Johnson on a few tracks. There are a few guest appearances, including English vocalist Kate Bush on "My Computer" and dancer Savion Glover on "Joint 2 Joint."

There's no one song here that's a sure shot to factor in a career-long greatest-hits collection ("The Love We Make" and the title track are on 2018's *Anthology: 1995–2010*), but there are several lesser highlights. On the upbeat/dance side, "Jam of the Year," "Joint 2 Joint," "Slave," and "Style" are keepers. "Courtin' Time" gets individual props as Prince's best Glenn Miller–era "Delirious" rewrite. On the mellow/ballad side, "White Mansion," "Sex in the Summer," "The Holy River," and "The Love We Make" get the job done, the latter improving much with age. The second half of the second disc sags with a bit too much gooey Mayte worship and the inclusion of a snippet of the NPG's Orchestra's "The Plan" (edited to ensure that the second disc was exactly sixty minutes).

For the first time on LP, Prince included cover songs. Both the Stylistics's "Betcha by Golly Wow!" and the Delfonics's "La, La, La Means I Love U" keep pace with the soul originals (albeit with a bit too much gloss), but the Bonnie Raitt–associated "Eye Can't Make U Love Me" and the Joan Osborne–associated "One of Us" are flaccid.

The album reached number eleven on the top 200 and number six on the R&B charts. It went double platinum on shipments of about 666,666 units of the triple LP and, based on the deal with EMI, earned Prince a cool $5 million from actual sales of around 450,000 units. While the actual numbers weren't as impressive as they were in the past, the numbers didn't matter because the profits were real.

There were no conventional commercial singles released in the United States. The United Kingdom and Australia saw the release of album versions of "Betcha by Golly Wow!," Prince's first cover-version single, backed with "Right Back Here in My Arms." An edit of "The Holy River" backed by a "Somebody's Somebody" edit followed. A first CD maxi-single added "Somebody's Somebody," "Livestudio Mix," and "Ultrafantasy Edit" versions, while a second included an *Emancipation* ad, "On Sale Now!" (forty-eight seconds). The three "Somebody's Somebody" mixes and the ad ended up on a US promo twelve-inch and CD on January 13, 1997. In spite of the lack of commercial product, "Betcha by Golly Wow!," "The Holy River," and "Somebody's Somebody" all charted in the United States based on radio play.

The United States also saw the release of *NYC*, a direct-order cassette containing live versions of "Jam of the Year" and "Face Down" from a January 11, 1997, show at New York's Roseland Ballroom. *NYC* retailed for $20 for a cassette. The studio version of "Face Down" was released as a US promo twelve-inch and CD in April 1997, with three new versions spread across the two formats: "X-tended Rap Money Mix," "Instrumental Money Mix," and "A Cappella." EMI-Capitol shut down the same month, thwarting any promotion of *Emancipation* or its potential singles. None of the non-LP tracks have been collected on CD.

Prince officially kicked off the *Emancipation* era with an eight-song, twenty-five-minute performance from Paisley Park on November 12, 1996. The show, which tellingly featured only four new songs, was broadcast on MTV, VH1, and BET. He followed with two North American tours. The thirty-five-date Love 4 One Another Charities tour opened in January 1997 at the Tower Theater in Upper Darby, Pennsylvania, continuing in Hit N Run style until June in Chicago. The full-blown sixty-plus-date Jam of the Year tour ran from July to January 1998.

During the first tour, Prince was playing about half a dozen new songs on a more or less regular basis: "Get Yo Groove On," "Face Down," "Jam of the Year," "One of Us," "Sleep Around," and "Mr. Happy." On the Jam of the Year tour, only "Jam of the Year" and "Face Down," were played regularly, with "One of Us" and "Sleep Around" played occasionally. More than half of the *Emancipation* songs, nineteen of thirty-six, were never performed live, and none made a lasting impact on set lists. What had started in the freedom to do anything ended up, disappointingly, with a rejection of the new and a return to rote performances of tired hits. Fans in sheds and arenas wanted Prince, not Symbol, and it appeared that Symbol wanted Prince, too.

18

I Don't Need U 2 Tell Me I'm in the Band

1990s Band Members

Prince entered the 1990s with his no-name band featuring Michael B., Levi Seacer Jr., Miko Weaver, Rosie Gaines, Dr. Fink, and the Game Boyz. He dropped Weaver and Fink and added Tommy Barbarella, Sonny Thompson, and Tony Mosley, and on January 6, 1991, the NPG was born. The eventual NPG core of Michael B., Barbarella, and Sonny T. was let go in 1996 as the continuing Morris Hayes anchored Prince's late 1990s NPG.

Rosie Gaines (1990–1992)

Although her tenure was brief, Rosie Gaines is fondly remembered as a commanding stage presence and captivating vocal foil in the first NPG. Gaines first played live at the 1990 Huntsberry benefit and appeared on the *Nude* and the *Diamonds and Pearls* tours. She was typically featured vocally, often on Aretha Franklin covers, such as "Dr. Feelgood" or "Chain of Fools." Gaines left Prince in 1992 on uneven terms, disappointed at the direction of her career and sexism in the band, but returned live a few times, most notably for *Rave Un2 the Year 2000*.

Starting with "vocal icing" on "New Power Generation," Rosie appeared on around twenty Prince songs on keys and vocals, most prominently on the *Diamonds and Pearls* and *Chaos and Disorder* LPs, the latter four years after leaving the fold. She's most conspicuous on the duets "Diamonds and Pearls" and "Nothing Compares 2 U," "Jam of Year," and "1999: The New Master." With Prince, she cowrote "Push" and three songs that appear on her post–Paisley Park LPs: "I Want U (Inner City Blue)," "My Tender Heart," and "Hit U in the Socket." Gaines also cowrote "I Hear Your Voice" and "The Voice" with Prince (and her husband deejay Francis Jules on the latter track), and "House in Order" on Mavis Staples's *The Voice*. She also played keys and/or sang on five additional Prince-associated LPs. Her debut album, *Caring* (1985), featured Levi Seacer Jr. on guitar.

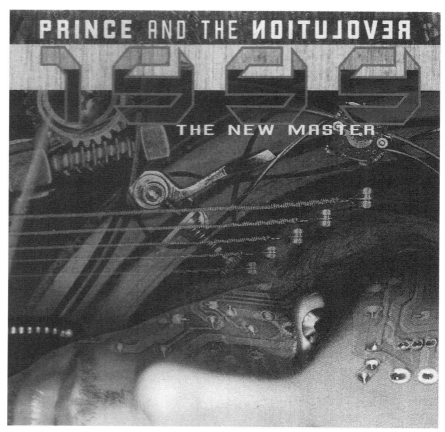

Symbol released "1999: The New Master" on NPG Records as Prince and The Revolution in a move designed to counter Warner Bros.'s reissue of Prince's original "1999" single. The unlistenable re-recording strangely features no members of The Revolution, but includes a return visit from Rosie Gaines, bass from 1990s pal Larry Graham, and contributions from actress Rosario Dawson and hanger-on Doug E. Fresh. A total mess.   *(Author's collection)*

Tony M. (1990–1993)

Along with Kirk Johnson, Tony M. (Mosley) is among the most disliked Prince associates among fans. For many, he's disdained because he foregrounded rap in Prince's early 1990s music. For others, he's disdained because he had about as much flow as the Los Angeles River in mid-July. When he yells he's gonna "get stupid," you believe him.

Like Gaines, Tony first featured on the 1990 "NPG" maxi-single, mainly on "Brother with a Purpose," originally titled "Tony's Iggnant Mix." He was highlighted on the "Cream" maxi-single on "Things Have Gotta Change (Tony M. Rap)" and credited on raps and vocals on a baker's dozen of tunes on *Diamonds* and *Pearls* and *Symbol*. He's also the lead vocalist on the NPG's *Gold Nigga*. He cowrote half a dozen songs with Prince on the *Carmen Electra* LP. His Paisley Park album *True Confessions* was released on May 28, 1991. The LP includes "Miss Thang," which Prince wrote and plays on; "Girl O' My Dreams," which Prince wrote; a rap cover of "Bambi"; and the title track, which is a version of Mosely's "NPG" single rap. He and Seacer Jr. eventually sued for Prince for royalties for cowritten songs.

Tommy Barbarella (1991–1996)

Often underestimated as nothing more than eye candy when Prince was loading the stage with sexy guys, keyboardist Tommy "Barbarella" Elm skillfully filled out the sound with his melodic but funky fills. And often he stepped center-stage on the Purpleaxxe, the patented keytar Prince created for Barbarella in 1994.

Kicking around Minneapolis cover bands in the late 1980s, Barbarella backed The Steeles when they went secular. Prince brought him in the fold for the unreleased Flash project. Barbarella doesn't appear on Flash studio songs, but the band opened two Minnesota Prince shows in the spring of 1990. Barbarella and Flash singer Margie Cox were also members of Mavis Staples's band that opened UK and Irish Nude tour dates in the summer of 1990. Barbarella was a member of the NPG at their first gig on January 6, 1991, at Glam Slam Minneapolis. His last gigs were the three Hawaiian honeymoon shows in February 1996.

Barbarella plays keys on about forty studio songs of new-material Prince LPs from *Diamond and Pearls* (where he's credited as "sex symbol") through *Emancipation* plus the *Crystal Ball* and *The Vault* collections. He's also on the first two NPG albums and side projects such as *Carmen Electra* and Mavis Staples's *The Voice*. On the later album, he's given cowriting credit on "The Undertaker." He recorded the demo for "Girl 6" at his home studio and received music-writing credit but doesn't appear on the song. After leaving NPG, Barbarella toured with Art Garfunkel and was part of numerous bands, including Greazy Meal and Sons of Almighty, both with other ex-NPG members.

Sonny T. (1991–1996)

Sonny Thompson was the bassist who best completed Prince's live sound. According to Prince's guitar tech Takumi Suetsugu, he was also the biggest bass-playing influence on Prince. In the mid-1970s, Prince loved watching the slightly elder Sonny sizzle onstage with the local band Family. Prince jammed with Sonny and appears on Sonny's composition "Got to Be Something Here" for local artist the Lewis Brothers. This 1976 recording on the Lewis Connection's 1979 LP is the first time Prince appeared on someone else's released recording. Sonny eventually joined Dr. Mambo's Combo, a Minneapolis mainstay formed in 1987. The Combo morphed into Prince side project Flash, which morphed into the NPG. Sonny has the same live history as Barbarella, although he also subbed in Carmen Electra's opening band for two Earl's Court dates in 1992 and returned for the "rock" Conga Room performance on March 28, 2009.

Sonny T. appears on more than fifty Prince studio tracks, first from *Diamond and Pearls* through *The Vault* (except *The Truth*), then on *3121*, *Planet Earth*, and *Lotusflow3r*. He contributed some of Prince's most memorable bass licks, including "Cream," "Calhoun Square," "Days of Wild," and "Ripopgodazippa," and was down low on the New Power Trio's *The Undertaker* DVD. He played on half a dozen Prince protégé projects, was bassist and then lead vocalist on the first two NPG albums, and was bassist for the failed "New Power Madhouse" *24* LP in 1994. After leaving the NPG, Sonny was involved in numerous projects, most notably a sampling *Funky-ass Loops* (1998) (with Michael B.) that Prince used on Chaka Khan's *Come 2 My House* and as bassist for Nick Jonas and the Administration, joining Michael B. and Tommy Barbarella behind the erstwhile Jonas Brother.

NPG Hornz/Hornheadz (1991–2001; 2014–2015)

Trombonist and arranger Michael B. Nelson is an unsung hero among Prince musicians. As leader of the NPG Hornz, he provided a full-funk brass sound woven into the texture of the grooves rather than a modified jazz sound layered over the top. NPG Hornz also includes Dave Jensen (trumpet), Kathy Jensen (saxophone), Steve Strand (trumpet), and Brian Gallagher (tenor saxophone), the latter replaced in 1996 by Kenni Holmen.

In the late 1980s, Nelson worked as an arranger at Rupert's Night Club and for the Minnesota Vikings Band. He and the group hooked up with Prince as the Hornheadz, first joining the live NPG on June 3, 1991, at a Warner Bros. Studio Lot performance—Prince's attempt to get the label behind the forthcoming *Diamonds and Pearls*. The band went on the road for the subsequent tour, followed by the 1993's Act I and Act II tours. The group's work at the 1993 Bagley's Warehouse gig, especially on the Prince-written Mavis Staples song "House in Order," which segues into Nelson's original "Intermission," shows the horn section at the top of their game. Prince used group members though 2001, most interestingly on ten European TV broadcasts in November 1999.

The Gallagher Hornheadz appeared on around twenty-five Prince tracks between 1992 and 1998, most notably "Sexy M.F.," "The Sacrifice of Victor," and "Courtin' Time." With Holmen on sax, they appear on about fifteen LP tracks from 1999 to 2001 and 2014 to 2015. Kathy J. and Gallagher played sax on *The*

Hits version of "Nothing Compares 2 U." Nelson cowrote "Billy Jack Bitch" and NPG's "Oil Can" with Prince. The Hornheadz appear on nine protégé albums plus the NPG albums, most notably on "Black M.F. in the House," "The Exodus Has Begun," and "Mad Sex."

Mayte (1991–1996)

Dancer Mayte's NPG stint began at the August 16, 1991, one-off Chicago gig and ended at the February 19, 1996, Hawaii Honeymoon show. Mayte danced occasionally through 1999. She appeared in multiple Prince videos, including *3 Chain o' Gold* as the belly-dancing princess. Mayte is credited with vocals on ten Prince songs, most notably "Love 2 the 9's," "The Max," "Pope," and the Spanish on "Damned If Eye Do" (as Janelle, her middle name). In addition to the twelve songs on her only LP, 2005's *Child of the Sun*, she sang on a number of songs left unreleased or given to other artists. Like many other Prince-associated dancers, Mayte dabbled in film and TV after leaving the NPG, most notably on VH1's reality show *Hollywood Exes* (presumably *Minneapolis Divorcees* was taken), and wrote a post-death Prince-related autobiography: *The Most Beautiful*.

Morris Hayes (1993–2012)

Funk-rock keyboardist and band leader Morris "Mr." Hayes had the longest connection with the NPG. Hayes entered the Purple realm in the late 1980s when Brown Mark recruited him for post-Prince Mazarati. He appeared in *Graffiti Bridge* as a member of George Clinton's Funkestra, then joined The Time for two Japanese *Pandemonium* shows in February 1991. Back in Minneapolis, Hayes formed G Sharp and the Edge with fellow keyboardist Greg Sain (GSharp). This group served as Carmen Electra's band for the 1992 *Diamond and Pearls* tour.

Hayes was promoted to the NPG around the time of a February 18, 1993, Glam Slam Minneapolis gig. He joined the band full-time for the Act I tour, missed the *One Nite Alone* and *Musicology* tours while on tour with Maceo Parker, and then worked through September 27, 2012, at the House of Blues in Chicago, the end of the Welcome 2 tours.

For all his time with Prince, Hayes appears on remarkably few released studio songs (around thirty) and, more incredibly, only on Andy Allo's *Superconductor* side project (although he did provide additional production on Bria Valente's *Elixir*). He's also on *Indigo Nights* and the NPG albums. Hayes has performed with many other artists, including Kanye West and Stevie Wonder, and was inducted into the Arkansas Black Hall of Fame in 2013. He served as musical director for the Official Prince Tribute Concert in the fall of 2016.

Rhonda Smith (1996–2004)

Rhonda Smith is a hard-rocking Canadian bassist with jazz roots who hooked on with Prince through Sheila E. She's high in the NPG pantheon as one of the longest-serving members and a musical mainstay throughout Prince's roughest period. Smith debuted on July 2, 1996, as part of the new NPG performing "Dinner with Delores" on *The Late Show with David Letterman* alongside fellow instrumental newcomers Kat Dyson and Kirk Johnson. Although briefly replaced by Larry Graham in 1999, she would last through the *Musicology* tour, ending her tenure on September 11, 2004, in San Jose, California. During the *One Nite Alone* tour, she often sang Erykah Badu's "Didn't Cha Know."

She returned to the live fold in the summer of 2009 for half a dozen performances, including the jazz show of the three shows in one day in Los Angeles. Smith appears on more than twenty studio tracks from *Emancipation* through *Musicology*, including all of *N.E.W.S.* and the eight band tracks on *Xpectation*, and cowrote the music for *The Truth* tracks "Man in a Uniform" and "Animal Kingdom." Smith toured Europe with C.O.E.D. in 2007, has released two solo albums, and is Jeff Beck's longtime live bassist.

Kat Dyson (1996–1998)

Kat Dyson is an American guitarist/vocalist for the Mach II NPG. After moving to Montreal, she hit the top of the US dance charts for seven weeks in 1980 as cowriter of Geraldine Hunt's "Can't Fake the Feeling." Dyson was working for Canadian guitar maker Godin at a trade show in Germany in the mid-1990s when she met Sheila E., who sent her digits to Prince. Featured on the *Emancipation*-era Love 4 One Another and Jam of the Year tours, Dyson tended to keep her gospel/soul stylings in the background on shows that were tight and somewhat uninspired. She debuted in 1996 on the *Letterman* show and checked out in February 1998.

Dyson contributed guitar and vocals to a handful of *Emancipation* songs and vocals/percussion on "Fascination" from *The Truth*. She's also on the NPG's "Come On" (bottleneck acoustic guitar) and Graham Central Station's "Utopia" (vocals). After leaving the NPG, she toured Europe with C.O.E.D in 2007; enjoyed a deep career as a hired hand for scores of artists, including Cyndi Lauper, Mick Jagger, and Italian legend Zucchero; and was an active member of the Black Rock Coalition.

Mike Scott (1996–1999; 2004)

Mike (Rev.) Scott is an American guitarist who served a few stints in the NPG. He jump-started his career with a move in the late 1980s to Minneapolis, where he was hired by Jimmy Jam and Terry Lewis for session work. He made his NPG debut at Paisley Park on December 28, 1996, and was a regular member of the band through the New Power Soul Festival tour in 1998. He was a part of the non-touring 1999 band through his final December 18, 1999, *Rave Un2 the Year 2000* gig. In 2000, he joined Fonky Bald Heads and periodically joined Prince for one-off gigs, then rejoined the NPG for the February 8, 2004, Grammy Awards performance and stayed through the September 11, 2004, end of the *Musicology* tour. He sat in a few times before returning in 2012 for five September shows in Chicago and a one-off date in Los Angeles in October.

Scott played on a handful of Prince studio releases, most notably "The Greatest Romance Ever Sold" and "Beautiful Strange." He shines on the *Beautiful Strange* video and is on Mayte's version of "Love's No Fun." His most notable outside work was joining John Blackwell on Justin Timberlake's 2007 *FutureSex/LoveShow* tour.

Kirk Johnson (1996–2000; 2015–2016)

Kirk Johnson, aka Kirky J and KAJ, was an NPG drummer, Prince's best man at his first wedding, and a longtime associate deeply involved in Prince's last days. Kirky J got his start on the set of *Purple Rain*, first as an extra with his dance crew 2 Be Rude and then, after being noticed by Prince, as a choreographer and casting assistant. With his renamed crew Game Boyz, he shows up in 1988's "Glam Slam" video, then as a member of Kid's Band in *Graffiti Bridge*, and eventually as a dancer/percussionist with the NPG starting at the April 1990 Huntsberry benefit through the September 1993 end of Act II.

Johnson latched on as the full-time drummer for the July 2, 1996, *Letterman* performance, toured on the *Emancipation*-era and New Power Soul tours, and lasted until a July 29, 2000, show at Paisley Park. Johnson performed percussion at several of the 2002 Paisley Park Xenophobia shows. He was drumming for Judith Hill when he reappeared on stage with Prince in the summer of 2015 and was behind the kit for a series of expansive, funky Paisley Park shows in the fall of 2015. He was also the drummer at the January 1, 2016, St. Barts show, the last full band show, and accompanied Prince at a number of sampler shows in the spring of 2016, the last on March 22 at Muzique in Montreal. Johnson and Hill were also part of the emergency "flu" plane landing in Illinois on April 15, 2016.

More than any other band member, Kirky J seems to have simply been present at numerous recording sessions and consequently has the most eclectic and often marginal set of credits. These credits typically include background vocals, percussion, and drum programming on most LPs from 1992's *Diamonds and Pearls* through 2001's *Rave* remix disc and all the NPG albums. His most conspicuous release was "Kirk J's B Sides Remix," included on the March 1995

Symbol released the "Purple Medley" single as Prince in March 1995 to coincide with the Ultimate Live Experience Tour. A pre-recorded video version of the tune opened the brief Japan '96 tour. The CD featured "Kirk J's B Sides Remix," the most high-profile gig for Prince drummer and professional pal Kirk Johnson.   *(Authors collection)*

"Purple Medley" single. He also remixed NPG songs and cowrote five songs with Prince.

Kip Blackshire (1999–2001)

Kip Blackshire is a keyboardist and sweet-voiced singer brought into the NPG fold in 1999 by hometown friend Morris Hayes. He joined Hayes on keyboards from his June 20, 1999, Paisley Park debut through the first Hit N Run tour until July 6, 2001, in Montreal, the last gig in the aborted A Celebration tour. Blackshire also sang for the Fonky Bald Heads; during their opening gigs on Hit N Run, Prince would join the band on "Passing Your Name." Prince tapped Blackshire for studio vocals on at least a dozen tracks, including co-lead on "Wedding Feast." He also acted in "The Daisy Chain" video and is on the *Rave Un2 the Year*

2000 video. Blackshire was part of Prince protégé Judith Hill's opening band for the April 9, 2015, 3rdEyeGirl Detroit show.

Other notable 1990s NPG members include the following:

- Damon Dickson (1990–1993) Dancer/percussionist
- Elisa Fiorillo-Dease (1990; 2009–2014) Vocalist
- Lori Elle (1991–1992) and Robia LaMorte (1991–92) Dancers, known as Diamond and Pearl
- William "DJ" Graves (1991–92) Deejay/turntablist
- Kelly Konno (1993) Dancer
- Jerry Martini (1997–1999) Saxophonist (from Sly and the Family Stone)
- Cynthia Robinson (1997–1999) Trumpet (also Family Stone)
- Marva King (1997–1999; 2007–2009) Vocalist
- Estaire Godinez (1999) Percussionist

19

Halfway through Her History Class

Intermission

One of my favorite books is *The Book of Lists*. This book would not exist if not for that book.

First published in 1977, *The Book of Lists* offered a reshuffled, unofficial view of history and culture that was at turns sassy, silly, and risqué—and endlessly entertaining, just like Prince.

With numbers popping from titles on every page, it was the original click-bait and best bathroom reader ever. And, just like Prince, it had to deal with moral outrage, banned in many communities for its list of, essentially, "23 positions in a one-night stand."

As a tribute to *The Book of Lists*, this hallway-through chapter is a chapter of lists.

Six Things That Didn't Fit Neatly into Other Chapters That Fit Here

Music Videos

Prince released about 120 promotional music videos plus another fifty or so with associated artists. These videos played a vital role in exposing Prince to audiences otherwise limited by segregated radio programming policies. But there's not a lot to say about them other than that they exist and that some are more entertaining than others—but not enough that they warrant a whole chapter. Prince won four MTV Video Music Awards, including Best Choreography for "Raspberry Beret," Best Male Video and Stage Performance for "U Got the Look," and Best Dance Video for "Cream."

While exact numbers are impossible to calculate, it seems likely that Prince is the popular artist with the most unreleased studio material in circulation among fans. *"The Black Album"* was available illegally on vinyl, cassette, and CD for seven years before its 1994 Warner Bros. release and is considered the bestselling bootleg of all time. Although other bootlegs and fake copies are easier to spot, Prince's graphics for this album made detection difficult.

(Author's collection)

Flash

Flash is an unreleased 1989 associated-artist album. Also known as MC Flash, the group featured vocalist Margie "MC" Cox and evolved from Minneapolis's still-thriving Dr. Mambo's Combo. Prince cowrote and played on all ten album tracks. The studio band, featured on "Good Body Every Evening," included Prince band members Michael B. and Levi Seacer Jr., joined by guitarist Billy Franze (vocalist on "Good Man") and bassist Doug Nelson. Warner Bros. rejected the album, and it was abandoned. The only song released was the hidden gem "Whistlin' Kenny," which appeared on a Margie Cox promo single in 1995. The group opened two 1990 Prince shows with Sonny T. on bass and Tommy Barbarella on keys.

Thank You

Mavis Staple
George Clinton
N.P.G.
The Steeles
Mayte
Margie Cox
Madhouse
Nona Gaye

Thank You

for making

1-800 NEW FUNK

a tremendous success

OVER 500,000 UNITS SOLD INTERNATIONALLY!

Stay Tuned For The Next Single from 1-800-New-Funk
"Standing at The Altar" By Margie Cox

NPG RECORDS

§ Appears Courtesy of Warner Bros. Records
Manufactured, Marketed and Distributed by Bellmark Records, Hollywood California 90028

Similar in intent to Warner Bros.'s various artist "loss leaders" LPs from the 1970s, NPG Records's 1994 release *1-800-NEW-FUNK* attempted to build a personality and brand loyalty for the label. All but one of the eleven tracks feature Prince/Symbol input and most are unavailable elsewhere, including the original version of the Symbol/Nona Gaye collaboration "Love Sign."

(Courtesy Ric Dube)

1-800-NEW-FUNK (1994)

The hidden gem "Whistlin' Kenny" was the B-side of Cox's "Standing at the Altar," the fourth single from 1994's NPG Records release *1-800-NEW-FUNK*. The LP features the only release of Symbol and Nona Gaye's original version of "Love Sign" plus exclusive Prince-penned tracks from Cox, Minneapolis (aka the Crayons) ("MPLS" and reprise), The Steeles ("Color"), Madhouse ("17"), and Nona Gaye ("A Woman's Gotta Have It"). While various-artist compilations would become common for the NPG Music Club Ahdio Show, this is the only VA CD release.

The NPG Orchestra *Kamasutra* (1997)

Kamasutra is Prince's mostly instrumental plunge into the New Age/light jazz/classical world. At its most engaging, the album is Madhouse plus Clare Fischer's orchestra. At other moments, it's background music. The eleven-track, forty-minute *Kamasutra* was released on February 14, 1997, on cassette, a Valentine's Day present to Mayte. The only release from the NPG Orchestra, it was included as the fifth disc in 1998's *Crystal Ball* CD package.

The Versace Experience (Prelude 2 Gold) (1995)

The NPG Orchestra also shows up on this fifteen-track promo-only cassette on "Kamasutra Orchestra #5," aka "Serotonin." The tape was distributed in July 1995 at the Versace Collection during Paris Fashion Week. It features several exclusive remixes and edits, including the only release of Madhouse's "Rootie Kazootie," from the unreleased *24*. Prince also worked with the fashion house on *Playtime by Versace* and Versace's 2016 collection, which featured an eleven-minute Prince audio compilation. *Experience* was rereleased on Record Store Day 2019 along with *His Majesty's Pop Life/The Purple Mix Club*, a reissue of a 1985 Japan-only two-disc compilation.

Dance and Stage Productions

Prince first tried to "put on a show" in 1993 with *Glam Slam Ulysses*, an adaptation of Homer's *Odyssey*. It was his first alternative media project after the name change. It featured thirteen then unreleased songs, Carmen Electra, and a mishmash of live dancing and video projections. It was bizarre. The same year, Prince contributed a ten-minute version of "Thunder" to the Joffrey Ballet for their Prince-themed *Billboards* production, which was released on video in 1994. He also set up Mayte as the NPG Dance Company in *Around the World in a Day*, which toured the United States in the fall of 1997.

Ten Minneapolis-Area Places Where Prince Recorded before He Built Paisley Park

1. Moonsound (1976–1977) Chris Moon's Studio
2. Sound 80 (1978–1978) Minneapolis's "real" recording studio
3. France Avenue Home Studio (1978–1980)
4. Wayzata Home Studio (1980)
5. Kiowa Trail Home Studio (1981–1985) "The Purple House"
6. St. Louis Park Warehouse (1983) Rehearsal space
7. First Avenue (1983) Basic live tracks for "I Would Die 4 U," "Baby I'm a Star," and "Purple Rain"
8. Flying Cloud Drive Warehouse (1984) *The Family* was recorded here
9. Washington Avenue Warehouse (1985–1987) Rehearsal space
10. Galpin Blvd. Home Studio (1986–1987)

Nine California Places Where Prince Recorded

1. Record Plant, Sausalito
2. Sound Labs, Los Angeles
3. Alpha Studios, Burbank
4. Hollywood Sound Recorders, Los Angeles
5. Sunset Sound, Hollywood
6. Larrabee Sound Studios, North Hollywood
7. Record Plant, Hollywood
8. 3121 Antelo Road, Los Angeles
9. 77 Beverly Park Lane, Beverly Hills

Thirteen Studio Songs by Prince and the Revolution That Feature Bobby Z., Matt Fink, Brown Mark, and Wendy and Lisa on Instruments

1. "Let's Go Crazy"
2. "Take Me with U"
3. "Computer Blue"
4. "I Would Die 4 U"
5. "Purple Rain"
6. "America"
7. "Pop Life"
8. "The Ladder

9.   "Girls & Boys"
10. "Mountains"
11. "Anotherloverholenyohead"
12. "It's Gonna Be a Beautiful Night"
13. "All Day, All Night" (Jill Jones)

Era-Spanning All-Star Band

1.   Lead guitar and vocals: Prince
2.   Guitar: Wendy Melvoin
3.   Bass: Sonny T.
4.   Drums: Michael B.
5.   Keyboards: Renato Neto
6.   Keyboards: Dr. Fink
7.   Horns: Michael Nelson's NPG Hornz
8.   Co-lead and background vocals: Rosie Gaines

Top Ten Songs of the 2000s

1.   "Beginning Endlessly"
2.   "Boom"
3.   "F.U.N.K."
4.   "Fallinlove2nite"
5.   "Judas Smile"
6.   "Love"
7.   "Rainbow Children"
8.   "Rocknroll Loveaffair"
9.   "Way Back Home"
10. "X's Face"

Twelve Prince Pseudonyms

1.   Jamie Starr
2.   The Starr Company
3.   Joey Coco
4.   Alexander Nevermind
5.   Rocker Happyfeller (Sheena Easton "Eternity")
6.   Freddie "The Phantom" (Sheena Easton "Eternity")

7.   Christopher
8.   Austra Chanel, John Lewis, Bill Lewis (Madhouse)
9.   Camille
10.   Paisley Park
11.   Tora Tora
12.   Symbol

Twelve Most Interesting Live Cover Songs from Artists Who Aren't Musical Influences

1.   "Creep": Radiohead
2.   "Crimson and Clover": Tommy James
3.   "Even Flow": Pearl Jam
4.   "Heroes": David Bowie
5.   "Let's Go": The Cars
6.   "Love Rollercoaster": Ohio Players
7.   "More Than This": Roxy Music
8.   "Now's the Time": Charlie Parker
9.   "Stratus": Billy Cobham
10.   "The Whole of the Moon": The Waterboys
11.   "Train in Vain": The Clash
12.   "Whole Lotta Love": Led Zeppelin

Fifty Must-Hear Unreleased Studio Songs

1.   "2020"
2.   "A Place in Heaven"
3.   "Adonis and Bathsheba"
4.   "All My Dreams"
5.   "American in Paris"
6.   "Big House"
7.   "Big Tall Wall"
8.   "Billy"
9.   "Boom Box"
10.   "Broken"
11.   "Can I Play with U?"
12.   "Check the Record"
13.   "Coco Boys"
14.   "Come Elektra Tuesday"
15.   "Dance with the Devil"

16. "Deliverance"
17. "Donna"
18. "Emotional Pump"
19. "Feel Good"
20. "God is Alive"
21. "Good Man"
22. "Grand Progression"
23. "Groove in G Flat Minor"
24. "Hard to Get"
25. "Junk Music"
26. "Heaven"
27. "I Spend My Time Loving You"
28. "I Wonder"
29. "I'll Do Anything"
30. "It's a Wonderful Day"
31. "Lisa"
32. "Lust U Always"
33. "Me Touch Myself"
34. "Others Here with Us"
35. "Rough"
36. "Schoolyard"
37. "She's Just a Baby"
38. "Slave 2 the System"
39. "Something Funky (This House Comes)"
40. "Soulpsychodelicide"
41. "Stone"
42. "Strange Way"
43. "The Ball"
44. "The Line"
45. "The Second Coming"
46. "Uh Huh"
47. "Wally"
48. "We Can Work It Out"
49. "Witness 4 the Prosecution"
50. "Your Love Is So Hard"

One Must-Not-Hear Unreleased Studio Song

1.   "Eggplant"

A Baker's Dozen of Live Concerts/Concert Series Worth Seeking Out

1. August 3, 1983, First Avenue, Minneapolis
2. June 7, 1984, First Avenue, Minneapolis
3. June 15, 1987, New Morning, Paris
4. December 31, 1987, Paisley Park
5. August 1988, Iron Horse, Den Hague
6. September 8, 1993, Bagley's Warehouse, London
7. February 13, 1994, Paisley Park, Minneapolis
8. March 23, 1996, The Emporium, London
9. June 21–28, 2002 (seven shows), Paisley Park
10. March 28–29, 2009 (three shows), LA Live Nokia Center, Los Angeles
11. July 18, 2009 (two shows), Auditorium Stravinski, Montreux, Switzerland
12. July 23, 2010, New Morning, Paris
13. January 16–18, 2013 (six shows), Dakota Jazz Club & Restaurant, Minneapolis

20

My Only Competition Is Well in the Past

Late 1990s LPs

Crystal Ball (1998)

Symbol spent much of 1997 touring and recording NPG, Chaka Khan, and Graham Central Station albums. But he didn't really record new Symbol material: it was time to hit the vaunted Vault for ready-to-release material.

But how to release without a label? On-demand pressing. NPG Records started preorders for the collection in May 1997 through the 1-800-NEW FUNK phone line and a new website, love4oneaonther.com. The collection would be housed in a fabulous crystal ball case and pressed once sales reached 100,000 copies. That number was reached by June. But people waited. Eventually, *The Truth* was added to the collection to ease the wait. And the NPG Orchestra's *Kamasutra*, released on cassette on February 14, 1997, was added to further sweeten the deal.

The first *Crystal Ball* shipments arrived in homes on January 29, 1998—but not in a fabulous case and without a color booklet. Fans were frustrated. A non-*Kamasutra* four-disc set was eventually released through Minneapolis-based Best Buy on March 21, 1998, and other retailers soon followed. This angered fans who thought that the online product would be exclusive but offered some relief to the many who never received their discs.

The music is fine, but the project gives off the same vibe as when you get an ugly Christmas sweater from your grandma: you're thankful for the gift, intrigued because you can always use a new sweater, but disappointed by the patterns and colors. With so much to choose from, how did Prince end up with this? And so little of it—just 150 minutes, enough to fill just two discs, but spread over three? Why these songs in this order from these periods?

Following on the heels of Symbol's kitchen-sink compilation *Crystal Ball* on NPG Records, Warner Bros.'s 1999 Prince release *The Vault: Old Friends 4 Sale* gathers ten songs from a disconnected decade of Prince's career, 1985–1994. The album was his last of new/unreleased material on Warner Bros. until *Plectrumelectrum* and *Art Official Age* in 2014.   *(Author's collection)*

The earliest track is from 1983, the collection highlight "Cloreen Bacon Skin," fifteen minutes of Prince and Morris Day jammin' and jivin'. The song eventually morphed into The Time's "Tricky." It's pure joy.

Nine songs come from the 1985–1986 period. Most were familiar to long-time fans. The highlights are the "Crystal Ball" and "Dream Factory" title tracks, kaleidoscopic suites that go places Prince otherwise never went, the light pop of "Last Heart," and the springy comedy of "Movie Star." These nine songs would have made a great one-disc collection.

Twenty songs come from the 1992–1996 period, with the Mach I NPG appearing on about half of the tracks. Six of the twenty songs are remixes, and none of these adds much to the originals. When the collection was released, fans were familiar with many of the tracks from live recordings and unauthorized sources, with the 1996 *Emancipation*-era tracks "Da Bang," "Poom Poom," "2Morrow," "She Gave Her Angels," and "Goodbye" the big prizes. In addition to the bluesy rocking of "Calhoun Square," the highlight among the mid-1990s tracks is the live linchpin "Days of Wild," already familiar from bootlegs and *The Beautiful Experience* TV special.

The twenty-nine-track *Crystal Ball* peaked at number sixty-two on the pop charts and number fifty-nine on the black charts, Prince's lowest charting since the debut. But it's assumed that Prince made money—costs were kept low by using available material, and he made 75 percent of the profits versus maybe 25 percent under his Warner Bros. deal.

Prince didn't tour *Crystal Ball* but spent a lot of 1998 on the road supporting the NPG's *Newpower Soul*. The mid-1980s and *Emancipation* material was performed infrequently, but the NPG material got a lot of work at mid-1990s one-off gigs.

The Truth (1998)

The mostly acoustic *The Truth*, the fifth Symbol album, was recorded in the fall of 1996 at Paisley Park. The twelve-track, forty-three-minute disc was intended as a discrete release, but that plan tanked when EMI-Capitol closed in April 1997. Prince had the disc pressed (which explains the disc's 1997 copyright) and was going to sell it through 1-800-NEW-FUNK or, at Mayte's behest, give it away. Neither happened, nor did a planned solo acoustic tour, canceled when Mayte urged him to get out and play the hits. Eventually, to assuage the anger of fans who had ordered *Crystal Ball*, he included it as a fourth disc in the January 29, 1998, release.

The Truth is among the more interesting works in Prince's catalog because it offers a chance to listen to Prince in the studio in a new way. While not totally unmodified, the tracks here offer Prince's vocals mostly unadorned. As with the latter *Piano & a Microphone 1983* release, the expression is in his range and tone, not in the twisting of a knob. Likewise, we know the awe-inspiring things he can do with an electric guitar, but here we find out he'd be just as comfortable if the electricity went out.

The most memorable tracks are the Delta blues title track, "Dionne," Prince in his finest chanteuse mode, and "Comeback," which works in part because of the multitracked vocals.

The album's chart fate was tied with that of *Crystal Ball*. The album produced one single, "The Truth," backed with "Don't Play Me." The single was released on Valentine's Day 1997 but at the mind-boggling price of $15.

There was no *The Truth* tour. Prince debuted an acoustic guitar set on June 24, 2002, at the Xenophobia Celebration but wouldn't regularly jam acoustic until 2004's *Musicology* tour. Only three songs from *The Truth* were performed live—"The Truth," "Don't Play Me," and "The Other Side of the Pillow"—the last of which appears on the first live album.

The Vault . . . Old Friends 4 Sale (1999)

Riding on the crest of goodwill and publicity surrounding the chart-topping rerelease of his millennium-closing anthem "1999" and the subsequent tour that combined spot-on interpretations of old hits with breathtaking renditions of songs from his new, groundbreaking number one LP, Prince, formerly known as Symbol, once again sat atop the music throne in 1999.

Oh, wait. None of that happened.

In 1999, Prince and The Revolution (without The Revolution) released "1999: The New Master," by far Prince's worst and most embarrassing release ever. To top that, Warner Bros. released the purposefully misguided *The Vault*. . . *Old Friends 4 Sale*, which Symbol tried to match with one of his weakest and most desperate albums: *Rave Un2 the Joy Fantastic*. Oh yeah, he also sued his biggest fans for infringing on his copyright, including the essential magazine *Uptown*; signed a deal with Arista, who refused to support the *Rave* album; and delivered a lackluster New Year's Eve pay-per-view event: *Rave Un2 the Year 2000*. Not quite hail the conquering Prince.

But just because *The Vault* is misguided—brief, inconsistent, and assembled in spite from the title on down—doesn't mean it's not a must-listen. The album was delivered to Warner Bros. on April 26, 1996, along with *Chaos and Disorder*, intended to fulfill the terms of the 1992 contract. It sat on the shelf for three years, or approximately until Warner Bros. got wind that Prince had secured a distribution deal with Arista.

Although not strictly a jazz album and more a collection of songs than a thematic album at that, *The Vault* offers lighter, often piano-based songs that serve as a sonic contrast to the bombast of *Chaos and Disorder*. The highlight is the direct, bluesy "5 Women," given to Joe Cocker in 1992. *Parade*-era bootleg favorite "Old Friends for Sale," replete with a grand Clare Fischer arrangement, shows up here in a 1991 recording with altered, less confrontational lyrics. "She Spoke 2 Me" from *Girl 6* shows up in a full-length version, the second half a disorganized jazz workout. Three slight tunes from early 1992 sessions for the scrapped *I'll Do Anything* project appear—"The Rest of My Life," "There Is Lonely," and "My Little Pill"—augmenting "Don't Talk 2 Strangers," also on *Girl 6*. "My Little Pill" bears more than a slight resemblance to Blur's "Intermission," released in 1993. "When the Lights Go Down" is a mellower cousin to "Willing and Able," thankfully with no Tony M. in sight. "It's About That Walk" has a decent horn riff, while "Sarah" and "Extraordinary" are ordinary.

The Vault was released album on August 24, 1999. The album reached number eighty-five on the US album charts and number thirty three on the R&B chart, and that probably overstates how little consumers actually cared about the release.

There were four non-charting promo singles with no non-LP material. There was no tour to support the album, and Prince performed outside of Minneapolis fewer than ten times in 1999. Half of the songs ("She Spoke to Me," "Five

Women," "When the Lights Go Down," "Old Friends 4 Sale," and "Extraordinary") were played live infrequently; the others were never played live.

Rave Un2 the Joy Fantastic (1999)

The twenty-month pause after *1999* produced *Purple Rain*. The twenty-three-month wait after the barely noticed *The Truth* produced *Rave Un2 the Joy Fantastic*, a "you can't call it a comeback if you don't comeback" release that found Symbol at his lowest point creatively, desperately clawing at relevancy.

Although he claimed to know nothing of the man, Prince probably knew that Clive Davis had signed his heroes Earth, Wind & Fire to Columbia Records

In 1999 Prince as Symbol joined his guitar hero Carlos Santana on Clive Davis's Arista Records. While Santana's *Supernatural* went on to outsell *Purple Rain*, Prince's *Rave Un2 The Joy Fantastic* languished. Prince blamed Davis's PR department and Davis blamed Prince's refusal to properly promote the album, including a reluctance to co-headline a tour with Santana.

(Author's collection)

in 1972. A quarter of a century later, Davis was on the verge of releasing an LP by another Prince hero, Santana, when he told Symbol he'd give him a number one hit and make him a star again, baby. Prince liked the idea and signed a one-disc deal for an $11 million advance and possession of the masters. There were high hopes on both sides, including dreams of pairing Santana and Prince on a promotional tour. But the to-be-number-one single "The Greatest Romance Ever Sold" and the album stiffed (while Santana's *Supernatural* went on to out-sell *Purple Rain*). Symbol claimed that Arista didn't support the disc, and Davis claimed that the Artist wasn't cooperative promoting it. The label de-prioritized the album, and Davis was left acknowledging associates' "I told you so" remarks about working with the temperamental artist.

Rave Un2 the Joy Fantastic is Symbol's sixth album. Produced by Prince (throw the public relations people a bone), it was released on November 9, 1999. It reached number eighteen on the pop charts and number eight on the black charts. In spite of Prince's insistence, there was only one commercial single: "The Greatest Romance Ever Sold." The song reached only number sixty-three on the Hot 100, but the multiple remixes hit number six on the maxi-singles sales chart. A US promo of "Man'O'War" included three uncollected edits.

While most of the album was recorded in 1998–1999, its roots lay in the title track from the late 1980s. The song, a tribute to then girlfriend Anna Garcia, aka Anna Fantastic, was the centerpiece of a project that spun off parts into *Graffiti Bridge*, *Batman*, and associated-artist projects. The distance between the sponta-neous, life-affirming 1988 live versions and the mechanical 1999 exercise is jarring.

The problems with the fifteen-song, eighteen-track *Rave Un2 the Joy Fantas-tic* are threefold. First, there's the production. There's clutter and distraction and way too much Kirky J. For the love of all that's holy, get that little tinkling bell out of "Wherever U Go, Whatever U Do!" Second, a lot of the songs are pander-ing, either assembled more than written to be radio friendly ("Baby Knows") or clearly designed with market tasks in mind: "Undisputed"—let's do rap right! "Hot Wit U"—we'll take back the dance floor!

Finally, for the first time, Prince has surrounded himself with other name artists. It's not a bad decision but is one poorly executed. The problem here isn't the choice of guest artists—Chuck D. ("Undisputed"), Eve ("Hot Wit U"), Gwen Stefani ("So Far, So Pleased"), Sheryl Crow ("Baby Knows"), Ani DiFranco ("Eye Love U, but Eye Don't Trust U"), and Maceo Parker (the hidden track "Pretty-man")—but that they seem to work for Prince rather than with him. I'll listen to hours of Prince tuning his guitar, but many of the solos here sound like they've been affixed to a song by a (failed) hit-making algorithm.

The one collaboration that does work is the overlooked ballad "Eye Love U, But I Don't Trust U." Along with equally quiet "The Sun, the Moon and Stars," it's unassuming and uncluttered. The cover song here, his third from a female pop singer, Crow's "Everyday Is a Winding Road," fails to breathe life into an average song. The other notable fact about this LP is that four songs use commas in the titles, which should give us all pause.

There was no *Rave Un2 the Joy Fantastic* tour, although Symbol made ten TV appearances in five European countries to promote the album, often performing "The Greatest Romance Ever Sold" and "Baby Knows." Those two songs were the only new songs performed at the December 18, 1999, Paisley Park show recorded as *Rave Un2 the Year* 2000.

Thankfully, Prince's affection for these songs knew some bounds. Most songs were played infrequently live, and half were played once or never.

All in all, an album best forgotten—although it wasn't, as it was packed along with the *Rave In2* remix LP and the live *Year 2000* DVD and released as *Ultimate Rave* on April 26, 2019.

Rave In2 the Joy Fantastic (2001)

Although Prince released a few songs online and recorded parts of two LPs (the unreleased *High* and *The Rainbow Children*), the year 2000 was a public look to the past for Prince. In April, he settled debts with Tony M. and Levi Seacer Jr., paying $80,000 in unpaid royalties. In June, he feted his past with "A Celebration" concert. In the summer, he met with members of The Revolution to revive a late 1990s reunion project: *Roadhouse Garden*. In November, on the night of the most confusing election in American history, he embarked on his first US greatest-hits tour. And, most important, he returned to using the name Prince. Eventually.

Ownership of the Arista masters proved handy when Prince followed up 1999's *Rave Un2 the Joy Fantastic* on April 29, 2001, with the remix album *Rave In2 the Joy Fantastic*. Available only through NPG Music Club and released on NPG Records, it is the last Symbol LP. It failed to chart, and there were no singles.

This disc is slightly more essential than its progenitor due to the inclusion of the long-cherished slow-burn "Beautiful Strange," a guitar companion to "Joy in Repetition." An alternate version was included in the *Beautiful Strange* home video.

The rest of the songs are either unimproved or unchanged.

"Hot Wit U (Nasty Girl Remix)" mixes it up with the Vanity song. This version was the lead track on a vinyl twelve-inch—*The Hot X-perience*—advertised online during the summer of 2000. The unreleased disc included hip-hop and dance/club mixes of the first track, a dance/club mix of "So Far, So Pleased," and the eventually released "Underneath the Cream," which originated in a "Hot Wit U" lyric.

Prince contributed exclusive songs to a handful of compilations, including the *Bright Lights, Big City* ("Good Love") and *Happy Feet* ("The Song of the Heart") sound tracks and a Jimi Hendrix tribute LP ("Purple House"), but avoided placing his otherwise-available songs on various artist collections. The 2000 BlackPlanet.com *Heavy Rotation* compilation, featuring a "Man'O'War" edit, is an exception. As with the presence of "2045: Radical Man" on the *Bamboozled* sound track in the same year, the *Heavy Rotation* inclusion was intended to shed light on the visibility and role of African Americans in the performing arts industry.

(Author's collection)

The Very Best of Prince (2001)

On May 21, 2001, Warner Bros. released *The Very Best of Prince* in the United Kingdom, around the same time that Prince's people announced on the NPG Ahdio Show that he was talking with a store about rerecording and releasing an album of twenty old hits. On June 15, 2001, Prince started the A Celebration tour in St. Paul. The tour was scheduled to last until August 5 in Anchorage, Alaska, but Prince stopped after six dates, on June 28, in Milwaukee, Wisconsin.

It was probably stopped because Prince didn't want to be seen as promoting this album, released on July 31 in the United States.

The Very Best of Prince offers seventeen less racy hits and could be subtitled *The Prince Songs You Already Have That Won't Offend People Very Much*. It's the first of two contractually obligated collections based on the 1992 contract. And it's on the bottom rung of the collections ladder. All the selections are duplicates from the previous *The Hits* albums, save for the inclusion of "Money Don't Matter 2 Night" (but not in otherwise unavailable edit form).

Perhaps most insulting to Prince's sensibilities: it wasn't even released on Warner Bros. but rather on subsidiary nostalgia label Rhino Records.

The album hit number two on the greatest-hits-friendly UK charts and number sixty-six in the United States, staying on the charts for twenty-five weeks. These aren't amazing numbers, but they were financially worthwhile for Warner Bros.

The concise and nonconfrontational nature of *The Very Best* served it well after Prince's death. The album hit number one for one week on the hits chart (charting for twenty-two weeks) and number one for eleven weeks (charting for thirty weeks) on the catalog sales chart. The album sold 668,000 copies in 2016, contributing in part to Prince's status as best-selling album artist of the year.

21

However Much U Want

Protégés, Part 2

Prince continued to produce protégé work alongside his own until the late 1990s, when he took a decade-long break between projects. This chapter covers protégé albums released over the last twenty-five years of Prince's life.

Ingrid Chavez's *May 19 1992* (1991)

Prince went to Rupert's Nightclub on December 1, 1987, to deejay *"The Black Album"* and met up with artist/fan Ingrid Chavez. Legend has it that their spiritual discussion sealed Prince's decision to cancel the December 8 *"The Black Album"* release. At the very least, it contributed to their entering the studio on December 10.

Prince on piano, as Paisley Park, recorded twenty-one talking poems with Chavez with the intent of producing an album. The songs languished, even as Chavez starred in *Graffiti Bridge*. She recorded two songs with Paisley Park engineer Michael Koppelman and brought them to Warner Bros. to get the project jump-started. It jump-started, with Prince handing production work to Koppelman. *May 19 1992* was finally released on September 24, 1991. Alan Leeds recounts Prince taunting him that his current project, Carmen Electra, would outsell Ingrid Chavez, although neither had to worry about any calculable sales.

Five minor Prince/Paisley Park–Chavez collaborative tracks ended up on *May 19 1992*, and a sixth includes Prince instrumentation. The unreleased song "Cross the Line" included a Chavez spoken part that was used on "Intermission," which opened the religious half of *Lovesexy* shows, much to the chagrin of band members.

Chavez is best known for an out-of-court settlement with Lenny Kravitz and Madonna over her lack of writing credit on Madonna's steamy 1990 hit "Justify My Love."

Eric Leeds's *Times Squared* (1991)

Eric Leeds received his own Paisley Park album only after Madhouse *24* fell apart in 1989. Prince got distracted by *Batman*, and Leeds didn't like the *24* mix. Prince gave Leeds three dozen songs to remix, dating back to still-unreleased songs, such as 1982's "U Should Be Mine" and 1983's "Wet Dream Cousin," and told him to see what he could do. The result was *Times Squared*.

Prince wrote/cowrote nine of the LP's eleven instrumental songs and plays on a tenth. The album is a strong, consistent record, marred slightly by a bit too much high end. It's a steady bridge from frenetic Madhouse to the more measured jazz of the early 2000s.

The album was released on February 19, 1991. By this point. Prince didn't care much about Leeds or this music. The album failed to chart and produced no commercial singles. Leeds didn't tour the album but did play some songs later in his career.

Carmen Electra (1993)

In the summer of 1990, Prince was in Los Angeles working with Rosie Gaines on her first solo album. He met Tara Leigh Patrick at a nightclub and soon lost interest in Gaines. Although juggling multiple projects, Prince fixated on Patrick, soon renamed Carmen Electra. As with Vanity and Apollonia, Prince didn't let the fact that Electra had neither stage presence nor discernible musical talent distract him from the fact that she was physically appealing. As writer Brian Morton says, she had "pneumatic talents."

Prince cowrote eleven of *Carmen Electra*'s fourteen songs and also performs on eleven. Unfortunately, these songs are among the most generic of Prince's career, something such as "All That," a pale echo of "Adore" or countless other ballads. And Prince's limp production, as Paisley Park, does nothing to distinguish these tracks from anything else of the period that relied merely on samples and gimmicks. This sounds like background music for a lazy TV series about urban college life in the early 1990s. Some have suggested that the album is a parody, and that might be the best-path mind frame for listening.

The first single, "Go Go Dancer," was released on June 18, 1992, and the album, *On Top*, was to follow soon afterward. Warner Bros. knew they had a dud, so they asked Prince to fix the album. Prince pulled five songs, all still unreleased, and Warner Bros. still had a dud. *Carmen Electra* was released on February 9, 1993. It failed to chart, and it's unclear at this point if even Prince cared, as he was busy opening soon-to-fail nightclubs and beginning his feud with Warner Bros.

Carmen Electra opened a dozen shows on the *Diamonds and Pearls* tour in the late spring of 1992. The shows were disastrous. Rather than holding

Electra accountable, Prince fired her band, except Morris Hayes, and installed the NPG for the final few shows. The NPG didn't improve her singing or her stage presence.

Carmen Electra went on to act in marginal movies, expose herself in *Playboy*, and date, marry, and divorce a series of high-profile celebrities, including basketball star Dennis Rodman and Jane's Addiction guitarist Dave Navarro.

Mayte's *Child of the Sun* (1995)

Prince was moving from weakness to weakness as he transitioned from non-singer Carmen Electra to non-singer Mayte. While Electra's only album is needlessly loud and aggressive, the offense of Mayte's only album is that it's hollow and uninspired, more passively mediocre than Electra's in-your-face bad—a minor improvement.

The sixteen-year-old Mayte and her mom went to Prince's Barcelona Nude tour show on July 25, 1990. The performance inspired Mom to send Prince a video of Mayte dancing to "Thieves in the Temple." Prince liked what he saw, invited her backstage to a German show a few weeks later, and told Rosie Gaines he was going to marry her. Prince and Mayte corresponded the next year, and she eventually moved to Minneapolis, joining the *Diamonds and Pearls* tour band on August 16, 1991, at a one-off Chicago show.

Mayte first entered the studio with Prince in late 1991, providing vocals on "Love 2 the 9's" and "The Max." It wasn't until September 1993 that the duo began work on Mayte's solo album, originally titled *Latino Barbie Doll*, a retread of the unreleased 1987 Sheila E. track. Apart from the new song "However Much U Want," this early version of the album consisted entirely of cover versions of songs Prince had given to female artists plus gender-flipped English and Spanish versions of Prince's own "The Most Beautiful Boy in the World."

For *Child of the Sun*, completed early 1995, Prince crafted tunes specifically for Mayte and dropped all but three self covers. He also added "House of Brick (Brick House)," an unlistenable alteration of the Commodores's classic. Prince is on all the tracks except "Mo' Better," which features Kirk Johnson. None of the tracks stand out, held back by Mayte's thin vocals and generic production.

The album was released on NPG Records in Europe on November 27, 1995. American audiences weren't afforded a chance to ignore the album, as Warner Bros. refused to release it. The album spawned three non-charting 1990s singles and a Mayte-released 2007 single.

Mayte opened a June 8, 1995, Glam Slam Miami show with a lip-synch performance of "Children of the Sun," "The Rhythm of Your ♥," and "Baby Don't Care." She also performed on December 16, 1995, at the same venue. In a late

1995 interview, she mentions a 1996 world tour with her opening, the NPG doing *Exodus*, and Prince headlining, but that was derailed with Prince and Mayte's 1996 Valentine's Day wedding.

Chaka Khan's *Come 2 My House* (1998)

Chaka Khan enjoyed multiple number one R&B hits as a solo artist and singer for Rufus before she hit the top in 1983 with Prince's "I Feel for You." In 1988, Prince contributed two songs to her *CK* LP—"Eternity" and "Sticky Wicked"—the latter recorded with Miles Davis. In 1995, Khan recorded the Prince-cowritten tune "Pain" for her *Dare You to Love Me* LP. The song appeared in 1997 on the *Living Single* sound track after Warner Bros. refused to release the album and dropped her from the label. Prince swooped in and signed Khan to NPG Records. *Come 2 My House* was completed in June 1998.

Prince wrote or cowrote ten of the album's fourteen tracks and coproduced thirteen with Khan. He played on all the tracks except Kirk Johnson's production "The Drama," with Rhonda Smith adding bass on "Eye Remember U." The album includes covers of Prince's "Don't Talk 2 Strangers" and Graham's "Hair."

Aside from some period-specific production annoyances, *Come 2 My House* is a success. Nothing's a Prince classic, but the album's diversity of styles and Khan's vocal talents carry the day.

The album was released on September 29, 1998, in the United States and on March 29, 1999, in the United Kingdom. It reached number forty-nine on the US R&B charts. Two singles stirred no public interest. During TV appearances at this time, Prince bemoaned the fact that *Come 2 My House* wasn't getting the love and all but begged a major distributor to pick it up.

Chaka Khan opened for and appeared with Prince through 1997 and 1998, punctuated by her London Café de Paris performance on August 28, 1998, featured in the *Beautiful Strange* video. Khan left the label in 2000, but she and Prince guested at each other's shows through the years, and Khan opened Welcome 2 America shows in 2011.

Graham Central Station's *GCS 2000* (1999)

Prince and Larry Graham met and played together at a Nashville Music City Mix Factory aftershow on August 23, 1997. The two became inseparable, and Graham Central Station was soon opening for Prince on the second leg of the *Jam of the Year* tour.

Graham made his mark in the late 1960s as bassist for Sly and the Family Stone, with "Thank You (Falettinme Be Mice Elf Agin)" the apex of his tenure. He left in 1973 to form Graham Central Station and in 1980 went solo and garnered a number one R&B single: "One in a Million You." In the decade prior to hooking up with Prince, he was primarily a live act without a label.

Like Khan and Mavis Staples and George Clinton, Graham was a childhood hero whom Prince could now claim as his own. But this relationship went beyond musical adoration, as Graham had a role in Prince becoming a Jehovah's Witness and functioned as Prince's surrogate father, mentor, and best friend.

Unlike Prince's deep involvement with Khan's project, Prince cowrote only one song here, "Utopia," although he coproduced and shows up on every track in some capacity. As solid as Khan's work is, this is equally uninspired. The major problem is the same one that plagued Graham his whole career: he's otherworldly on bass but is a weak songwriter and has little vocal range. One wishes Prince had channeled "Days of Wild" and given Graham some decent songs.

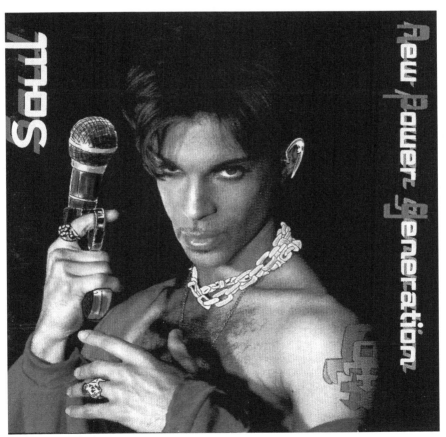

During the Paisley Park Records and early NPG Records days, Prince worked simultaneously with multiple artists, most unproven in the marketplace. By the late 1990s he changed tack and began working with and actively promoting known commodities, such as Chaka Khan and Larry Graham. Their late 1990s LPs were paired with the NPG's final album, *Newpower Soul*, as the New Power Pack.   *(Author's collection)*

GCS 2000 was released on February 2, 1999. The album failed to chart and only spun off the US promo single "U Move Me." Graham toured extensively, opening for Prince in 1998 on the New Power Soul tours as the New Power Graham Central Station.

Prince features on three songs on Graham's 2012 *Raise Up*, contributing drums, guitar, keys, and backing vocals on the title track and "Shoulda Coulda Woulda," and guitar on "Movin'."

Graham continues to perform live and for many is best known as Drake's uncle.

Bria Valente's *Elixir* (2009)

The monetary failure of the late 1990s Khan/Graham New Power product line seems to have reigned in Prince's impresario tendencies for a good half decade. He tried in 2006 with Tamar's *Milk & Honey*, but the album was never released after Prince blew off Universal's requests for a *3121* tour. Not uncoincidentally, Prince met Minneapolis-born Brenda Fuentes, aka Bria Valente, that summer and soon had her in the studio for "The Song of the Heart" and nascent recordings for 2009's *Lotusflow3r* and Valente's only album: *Elixir*.

Prince produced all and cowrote nine of *Elixir*'s ten tracks with Valente. Valente handles vocals, with Prince on everything else except C. C. Dunham (drums) and Joshua Dunham (bass) on "All This Love," "Something U Already Know," and "Kept Woman," the latter a recycled Tamar song written solely by Prince.

The album is generic adult contemporary—nothing offensive but nothing engaging either. It is, as Prince said, "nasty but not dirty." Prince himself

Prince mostly stepped back from the protégé business in the early 2000s, returning in 2009 with Bria Valente. In this instance, Prince forced Valente's *Elixir* on the buying public, bundling it in a three-CD set with his *Lotusflow3r* and *MPLSound* albums. Valente scored an inadvertent number two LP on the Billboard 200 and was never heard from again.   *(Author's collection)*

compared it to Sade, and Valente claimed the two were just trying to make some "elevator music." And it almost goes without saying that, as with those one-album lovers who came before her (Vanity, Apollonia, Carmen Electra, and Mayte), Valente can barely carry a tune—unless it's an auto-tune.

Elixir was released as a download on Lotusflow3r.com on March 24, 2009, and then as part of a Target-exclusive three-disc package with *MPLSound* and *Lotusflow3r*. Buoyed by the Prince albums and an $11.98 price, *Elixir* went to number two on the Hot 200 and number one on the R&B/hip-hop charts.

Bria Valente didn't play live. Prince played the Latin-jazz "All This Love" and the ballad "Elixir" at the first July 18, 2009, Montreux Jazz Festival show.

Prince and Valente started dating in 2007 (because she was good at scripture), and she converted to Jehovah's Witness in 2010. The couple seems to have broken up in early 2011, and Valente married in 2013.

Andy Allo's *Superconductor* (2012)

Andy Allo met Prince in early 2011 when the Africa Channel's chief executive officer, Elrick Williams, brought Allo to a party at Prince's house. Williams's station had run an hour-long show about Allo, and he thought the two would hit it off. He was right. By May, Allo was guesting live on "Crimson and Clover," and by June, she was part of the NPG, singing lead on covers and her own "People Pleaser," and co-lead on "When We're Dancing Close and Slow." She last played live with Prince in the fall of 2012.

Allo and Prince worked on *Superconductor*, Allo's second LP, from the summer of 2011 until early 2012. Prince serves as executive producer of the Allo-produced project and is probably on every track, but he seems more an oar than a rudder on this ship. Only three of the nine tracks are written by Prince: "The Calm" with Allo and the title track and "Long Gone" on his own. That's not to say there isn't a big Prince presence, as the current NPG, including new bassist Ida Nielsen and the Hornheadz, are all over the record.

The album's highlight is the super-funky "People Pleaser," a song Prince said he wishes he wrote. The rest of the light R&B album is pleasant enough and shows Allo working as a real artist rather than as a Prince puppet, but it doesn't want to get its hands dirty and rarely rises above pleasant. Allo kept Prince from adding strings on one song to keep the music raw, but her idea of raw is still a bit too precious.

Superconductor was released on NPG Records on November 20, 2012. Prince played "Superconductor" a few times as part of his show with a female vocalist other than Allo and sang co-lead on "People Pleaser" about a dozen times.

Allo posted twenty mostly live tracks on Facebook from July 15, 2011, to September 29, 2012, often moments after recording. The most interesting track is the demo duet with Prince of "U Will B." Allo found her way onto three *Art Official Age* tracks, singing background on "Breakdown" and co-lead on "What It Feels Like" and "Time."

Andy Allo's *Oui Can Luv* (2015)

Nine tracks recorded in 2011 and 2012 with Allo on vocals and Prince on acoustic guitar were pulled together for 2015's *Oui Can Luv* album. The album includes eight cover songs, including Prince's "I Love U in Me" and the title track: a reconceived version of "We Can Funk." The ninth song, "False Alarm," is assumed to be a Prince/Allo collaboration. The album is loose and listenable. It feels like hanging out with friends. The album was made available as a twelve-hour Tidal stream on November 7, 2015.

Judith Hill's *Back in Time* (2015)

Judith Hill worked with Michael Jackson, was a top-eight finalist on *The Voice*, and was featured in the 2014 Oscar-winning documentary *20 Feet from Stardom*. But Prince first noticed her on Sean Combs's Revolt TV talking about how she wanted to work with Prince. He gave her a call, and sometime in early 2015, the two recorded the eleven tracks that make up her debut LP *Back in Time*. Although clearly a protégé project, *Back in Time* sounds less like Prince than any other protégé release.

The album is a winner. The music recalls early 1970s R&B, with a few tracks echoing a crisper version of "Ol' Skool Company." Hill's slightly throaty vocals are a welcome change to the can't-sing-so-I-talk soprano efforts of many protégés.

Back in Time was released as a free twenty-four-hour download on March 23, 2015, through Prince's Live Nation mailing list and Hill's website, then as an NPG CD on October 23. The album's release was not without controversy. Prince was sued by former Universal Music Group and Sony executive Jolene Cherry, who claimed to hold the rights to Hill's music, with which Prince was "tortuously interfering." The case remains unsettled.

Hill opened for Prince several times in 2015. Hill's band included keyboardists Chance Howard and Kip Blackshire, Kirk Johnson, bassist MonoNeon, and Minneapolis guitarist Jesse Larson, another *Voice* top-eight finalist.

Hill was with Prince when his plane made an emergency "unresponsive passenger" landing at Quad City International Airport in Moline, Illinois, on April 21, 2015, less than a week before the performer's untimely death.

22

Slave to the System

Record Companies, Wrecka Stows, and Digital Distribution

In 1977, Prince signed a contract with Warner Bros. Records for $180,000 to record three albums. He soon spent all but $10,000 on his first album while learning how to record a record. It's unlikely he was thinking about contractual freedom as a defining aspect of his legacy, but this disdain for the established music industry order came to define who he was and how people understood him. This chapter touches on Prince's work with the traditional record industry, then explores his adventures in alternative and digital distribution.

Record Companies

Warner Bros.

Prince signed a recording contract with Warner Bros. Records (now Warner Records) on June 25, 1977. The initial contract secured unprecedented freedom: a three-record deal, the chance to play all the instruments, and the ability to coproduce. It also gave Prince the power to bring other artists to Warner Bros. He celebrated by recording the still-unreleased song "We Can Work It Out," which prophetically ended with an explosion.

Through the early 1980s, Prince and Warner Bros. enjoyed a mostly good relationship, encountering typical money and promotion squabbles. The good was especially true when Prince was making oodles of money for the label and he was buffered from label criticism by his management team of Bob Cavallo, Joe Ruffalo, and Steve Fargnoli, who later sued him for their buffering.

Things unraveled in the mid-1980s as Prince wanted to release an unprecedented amount of material, both his own and from protégés. The first cracks appeared in December 1986 when Warner Bros. rejected the three-LP *Crystal Ball*. Warner Bros.'s caution followed six months that saw the relative disappointment of the *Parade* record, the total failure of *Under the Cherry Moon*, and the dissolution of The Revolution. After a few years of détente, the relationship devolved into open warfare during the 1990s.

Prince released six albums (*For You* through *Purple Rain*) and twenty-two singles on the Warner Bros. imprint from 1978 to 1985 plus six albums and eighteen singles by protégé artists. *Batman* (1989) was also on Warner Bros.

From 1994 to 1999, Warner Bros. released five Prince (as opposed to Symbol) albums: *Come*, *The Black Album*, *Chaos and Disorder*, *The Vault*, and the sound track *Girl 6*. As part of the renegotiated contentious 1992 contract, they also released the hits collections *The Very Best of Prince* (2001) and *Ultimate* (2006).

Prince and Warner Bros. made peace in 2014 with the company distributing the NPG releases *Plectrumelectrum* and *Art Official Age*. Prince also gained control of his back catalog at that time. The Estate released 1978–1993 back-catalog and Warner Bros. material posthumously, resulting in six physical posthumous releases through 2019's *1999 Super Deluxe*.

Paisley Park Records

Prince leveraged *Purple Rain*'s success into his own label, Paisley Park Records, which operated like an independent label but was funded and distributed by Warner Bros.

Prince released seven albums on Paisley Park Records, from 1985's *Around the World in a Day* through 1992's *Symbol* plus the three-LP *The Hits/The B-Sides* in 1993 and twenty-eight singles. Paisley Park Records released twenty-two non-Prince LPs, four of which—*Good Question*, *Tony LeMans*, George Clinton's *The Cinderella Theory*, and Eric Leeds's *Things Left Unsaid*—had no Prince input, and at least fifty singles. While the Prince albums sold well, the other releases were mostly failures aside from *Sheila E. in Romance 1600* and the *Graffiti Bridge*–associated releases from *The Time* and *Tevin Campbell*.

Warner Bros. shut down Paisley Park Records on February 1, 1994, a casuality of poor A&R and marketing decisions, such as spending $2 million on the atrocious *Carmen Electra* album, and Prince's legal battles with Warner Bros.

NPG Records

The first album released on NPG Records was NPG's *Gold Nigga* (1993), an album that Warner Bros. refused to release. Prince started the label while still running Paisley Park Records and signed to Warner Bros. Unlike Paisley Park Records, which had the trappings of a functioning label, NPG Records was often nothing more than a literal label slapped on a disc released by whomever was offering the best distribution deal at the moment. Like many NPG releases, *Gold Nigga* never had an official distributor.

The first NPG release with widespread distribution was Symbol's "The Most Beautiful Girl in the World," released on February 1, 1994, less than two

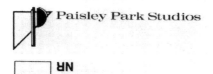

Digital Audio Tapes (DAT) were the digital recording medium of choice in the late 1980s and early 1990s, but the format all but disappeared by 2005, killed off by more accessible digital formats. Paisley Park was set up for DAT recording and provided custom case inserts, as shown. The 1990 *Nude* tour opened with a recording that has come to be known as "DAT Intro."   *(Courtesy Jeff Munson)*

weeks after Paisley Park Records closed. The wildly popular "TMBGITW" and *1-800-NEW-FUNK* were distributed by Bellmark Records, created by Al Bell of Stax Records fame, which explains the "Staxowax" "TMBGITW" remix.

Symbol's first album, 1995's *The Gold Experience*, was distributed by Warner Bros., but after that, a dozen distributors released twenty-six Prince/Symbol LP and twelve protégé projects plus Jacob Armen's *Drum Fever*, a jazz/rock instrumental album by the only non-Prince NPG artist. Distributors ranged from the multinational powerhouses EMI (*Emancipation*), Arista (*Rave Un2 the Joy Fantastic*), Columbia (*Musicology*), and Universal (*3121*) to otherwise obscure independents, such as Redline Entertainment (*The Rainbow Children*), MP Media (*N.E.W.S.*), and Because Music (*MPLSound/Lotusflow3r*). NPG's *Exodus* and Mayte's *Child of the Sun* were distributed by Edel Records, and the 1998–1999 New Power Pak (NPG's *Newpower Soul*, Chaka Khan's *Come 2 My House*, and Graham Central Station's *GCC 2000*) was released through BMG Music.

Universal Music Group acquired the rights to distribute much of this material on February 9, 2017, but the deal was voided on July 13 after Universal Music Group had questions about rights conflicts with Warner Bros. In June 2018, Sony's

Legacy Recordings secured immediate rights to 1995–2010 recordings, acquiring rights to the complete catalog by 2021. Legacy Recordings released *Anthology: 1995–2010* in 2018 and *The Versace Experience (Prelude 2 Gold)* in 2019.

Alternative Distribution

From 1993 on, Prince was continually experimenting with different forms of distribution. These ranged from old-fashioned stores to, at the time, cutting-edge online subscription services.

Glam Slam Clubs

Prince opened Glam Slam Minneapolis on October 16, 1990, with a Rosie Gaines performance. MPLS was followed by Glam Slam Yokohama, East (Miami Beach), and West (Los Angeles). All sold some Prince merchandise, but all were shut down by February 1996 as Symbol transitioned toward *Emancipation*.

NPG Stores

NPG MPLS opened on August 3, 1993, followed by NPG London in Camden Town on April 30, 1994, with Symbol and Mayte attending the opening. A Mall of America kiosk opened on August 15, 1994. These brick-and-mortar outlets sold Prince and NPG records and posters plus jewelry, perfume, and other memorabilia. MPLS closed in early 1996, and London soon followed.

1-800-NEW-FUNK

This direct-marketing phone number hooked fans up with materials otherwise available only at shows or the NPG Stores, such as the *Gold Nigga* LP, the Prince *NYC* cassette EP, and "The Truth" single. While the intention was good, the pricing wasn't, as the four songs total on the EP and single would set you back $35.

Concerts

Every ticket on the *Musicology* Live 2004ever tour came with a "free" copy of *Musicology*. The wildly popular tour boosted *Musicology* numbers enough that Billboard stopped included giveaways in sales counts.

Verizon.com

Prince joined forces with telecom giant Verizon to release "Guitar" on May 31, 2007. He got exposure for the single and upcoming *Planet Earth*, and they got

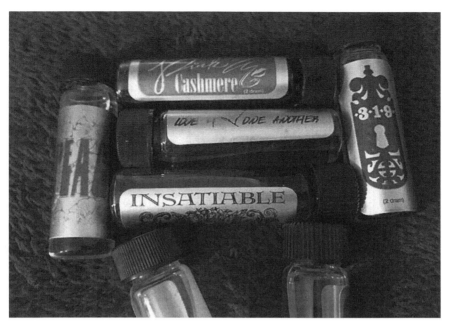

The NPG Stores sold all manner of Prince memorabilia, including five versions of Prince-themed essential oils aka "pheromone oils." The Camden, UK, Chalk Farm Road NPG Store location is now the "Home of the Waffle Burger," a decidedly un-Prince culinary choice.

(Courtesy Bob Poppo)

to promote their now arcane V CAST Song ID program: basically an app that could identify songs if you hold your "phone close to the PC speaker" and then give download options.

Newspapers

Prince distributed *Planet Earth* via the *Mail on Sunday* in the United Kingdom and Ireland on July 15, 2007, and *20Ten* was released with half a dozen European publications in July 2010. These deals avoided traditional distribution and got the music into fans' hands, and Prince got paid up front.

Websites

TheDawn.com

TheDawn.com was Prince's first website, lasting from February 14, 1996, his Mayte wedding day, until May 1997. The site contained no exclusive content, offering much of the same product as the withering NPG Stores.

1800Newfunk.com

Prince rebranded TheDawn.com in 1997, pairing it with the toll-free phone line as a central product location. The site offered no exclusive material but served as a launching point for Love4OneAnother.com and the *Crystal Ball* and *Kamasutra* websites. The *Crystal Ball* website contained exclusive album lyrics.

Love4OneAnother.com

Prince kept the retail site operating and opened Love4OneAnother.com from 1997 until December 31, 1999. The site started nominally as a charity site but soon operated as a blog-type venture that didn't want to be a stodgy official artist website. Prince recruited fans to help curate the site, which in part led to his filing lawsuits against fan magazines and websites for copyright infringement.

Love4OneAnother.com included an audio stream. At first, the site offered brief edits of songs, such as a thirty-five-second bit of NPG's "Shooh-Bed-Ooh," but by 1999, full songs were available, such as "U're Still the One," Prince's duet with Marva King, and a live "Purple Rain." Nothing essential was exclusive to this site.

One Song

From January 1 until March 3, 2000, Love4OneAnother.com was replaced by a video for the otherwise unreleased "One Song." The first 5:45 of the 9:00 clip is Prince reciting a speech about creation, while the balance is Prince belting out the raw-throated power ballad.

NPGonlineLTD.com

NPGonlineLTD.com opened on March 4, 2000. It had more of an official feel than previous sites and was more oriented toward NPG business. As with the previous site, the music was more tantalizing than satisfying, with occasional edits of unreleased songs popping up on the audio stream.

NPG Music Club

Prince finally pulled it all together with the NPG Music Club. Launched on February 14, 2001, the subscription site included not only the standard material available on earlier sites but also exclusive audio and video content and access to exclusive events, such as sound checks. The initial version of the site required the user to download a Real Audio player to access material, but later incarnations stuck to Web-based audio and video reproduction. The site went through multiple iterations before shutting down on July 4, 2006, three weeks after Prince received a Webby Lifetime Achievement Award for innovative use of the Internet.

The site was free for retail traffic, but fans could subscribe at two levels for extra content. During the first years, for $7.77 per month, you'd get three new songs plus a 45–60 minute, non-tracked NPG Ahdio Show. For a $100 premium membership, fans got all this, extra audio/video downloads, and VIP access to concerts and special events plus a copy of *Rave In2 the Joy Fantastic*.

The first year—from Adhio Show #1, released on February 18, 2001, through Adhio Show #11, released on January 17, 2002—was an unprecedented bounty of unreleased studio, rehearsal, and live audio and video material from both Prince and satellite acts. Almost all the live and rehearsal material remains unavailable (a 1988 "Rebirth of the Flesh" rehearsal is otherworldly). Most of the studio songs have been released, but at least twelve studio alternates, edits, or remixes remain unavailable:

1. "The Holy River (Instrumental)"
2. "Love Sign (Ted's Funky Chariot Mix Edit)"
3. "Seventeen" Madhouse rerecording of *Kamasutra*'s Overture #8
4. "Superfunkycalifragisexy (Instrumental)"
5. "Race (Alternate)"
6. "Silicon" (unedited)
7. "Sex Me Sex Me Not" (edit)
8. "Golden Parachute" (edit)
9. "Judas Smile" (alternate)
10. "Vavoom" (edit)
11. "Willing and Able" (alternate)
12. "Hot Wit U (Remix)"

In addition to the opening "NPG Commercial," ten songs remain unreleased, although three are less-than-a-minute edits:

1. "1, 2"
2. "Habibi" (two versions)
3. "Van Gogh"
4. "One Song"
5. "We Gon' Make It Funky (Live)"
6. "Eye Like 2 Play"
7. "Asswhuppin' in a Trunk" Madhouse
8. "Contest Song"
9. "Jukebox with a Heartbeat"
10. "Bay Girl"

The October 16, 2001 release was a single-stream, untracked copy of *The Rainbow Children*.

In March 2002, the NPG Music Club relaunched, with the non-subscription public site and the retail site consolidated. For members, the monthly downloads were gone, replaced by a promise of four LPs. Two LPs were mailed to members: *One Nite Alone* in May and the three-CD *One Nite Alone . . . Live!* collection in November. January 1, 2003, saw the surprise release of *Xpectation*, followed by the *C-Note* tracks, followed by yet another site revamp.

The site relaunched in April 2003. The interface reverted from a text-oriented website to an entering-a-building vision that resembled the *Interactive* CD-ROM and many 1990s straight-to-video projects. A lifetime membership was now $25. This included former VIP perks but didn't include music, available at an extra cost through the Musicology Download Store.

The NPG Music Club had a final relaunch in March 2004 to coincide with the release of *Musicology*. On March 29, the Musicology Download Store opened, featuring *Musicology*, *The Chocolate Invasion*, *The Slaughterhouse*, and *C-Note* and the singles "Controversy (Live in Hawaii)" and "Bataclan" (a medley of "NPG in This Funky House/All the Critics Love U in Paris"). A year later, the store added *Crystal Ball*, *Kamasutra*, *The Truth*, and "The War."

The United Kingdom's Nature Publishing Group filed a copyright infringement lawsuit against Prince on July 3, 2006. The NPG Music Club closed the next day, although Prince's lawyers claim a coincidence. Before the July 4, 2006, closing, the site offered several exclusive streams and downloads. Many were live versions of available songs, but these studio songs remain unavailable:

1. "Magnificent"
2. "The United States of Division"
3. "Silver Tongue (Demo)"
4. "Glasscutter"
5. "S.S.T."
6. "Brand New Orleans"

3121.com

Prince replaced the NPG Music Club with 3121.com in the summer of 2006. It was created to promote the new LP and the Las Vegas residency but ended up as the low-fi official site for just under three years. The site was free, but there was little innovation. It wasn't a living blog or a club, just a website. The Jam of the Week offered a mixed bag of songs, with the only rarities a remix edit of "Eye Wish U Heaven" and an acoustic version of "Love."

Lotusflow3r.com

Prior to the 2009 3121.com shutdown, Prince briefly opened MPLSound.com. It offered "(There'll Never B) Another Like Me (Instrumental Short Edit)" on December 16 and not much else.

Lotusflow3r.com started streaming on January 6, 2009, with "Disco Jellyfish," an alternate mix of "Chocolate Box." It became his official website on January 31. The site moved to a subscription model to promote the 2009 LPs on March 24, the day the albums were available for download. The subscription cost $77 and was good for 365 days. Aside from the LPs, a few live downloads and the otherwise unavailable "Cause and Effect," the site was, at best, bells and whistles. Prince proclaimed that the Internet was dead, and the site stopped on March 23, 2010.

Radio Silence

Even before shuttering 3121.com, leading to three years without an Internet presence or a real record label, Prince began relying on other websites, including YouTube, to distribute his music. While much of this was live material, such as "Y U Wanna Treat Me So Bad," released on September 29, 2009, on Drfunkenberry.com, and rerecordings, such as "Dark" from Andy Allo's Facebook page, several relevant studio tracks remain uncollected:

1. "Purple and Gold," Vikings.com, January 21, 2010
2. "Hot Summer," Thecurrent.org, June 7, 2010
3. "Rich Friends," Ktu.com, October 14, 2010
4. "Guitar (Acoustic)" with Andy Allo, Thisisrealmusic.com, July 7, 2011
5. "Same Page Different Book," YouTube.com, January 6, 2013
6. "Chapter & Verse" (live), YouTube.com, January 20, 2013
7. "What If," Live Nation e-mail, March 14, 2015

Wolfgangsvault.com

It's unclear who owns the license for these recordings, housed at the online live recording mecca Wolfgang's Vault. The site began offering audio for the April 12, 1993, San Francisco DNA Lounge show in September 2010, followed by the September 26, 1998, NYC Tramps show in November 2012. Video for the January 30, 1982, Capitol Theater show in Passaic, New Jersey, came online on December 19, 2013. The video is also available on the Capitol Theater's extensive YouTube channel.

20pr1nc3.com

Prince briefly jumped back online on January 22, 2013, the week after 3rdEyeGirl's live debut. The site was designed to sell the lyric video for "Screwdriver" and Andy Allo's *Superconductor* and promote a never-released live video from the two July 18, 2009, Montreux shows.

3rdEyeGirl.com

3rdEyeGirl.com opened on February 5, 2013, in time for the Super Bowl, offering four downloadable tracks at $0.88 each. Videos sold for $1.77. A few more tracks were added before June 28, when it became an information site, with downloads available at 3rdeyetunes.com. The main site was deleted in August 2014, pointing toward a Warner Bros. *Plectrumelectrum* site. Songs were posted on 3rdEyeGirl.com, 3rdeyetunes.com, and multiple social media sites. To call this approach haphazard would be to give it too much credit.

Exclusive full-length studio material from 3rdEyeGirl.com are the following:

1. "Screwdriver (Remix)"
2. "Rock and Roll Love Affair (Remix7)"
3. "Boyfriend (demo)"
4. "That Girl Thang"
5. "Live Out Loud"
6. "Ain't Gonna Miss U When U're Gone"
7. "Da Bourgeoisie"

3rdEyeGirl's Twitter offered a "The Sweeter She Is" rehearsal on October 16, 2013, and 3rdEyeGirl's and Prince's SoundCloud offered the instrumentals "Menstrual Cycle" and "Octopus Heart" plus Tidal's *Dance Rally 4 Peace*, forty-one minutes of the May 9, 2015, Baltimore show.

3rdEye TV

3rdEye TV broadcast twenty episodes via Livestream.com on a more or less regular basis from June 19 to August 12, 2013, and additional episodes October 5, 2013, and July 26, 2014. The shows were short on studio material, typically a mix of live performances, including numerous cover versions and essential rehearsal material from Paisley Park. The non-live exclusive songs are the following:

1. "Midnight Blues"
2. "Moon Drop" (rehearsal)
3. "The Third Heart of the Octopus Menstrual Cycle Originally Dropped from the Moon" (rehearsal)
4. "What It Feels Like" (alternate)
5. "Rock and Roll Love Affair" (reloaded instrumental remix)

Tidal.com

Prince joined Jay-Z's Tidal service on July 1, 2015, pulling his catalog from iTunes and Spotify. This served as a prelude to the September 7 streaming of *Hitnrun Phase One*, which also saw the introduction of the Purple Pick of the Week and the video stream for "Indifference." *Hitnrun Phase Two* became available on Tidal on December 12 but oddly was available on iTunes three days later. The Purple Pick of the Week offered three exclusive studio tracks unassociated with any LP: "Free Urself," Prince's last single; "Pretzelbodylogic Reloaded"; and "If Eye Could Get Ur Attention." Tidal shut down the Purple Pick when Prince died and added fifteen post-1993 albums on June 7, 2016.

Prince's music returned to multiple platforms on February 12, 2017.

23

Reproduction of the New Breed Leader

Early 2000s LPs

The Rainbow Children (2001)

Prince abruptly stopped the A Celebration tour on June 28, played a Montreal show on July 6, and then stayed off the stage for the rest of 2001. But that doesn't mean he wasn't working. He finished *The Rainbow Children* in the spring, recorded *One Nite Alone* and some of *Xenophobia* in the fall, and laid down tracks for his major project of the year: the NPG Music Club's monthly Ahdio Show. The Ahdio Show featured new Prince songs mixed with old songs, live tracks, commentary, and tunes from associate artists.

Perhaps the biggest events in 2001 were two life transitions. On August 25, Prince's father, John L. Nelson, died. It's hard not to see a connection between the elder Nelson's passing and Prince's almost immediate recording of a solo piano album and a two-year plunge into jazz. On New Year's Eve, he married his assistant, Manuela Testolini, in Hawaii.

The Rainbow Children is Prince's first album of new material as Prince since 1994's *Come*. It appeared as a single, untracked stream in place of the October 2001 Ahdio Show. The CD hit the market on November 20 on NPG Records through a Redline Entertainment distribution deal, making it Prince's first independent album. It reached only number 109 on the top 200, his worst showing since *For You*.

The Rainbow Children is among Prince's best work and his most underrated. The disc doesn't follow the marketplace (neither does it set it) but rather goes in musical and lyrical directions previously unknown or unavailable. It feels like he's not looking for something (a hit, respect, or publicity) but rather sharing what he's already found. *Emancipation* may have been the album that Symbol had to make, but *The Rainbow Children* final sets Prince free.

With 2001's *The Rainbow Children*, the name-restored Prince explored musical and lyrical directions that challenged many fans. He also took a new turn visually, using the jazz–era-influenced work of St. Louis-based artist Cbabi Bayoc. In keeping with Prince's revived African American awareness of the time, the artist's names are acronyms for Creative Black Artist Battling Ignorance and Blessed African Youth of Creativity.   *(Author's collection)*

Fans and critics grumble about *The Rainbow Children*'s musical direction and, more often, lyrical content. The major complaint musically seems to be that it's different. And that means jazzier. But the jazz here is cautious at best, either R&B tinged, as on "Mellow," or tending toward New Age, as on the less successful "The Sensual Everafter." But the album's musical centerpiece, "The Work Part 1," anchors Prince's jazz tendencies in early 1960s James Brown orchestral and instrumental work. And this hooks up with the jazz funk of "1+1+1 Is 3" and "The Everlasting Now." And it's difficult to understand how any Prince fan couldn't love the altered voice of the narrator and the freewheeling, funkadelic joy of the opening title song.

But the bigger complaint was lyrical. The songs about dumping Mayte and hooking up with Testolini are no problem for most fans. But *The Rainbow*

Children is a concept album about a religious struggle between the title characters and the Banished Ones. (Spoiler alert: The Rainbow Children win, and Christ reigns in the everlasting now.) The basic narrative is not that far off from or any more successful than previous conceptual projects, such as *Graffiti Bridge*, the *Symbol* LP, and *Glam Slam Ulysses*. But what is different is the explicit and, some would say, exclusionary Christian nature of the project. But this criticism seems misplaced. To enjoy this work, you don't have to put yourself in the role of a believer in this version of a Christian God any more than you needed to endorse incest by enjoying "Sister." This doesn't excuse the sexism and anti-Semitism, but it does remind us that our relationship to artists and their creations will always be complex.

The Rainbow Children is almost entirely Prince and John "The Magnificent" Blackwell, who drums on every track except the vocal flourish "Wedding Feast." Larry Graham adds bass on "The Work Part 1" and "Last December," the Hornheadz show up on four songs, and numerous artists, including Milenia, provide vocals.

A different-mix version of "The Work Part 1" preceded the album by six months and was available only online. The B-side "U Make My Sun Shine" later appeared unedited on *The Chocolate Invasion*. Neither has been collected on CD. "She Loves Me 4 Me" was available as single-track US promo CD and as the lead track on a four-track *Jazz Sampler* promo, along with album versions of "The Sensual Everafter," "Rainbow Children," and "Digital Garden." The epic "Last December" was released to radio in Japan.

Prince toured *The Rainbow Children* during 2002's *One Nite Alone* tour, which hit more than sixty dates in North America, Europe, and Japan plus dozens of aftershows and NPG Music Club–member preshow sound checks. The tour ran from March to November. Seven *Rainbow Children* songs constitute the core of the 2002 set: the title song, "The Work Part 1," "Mellow," "1+1+1 Is 3," "Family Name," "The Everlasting Now," and "Muse 2 the Pharaoh." Other songs were played sporadically, and "The Sensual Everafter," "Digital Garden," "Deconstruction," and "Wedding Feast" never took it to the stage.

One Nite Alone . . . Solo Piano and Voice by Prince (2002)

Sometime after the death of his father in the fall of 2001, Prince recorded the ten tracks for *One Nite Alone… Solo Piano and Voice by Prince*. It's a sparse, almost claustrophobic record that's more a performance than a peek into Prince's soul (as the subtitle subtly suggests). The piano almost acts as a barrier protecting Prince's exploring, fragile falsetto. The disc never feels intimate or personal, two qualities typically expected in a collection of this nature. This doesn't mean it's a bad album, just that there's not much here to love: it's not the warm-and-fuzzy vibe of later live piano sets.

Contextually, *One Nite Alone* serves as a (mostly) solo piano companion piece to *The Truth*'s (mostly) solo guitar collection. Drummer John Blackwell appears on "Here on Earth" and Joni Mitchell's "A Case of U." The songs are slight and less developed than their guitar counterparts, more content to ride vocal and piano flourishes than develop structure and themes. The best songs here are the Mitchell cover (finally!), "U're Gonna C Me" (redone on *MPLSound*), and "Avalanche," which controversially calls Abraham Lincoln a racist. The other songs are interchangeable curios, except the closer "Arboretum," a light instrumental that's in the running for Prince's most insignificant composition.

The *One Nite Alone* CD was mailed to NPG Music Club members on May 14, 2002, and later included as a bonus in the live box set. It never received a physical commercial release but showed up on Tidal in 2015. The album produced no official singles.

The release was paired with the *One Nite Alone* tour, although the tour started six weeks before the album release. "One Nite Alone..." and "Avalanche" were semi-regulars on the tour, and "A Case of U" appeared from 1983 to 2016. "Have a ♥," "Objects in the Mirror," "Young and Beautiful," and "Arboretum" were never performed live.

One Nite Alone . . . Live! (2002)

One Nite Alone . . . The Aftershow: It Ain't Over (2002)

The two-disc *One Nite Alone... Live!* and the single disc *One Nite Alone... The Aftershow: It Ain't Over* are Prince's first and second legal live albums, although home videos had included live performances. The collections are technically two different releases, but, as with *The Truth*, the latter disc was available only as part of a set with the former.

The albums are the first credited to Prince and the NPG since 1992's *Symbol*. The collection features a stripped-down version of the NPG with Prince on vocals and guitar, John Blackwell on drums, Rhonda Smith on bass, and Renato Neto on keyboards, with Maceo Parker, Candy Dufler, Najee, and Greg Boyer rotating on horns.

The twenty-seven tracks on the *Live!* collection were recorded at eight American venues during the *One Nite Alone* tour. It's representative of the standard concert minus periodic cover songs. Eight tracks were culled from *The Rainbow Children* and *One Nite Alone*. Most other tracks were standard pre–name change hits, but a few surprises popped up. "Xenophobia," the discarded title song of Prince's post-9/11–influenced jazz project, makes its only commercially released appearance—loose, long, and luxurious. *The Vault*'s likable "Extraordinary" finally gets some surprise love from Prince. And "Anna Stesia," never a hit but well loved expands nicely.

Like the later *Indigo Nights*, *Aftershow* seems to promise a lot—the excitement and mystery of a surprise gig—but it's strangely tepid. This might be in part because the joy of listening to an aftershow is often not only in the individual songs but also in the structure and surprises as the set develops free from arena constraints. Lesser parts can produce a greater whole. The guitar-drench anthem "Joy in Repetition" and dance-pop "Peach (Xtended Jam)" are interpretive highlights, while the rockabilly "Alphabet St.," meandering "Dorothy Parker," and perfunctory "Girls and Boys" don't add to the almost perfect originals. The major downers are "We Do This," featuring George Clinton, and the "Just Friends (Sunny)/If You Want Me to Stay" medley, featuring Musiq Soulchild and Questlove on vocals. No knock on the vocalists, but it's a letdown when Prince isn't singing lead.

The sets were first mailed to NPG Club members on November 24, 2002. The collection was released to retail stores on December 17, 2002. The albums did not chart.

Xpectation (2003)

On New Year's Day 2003, NPG Music Club members woke up to a complete surprise: *Xpectation*, a full-length instrumental jazz album from Prince. This treat appeared only five weeks after the arrival of the three-disc *One Nite Alone* live collection. Two weeks later, a digital cover appeared for the album. A year later, it was made more widely available through the Musicology Download Store and, finally, offered as a Tidal download on December 3, 2015. *Xpectation* never received a physical release.

By the time of *Xpectation*'s release, it's believed that most of the material was about a year old, recorded in the fall of 2001 after the death of John Nelson. The album was originally called *Xenophobia*. It's unclear if that title song was left off because it was on the live collection or because it seems to be a Madhouse leftover among otherwise new material.

Eight of the nine songs feature Prince on keyboards and guitar along with the current NPG rhythm section of John Blackwell and Rhonda Smith, augmented by Candy Dulfer on sax. Classical violinist Vanessa Mae appears on seven songs, skipping "Xotica" and "Xpand" but accompanying Prince alone on the opener "Xhalation." Silence is also credited with being itself.

While the album routinely ends up at the bottom of Prince album rankings, taken on its own, it's worth more than an occasional listen. The songs are generally entrenched in the 1970s. At its worst, this means tunes that call to mind the light alto sax "jazz" of Paul Simon's "Still Crazy after All the Years." At its best, this means echoes of Weather Report and harder fusion on guitar crunchers like "Xpand" and workouts like "Xpedition." But there's some looking further back, too, on tunes such as "Xemplify." Aided by Mae's violin, this creeps into 1930s Hot Club territory à la Stéphane Grappelli, although Prince never gets his Django Reinhardt on. The title track sticks the closest to the Madhouse pop-jazz formula.

There was no *Xpectation* tour, and only two songs were performed live. "Xemplify" was played twice in October 2003 in Australia, while "Xpectation" was performed at NPG Music Club sound checks in 2002, then twice on January 16, 2013, at the Dakota residency and once at a November 2015 Paisley Park session.

C-Note (2003)

Just two days after *Xpectation*, on January 3, 2003, Prince dropped *C-Note*, five songs pulled from NPG Music Club sound checks in October and November 2002. The collection is the third live set from the *One Nite Alone* tour and the sixth and final Prince and the NPG album.

The title is an initialism for the song titles, which reflect the city in which the first four songs were recorded ("Copenhagen," "Nagoya," "Osaka," and "Tokyo") plus "E" for "Empty Room." The title is also slang for a US $100 bill. And $100 is how much the complaining NPG Music Club members paid in 2002 for a guaranteed four albums. *Xpectation* was number three. This was number four.

"Empty Room" features the core *One Nite Alone* live band, while the "city" tracks add Eric Leeds and Candy Dulfer on horns and deejay Dudley D. on "scratches." The city tracks are mostly instrumentals ("Tokyo" has some vocal chants) that are open, organic, and fun. The first two tracks tend toward funk/fusion, while the second two are more mellow and introspective. The collection highlight is the (bootleg) fan favorite power ballad "Empty Room." "Empty Room" was first recorded in August 1985, then rerecorded in 1992 for the failed *I'll Do Anything* project. There still hasn't been a studio release, although the 1985 version circulates in a 1994 video featuring Mayte.

"Copenhagen" was available as a members-only download on October 29, 2002, four days after it was recorded. Four days later, it was edited, excising a quote from Miles Davis's "Jean Pierre." This track was also e-mailed to European NPG Music Club members. The three Japanese tracks were released with "Empty Room" on January 3, 2003, and were e-mailed to Japanese and European members.

Sources disagree about *C-Note*'s official release date. Some give the January 3, 2003, date, while others give March 29, 2004, when it was collected as a download alongside *The Slaughterhouse* and *The Chocolate Invasion*. I put it here as part of 2003's jazz trilogy.

There was never a physical release, but in 2015, the album finally received widespread release on Tidal. This was the first appearance of the $100 cover, echoing the cover of Funkadelic's 1972 release *America Eats Its Young*.

There was no *C-Note* tour and no singles (or only singles, depending on your point of view). Except "Empty Room," which was played as a majestic guitar anthem about twenty-five times from 2002 to 2015, no *C-Note* song was reproduced in the studio or live.

N.E.W.S. (2003)

A YouTube search of Prince and any *N.E.W.S.* song turns up unauthorized remixes that run from just under forty-five minutes to just over ninety. The remixes are described as "homework edits" and are good for ambient music even if you're trying to have a conversation. That, concisely, summarizes the four tunes on Prince's second jazz LP (although I find they're good for napping, too).

N.E.W.S., its songs named after the four compass points, offers multiple intriguing melodies, about two or three in each of the four exactly fourteen-minute songs. But often those melodies are only as intriguing as they are long, quickly forgotten as the next one arrives. While it's encouraging to hear the band expand, it also leaves the listener wondering what could have been if each idea were fully developed. The recordings also have the same warmth problem as *One Nite Alone*: there is none. For all their illusion of jazz freedom, these are expressly performances for recording devices, not performances luckily captured by recording devices.

The album was recorded at Paisley Park in one session on February 6, 2003. Prince, John Blackwell, and Rhonda Smith return from *Xpectation*, with Eric Leeds replacing Candy Dulfer and Renato Neto joining on keyboards. Unlike the previous two releases, a CD was pressed and then distributed to the NPG Music Club starting on June 19, 2003, with a retail release on July 29. While the album didn't chart in the United States, it did receive a Grammy nomination for Best Pop Instrumental Album. It lost to Ry Cooder and Manuel Galban's *Mambo Sinuendo*, but Prince used the nomination and his performance at the awards show with Beyoncé as a springboard back into the spotlight.

There was no single from *N.E.W.S.*, although there is a purported "North" video.

While there wasn't a tour to support *N.E.W.S.*, Prince undertook his only official 2003 shows in October and November. World Tour 2003 included eight scheduled dates in Hong Kong, Australia, and Hawaii accompanied by seven aftershows. The scheduled shows were heavy on the hits, a dry run for 2004's epic *Musicology* tour. The October 23 Melbourne Metro aftershow included the only known performance of "South." "North" was never played live, but it's believed "East" and "West" were performed on August 18, 2003, at B.B. King's Blues Club in Universal City, Prince's first live show since December 16, 2002. "West" shows up on 2018's *Anthology*.

Save for an occasional live jazz set, this marks the end of Prince's flirtation with jazz.

Time to be a people pleaser.

24

If U Wanna Just Clap Yo' Hands

Prince and the Band, 2000s

The New Power Soul Festival tour ended on December 28, 1998. In 1999 and 2000, Prince played only a dozen shows outside of Paisley Park, resuming semi-regular touring with the November 8, 2000, Palladium gig in Worcester, Massachusetts. Bassist Rhonda Smith and keyboardist Morris Hayes continued with the NPG during this transitional period, but Kirk Johnson, Mike Scott, and Marva King were dropped. Prince resumed exclusive guitar duties, Johnson was replaced by John Blackwell, and Kip Blackshire, who started gigging in 1999, became a full-time member. Najee and Geneva also joined the fray. From this point, members cycled in and out of the NPG until 2013 when 3rdEyeGirl debuted.

John Blackwell (2000–2004; 2010–2012)

John "The Magnificent" Blackwell gigged in early 2000, then became the regular drummer on September 9, 2000, at a Paisley Park gig. He manned the kit from the 2000 Hit N Run tour through Musicology Live 2004ever. After joining Justin Timberlake for a few years and appearing at 2009 Los Angeles, Montreux, and Monaco Prince gigs, Blackwell returned for European Live 2010 through the May 2012 Welcome 2 Australia tour. He played his last gigs in the fall of 2012, overlapping with replacement Hannah Ford until his final show on October 26, 2012, at the Sayers Club in Los Angeles. Prince guested with Blackwell's New Power Generation Quartet at Paisley Park on August 10, 2014.

Blackwell appeared on more than forty Prince studio tracks, including all of *N.E.W.S.*, two tracks on *One Nite Alone*, and most of *The Rainbow Children*, *Xpectation*, and *HNR Phase Two*. He anchored the two *One Nite Alone* live albums and *C-Note* as well as Judith Hill's *Back in Time*. Blackwell died on July 4, 2017, as the result of brain tumors.

Greg Boyer (2001–2009)

Trombonist Greg Boyer was in Maceo Parker's band when he played at 2001's A Celebration dates. The funk giant joined NPG full time on the *One Nite Alone* tour, sat out Tamar, and then was the "3121" "elephant man" through the 2007 21 Nights London residency. Boyer appeared on ten songs spread over five LPs, including "Chelsea Rodgers," "$," and "Compassion."

Maceo Parker (2001–2007)

Maceo Parker is the king of funk saxophone, leading his own bands and backing legends including James Brown and George Clinton. Employing Parker, Prince was able to work with not only a master but also a lifelong musical influence, much like his time with Larry Graham.

Parker first recorded with Prince on January 26, 1991, on the unreleased Clinton track "My Pony." Parker was in Ani DiFranco's band when Prince caught him in Minneapolis on July 3, 1999. DiFranco and Parker returned with Prince to Paisley Park, where she added guitar to "Eye Love U but Eye Don't Trust U" and he added sax to "Prettyman."

Parker first played live with Prince on September 6, 1999, at the Warehouse District in Minneapolis, guesting on "Purple Rain." He then worked the December 17 Paisley Park Morris Day aftershow before appearing later in the day for the *Rave Un2 the Year 2000* filming.

Maceo was a periodic NPG member from 2002's *One Nite Alone* tour through 2007's 21 Nights in London dates, then guested several times through the 2012 Sayers Club dates in Los Angeles.

In addition to "Prettyman," Parker appeared on nine studio tracks stretching from *Musicology* tracks to *20Ten*. He's also on all *One Nite Alone* tour live albums. Prince appears on "Baby Knows" and "The Greatest Romance Ever Sold" on Parker's 2000 release *Dial M-A-C-E-O*. Maceo plays alongside Prince on "If I Was King" from Andy Allo's *Superconductor*.

Renato Neto (2002–2011)

Brazilian keyboardist Renato Neto came to the United States in 1991 and gained recognition in Los Angeles–area bands, finding his way to Prince through Sheila E. Neto joined the NPG on January 5, 2002, for a Paisley Park gig and was a part of the live band consistently through the May 29, 2011, final night of *Welcome 2 America*'s 21 Night Stand in Los Angeles. A highlight from this time was a duet with sax player Mike Phillips on "What a Wonderful World." Neto's playing runs more jazz than funk, and his keyboards are central on *N.E.W.S.* and *C-Note*.

He is featured on all the *One Nite Alone* live discs as well as *Indigo Nights* and the *Live at the Aladdin Las Vegas* DVD. Neto plays Fender Rhodes on "Dear Mr. Man" and keyboards on "Somewhere Here on Earth."

Chance Howard (2003–2004)

Keyboardist/vocalist Stanley "Chance" Howard was a member of The Time until he joined the NPG for October's world tour in 2003, staying on through *Musicology*. Howard's live highlights included solo leads on "Soul Man" and a nasty version of Blackstreet's "No Diggity." He sat in on 2007 Las Vegas shows and was in Judith Hill's band that opened Prince shows in April 2015. Howard added vocals to *Musicology*'s "Life 'O' the Party," "Call My Name," and "Cinnamon Girl."

Mike Phillips (2004–2008)

Saxophonist/vocoder master Mike Phillips joined the NPG at a San Francisco Fillmore aftershow on February 16, 2004. He stayed through *Musicology* Live 2004ever as music director until a Paisley Park aftershow on June 19, 2004. He returned for a March 2006 Tamar date and played one-off shows and the Las Vegas and London residencies before a final February 25, 2008, Beverly Park show. Phillips's vocoder performances were showstoppers, with highlights including 2007 aftershow performances of "3121" and numerous covers, including Tupac's "California Love." In the studio, Phillips contributed to "Chelsea Rodgers" and "$" and appears on a few live-stream songs. Phillips was a part of the Cirque de Soleil Michael Jackson show and tours as a saxophone headliner.

C. C. Dunham and Josh Dunham (2005–2010)

Drummer Cora Coleman-Dunham (aka C. C. Dunham and currently Queen Cora) and bassist Josh Dunham were Prince's funk rhythm section in the late 2000s. Prince saw Cora at a Frank McComb (Buckshot LeFonque) show and invited her to join the band. She convinced Prince to add her then boyfriend Josh. They were on board for Prince's *3121* private West Hollywood shows in 2005 and stayed until a July 26, 2010, aftershow at the Palais Club in Cannes. Although they kept busy, the duo never embarked on a full-fledged Prince tour, playing Los Angeles, Las Vegas, and London residencies and a very brief seven-date European 20Ten tour. The highlight of their time with Prince was at London Indigo aftershows, which included the performance of Cora's composition "Mind in 7" and a power-trio version of the band on August 29, 2007. The duo appeared on two *3121* tracks, four from both *Planet Earth* and *Lotusflow3r*, and all of *Indigo Nights*. They are also on three songs from Bria Valente's *Elixir* and two from *Prelude to Tamar*. Cora toured with Beyoncé in 2013 and opened a modular building construction company in 2017.

Shelby J. (2006–2014)

Singer/songwriter Shelby J. was fronting blackgypsy in the mid-2000s when Larry Graham asked her to join GCS. Prince guested with GCS on May 26, 2006, at Club Rio in Las Vegas, and Prince snagged her for the NPG. Her first gig was in Las Vegas on December 30, 2006, and she was around until the blowout 2014 Essence Music Festival. Shelby enjoyed a prominent place onstage, swapping leads with Prince ("Nothing Compares 2 U") and singing solo cover tunes, such as "Love Changes" by Mother's Finest. On occasion, she used the NPG as a backing band, such as her ten-song aftershow opening set in Amsterdam on July 25, 2011. Shelby shares co-lead on "Chelsea Rodgers" and appears on fifteen studio tracks spread over *Planet Earth*, *MPLSound*, and *20Ten*; all of the live *Indigo Nights*; and many streamed tracks, often released through her Soundcloud. Prince co-wrote and produced "North Carolina," the single from Shelby's never-released *Just Shelby* album.

Liv Warfield (2008–2015)

Liv Warfield was reluctant to send an audition tape to Prince, so in the summer of 2008, a friend sent in a video of "Portland's most soulful singer" belting out the Rolling Stones's "Gimme Shelter." She visited Paisley Park on October 4, and a few weeks later she was a singer in the NPG.

She first played with Prince on January 12, 2009, at his Beverly Park home, then at about a dozen shows and TV appearances that year, taking lead vocal duties on cover songs such as "When Will We B Paid," often when Shelby J. wasn't around.

Warfield was a full member of the NPG for six tours from the Prince 20Ten tour through 2012's Welcome 2 Australia tour and joined occasionally after that. Her final appearance with Prince was January 1, 2016, on St. Barts, where she sang lead on five songs, about a quarter of the show.

Warfield's released output with Prince originates with 2010 studio work. For LPs, she's on seven tracks on 20Ten and two—"Big City" and "Black Muse"—from *HNR Phase Two*. She's also on the studio online tracks "Purple and Gold," "Hot Summer," "Rich Friends," and "Same Page Different Book" and a cover of Emeli Sandé "Next to Me" in addition to many live and rehearsal songs. She wrote the lyrics to Prince's music for 3rdEyeGirl's "Live Out Loud."

Warfield sings background on Andy Allo's 2012 effort *Superconductor* and in 2014 released her second solo album: *The Unexpected*. Prince wrote the title track, which shows up on *Plectrumelectrum* as "Wow," and cowrote and plays on "Your Show."

PRODUCED, ARRANGED, COMPOSED AND PER4MED BY
PRINCE & 3RDEYEGIRL
ALL FUTURE RIGHTS RESERVED © NPG 2014

Prince debuted his new band, 3rdEyeGirl, in January 2013 and released the co-credited *Plectrumelectrum* LP in September 2014. While drummer Hannah Ford Welton's tenure with Prince ended at the June 2015 Washington shows, bassist Ida Nielsen and guitarist Donna Grantis jammed as part of the NPG through January 2016.   *(Author's collection)*

Warfield worked with the band Blackbird in 2014 and 2015, with Prince guesting at a few gigs, and in 2017 formed Roadcase Royale with former Heart guitarist Nancy Wilson.

Cassandra O'Neal (2009–2016)

Cassandra O'Neal is a gospel/R&B keyboardist and arranger who has worked with numerous artists, including Jay-Z. After being introduced by Sheila E., O'Neal debuted with Prince on March 19, 2005, celebrating Prince's NAACP Image Lifetime Achievement Award. She toured Europe with C.O.E.D. (Chronicles of Every Diva) with fellow NPG musicians Rhonda Smith, Kat Dyson, and Sheila E. before joining the NPG on a regular basis on October 11, 2009, at Paris's Grand Palais. She toured through HNR II in 2014–2015, often playing an untitled piano interlude. O'Neal played keyboards at Prince's last public group performance, a January 1, 2016, St. Barts bash. O'Neal is on a number of streamed live songs and the studio version of "Big City."

Ida Nielsen (2010–2016)

Danish bassist/vocalist Ida Nielsen enjoyed early 2000s success with Belgian band Zap Mama and as the solo artist Bassida. Based on this work and her MySpace, Prince summoned Nielsen to Minneapolis in 2010. After twenty minutes of jamming with Prince and John Blackwell, he told her they were touring. Nielsen, aka Ida Funkhouser, played her first gig with the NPG on October 18, 2010, in Bergen, Norway, the first date of the Prince Live 2010 tour. She was his anchor on bass (and occasional guitar and keyboards) first with the NPG and then 3rdEyeGirl through 2016.

In the studio, Nielsen is featured as a member of 3rdEyeGirl on every *Plectrumelectrum* track, on bass on the e-mail download cover song "What If," and for background vocals on "Ain't About to Stop" from *HNR Phase One*. As a member of NPG, she contributes bass to "Rocknroll Loveaffair," "Screwdriver," and "Big City" on *Phase Two* and, as a solo artist, Danish vocals on "Art Official Cage" and bass on Andy Allo's "People Pleaser." She also appeared on numerous live streams, the earliest a cover of "Stratus" streamed through Drfunkenberry.com from her fourth gig on October 22, 2010, in Herning, Denmark: a triumphant homecoming.

Hannah Welton-Ford (2012–2015)

Louisville native Hannah Welton-Ford literally put on a drum clinic in the early 2010s. Her online videos attracted Prince's attention in 2012, and after she delivered some videos of her playing along to his songs, she received an invitation to Paisley Park. She jammed with bassist Nielsen, and soon after, Prince had two-thirds of his latest creation: 3rdEyeGirl.

Ford's first live appearance was on "Stratus" at a House of Blues aftershow in Chicago on September 26, 2012. She then played on "Rock and Roll Love Affair" on *Jimmy Kimmel Live!* on October 23, swapping out the kit with the soon-to-depart John Blackwell before appearing at the October 24 and 26 Sayers Club shows in Los Angeles. Ford made her formal 3rdEyeGirl debut at the first of two January 18, 2013, Dakota shows. She was behind the kit for the Live Out Loud and HNR II tours and most one-off shows through two Warner Theatre shows in Washington, DC, on June 14, 2015.

As a member of 3rdEyeGirl, Ford drums on all *Plectrumelectrum* tracks; sings lead on "Aintturninround," "Whitecaps," and "Stopthistrain"; and co-leads on "Pretzelbodylogic." She also sings background on *HNR Phase One*'s "Ain't About to Stop" and drums on *Art Official Age*'s version of "Funknroll." She's on numerous streamed 3rdEyeGirl live versions of previously released tracks. Ford and Prince recorded the online song "Da Bourgeoisie" in November 2013. She is married to producer/instrumentalist Joshua Welton.

Donna Grantis (2012–2016)

Canadian guitarist Donna Grantis had been a working musician for years, touring Europe with her Donna Grantis Electric Band, when she got an e-mail in November 2012 from Joshua Welton inviting her to Paisley Park to jam. Prince was impressed by online videos of Grantis playing "Stratus," a Prince cover favorite, and "Elektra," an original that eventually morphed into "Plectrumelectrum." She learned a half dozen Prince songs, they jammed, and on November 30, a rehearsal of "I Like It There" was streamed on Ford's Facebook page with the message "2 C the rest of Donna's audition holla at ya girl! We've got bootlegs 4 daazzzzzze every good thing in the vault.... Coming 2013." Unlike any past Prince guitarist, except Prince himself, Grantis was never afraid of cranking the amp to eleven.

Grantis joined 3rdEyeGirl for the pair of January 18, 2013, Dakota shows. She was on the 2013 North American Live Out Loud and 2014 European HNR II tours. Grantis was at most one-off performances during 2015 and on guitar at the final 3rdEyeGirl show on June 14, 2015. Grantis played at a series of six somewhat experimental Paisley Park shows in October and November 2015. With Nielsen, she was playing on January 1, 2016, in St. Barts for Prince's final band show.

Minus the "Da Bourgeoisie" duet and the *Plectrumelectrum* LP vocals but adding a guitar solo on "Ain't About to Stop," Grantis essentially shares the same recording history as Ford.

Joshua Welton (2012–2015)

Joshua Welton climbed aboard the Paisley Park train in the summer of 2012 when his wife, drummer Hannah Welton-Ford, was rehearsing for what would become 3rdEyeGirl. Welton walked into the room, Prince came offstage and hugged him, and soon after, the two spent a lot of time talking about God. Welton was deputized, working to recruit guitarist Donna Grantis, and not much later found himself coproducing 2014's *Art Official Age* and cowriting and coproducing 2015's *HNR Phase One*.

Welton made his debut with the NPG along with Ford on keyboards on the October 23, 2012, *Jimmy Kimmel Live!* performance of "Rock and Roll Love Affair." His first live show was at the October 26 Sayers Club show in Los Angeles. Although never officially part of 3rdEyeGirl, Welton contributed on cowbell, keyboards, vocals, and tambourine on the band's 2013–2014 tours with Prince and participated in the one-off 3rdEyeGirl and NPG shows in 2015. His last show was on October 15, 2015, a Paisley Park show celebrating the Minnesota Lynx winning the Women's National Basketball Association championship.

In addition to the Prince albums, Welton worked with Prince on "Angel in the Dark" and the title track on Judith Hill's 2015 LP *Back in Time*. He also coproduced the unreleased Prince track "The Single Most Amazing" by Rita Ora and the streamed "Stones," a collaboration with Prince and the Golden Hippie.

MonoNeon (2015–16)

Dywane "MonoNeon" Thomas Jr. was a bass player in the Judith Hill Band who hooked up with Prince for half a dozen jam-filled Paisley Park shows in the fall of 2015, accompanied by Kirk Johnson on drums and Donna Grantis on guitar. This group recorded the unreleased "Soul Patch," played by tour guides at Paisley Park. Prince wrote, produced, and played on MonoNeon's "Ruff Enuff," recorded on January 6, 2016, and released on Tidal instrumentally, with Adrian Crutchfield on sax, on January 11 and with Crutchfield vocoder vocals on January 12. It's unknown if these songs were recorded as part of a larger project. "Ruff Enuff" was the last new studio song featuring Prince released during his lifetime.

Other NPG members are the following:

- Najee (2000–2002) Saxophonist/flautist
- Geneva (2000–2001) Dancer
- Milenia: Mikele, Malikah, Niyoki, and Tia White (2001 Singers
- rad. (2003–2004) Keyboard/vocals
- Dudley D. (2002) Deejay/turntablist

- Ray Monteiro (2005–2006) Trumpet
- Steve Baxter (2005): Trombonists
- Garrett Smith (2006): Trombonists
- DJ Rashida (2006, 2011): Deejay
- Maya McClean and Nandy McClean (2006–2008, 2011–2012): Dancers/ singers as the Twinz
- Lee Hogans (2007–2009): Trumpet
- Frederic Yonnet (2008–2011): Harmonica
- Andy Allo (2011–2012): Guitarist/singer
- Damaris Lewis (2012–2014): Dancer
- NPG Hornz (2012–2015)
    - Marcus Anderson, Adrian Crutchfield, Sylvester Onyejiaka, BK Jackson, and Keith Anderson Saxophone
    - Roy Agee and Joey Rayfield Trombone
    - Lynn Grissett, Steve Reid, Phil Lassiter, and Nick Marchione Trumpet
- Saeeda Wright (2014–2015): Singer
- Ashley Jayy (2014–2015): Singer

25

Just as Long as We're Together

Songwriting Collaborators

The cover image for 1978's debut LP *For You* is nothing special. It shows Prince slightly out of focus with his features elongated and streaked into blackness. The darkness is countered by a bright light glowing behind him just out of view over his shoulders. Maybe it's the dawn we're repeatedly welcomed to later in his career. But, unlike most albums, the attraction here isn't the altered cover photo of a precocious nineteen year old—it's the declaration on the jacket back that reads "Produced, Arranged, Composed and Performed by Prince." That, in a concise phrase, is what transforms Prince into PRINCE.

The inner sleeve, designed by Prince, elaborates on this singular theme. On one side, a black-and-white image shows Prince sitting on the edge of a bed playing a big ol' acoustic guitar. And there are three of him in the picture. Yeah, he's on a bed playing with himself.

The other side of the sleeve? A track-by-track list of the instrumentation for album details about thirty different instruments used to create sounds on the album in addition to lead and background vocals and "Handclapsandfingersnaps." The only musician listed? Prince.

Of course, the phrase on the back of the jacket includes an asterisk on "Composed," which leads to a lyric cowriting credit by C. Moon on "Soft and Wet," the album's first single. And that asterisk is the focus of this chapter: a look at ten artists who helped to write tracks on Prince albums. This chapter excludes songwriting collaborations with band members and protégés, too numerous to discuss here.

Pepe Willie

Like most young musicians, early career Prince was in many bands with fluid membership; 1973's Grand Central, featuring The Revolution's Andre Cymone, became 1974's Grand Central Corporation, featuring The Time's Morris Day, which, in turn, became Champagne in 1976. It was during this middle incarnation that Prince's first manager, Day's mother LaVonne Daugherty, hooked him up with Pepe Willie, husband to Prince's first cousin Shauntel Manderville.

Willie is the nephew of Clarence "Wa-hoo" Collins, the founding member of Little Anthony and the Imperials (1958's "Tears on My Pillow"). Willie acted as a gofer for the band and got a hard-knocks degree in the music business. Prince turned to Willie for advice about the legal aspects of the music publishing and copyright, first on the phone when Willie lived in New York and then in person when Willie moved to Minneapolis.

In 1975, Willie took note of Prince's talents and invited him and Cymone into the studio to record with his band 94 East (named after the US interstate highway in the Twin Cities). These Prince-fueled recordings helped 94 East land a record deal with Polydor. After 94 East was signed, Willie tried to forge his own path, rehearsing a live set with future Revolution drummer Bobby Z. in New York and recording a single for Polydor (with Prince on guitar) in 1976. But a management change at Polydor led to 94 East being dropped, and it would be another decade before any of the material would be released.

Even as Willie's and Prince's career paths diverged, Prince seemed to use Willie as a safe haven, the father he wouldn't have until a few years later. When Prince's equipment was stolen from Del's Tire Mart in 1978, Pepe Willie let him and his band rehearse in his basement. When Prince's first real manager, Owen Husney, quit in December 1978, Willie picked up the slack and acted as an interim manager. During this time, Willie arranged Prince's first two live shows—January 5 and 6, 1979—at the Capri Theater in Minneapolis. These shows were staged for Warner Bros. executives to decide if Prince was ready to tour. He wasn't.

As Prince enjoyed more success, Willie settled back into the role he served with his uncle's band: gofer. As even this role dwindled, Willie decided to take advantage of Prince's success and released *Minneapolis Genius* on February 12, 1986, a week after the release of "Kiss." Trying too hard, the cover featured not only the hit-you-over-the-head title and Prince's name (along with those of Willie, Cymone, and Alvin Moody, a noted dance and jazz bassist) but also a white dove on a purple backdrop. The LP featured six songs recorded between 1975 and 1979, all featuring instrumentation by Prince and including the Willie/Prince-cowritten tune "Just Another Sucker." This LP led to not only a public confrontation between Prince and Willie at First Avenue but also at least five rereleases of the same material. The year 2002 saw the release of an album of new 94 East recordings with the unreleased Prince Polydor single "10:15" and "Fortune Teller" (not the Naomi Neville/Allen Toussaint song) tacked on.

Willie received the Minnesota Black Musicians Hall of Fame Award in 1988. In 2016, he was again working with Little Anthony and the Imperials.

Riding comfortably on the *Purple Rain* coattails, early Prince collaborator Pepe Willie released 94 East's *Minneapolis Genius* in February 1986. The release caused a rift between the two men that culminated in an animated conversation at First Avenue. The six-track collection of songs from the late 1970s includes Prince on guitar and keyboards and one Prince co-composition ("Just Another Sucker"). The songs have been repackaged and rereleased at least five times.

(Author's collection)

Chris Moon

As with Pepe Willie, Chris Moon was there before the beginning, and he's here after the end. Like Willie, he takes credit for discovering Prince.

Engineer, writer, and publicist Moon seemed to have Svengali-like ambitions in those days. He offered free studio time to local young bands in exchange for the possibility that the band would record his songs, which he would then produce and promote. Moon first met Prince in early 1976 when Morris Day's mom brought Grand Central Corporation to his Moonsound Studio to record. Recognizing Prince's talent, Moon offered Prince an exclusive collaboration deal in exchange for the keys to the studio and lessons on how to use the studio. It was a great eighteenth-birthday present for Prince.

The Prince/Moon collaboration resulted in fourteen songs recorded during the summer of 1976. Five of the songs ended up in some form on *For You*. From these fourteen songs, Prince used four as a demo tape that he used in New York to try to secure a record deal. Three songs were cowritten with Moon ("Soft and Wet," "Aces," and "Love Is Forever"), while the fourth, "Baby," was a Prince original. When Prince returned from New York empty-handed, Moon introduced him to Owen Husney, who became his manager. Husney gave Prince an allowance and booked him time at Minneapolis's Sound 80 Studios, marking the beginning of the end for Moon.

Moon collected the lyric cowriting credit on "Soft and Wet" but not much else (and certainly not "My Love Is Forever," for which he cowrote the lyrics). He claims that after *For You* was released, he got a call from Prince asking for help making his dad famous. Days later, John L. Nelson left Moon's office without a path to future fame, and Moon never again heard from Prince.

In 2018, Moon attempted to sell his rights to "Soft and Wet" on eBay for a "Buy It Now" price of $490,000. He eventually pulled the offer.

John L. Nelson

Leaving aside all the family and father issues that plagued Prince's childhood (and adulthood for that matter if we're to read *Purple Rain* as semiautobiographical), John L. Nelson's creative influence on Prince is undeniable—or, at least, that the importance of that influence meant something to Prince. At the very least, John L. Nelson left a piano hanging around the house and gave Prince his first electric guitar. Those things happened.

John L. Nelson was a jazz performer who headed the Prince Rogers Trio in the 1950s. He worked as a plastic molder and moonlighted playing the piano at strip clubs. Legend has it that Prince started on his music career at age five after seeing his father onstage showered with applause and surrounded by attractive, fancy women. He knew at that moment what he wanted to do with his life, just as he confirmed later in his high school yearbook when he said that his occupation was "music." If this origin story is true, or even if it's just wishful thinking on Prince's part, it's enough to give Nelson some serious props.

Long estranged, Prince attempted to repay the props by playing his father's music to members of The Revolution as inspiration. He also credited his father with cowriting seven songs from 1984 to 1989: "Father's Song," "Computer Blue," "Around the World in a Day" (with David Coleman), "The Ladder," "Christopher Tracy's Parade," "Under the Cherry Moon," and "Scandalous." It's unlikely that

Nelson actually wrote much if any of these songs, and it's assumed that Prince gave his father credit for monetary reasons.

John L. Nelson died on August 21, 2001.

David Coleman

David and Jonathan? It doesn't have quite the same ring as Wendy and Lisa, does it? But David Coleman, Lisa's brother, and Jonathan Melvoin, Wendy's brother, recorded together in the summer of 1984. David received studio time as a present from Prince, and the duo used the time to create a demo tape that included David's song "Around the World in a Day." The sisters played the tune for Prince, who loved it. Prince and (some of) The Revolution eventually rerecorded it and used it for the title song for the *Purple Rain* follow-up LP, with cowriting credit going to Prince and his father. Coleman was never an official member of The Revolution, but he was around the band on occasion and played cello on a number of important songs, including "Purple Rain" and "Raspberry Beret." Coleman died in 2004 at the age of forty-two.

Carole Davis

Carole Davis is a British actress (*The Flamingo Kid*), songwriter, and writer credited with cowriting *Sign 'o' the Times*'s "Slow Love" with Prince. Davis had auditioned for *Purple Rain*, and the duo were supposedly dating when Prince came calling for the song. According to Davis and a side-by-side comparison of the tracks (she released her own version in 1989), Prince's contribution to the song is more adaptation than collaboration, but she legally signed away half the rights in exchange for getting it on a Prince album (and the expectation of royalty checks).

David Henry Hwang

David Henry Hwang is an award-winning playwright and lyricist best known for *M. Butterfly*, his Puccini-based story of the relationship between a French diplomat and a male Chinese opera singer posing as a woman. Hwang had turned on to Prince with the *Dirty Mind* album and considered himself a fan, one who was more than flattered when he saw a photo of Prince leaving an *M. Butterfly* performance. A few years later, he received a request from Prince to work on a stage musical. They met, and Prince requested a libretto for a musical about two lovers who never meet (called *Come*) and a poem. The musical never materialized, but the poem made its way back to Prince, who put it to music as "Solo," which ended up on the *Come* LP and the B-side of the single "Letitgo." Prince would go on to stage his own musical *Glam Slam Ulysses*.

Nona Gaye

Nona Gaye is the daughter of Marvin Gaye, the late Motown superstar who bridged the spiritual and sexual in his songs in a way similar to Prince. Gaye dated Prince for about three years in the mid-1990s, and at one point the two were engaged. *The Undertaker* project was originally developed as a feature-length movie with Gaye in a co-lead role. The high point of Gaye's career with Prince was "Love Sign" from the *1-800-NEW-FUNK* NPG Records sampler. The single wasn't commercially released but reached number thirty-two on the US R&B charts in 1994.

Gaye shared vocals on and is credited with cowriting the freedom anthem "We March," which appeared on *The Gold Experience*, but, as usual, her contribution is unclear. A recorded version of "We March" was the first tune played on the PA during the May 10, 2015, Baltimore concert that Prince played to ease the city's racial tensions after riots caused by the death of Freddie Gray at the hands of Baltimore police.

Gaye once described her time with Prince as "head trips and mind screws."

Sandra St. Victor and T. Hammer

Sandra St. Victor was the lead singer of the Family Stand, a Dallas trio that had a number three *Billboard* R&B hit in 1990 with "Ghetto Heaven." As with the Hwang collaboration, St. Victor and Prince seem to have had a pen pal–like collaboration, with the songwriter and her collaborator (the mysterious) T. Hammer sending Prince the lyrics to five songs in the summer of 1995. Prince tinkered with the lyrics to "Sanctuary" and released "Soul Sanctuary" on 1996's *Emancipation* (without crediting T. Hammer). Three of the other four songs would be released but not without some controversy.

St. Victor's "Love Is" was reworked as "Van Gogh" and first released by the band Van Gogh. Prince gave the track to the Atlanta-based Van Gogh (not the Serbian band), the members of which are all in wheelchairs, to help disabled musicians. However, he forgot to help St. Victor, leaving her name off the songwriting credits. "I'll Never Open My Legs Again" was restyled as "Eye'll Never B Another Fool" for Chaka Khan's 1998 NPG Records LP *Come 2 My House*. St. Victor was included on these cowriting credits. Prince also recorded St. Victor's

"How We Livin'" (renamed "Livin' 2 Die") and "Nothing Left to Give" (retitled "Stone"). All but "Livin' 2 Die" were featured on 1995's not-commercially-released *Playtime by Versace* CD, and Prince's "Van Gogh" appeared as an NPG Music Club download in 2001.

St. Victor reportedly considered legal action against Prince for the lack of songwriting credits but decided against suing him. On falling out of favor with Prince, she's quoted as saying, "You've never known cold like that."

Brenda Lee Eager and Hilliard Wilson

Brenda Lee Eager is an American soul singer who has enjoyed a long and varied career, including a stint with Graham Nash that landed her a role on the LP and film *No Nukes*. Her greatest success was in the early 1970s as part of soul giant Jerry Butler's group. Eager and Butler charted six singles from 1971 to 1973, with "Ain't Understanding Mellow" hitting number three on the R&B charts.

Hilliard Wilson is a bassist, vocalist, and composer who has worked with many artists, including The Manhattans and jazz vocalist Nancy Wilson.

Eager and Wilson cowrote two songs with Symbol—*Emancipation*'s "Somebody's Somebody" and *Crystal Ball*'s "Hide the Bone"—on which they're given lyric credit. "Somebody's Somebody" received a promo-only release in the United States, reaching number fifteen on the R&B charts.

There is no record of how this collaboration was developed or conducted, but, on the plus side, there's also no record of hard feelings or potential legal action.

Cornel West

Dr. Cornel West is an American race theorist and activist best known for his groundbreaking 1994 book *Race Matters* and frequent media appearances. West is as important in intellectual circles as Prince was in entertainment circles. West contributed additional lyrics to "Dear Mr. Man" from *Musicology* and released it, with overdubs, as "Mr. Man" on his 2007 debut LP *Never Forget: A Journey of Revelations*, which explores the contemporary African American condition. While this collaboration likely didn't even reach the pen pal level, according to a West *Playboy* interview, he and Prince welcomed the dawn with conversation after one of the latter's 2009 Montreux performances.

26

Willing 2 Do the Work

2004 LPs

Musicology (2004)

After a 2003 with little activity until an eight-date world tour in the fall, 2004 saw Prince will himself into the spotlight with a strong TV presence, three albums, and a lengthy greatest-hits tour.

TV first.

On February 12, Prince was interviewed and performed "Reflection," with Wendy, on PBS's *The Tavis Smiley Show* (broadcast on February 19). The next day, accompanied by Beyoncé, he stole the Grammy broadcast with an opening performance of "Purple Rain," "Baby I'm a Star," "Let's Go Crazy," and Beyoncé's "Crazy in Love." On February 26, he performed "Musicology/Tighten Up" on *The Tonight Show* and a week later was interviewed and performed a four-song set for *The Ellen DeGeneres Show*.

He powered through a three-song set as he was inducted into the Rock and Roll Hall of Fame on March 15, which served as prelude to his scorching solo on "While My Guitar Gently Weeps" during a George Harrison tribute. He then recorded a nine-song medley on March 19 for the March 25 broadcast of the thirty-sixth NAACP Image Awards. He also performed a forty-minute show at New York City's Webster Hall that was recorded, edited, and broadcast on MTV Networks as *The Art of Musicology*. The highlight was an acoustic guitar set, soon a standard feature of the *Musicology Live 2004ever* tour

So what was Prince promoting aside from Prince? *Musicology* is a straight-ahead R&B album that excels mainly in not offending anyone. It's not too nasty. It's not too rocking. It's a little political. It's just enough flirty and sexy. You've heard it all before and often better. The title track is a nostalgic callout that shuffles along doing the James Brown, last heard on "The Work Part 1," as does "Life 'O' the Party," featuring vocals by sax player Candy Dulfer. "Call My Name" has sweet vocals, but so did "Shhh" and numerous other ballads. Both "Cinnamon Girl" and "Dear Mr. Man" get political, with the former's post-9/11 surveillance

Continually searching for innovative ways to distribute his music, Prince included a flimsy-but-functional copy of *Musicology* as part of the ticket price for the *Musicology Live 2004ever* tour. This practice helped bump the LP to number three on the US *Billboard* 200 charts, his highest showing since 1991's *Diamonds and Pearls*. While this type of free distribution is de rigueur for aging rock artists as the 2020s approach, *Billboard* stopped counting free copies toward the charts after *Musicology*.   *(Author's collection)*

message almost lost in the generic light rock. There's nothing here that's bad, only forgettable.

Eight of the twelve tracks are essentially Prince solo affairs with occasional background vocals and horns by studio stalwarts. John Blackwell drums on four tracks.

A low-tech version of *Musicology* was given away with every concert ticket. These look like Prince made a band member use the low-on-ink arena copier to make covers every night before bed. On March 29, the album was at the NPG Music Club's Musicology Download Store, along with *The Chocolate Invasion* and *The Slaughterhouse*. On April 19 in the United Kingdom and April 20 in the United States, fully outfitted CDs hit retail. This version includes twelve songs

Prince released three albums on March 29, 2004, but only focused on the new-material *Musicology* LP on the *Musicology Live 2004ever* tour. The tour was among Prince's longest (ninety-six shows) and most successful (almost $90 million) and was his last extended traditional tour of the United States.   *(Author's collection)*

plus a "Musicology" video track. The retail album was released on Columbia Records, Prince's first distribution deal with a major label since 1999's Arista debacle. Aided by the free concert copies, *Musicology* hit number three on the pop charts and number one on the R&B charts, staying afloat for twenty-six weeks and thirty-eight weeks, respectively. *Billboard* and bean-counting company Nielsen SoundScan soon announced that free concert CDs would no longer count toward the charts.

The album produced three singles, although by this point, the concept of a single is rather fluid. The first single is the LP version of "Musicology," released as a physical CD in the United Kingdom with "On the Couch" as a B-side. It was also released as a CD-R promo with three edit mixes. Online, the single included a virtual B-side, "Magnificent." The album version of "Cinnamon Girl" was the second single in both countries. In the United States, it appeared on CD with its video and "Cinnamon Girl: Xposed (Making of The Video)." "United States of Division" was the virtual B-side and one of four tracks on the UK CD. In addition to the studio version of "Cinnamon Girl," the UK disc included "Dear Mr. Man (Live at Webster Hall)" and its video.

The third single was the US-only promo of "Call My Name (Single Version)," "backed" with another virtual B-side: "Silver Tongue." "Call My Name" was also released in a "DLM Mix" on CD-R, presumably the work of someone at the Belgian Studio. "Call My Name" hit number twenty-seven on the R&B/hip-hop singles and airplay charts and won a Grammy Award for Best Male R&B Vocal Performance.

An Italian-free "What Do U Want Me 2 Do" was available online in 2003.

Prince performed seven Hit N Run–type shows in the winter of 2004 before *Musicology Live 2004ever* opened March 27. The tour lasted ninety-six shows, two short of *Purple Rain*'s ninety-eight, ending on September 11. It was the last major full-scale tour Prince would mount. The tour marked the end of the John Blackwell and Rhonda Smith NPG rhythm section although not Prince's association with either artist.

Unlike the more challenging *One Nite Alone* tour, *Musicology* was a treat for casual fans. The shows opened with a recording of Alicia Keys's Prince Rock and Roll Hall of Fame induction speech, which was followed by a two-hour-plus celebration of Prince's long musical history. "Musicology" and "Life 'O' the Party" were the only new songs played at almost every show, with "On the Couch" figuring in about half. Other new songs played occasionally during the tour include "A Million Days," "Call My Name," and "Dear. Mr. Man."

Two songs were played live twice. "Reflection" was performed on *Tavis Smiley* and in June 2007 at the Hollywood Roosevelt Hotel. "Illusion, Coma, Pimp & Circumstance" was played at an October 2003 Hong Kong aftershow and on June 17, 2004, at Paisley Park. This sizzles, highlighted by Mike Philips's scorching vocoder romp. This show was one of three shows that would mark Prince's last live appearances at Paisley Park until October 24, 2009. Four songs were never performed live: "Cinnamon Girl," "What Do U Want Me 2 Do?" (thankfully), "The Marrying Kind," and "If Eye Was the Man in Ur Life."

The comic/improv tour pieces, variously named "Telemarketer Blues," "Bill Collector Blues," "The Rules," and "12:01," have never surfaced in a studio version. Prince inserted snatches of "The Ballad of Jed Clampett" (aka "The *Beverly Hillbillies* Theme") into the set, and this makes sense. You can hear echoes of Perry Botkin Sr.'s beautiful jazz sound track work from the first years of the TV show on *Xpectation*, and Prince would soon become a Beverly Hillbilly himself.

The Chocolate Invasion: Trax from the NPG Music Club Volume One (2004)

The Slaughterhouse: Trax from the NPG Music Club Volume Two (2004)

The two *Trax from the NPG Music Club* albums were released as NPG Music Club downloads on March 29, 2004. They're compilations of 2001–2002 online tracks, often in slightly altered form. NPG Music Club members already had access to most of the songs as part of the $100 yearly "admission" fee, but the LPs were newly assembled and available to the public through the Musicology Download Store at a price of $9.99 per disc. Neither album was available in physical form, but both were available on Tidal starting on December 3, 2015.

The songs are primarily Prince solo songs recorded from 1998 to 2001. The compilations lack internal coherence, with the twenty-one songs primarily castoffs from more fully realized unreleased projects. *High* was completed on

August 8, 2000, and some version of all ten intended tracks show up here. *Peace* was billed as a forthcoming NPG album on the 2001 "Peace" single.

Both *The Chocolate Invasion* and *The Slaughterhouse* were tapped for the never-released seven-disc *Chocolate Invasion* set, along with *One Nite Alone, C-Note*, *Xpectation*, "The War," and the ten-track *Glam Slam Club Mix* (NPG Ahdio Show #11 in January 2001). They are the third and fourth collections of unreleased archival recordings, following *Crystal Ball* and *The Vault*.

Neither album has a personality distinct from the other, although *The Slaughterhouse* is a bit more loose and groovy and lyrically tends to be a bit more bitter and political. Musically, the collections steer clear of the more organic R&B of *Musicology*, definite products of studio work trending more toward the electronic, programmed sounds of the second and third NPG "solo" albums. They're not masterpieces, but they're more rewarding than *Musicology*.

The Chocolate Invasion

The centerpiece of *The Chocolate Invasion* is "Judas Smile," a rocking dance screed against the music industry. Other highlights include the ballads "When Eye Lay My Hands on U" and "Underneath the Cream" and the gospel-ish duet with Angie Stone "U Make My Sun Shine." The more dance-oriented numbers, such as "Sexmesexmenot" and "High," tend to be a bit long in the tooth. And "Vavoom" isn't "Cream" or even "Baby Knows."

Two singles were associated with *The Chocolate Invasion*. A "U Make My Sun Shine" edit was released as a download on December 21, 2000, and as a physical CD on April 10, 2001, backed with "When Will We B Paid." The song hit number fifty-nine on the singles charts and number fifty-three on the R&B charts. The full-length version of the A-side appears on *The Chocolate Invasion*, and the B-side remains uncollected. "Supercute" backed with "Underneath the Cream" was sold as a physical CD at 2001 shows. All four of these songs were originally intended for *High*.

Alternate NPG Music Club versions of three songs exist: "Judas Smile," "Sexmesexmenot" as "Sex Me Sex Me Not," and "Vavoom," here with extra vocals. "The Dance," rerecorded for *3121*, was pulled from the album for the Tidal stream, replaced by "My Medallion."

Only four of the ten *The Chocolate Invasion* songs were played live, all less than a dozen times: "Vavoom," "When Eye Lay My Hands on U," "The Dance," and "U Make My Sun Shine."

The Slaughterhouse

The closest thing to a home run here is "Northside," a nice piece of mid-1970s Stevie Wonder pop. Many tunes encourage you to get freaky and let your head bop, including "S&M Groove," "Silicon," "2045: Radical Man," and "Props N Pounds," the last three railing against differing forms of systemic injustice. The lighter songs here are open and dreamy, including "Golden Parachute" and the slightly more driven "Hypnoparadise"—nothing groundbreaking but all listenable.

Two singles were associated *The Slaughterhouse*, both credited to the NPG. The LP versions of "Peace" and "2045: Radical Man" were paired on a CD first sold at a 2001 Atlanta Hit N Run show. "Peace" was part of NPG Music Club #1, and the B-side first appeared on the September 2000 sound track to Spike Lee's *Bamboozled*. "The Daisy Chain," backed with *The Chocolate Invasion*'s "Gamillah," was also sold on CD at the Atlanta show. The A-side was available online in alternate, video form on March 22, 2001.

Half the songs here are altered from their original online release. "Silicon" is an edit of the NPG Music Club #11 version. "S&M Groove," featuring Marva King on vocals, is an edit/remix of the NPG Music Club #6 version. "Golden Parachute" is slightly different than the version on NPG Music Club #7 version. Different versions of "Props N' Pounds" are found here and on NPG Ahdio Show #4. The most radically different is the LP version of "Northside," preceded by an instrumental version found on NPG Ahdio Show #9.

Three songs were never played live: "Silicon," "S&M Groove," and "Props N' Pounds." Five were only played once: "Peace" on May 20, "Golden Parachute" on July 8, and "Y Should Eye Do That When Eye Can Do This?" on July 15, all in 2000 at Paisley Park; "Hypnoparadise" was played completely on December 27, 1998, in Cologne, Germany, and "2045: Radical Man" showed up at the epic July 23, 2010, New Morning show in Paris. "The Daisy Chain" was played twice in 2001, including a twenty-minute version on April 29 at the Fillmore in San Francisco. "Northside" was the most enduring song, appearing about a dozen times between 2000 and 2015.

27

Everybody Keeps Tryin' 2 Break My Heart

Rifts, Rivals, and Lovers

I n "All the Midnights in the World," Prince bemoans "those prickly fingered scallywags" who are jealous of his latest relationship. This chapter covers both the scallywags and the relationships, with the latter serving as a brief but necessary antidote to the nastiness of the former.

Rivals and Rifts

Rick James

"The Battle of Funk" tour pitted established R&B heavyweight Rick James against concert novice Prince. James had seen it all—army desertion, Motown contract, not getting killed by Charles Manson—and had finally achieved chart success. But he hadn't seen Prince. James held court early in the tour as the conservative US South reacted negatively to Prince's mixed-race band and his bikini briefs. But Prince volleyed by giving the audience what they wanted. He put Gayle Chapman in a nightgown. Matt Fink became Dr. Fink. In a twist straight out of *Glee*, Prince made the headliner's moves his own to make it look like James was copying him. Prince perfected his stagecraft with high-energy shows, while James's indulgent, drug-fueled performances lagged. Decision: Prince. Backstage, there were confrontations between James and Andre Cymone, sit-downs to clear the air, and James forcing cognac into Prince's mouth, but the tour ended with nothing more than hard feelings. Those hard feelings almost resulted in James assaulting Prince at a 1982 American Music Awards aftershow when Prince refused an autograph for James's mom. This was also the night that Prince met Denise Matthews, aka Vanity, who had been dating James. James never got over Prince's success and seemed to compensate by calling him a "little bitch" whenever possible. James died of heart failure in 2004.

Paisley Park Enterprises

MEMORANDUM

TO: *All PPE Employees*

FROM: *J. Carr*

DATE: *November 1, 1993*

RE: **ART DEPARTMENT (We now have one!)**

Jeff Munson and Chuck Hermes will be handling as many of our needs as possible "in-house." Please contact either one of them if you have a project that requires their assistance. Furthermore, the use of any outside printers, designers, etc. should be coordinated through them, so the use of outside services is properly managed.

FYI
(I have noticed several invoices come through for very basic office needs, such as the printing of purchase orders, fax cover sheets, and so forth, that were ordered through very expensive advertising companies, etc., instead of an office supply company).

JC/mrh

jcm-091

Paisley Park Enterprises endured multiple administrative changes in the early 1990s, but according to some insiders, often no one was in charge. In late 1993, Chief Financial Officer Jennifer Carr attempted to rein in spending across the organization, but when Prince heard "no" in response to a financial request, he simply found some other way to fund his project.

(Courtesy Jeff Munson)

The Time

Prince loved *The Godfather* and its behind-the-scenes boss pulling the strings of success. But his relationship with The Time was less Don Corleone and more Victor Frankenstein, Bobby Z. noting that he made a creature "he could no longer control." The major beef between Prince and The Time was about creative freedom: they had none. Prince almost single-handedly wrote, produced, and played on The Time's studio songs, while the band members were hired hands who played the songs live, opening for Prince. Often, they'd contribute a lick to a song and receive no songwriting credit. They needed more. Everything came to a head in 1983 on the *1999* tour. Jimmy Jam and Terry Lewis began a successful production company and missed a tour date. Prince fined them $3,000 each. Resentment followed. At the last show in Cincinnati, Ohio, Prince's band threw eggs at The Time and captured Jerome Benton, slathering him with honey and pelting him with garbage. After the show, Prince's bodyguard Chick Huntsberry handcuffed Jesse Johnson to a radiator, and Prince threw food at him. The Time retaliated, throwing eggs at Prince's band onstage. The battle continued at the hotel, where the bands' managers tried to diffuse the situation by providing ammunition: cream pies. Hotel rooms were damaged, and Prince made Morris Day pay. Jam and Lewis were fired at the tour's end, in part for their infraction, in part because they were offering Prince legitimate stage competition. Amazingly, Jesse Johnson hung around for a while, but, feeling slighted artistically and economically and believing that Prince's tendency was to "discourage people," he left in 1984. Day left in 1984 in search of more money, and the band totally dissolved. Prince leveraged a reformed Time to get financing for *Graffiti Bridge*, but the same creative tensions arose, and the band split again.

Parent's Music Resource Center

Before her husband Al Gore made it his mission to save the planet, Tipper Gore wanted to save America's youth. She cofounded the Parents Music Research Center, a group designed to let parents know that pop music was leading their kids straight to Hell. The center's opening salvo was the "Filthy Fifteen," a 1985 list of the most sexual, violent, and drug-addled songs. Prince claimed the top two spots—"Darling Nikki" and Sheena Easton's "Sugar Walls"—and Tipper singled out the *Purple Rain* song for its embarrassing and vulgar lyrics. The list developed into congressional hearings, dominated by musician Frank Zappa (Prince connection: Dale Bozzio was in his band). The hearings developed into "parental advisory" stickers. Although major retailer Walmart wouldn't carry albums with the sticker, warnings did more to fine-tune than discourage youth music purchases. And, according to Bob Cavallo, "bad publicity" was good for Prince. Gore won in the end, as Prince eventually stopped swearing and toned down more sexually provocative lyrics.

"We Are the World"

Prince ruled the January 28, 1985, American Music Awards, winning three awards and unleashing a monster "Purple Rain." But he declined the invitation to sing on the star-studded USA for Africa "We Are the World" recording after the Los Angeles show. He offered to play guitar but was rebuked. Prince believed that his album contribution of "4 the Tears in Your Eyes" and his reluctance to sing in large groups would be enough. He was wrong. A backlash ensued in the press, and Prince was the bad guy who didn't care about starving kids. Part of the bad press was that his bodyguard Chick Huntsberry threw a photographer out of Prince's limo outside a Mexican restaurant at the same time as the recording. Huntsberry quit after the incident, one of many overzealous encounters. Huntsberry surfaced a few months later with the tell-all *National Enquirer* exposé "The Real Prince: He's Trapped in a Bizarre Secret World of Terror," and Prince wrote the "Pop Life" B-side "Hello" in response to the whole disheartening experience. Prince held a benefit show for Huntsberry's family in 1990 after he died without life insurance but refused to sing on a twentieth-anniversary American Music Awards "We Are the World" performance in 1995, preferring to suck on a lollipop.

Prince wrote "Hello" in response to the criticism he received after his failure to participate in the "We Are the World" recording session that took place after the American Music Awards show in January 1985. The song was featured on the B-side of "Pop Life" in the United States and "Raspberry Beret" in Europe, with an extended "Fresh Dance Mix" on the respective twelve-inch versions.   *(Courtesy Ric Dube)*

Michael Jackson

No one got under Prince's skin more than Michael Jackson, and we'll skip this opportunity to talk about Michael's skin. What is known as "the rivalry" often seems more like ego and insecurity on Prince's part, somehow coveting Jackson's larger record sales rather than valuing his own artistic superiority—understandable but a waste of brain space when they were really playing different games.

Some highlights follow.

Jackson tore it up at a 1983 James Brown show and then got Brown to invite Prince onstage. Prince tripped on the stage and looked like a fool. Advantage Jackson. In January 1985, Prince avoided the "We Are the World" recording sessions. Cowritten by Jackson, the song sold more than 20 million copies, and Prince was sold out by his bodyguard. Advantage Jackson. Later that year, Jackson stopped by when Prince was in a Los Angeles studio and got his ass kicked at ping-pong, reportedly playing like "Helen Keller." Advantage Prince?

Jackson producer Quincy Jones brought the duo together in early 1987 to talk about recording "Bad" as a duet, but Prince nixed it, wanting no part of the lyric "Your butt is mine." Prince also said that *Batman* was conceived as a duet between the two. After this point, the rivalry was one-sided, with Prince knocking Jackson in songs such as "My Name Is Prince" and "Life 'O' the Party" and, at a 2006 Las Vegas gig, playing some aggressive bass in Jackson's face. The day after the bass incident, Jackson told his pal will.i.am that Prince was a "big meanie." And he was probably right. Jackson nicknamed his son Prince, which is just weird, and was probably excited about eclipsing Prince's twenty-one shows at the O2 in London with his fifty scheduled for 2009–2010, but he died on June 25, 2009.

Managers

Prince's managers, publicists, and Paisley Park executives typically bore the brunt of the friction between Prince and Warner Bros., blamed for not securing the next album deal or pushing for enough money or publicity or, in the case of Owen Husney, fired because he wouldn't bring Prince a space heater. Combined with his distrust of authority, this led to *Purple Rain* director Albert Magnoli becoming his manager, bodyguard Gilbert Davison becoming head of Paisley Park Enterprises, and bass player Levi Seacer Jr. heading NPG Records. They all left on uneasy terms, and many other administrative types left with lawsuits. The most significant lawsuit was filed by mid-1980s managers Cavallo, Ruffalo, and Fargnoli, who sued in 1991 for $600,000 severance pay and punitive damages, accusing Prince of trying to release too many records in weird ways without supporting the record releases through marketing campaigns. Well, yeah. The suit was settled out of court.

Warner Bros.

As with the Michael Jackson rivalry, the battle between Prince and Warner Bros. can seem one-sided, with Prince constantly kicking at their shins. The genesis of Prince's Warner Bros. problems is probably in 1985's creation of Paisley Park Records, which seemed to give Prince carte blanche to release material at will, and Warner Bros.'s December 1986 refusal to release the three-LP *Crystal Ball*. From that point, Prince was continually in a catch-22 with Warner Bros., arguing to release more mediocre material more frequently rather than saving up good material for more infrequent releases and then complaining that Warner Bros. didn't do enough to promote the inferior material. And it's not vastly inferior material. But if the ten discs of new material released from 1989 to 1996 had been released every other year as four single LPs, we'd be talking about four masterpieces. Not that I mind having all the songs.

But if we push it beyond the early struggles, August 31, 1992, becomes the day of contention, when Prince signed a new contract with Warner Bros. Why sign that contract when you know that there will be trouble going in? Soon, Prince not only wasn't pleased with the amount of material he could release but also wasn't happy with Warner Bros.'s promotion of *Symbol*. And Warner Bros. wasn't happy dumping money into dead-end Paisley Park products like *Carmen Electra* and Eric Leeds's *Times Squared*. On April 27, 1993, announced his retirement and told Warner Bros. they'd receive no new material, and then he changed his name on June 7. He started writing "slave" on his face for public appearances and tried to embarrass Warner Bros. into giving him his freedom. Warner Bros. closed Paisley Park Records on February 1, 1994, but that probably would have happened without the protest, as the business was being run by Prince's bodyguard.

For all of Prince's public protestation, Warner Bros. kept an even keel during the name change period. As Warner Bros. executive Bob Merlis says, "It was not in our interest to be confrontational" with Prince. By October 25, 1994, Prince needed money, and he let Warner Bros. release *"The Black Album"* for $1 million, outside of the contract. On April 26, 1996, the company cut him some slack on his contract, terminating his contract and accepting just two new albums plus two greatest-hits albums to complete the deal. It wasn't until 2014 that he had another new album on Warner Bros. and a deal for control of his back catalog.

Cheryl Johnson

Cheryl Johnson was a Minneapolis gossip columnist who started calling Prince "Symbolina" when he changed his name in 1993. Symbol didn't like the remark and wrote the bitter "Billy Jack Bitch" in response. Prince made fun of other people in his songs, such as manager Bob Cavallo and writer Nelson George in "Bob George," but this was his most forthright attack. Johnson met Prince in 1997, and he called her his "biggest enemy," but he also said she was an old girlfriend and that they'd work together in the future—none of which, according to Johnson, is true. "Billie Jack Bitch" is Johnson's favorite Prince song.

The Internet

Prince had a love/hate relationship with the Internet. On the one hand, it seemed to offer an answer to his independent distribution problems. He even won a Webby Lifetime Achievement Award in 2006 for his visionary use of the Internet. On the other hand, it reified his ultimate fear: not being in control of his music. And, back to the first hand, he could never quite get the distribution model to work efficiently: less than a month after winning the Webby, he shut down his NPG Music Club website, saying it had gone "as far as it can go."

But Prince's biggest online battles were with fans. In 1999, Prince sued unofficial Prince information site *Uptown* and ten other websites for trademark and copyright infringement. Nine of the sites immediately closed shop, but *Uptown* worked with Boston lawyer Alex Hahn, coauthor of *The Rise of Prince: 1958–2016*, to countersue, arguing that Prince's lawsuit stifled fair and protected speech. The suit would have deposed Prince. He backed down and said he only didn't want the sites to discuss bootlegs. *Uptown*'s progeny, princevault. com, still doesn't discuss bootlegs.

On November 5, 2007, he issued cease-and-desist letters to multiple websites over the use of his image. The websites housequake.com, prince.org, and princefams.com formed Prince Fans United (PFU—think about it). Three days later, Prince released his anti-fan response, "PFUnk," later retitled "F.U.N.K." Only prince.org exists today. The same year, Prince and Universal Music filed suit against Stephanie Lenz for using a twenty-nine-second clip of "Let's Go Crazy" in the background of a YouTube clip of her son. That was settled in Lenz's favor in 2015, with Prince enduring eight years of jokes about picking on a two-year-old enjoying his music.

In 2008, he sent off takedown notices for his Coachella performance of "Creep." But he didn't write the song and didn't have the right to remove the clip. Radiohead's singer and writer Thom Yorke told him to "unblock it." In 2014, he sued twenty-two fans for providing online links to bootlegs, a year after suing someone for a six-second Vine. He withdrew the 2014 suits after a public uproar, oddly claiming to the BBC that "nobody sues their fans." Did Prince change his name to "Nobody"? The Prince Estate sued a group of European bootleggers, including the owner of Eye Records, in the fall of 2018.

Just seven years after receiving his Webby for online contributions, Prince was inducted into the Electronic Freedom Foundation's Takedown Hall of Shame with their Raspberry Beret Lifetime Aggrievement Award.

Lovers

Prince was married twice but was connected romantically with more than two dozen other women. There are reports of proposals (Sheila E.) and engagements (Susannah Melvoin), but objectively naming the official status of other people's relationships is a losing game, to paraphrase Amy Winehouse. With that in mind, here's a roughly chronological list of thirty of Prince's significant others. All but the last five also worked professionally with Prince. All these women led robust lives before and after their time with Prince and, outside of this chapter section, can't be reduced to the singular function of "Prince girlfriend."

Wives

> Mayte Garcia—Mayte and Prince were married from 1996 to 2000. She released *Child of the Sun* (1995) and was a member of the NPG, touring and appearing on multiple mid-1990s Prince albums.
>
> Manuela Testolini—Canadian businesswoman Testolini was married to Prince from December 31, 2001, until May 2006. She married singer Eric Benet in 2011.

Significant Others

- Patrice Rushen—Keyboardist on "Baby"; Prince had a crush on her and wrote "I Wanna Be Your Lover" for her, but they never dated.
- Susan Moonsie—Vanity 6 and Apollonia 6 singer. Prince wrote "Private Joy" for her.
- Vanity (Denise Matthews)—Singer/actress who released *Vanity 6*.
- Jill Jones—Singer who released *Jill Jones*; inspired "She's Always in My Hair."
- Apollonia Kotero—Singer who released *Apollonia 6*; Prince wrote "This Could Be Us" about her.
- Susannah Hoffs—The Bangles singer received "Manic Monday" as a gift in 1984.
- Madonna—She's Madonna. Their first date was at a 1985 Prince Los Angeles Forum show. After they broke up, she referred to Prince as a "little troll."
- Sheena Easton—Singer who appears on "U Got the Look." She recorded numerous Prince originals.
- Susannah Melvoin—Singer-songwriter and twin sister of Revolution guitarist Wendy Melvoin. She appears on multiple mid-1980s recordings, and at least three songs are known to be inspired by her: "Nothing Compares 2 U," "Empty Room," and "Wally."
- Cat Glover—Dancer/singer who toured with Prince in the late 1980s and appears on *Lovesexy*.

- Sheila E.—Prince drummer and solo artist. Prince proposed to her during a "Purple Rain" performance in 1987.
- Ingrid Chavez—Poet/talker who appeared in *Graffiti Bridge* and released *May 19 1992*.
- Kim Basinger—Actress who appears on 1989's "The Scandalous Sex Suite."
- Anna Fantastic (Anna Garcia)—Actress who inspired "Rave Un2 the Joy Fantastic" and sings sampled vocals on "Partyman."
- Troy Beyer—Actress who appears in the "Sexy M.F." and *3 Chains O' Gold* videos and sings Spanish vocals on Mayte's "Baby Don't Care."
- Carmen Electra (Tara Leigh Patrick)—Singer who released *Carmen Electra*.
- Nona Gaye—Singer and model who appeared live with Prince in the mid-1990s and on studio songs, including "Love Sign" and "Acknowledge Me."
- Vanessa Marcil—Actress who appears in *The Undertaker*.
- Ananda Lewis—MTV veejay who appeared onstage at the December 18, 1999, Paisley Park recording for *Rave Un2 the Year 2000*.
- Bria Valente—Released *Elixir* and packaged with *Lotusflow3r* and *MPLSound*.
- Misty Copeland—Ballet dancer who appeared in the "Crimson and Clover" video and guested at 2010 shows.
- Damaris Lewis—Dancer/model who never dated Prince but served as his "Black Muse."
- Judith Hill—Singer-songwriter who released *Back in Time*.
- Sherilyn Fenn—*Twin Peaks* actress from in the mid-1980s who was at the infamous Michael Jackson ping-pong match.
- Devin DeVasquez—*Playboy* centerfold from the mid-1980s.
- Tatiana Thumbtzen—Actress in Michael Jackson's "The Way You Make Me Feel video" who dated Prince in 1989.
- Heidi Mark—Actress and ex-wife of Mötley Crüe's Vince Neil in 1991.
- Delilah—British singer whom Prince discovered on YouTube in 2012.

28

Daddy Pop Is the Writer

Covers of Prince Songs

Prince songwriting falls broadly into three categories: songs he wrote for himself, those for associated artists (such Vanity #6), and those for outside acts (such as the Bangles). This chapter looks at songs he wrote for himself that others covered and generally studio rather than live versions.

In a 2011 George Lopez interview, Prince claimed that when songs were covered, the originals no longer existed. His main beef seemed to be with the fact that when a song such as "I Feel for You" was mentioned, fans were more likely to think of Chaka Khan than him. So, this is a list of songs that no longer exist in the original form.

"When You Were Mine": Bette Bright and the Illuminations (1981)

Bette Bright's and the Illuminations's 1981 "When You Were Mine" is both the earliest Prince cover and the version that best highlights the original's New Waviness. The song's been covered often. The best-known versions are Cyndi Lauper's and Mitch Ryder's, both radio hits from 1983. The most unsettling variation goes to Lambchop's 2017 version, which turns the tune into Bryan Ferry on auto-tune.

"How Come You Don't Call Me Anymore": Stephanie Mills (1983)

This 1982 "1999" B-side became Stephanie Mills's second single from her self-titled 1983 solo release. Mills brings a fuller sound to the piano ballad and highlights the gospel undertones, more a lamentation of empowerment than melancholy. It bests the better-known 2001 Alicia Keys version, retitled "How Come You Don't Call Me," which is more about Keys and her talents than it is about the song.

"Purple Rain": Denice Brooks (1984)

Denice Brooks began the "Purple Rain" deluge with an unremarkable European single soon after the song's debut. Over the years, the song became one of Prince's most covered tunes, performed by everyone from blues legend Etta James to unexpected country star Darius Rucker to parody king Big Daddy. After Prince's death, "Purple Rain" became the National Anthem of Prince, with artists from Bruce Springsteen to low-fi all-star Sufjan Stevens to country icon Dwight Yoakam paying tribute.

"I Feel for You": Chaka Khan (1984)

While Prince was riding high in 1984 with *Purple Rain*, Warner Bros. and super producers Arif Marden and David Foster relaunched Chaka Khan's career (something Prince would try to do again next decade). The strategy was to tap a tune from the biggest artist and hook the tune into the hottest trend: rap. Thus, the fall of 1984 saw the release of Khan's "I Feel for You" with rapping by Grandmaster Melle Mel and harmonica by Stevie Wonder. And the video had a lot of break dancing! The result borders on novelty, but no one can ever unhear either Melle Mel's introduction or Stevie's solos. The song hit number three on the *Billboard* Hot 100 and number one on the dance and black charts and won Prince a songwriting Grammy.

The Pointer Sisters beat everyone else to "I Feel for You," offering a workable R&B version of the song on their 1982 LP *I'm So Excited*. Strangely, while the album also contained the hit title song, which went to number thirty, it didn't contain the big-hit version, which showed up the next year on *Break Out*, hitting number nine. *Break Out* also included the hit "Automatic," which Prince liberally borrowed for *20Ten*'s "Lavaux," although one could argue that "Automatic" liberally borrowed from Prince in the first place.

The less said about Rebbie Jackson's 1984 version, the better.

"Let's Pretend We're Married": Tina Turner (1985)

Tina Turner owns this song like she owns the Rolling Stones's "Honky Tonk Women." In both cases, she flips the tables on the guys and takes control, not afraid to lead with her hips rather than her heart. This pulsing live version gets by mostly on bombast, and that's not bad. It was recorded in 1984 during her wildly successful *Private Dancer* tour, the B-side of the LP's sixth(!) single. Turner also covered "Baby I'm a Star," most notably in a 2000 Target ad.

"Kiss": Age of Chance (1987)

Mid-1980s bands were quick to jump on the Prince hit train, and multiple versions of "Kiss" sprang up soon after the song's release. The UK indie Age of Chance struck first with a geeky industrial-light version featuring jerky, Johnny Lydon–like vocals. The Art of Noise ran with the same basic premise, adding legendary singer Tom Jones to the mix in a 1988 release that hit number thirty-one on the US charts. Other notable versions of "Kiss" include the 1987 release from Italian bombshell Sabrina, which is at best tuneless; the Nicole Kidman and Hugh Jackman version from 2006's *Happy Feet*; and Matthew Morrison and Gwyneth Paltrow's version from the 2011 "Sexy" episode of *Glee*. At some point, the song became a duet.

"Sign 'o' the Times": Billy Cobham (1987)

Jazz drummer Billy Cobham copped "Sign 'o' the Times" for his 1987 LP *Picture This*. Although drums are expectedly more forward and the production is lighter, this could easily be mistaken for a Madhouse outtake. Cobham was on Prince's jazz radar for his work in the early 1970s with Miles Davis and as a member of fusion powerhouse Mahavishnu Orchestra. Prince covered Cobham's "Stratus," from 1973's *Spectrum*, from January 2007 on.

Simple Minds released a version in 1989 that emphasized the song's fragmented, electronic nature, severely damaged by Jim Kerr's unintentionally disjointed vocals, while Minneapolis trio Arcwelder put out a quick funk version in 1992 as a B-side to "I Am the Walrus." It sounds like what Zappa might have done with the song.

The other important version is Nina Simone's. I would call Simone a jazz singer, but to categorize her is to fail to do her justice: She is simply Nina Simone. As with any tune, she makes "Sign 'o' the Times" her own, singing, talking, and phrasing in a way that convinces the listener she's reporting her own life, interpreting idiosyncratically on piano while cleverly orchestrated like a blaxploitation theme song.

"Batdance": Allen Toussaint Orchestra (1989)

Multiple LPs were issued in Europe the late 1980s under the Allen Toussaint Orchestra name, but it's unclear that the New Orleans music legend had anything to do with the music. In this case, we're treated to a musically competent note-for-note version of "Batdance." The song comes from 1989's *20 Superhero Themes*, hoping to cash in on Batmania. Prince did a few live mentions of

Toussaint's "Yes We Can Can" and included his "Country John" and "Back in Baby's Arms" on his *New Girl* house-party play list.

"The Black Album": The Black Album Band (1989)

Soon after Prince canceled the December 1987 *The Black Album* release, cassette copies flooded the secondary market. One copy made its way to Ralf Thomas. Thomas pulled together a group and banged out a rough approximation of *The Black Album*, releasing the record in Europe on his maybe legal TNT Enterprises label. The record fooled many consumers, at least until the colored disc hit the turntable.

"Pray": MC Hammer (1990)

No, not a cover but the first song that legally samples Prince. It's unclear why the "When Doves Cry" sample was needed unless Hammer was afraid listeners would get bored with hearing "pray" repeated 110 times during the five-minute song. There's no truth to the rumor that Prince waived his licensing fee in exchange for letting Tony M. raid Hammer's closet. Prince has since been sampled hundreds of times by artists ranging from Public Enemy to Kanye West to Justin Timberlake.

Ginuwine's 1996 "When Doves Cry" doesn't mess with the song's DNA as much as perform minor cosmetic surgery (altering the lyrics, to Prince's chagrin). Ginuwine gave the song a bland, mid-1990s light reggae treatment made popular by Big Mountain's 1994 cover of "Baby I Love Your Way." Patti Smith's 2002 version sounds like nothing so much as Patti Smith covering "When Doves Cry."

"Raspberry Beret": Hindu Love Gods (1990)

Hip, drunken cover songs were all the rage for late-1980s college rock bands, with Minneapolis's Replacements pioneering the genre (track down their "I Could Never Take the Place of Your Man"). In early 1987, R.E.M. guitarist Peter Buck, bassist Mike Mills, and drummer Bill Berry were recording singer Warren Zevon's *Sentimental Hygiene* when they set to tape a night of drunken revelry. The resulting ten cover songs were released in 1990 as *Hindu Love Gods*. "Raspberry Beret" is brash and unsubtle, lending support to the "drunk" angle.

"1999": Big Audio Dynamite II (1990)

Singer/guitarist Mick Jones formed Big Audio Dynamite in 1984 after leaving/getting fired from seminal English punks The Clash. While Joe Strummer's remaining group limped along for one last album of croaking, stale punk, Jones's Big Audio Dynamite innovated for the better part of a decade, merging rock, rap, funk, and electronica. This expansive, keys-and-guitar version of "1999" comes from the band's live promo disc *Ally Pally Paradiso*. The disc was available as a free mail-in from UK music magazine *New Musical Express* (who would give away an LP with a publication?).

Some Prince/Clash notes: The Clash was heavily involved in London's late 1970s rude boy culture, musically a mix of English rock and Jamaican roots/reggae. They starred in (but eventually disowned) the 1980 film *Rude Boy*. Prince wore a two-tone rude boy pin on the cover of *Controversy*. Around the same time, the Clash fought their record company, CBS, because they were releasing too much music. In December 1979, they released the nineteen-track, two-LP *London Calling* for the price of one LP. In September 1980, they released a budget-priced ten-track disc: *Black Market Clash*. And in December 1980, they released their magnum opus (and many critics' pick as the best album of the 1980s): the thirty-six-track, three-disc *Sandinista!* What artist in their right mind would release six discs of new material in one calendar year? In 2014, Prince returned the "1999" favor, covering Jones's Clash classic "Train in Vain" at a few shows.

"U Got the Look": Gary Numan (1992)

Gary Numan hit big in 1979 with "Cars." Musically, its punk-influenced, keyboard-central, beat-heavy New Wave sound helped pave the way for *Dirty Mind*, *Controversy*, and *1999*. But vocally, Numan was about as warm as those Minnesota winters Prince claimed kept the bad people away. That shtick holds in this "U Got the Look" cover—fairly funky, famously unfriendly. The LP *Machine + Soul* also includes "1999."

In 1999, "U Got the Look" was part of the Cleopatra collection *Party O' the Times (A Tribute to Prince)*. This unholy thirteen-track collection gathers the house, techno, and hip-hop versions of Prince songs that fans had never been clamoring for. Most recordings are little more than excuses for the artists to explore their own tendencies, such as Ice-T's "Head" and Sigue Sigue Sputnik's "I Could Never Take the Place of Your Man." But Dead or Alive, best known for "You Spin Me Round (Like a Record)," really makes "Pop Life" work, sounding a bit like what a not-for-laughs Weird Al version would sound like. Prince worked with two here. Dale Bozzio and Missing Persons show up with a remix misfire of "I Would Die 4 U," and Buddy Miles, who joined Prince onstage a few times, comes out of left field with a country blues reading of "Baby I'm a Star."

"If I Was Your Girlfriend": TLC (1994)

TLC was the protégé act Prince probably wishes he created. Instead, the trio worked for producer L. A. Reid, whose sound Prince had been chasing for half the decade by 1994. Oozing well-crafted, contemporary R&B goodness, TLC ruled the mid-1990s with their second LP, *CrazySexyCool*, selling more than 7 million copies. The group's "If I Was Your Girlfriend" sticks close to the Camille original but benefits from the female harmonies. Both of the two big hits from the disc—"Creep" and the gorgeous "Waterfalls"—purposefully sound like late 1980s Prince to the point that the latter is often mistaken as a Prince original. Prince incorporated "Waterfalls" into "Letitgo" at an August 5, 1995, Paisley Park show and joined the trio on guitar on "No Scrubs" on January 21, 2000, at Madison Square Garden. He also identified with TLC's legal battle with their former manager, bankruptcy laws, and their record company (Prince's future bedfellow Arista), announcing "Free TLC" on a 1996 appearance on *The Late Show*.

"Alphabet Street": Jesus and Mary Chain (1994)

Jesus and Mary Chain hit the UK charts and US college radio when Prince was collecting award hardware for *Purple Rain*. The group made their name by writing effortless pop tunes and drenching them in the waves of grinding noise and feedback. Their 1994 cover of "Alphabet Street" follows this pattern, which, surprisingly, doesn't get old. Indie darling Sufjan Stevens included a brief, computer-heavy version on his 2012 collection *Silver & Gold: Songs for Christmas, Vols. 6–10*. Nothing really says Christmas about "Alphabet St.," but it works.

"Jack U Off": Pansy Division (1995)

Founded in 1991, Pansy Division was the first openly gay rock band. Their punkish music addresses LGBT issues in a self-knowing and usually humorous light. Their biggest success was a 1994 tour with Green Day. The band unwinds the rockabilly twist of "Jack U Off" into something almost cow punk and reimagines the lyrics in a more typical gender usage of the title term. Why the band left "I Love U in Me" on the table I'll never know. "Jack U Off" is found on the band's compilation album *Pile On*, which includes catchy originals, such as "Homo Christmas," and an array of fascinating covers, including Spinal Tap's "Big Bottom," Joe Jackson's "Real Men," and a rewritten Nirvana tune: "Smells Like Queer Spirit."

"Thieves in the Temple": Herbie Hancock (1995)

Keyboard legend Herbie Hancock strips away the fussy New Jack *Graffiti Bridge* production from "Thieves in the Temple" and reimagines the song as a jazz standard. Flanked by Michael Brecker on tenor sax and Jack DeJohnette on drums, it works as an instant instrumental classic, luscious at well over seven minutes. At least two other jazz versions followed this, and jazz/funk interpretations of Prince tunes proliferated, such as Marcus Miller's 2005 "Girls and Boys" featuring Macy Gray.

"The Cross": Laibach (1996)

Slovenian industrial band Laibach made its name as social disruptors in mid-1980s Yugoslavia. They first attracted US attention in 1998 with a cover of the Beatles's *Let It Be*. Their slow, menacing version of "The Cross," with a video of Jesus weighted down by a commercialized crucifix, appears on their ironic 1996 effort *Jesus Christ Superstars*. Many artists over the years have covered the simple song with more traditional gospel interpretations.

"Erotic City": Arto Lindsay (1997)

Experimental artist/guitarist Arto Lindsay recorded "Erotic City" for his 1997 LP *Mundo Civilizado*. Featuring funk legend Bernie Worrell on organ, Lindsay deconstructs the song, turning it into a bossa nova dreamland punctuated by "Sign 'o' the Times" martial drums. "Erotic City" started life as a George Clinton tribute of sorts, written after Prince went to a Parliament/Funkadelic gig. Clinton took it back in 1994 for the sound track to the thankfully forgotten film *PCU*. Clinton's version is competent but mainly makes you miss the original.

In 1998 Yo La Tengo bassist James McNew released *That Skinny Motherfucker with the High Voice?*, a seven-track cassette of Prince covers by his one-man side project Dump. Three years later he expanded the set to a twelve-track CD, maintaining the "Bob George" quote in the title. McNew's project is one of the most interesting and ambitious Prince cover projects, reimagining standards ("1999," "Pop Life") and obscurities ("An Honest Man," "Another Lonely Christmas") alike.

(Courtesy Ric Dube)

That Skinny Motherfucker with the High Voice: Dump (1998/2001)

Dump's twelve-track CD of mid-1980s Prince songs is the Valhalla of Prince covers. Dump was a side project for James NcNew, bassist for indie-rock giants Yo La Tengo. In 1998, he didn't want to lose his own songs while testing new recording equipment, so he set down four-tracks of Prince songs culled from a bootleg compilation. The songs are breezy, unpretentious, and often poignant, wringing a melancholy and longing that's just under the surface of many mid-1980s Prince tunes. The highlights are a swirling, sample-heavy "Dirty Mind"; a punk/New Wave "Erotic City" (think Devo's "Uncontrollable Urge"); and "Another Lonely Christmas" reimagined as a Neil Young anthem.

"Peach": Rod Stewart (2001)

I love "Peach" even though (or because) it's one of Prince's stupidest songs. But Rod Stewart's version dumbs it down a notch, erasing any hint of irony or humor or fun. The song intrigues with Slash on guitar but puzzles with a

Sínéad O'connor

I do not want what I haven't got.

Irish singer Sinead O'Connor topped the charts worldwide in 1990 with Prince's "Nothing Compares 2 U," her only US top 40 single from her only US number one album. Originally released by The Family in 1985, Prince offered a live duet with Rosie Gaines on *The Hits / The B-Sides* in 1993. Prince's 1984 original version was released as a single in 2018 and turned up on *Originals* (2019). (Author's collection)   *(Author's collection)*

Stewart vocal that recalls Stephanie Mills with strep throat. While "Peach" will never enter the Great American Songbook, Stewart covered a possible entry, "Nothing Compares 2 U," live.

"Darling Nikki": Foo Fighters (2003)

Dave Grohl's Foo Fighters snuck "Darling Nikki" onto 2003's "Have It All" CD single. While the A-side did little, the Prince song hit number fifteen on the alternative songs chart. In a 2004 *Entertainment Weekly* interview, Prince was angry about the cover, telling Grohl to "write your own tunes." Prince felt he "got back" at the Foos by covering "Best of You" at the 2007 Super Bowl, but it's unclear if they put the double jinx on him by performing "Darling Nikki" in September 2007 at the MTV Video Music Awards, with CeeLo Green on lead. Prince and Grohl jammed before a 2011 Prince gig, but nothing more came of the meeting except a long, enjoyable Grohl story about the meeting that can be found online.

"Walk Don't Walk": Robert Randolph and the Family Band (2011)

With few exceptions, artists have covered Prince hits. Robert Randolph and the Family Band turned off this path with their 2011 cover of "Walk Don't Walk." This version doesn't lean much on Randolph's famous pedal steel guitar but does highlight the female vocals of the original. This track is also noteworthy because it was produced by Lenny Waronker, the A&R man instrumental in convincing Warner Bros. to sign Prince in 1977 and thrown out of the studio by Prince for suggesting more bass on "So Blue." By 1984, Waronker was copresident of the company, overseeing the release of *Purple Rain*.

29

U Can Let Ur Hair Down

Mid-2000s LPs

Like 1996 and 1999, 2005 was a transition year for Prince. Prince wrapped up the *Musicology* Live 2004ever tour on September 11. The most successful tour of the year and the longest of his career, it marked the end of Prince's extensive multiple-city tours. Future (baby) tours would focus on either residencies or briefer excursions, such as the seven-date 20Ten tour.

What happened between September 2004 and the January 2006 Tamar tour is at best murky. We know Prince rented Beverly Hills and West Hollywood mansions, transforming them into "3121" residences and throwing $50,000 parties. In between these Los Angeles adventures, his marriage with Manuela hit the wall as evidenced by the fact that he locked her out of the Chanhassen house in May 2005 and cut her off financially. She would file for divorce in May 2006. There are also rumors the Prince had a hip replaced, but this has never been confirmed.

Musically, in November 2004, Prince revived the New Power Trio with Michael B. and Sonny T., recording songs that would give him the title track for his next LP and five songs for 2009's *MPLSound*. During 2005 and into 2006, he recorded the rest of *3121* and Tamar's still-unreleased *Milk & Honey* LP.

In terms of public music engagement, 2005 was dry. In Los Angeles, he presented Album of the Year on February 13 at the Grammys and performed at the Thirty-Sixth NAACP Image Awards on March 19. After these types of events, he hosted parties and played in-home shows featuring celebrities including Justin Timberlake and Stevie Wonder. These were his only live appearances of the year.

By this point, NPG Music Club releases almost seemed by error. "S.S.T." and "Brand New Orleans" were released on September 3 in response to Hurricane Katrina. On December 13, "Te Amo Corazon" was released as a download and a week later as a CD single, distributed by Universal, Prince's new strange bedfellow. One year, three songs.

Prince started 2006 with the passive-aggressive move of touring as a sideman for Tamar on a baker's dozen of *Milk & Honey* shows from January through March. In the midst of these dates, the two performed "Fury" and "Beautiful, Loved and Blessed" on *Saturday Night Live*. After about seventeen months out of the spotlight, this performance would mark the beginning of about nineteen months back in the public gaze.

3121 (2006)

Prince released 3121 on March 31, 2006, on NPG/Universal. It shot to number one its first week of release, his first album to do so and his first number one since *Batman*. It also hit number one on the R&B charts. It is his last release of new material to go gold in the United States.

Willy Wonka (ah, Prince) included "Purple Tickets" in the first pressings, entitling the receiver to an all-expenses-paid trip to the 3121 residence for a concert on May 6. When Augustus Gloop and others failed to locate these tickets in time, secondary lotteries ensured a full house although not a full stomach, as a reported meal turned out to be just appetizers. It's unclear if any of the attendees were turned into giant blueberries, but they did endure an hour of Tamar to enjoy an hour of Prince hits.

3121 offers Tamar on five tracks and Sheila E. on the Latin-tinged "Get on the Boat." That track and "Te Amo Corazon" feature the new husband-and-wife rhythm section of bassist Joshua Dunham and drummer Cora Coleman-Dunham, both part of the band through July 2010. Michael B. and Sonny T. are on "3121."

3121 rates at the head of the Prince B-list, clearly below the masterpieces but leading the strongest of the rest. While the quality of the songs is higher here than in many years, the production is probably the most satisfying element. It's clean and contemporary, competing with trends rather than chasing them.

The title song ranks among Prince's classics, the monumental dance anthem Prince had been trying to write for years. And the nasty "Black Sweat," reminiscent of *Controversy*-era dance tracks, comes close. The uplifting "Satisfied" features some of Prince's finest vocals—why isn't it longer? The album is awash in concise, catchy pop tracks, including "Love," "The Word," and the Tamar duet "Beautiful, Loved and Blessed." The reworking of "The Dance" is a sweeping ballad with the Latin overtones that feature centrally in the tender "Te Amo Corazon" and the more raucous "Get on the Boat." The misfires here aren't dreadful, just misguided: the meandering, vocally altered "Incense and Candles"; the dull rock of "Fury"; and the arena-jock-rock anthem wannabe "Lolita."

3121 produced three singles. The first was "Te Amo Corazon." In addition to the download/CD releases, the album version of the song also saw a DVD release on February 14, 2006. The song reached number sixty-seven on the Hot R&B charts. There was no B-side.

The second single, the album version of "Black Sweat," was released via download on February 21 and physically in March. The UK CD included a video for the song and a non-LP version of "Beautiful, Loved and Blessed." The single reached number sixty in the United States. "Black Sweat" is also available in a two-minute, fifty-two-second, non-LP edit on a white label promo. A live version of the song from April 14, 2016, in Atlanta at Prince's last show was released on Tidal on April 18, 2016, the last release during Prince's lifetime.

The final single was a May UK/Europe-only release of "Fury" backed with audio and video of "Te Amo Corazon/Fury" live at the Brit Awards on February 15. A UK off-label CD-R offered an otherwise unavailable "Fury" edit. The single did poorly across Europe.

After the Tamar tour, Prince played a number of one-off dates around the United States (and one in Milan) with his band, now composed of the Dunhams, Morris Hayes, Renato Neto, and Greg Boyer, Mike Philips, and The Twinz. Prince didn't undertake a proper *3121* tour. Instead, after moving from Chanhassen in early October, between November 10, 2006, and April 28, 2007, he performed forty shows on the Per4ming *3121* Live residency at the 3121 Club at the Rio Hotel and Casino in Las Vegas (plus an additional twenty-six aftershows at the 3121 Jazz Cuisine venue). He also played a few gigs in Miami in early February 2007 in conjunction with the Super Bowl. The shows were heavy on hits, typically featuring just three or four *3121* songs and often only one other Prince song from the past fifteen years: "Musicology." The album was relevant, but the live show didn't keep pace. It's disappointing that this fine album wasn't better used live.

Ultimate (2006)

Sometime in 2005, Warner Bros. decided to assemble their second 1992-contract hits collection. While the first (*The Very Best*) was an artistic disappointment but an economic success, they decided to do this one for real fans. So the label hired two real fans, Geoffrey Decker and Mathieu Bitton, to assemble the songs and the packaging. By late 2005, the duo had assembled a classy, two-CD, twenty-nine-track collection that opened with "Purple Medley" and went back and forth between sixteen LP/single tracks and twelve remixes. Then Warner Bros. asked Prince for his input. He nixed the naughty cuts "Erotic City" (twelve-inch version) and the already muted "Sexy Mutha." And he wanted the singles on one disc and the remixes on another. Prince got his way.

Warner Bros., through its nostalgia subsidiary Rhino, scheduled the *Ultimate* release for March 14, 2006, one week before *3121*. Prince asked Rhino to change the date, and Prince once again got his way, although some copies leaked out. Rhino rescheduled for May 22, then canceled that date, perhaps hoping for a Prince tour to materialize. It never did, and the album was finally

Warner Bros. released its fifth Prince greatest hits collection, the two-CD Ultimate, in the United States in August 2006. The seventeen-track first disc was an almost total repeat of *Hits 1 / Hits 2* material, but the second disc included eleven extended or remixed tracks, none of which had been collected at the time of *Ultimate*'s release.   *(Author's collection)*

released in August. It reached number six in the greatest-hit-hungry United Kingdom but only number sixty-one in the United States.

Prince's relative comfort with this collection and Warner Bros. makes sense. By this point, he had worked with three other international music conglomerates (Arista, Columbia, and Universal) and no longer had a pony in the race after he flipped the switch on the already-past-life-support NPG Music Club website on July 4 (he soon opened 3121.com but not as a subscription site). In addition, he was working with the Warner Bros. film arm, recording "The Song of the Heart" for *Happy Feet*.

Ultimate ended up as a two-disc collection with seventeen hits on the first disc and eleven remixes on the second disc. All seventeen of the hits on the first disc are available on the other hits collections and only one ("Money Don't Matter 2 Night") wasn't on *The Hits/The B-Sides*. All eleven of the remixes appear collected for the first time, although "Let's Go Crazy (Special Dance Mix)" and "Little Red Corvette (Dance Remix)" have subsequently appeared on the *Purple Rain* and *1999 Deluxe* releases, respectively. The remix edit of "Cream (N.P.G. Mix)" appears for the first time anywhere.

The first disc is tired, but the second is essential.

This was the end of Prince's relationship with Warner Bros. until they joined forces again in 2014.

Planet Earth (2007)

The Las Vegas *3121* residency ended on April 29, 2007. Between then and the August 1 opening of the 21 Nights in London: The Earth Tour, Prince played about twenty shows. These included eight shows at the historic Roosevelt Hotel in Los Angeles, a few hometown gigs (first since 2004), a couple of private shows (including a gig for Russian "businessman" Leonard Blavatnik, who paid either $1 million or $2 million, depending on the report), and Prince's first stop at the Montreux Jazz Festival. The *3121* live band continued on this tour.

The run-up to the London residency began with the usual chaotic jockeying over album distribution. Prince struck a global distribution deal with Columbia, including its UK arm Sony BMG. In addition to regular UK retail distribution, scheduled for Monday, July 16, he offered *Planet Earth* in the price of each 21 Nights concert ticket. Then he struck a deal with the *Mail on Sunday* to include a free copy on the cover of the July 15 edition. This was the first time that new studio music from a major artist had been distributed in this way. This didn't go over well with Sony BMG, which refused to release the album in the United Kingdom, or retailers, although HMV stocked the newspaper for that one day. Prince reportedly received £500,000 for the deal plus royalties and distributed 3 million copies of his new LP overnight, ahead of the half million in ticket sales—overall, a successful if not sustainable way to release an album.

And one that raised concerns. At this point, the new songs seem almost an afterthought to the marketing and live shows. The album is a mixed bag—a string of guilty pleasures that quickly devolves into silliness and self-indulgence or one that starts with silliness and self-indulgence and soon moves elsewhere. The album's first four songs are keepers. *Planet Earth* opens with the bombastic title track, Prince once again mining a very "Purple Vein" of "Gold." It's musical and lyrical theatrics we've heard countless times, and it's a bit embarrassing—but it's wonderful. The funky phased rhythm guitar deep in the mix on the second chorus clinches it. "Guitar," with Michael B. and Sonny T., is a close cousin of U2's "I Will Follow." It's a dumb but fun rocker. Prince channels Billie Holiday (or at least Eartha Kitt) following the album theme on "Somewhere Here on Earth." It's his most convincing jazz number that's not on one of his

Prince's fourth live album, Indigo Nights, was released in 2008. It was available exclusively as part of the Prince/Randee S. Nicholas 21 Nights photo book. The 15-track collection featured selections from the Indigo aftershows that took place during *21 Nights in London: The Earth Tour*.

(Author's collection)

jazz collections. "The One U Wanna C" heads into uncharted territory: country music. In a different world, this would be a regular line dance at wedding receptions.

From here, it's slowly downhill. "Chelsea Rodgers," a slick dance disco number, rewards repeated listens, although co-vocalist Shelby J. is given too much space. The closer "Resolution," featuring Wendy and Lisa, is an inoffensive sing-along that masks some potentially offensive sentiments. "Lion of Judah" has a jagged guitar solo and lots of preachiness, while "All the Midnights in the World" borders on tunelessness. "Future Baby Mama" borders on parody, but "Mr. Goodnight" is simply embarrassing. It's hard to tell if its smooth early 1970s soul bravado is meant to be taken seriously: is it a parody? It's at least as funny as National Lampoon's 1978 masterpiece "Kung Fu Christmas."

Planet Earth didn't chart in the United Kingdom since it wasn't formally released. It finally saw the light of day in the United States on July 24. It reached number three on the Hot 200 chart and number one on the R&B chart.

The album has four associated single releases. "Guitar" was released three times prior to the LP release. A three-minute, twenty-eight-second version was made available as a 3121.com download on February 2, 2007. This was followed by the three-minute, forty-five-second album version on May 31, available through a Verizon.com download. Finally, the LP version was released in Europe on CD, backed with "Somewhere Here on Earth," on July 9. An acoustic version with Andy Allo was released online in 2011.

Three promo releases offered LP versions of songs. In the United States, "Chelsea Rodgers" was backed with "Mr. Goodnight," while Holland was treated to "The One U Wanna C," and France weathered "Future Baby Mama." None of these songs charted.

Prince played 21 Nights in London: The Earth Tour in conjunction with *Planet Earth*. The residency took place at the 02 Arena (aka the Millennium Done), capacity 16,739. The main shows were followed fourteen times by shows at Indigo2, an attached, 2,500-capacity version of Club 3121. During the residency, Prince had about as much interest in playing *Planet Earth* music as the average fan had in hearing it. More accurately, the concert grouping should be called 35 Shows in London: Avoiding *Planet Earth*.

"Guitar" was the only *Planet Earth* song played regularly in London, and it was played more than 100 times after as a showcase, its last appearance on New Year's Day 2016. Beyond that, the other songs were played, total, about fifty times throughout the course of Prince's career.

Prince closed out 2007 with two private concerts: one in Moscow and one at an executive airport in Miami. Each show reportedly brought in $2 million. While the set lists from these shows are unknown, one can presume that the audiences weren't composed of billionaires demanding a thorough airing of *Planet Earth* songs. If one didn't know better, one would think that Prince had forgotten that there was actually music on those 3 million discs he spread around London.

Indigo Nights (2008)

The year 2008 was a quiet one. Prince played about ten concerts, all in the United States and mainly at his new residence: The "77" in Beverly Park in Los Angeles. Included in his live appearances were an April 26 headlining Coachella appearance and two October shows at the Gansevoort Hotel in New York City as part of the *21 Nights* book launch. He also appeared on February 10 at the Grammys, where he picked up a Best Male R&B Vocal Performance for "Future Baby

Mama," and on April 25 on *The Tonight Show*, where he debuted the still-un-released "Turn Me Loose." There was no new studio music until December, when two versions of "(There'll Never B) Another Like Me" were streamed on mplsound.com and four *Lotusflow3r* tracks leaked on radio.

Indigo Nights was released on September 30. It was available only as part of *21 Nights* book. It's a live collection, Prince's fourth, that brings together fifteen tracks from September 17 and 22 London *Indigo Nights* aftershows. The album never received an independent release, never charted, and wasn't associated with any singles. In early 2009, plans for an updated version of the book, to be titled "Prince Opus," were revealed. This included a leather-bound version of the book and a Prince iPod containing *Indigo Nights* and a forty-minute documentary. As of 2017, new copies were still available for £1,750.

Indigo Nights serves as an inoffensive reminder of the 21 Nights aftershows but falls flat as a cohesive live document. Even more so than with the *One Nite Alone* aftershow disc, there's a sterility here that belies the looser, more organic nature of these well-documented shows. The band's tight. But too tight? Maybe it's something as simple as how the sound was captured that removes the vitality of the live experience. Where's the bass? Or maybe it's the songs—heavy on covers and light on adventure. Or the performers? Two Shelby J. songs and one Beverly Knight song? Out of the more than 100 songs played over the thirty-five shows in London, what fan really wanted to have a permanent record of Shelby J. singing "Baby Love" over, say, Prince juking "Calhoun Square?" None, I would hope.

There are three "new" songs here but none are essential. "Just Like U (Monologue)" is what it says it is, tacked at the end of a medley. "Beggin' Woman Blues" is a Prince-adapted cover of Cousin Joe's "Beggin' Woman." "Indigo Nights" is an attempt to get the crowd going based on "Get on the Boat."

Included as part of a vanity project, perhaps it's not surprising *Indigo Nights* was in vain.

30

Access Another Experience

Home Videos and TV Broadcasts

The moving image was always a big part of Prince's image. In addition to four theatrical movies, hundreds of TV appearances, and countless promotional videos, Prince released numerous home videos and offered multiple live broadcasts. This chapter takes a look at when Prince popped up on the home screen.

Live Home Videos

Prince and The Revolution: Live (1985)

Prince and The Revolution: Live is Prince's first home video. And it's marvelous.

The show was broadcast live via satellite in Germany on *Rockpalast Nacht*, an annual televised festival. The show is a standard *Purple Rain* show with an opening "Let's Go Crazy," hits followed by a piano set and "God," and then the closing seven *Purple Rain* songs. It was directed by Paul Becher, who went on to direct the Guns N' Roses *Use Your Illusion* documentaries.

The tape was released on July 29, 1985. It sold for $29.95 in the United States, reaching number one in rentals and number two in sales. It wasn't available on DVD until 2017 as *Live at the Carrier Dome, Syracuse, NY, March 30 1985*, the fourth disc in the *Purple Rain Deluxe Edition*.

Sheila E. Live in Romance 1600 (1986)

Not Prince per se but Prince and The Revolution perform on a killer "A Love Bizarre," recorded on March 8, 1986, at the Warfield Theater in San Francisco. The hour-long video features Sheila E. and her band, including Levi Seacer Jr., performing an additional five Prince-penned tunes. The show hasn't appeared on DVD.

Lovesexy Live (1989)

Many consider *Lovesexy* Prince's crowning live achievement, and some critics, such as biographer Matt Thorne, consider this release "the greatest concert film ever released." *Lovesexy Live* captures the entire two-hour show from September 9, 1988, in Dortmund, West Germany's Westfalenhallen (Halle 1), originally broadcast outside the United States and Japan. Prince and the 1987–1989 band are in top form, descending into the wicked ways of the world in the set's first half before finding funky redemption in the second half.

Lovesexy Live was released as two cassettes—*Live 1* and *Live 2*—although the show halves were reversed. It was released only in the United Kingdom and France and has never seen a US or a DVD release. It is the last Prince concert released intact and unedited until 2019 with the *1999 Super Deluxe* audio of the November 30, 1982, Detroit show at the Masonic Hall and DVD of the December 29, 1982, Houston show at the Summit.

Diamonds and Pearls Video Collection (1992)

The thirteen-track, fifty-eight-minute *Diamonds and Pearls Video Collection* sort of tries to tell the *Diamonds and Pearls* story, mixing eight videos with seven NPG interview segments and four live tracks. The live material was recorded in the late spring of 1992 in Sydney and London. The collection was released on October 6, 1992, in the United States on Paisley Park/Warner Reprise VHS and on DVD on August 22, 2006. Eight of the twelve songs were made available on the Official Prince YouTube Channel in 2017, including the live clip of "Live 4 Love." The material not available elsewhere includes a video for "Strollin'" and marginal material: the introduction and live clips of "Thunder," Rosie Gaines's cover of "Dr. Feelgood," and Tony M.'s "Jughead."

3 Chains O' Gold (1994)

3 Chains O' Gold is a seventy-three-minute video that tells the story of Mayte's Princess of Cairo. Her father is assassinated, so she turns to Prince for help. He decides to help her by interspersing eleven videos from the *Symbol* album with narrative segues before killing seven older versions of himself. Or something like that.

Much of the video was broadcast in the United States as *Act 1* on ABC's *In Concert* on December 18, 1992. *3 Chains O' Gold* was released direct to video in the United States and Japan on August 16, 1994, the same day as *Come*. It's hard not to see this convoluted release as an attempt to flood the market and undermine a Warner Bros. product. It's also not hard to see that spending on this marginal product, which included sending Mayte to Egypt for a photo shoot, necessitated Prince's October $1 million deal to release *"The Black Album."*

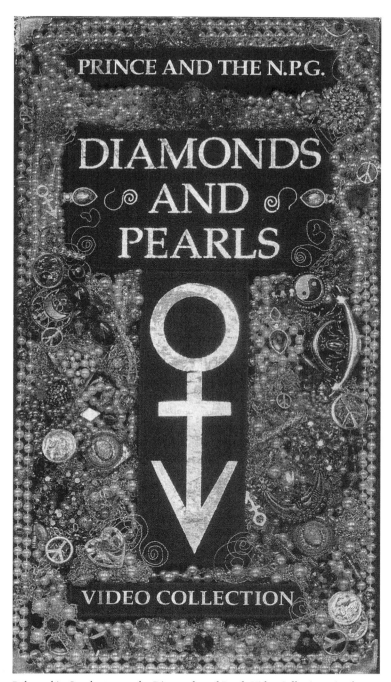

Released in October 1992, the *Diamonds and Pearls Video Collection* mixed commercial short videos and interviews with live footage from 1992's *Diamonds and Pearls* tour. Although the collection is commercially unavailable, most of the clips have been made available through the official Prince YouTube channel.

(Author's collection)

The video features most of the *Symbol* songs although not "3 Chains O' Gold." It also includes "The Call," which is Prince and Kirstie Alley chatting over Pete Rock and CL Smooth's "It's Not a Game." The full-length videos appeared on Prince's YouTube Channel in 2017 except "Eye Wanna Melt with U," "The Continental," and "7," the last an alternative version here.

Direction was credited to Paisley Park/Prince, along with video director Parris Patton, photographer/*21 Nights* coauthor Randee St. Nicholas, and Sotera Tschetter, whose design firm created the Prince symbol. A joint release with Warner Reprise Video, this was the last video on Paisley Park. It is not on DVD.

The Sacrifice of Victor (1995)

While *3 Chains O' Gold* was never more than a confused but well-intentioned public love note for Mayte, *The Sacrifice of Victor* had the potential to be a great concert film. The video was recorded at a Begley's Warehouse aftershow in London on September 8, 1993, an epic show featuring loads of, at the time, unreleased material. Unfortunately, it also included loads of guests, including Mavis Staples, The Steeles, the Hornheadz (who shine), and the NPG featuring lots of Tony M. So, an opportunity to share a two-hour, twenty-minute Prince show featuring guest artists ends up as a forty-six-minute video with lots of guests and Prince on vocals for well less than twenty minutes. It's not right.

Although he had changed his name at the time of the recording, *The Sacrifice of Victor* was credited to Prince when released in Europe (VHS) and Japan (Laserdisc) on March 6, 1995. It's never been released in the United States or on DVD. There's one exclusive song: a brief cover of Elvis Presley's hit "Jailhouse Rock."

The Undertaker (1995)

As a narrative video, *The Undertaker* has all the import of a freshman film, but musically, it ranks with Prince's best work of the 1990s. The video started out in the summer of 1993 as a feature film starring Nona Gaye and TV actress Vanessa Marcil. Gaye was phased out, and Marcil's parts were integrated into a weak story that finds her angry, doped up, and tripping out at the studio. Whatever.

The Undertaker features the New Power Trio, Prince joined by Michael B. and Sonny T. The trio recorded on June 14, 1993, playing a loose and loud seven-song set highlighted by slow and funky versions of "The Ride" and "The Undertaker." As a way of proving his guitar credentials, Prince intended to give *The Undertaker* CD away with the magazine *Guitar World*, an idea nixed by Warner Bros. He also pressed 1,000 copies of the CD that he was ordered to destroy.

The forty-minute video was released in Europe and Japan on March 6, 1995. It hasn't been released on DVD, but all videos except "Bambi" and the forty-four-second "Zannalee (Prelude)" were made available as NPG Music Club downloads in 2001.

Beautiful Strange (1999)

Like many of Prince's straight-to-video offerings, *Beautiful Strange* is frustrating. The first quarter of the eighty-minute video is entertaining, the Spice Girls's Mel B. interviewing Prince at Paisley Park, where we discover he has a blue, not purple, Weber kettle grill. The interview segues into a lyric video for the then unreleased title song, and then we get a parade of guest performances.

Beautiful Strange was recorded on August 28, 1998, at an invitation-only performance at London's Café de Paris. It was broadcast in a fifty-minute version on Channel 4 in the United Kingdom on October 4, 1998, before a VHS release through the NPG Music Club on August 24, 1999.

The fifty-five-minute concert segment features an opening eight-minute, three-song Prince set ("Push It Up," "Jam of the Year," and "Talkin' Loud and Saying Nothing"), followed by a twenty-five-minute, five-song interlude featuring Chaka Khan, Larry Graham, and Doug E. Fresh. Prince returns on the NPG's "Come On," which also closes the tape in video form, then shares the stage with Doug E. Fresh on "Mad." Why not just put out a whole Prince concert?

Rave Un2 the Year 2000 (2000)

Rave Un2 the Year 2000 represents the closest thing to a full concert video release since 1989's *Lovesexy Live*. The main portion of the video is a twenty-three-song, 113-minute concert from the December 31, 1999, pay-per-view designed to cash in on "1999." Twenty-one of the songs are from an epic twenty-nine-song December 18 Paisley Park show with Morris Day and The Time's "Jungle Love" and "The Bird" from a December 17 show.

Due to the length of the set, the guest damage is minimal here, with Day's two songs and Lenny Kravitz's "American Woman" and "Fly Away" the only intrusions, although Rosie Gaines, Maceo Parker, and George Clinton also performed. But the disc suffers from a dull performance by a too-slick group that feels like a failed late-night talk show band and unimaginative song selection, a string of greatest hits, tired covers, and only two recent songs. And there's a bigger issue that plagues all the live videos since 1989: they're atypical performances staged for video release rather than shows typical of the period. Why all the bells and whistles of one-off performances and special guests when all fans wanted (and still want) is professionally shot regular concerts? Yes, there were probably legal/copyright reasons, but it seems an insecurity that belies Prince's usual confidence.

Rave Un2 the Year 2000 was released on June 5, 2000, on VHS and DVD, almost the only release in a very down year. The DVD included bonus "Innerviews" with Prince, Kravitz, Day, and Parker; condescending "Freedom Newz" about copyright law and the music industry; and "Peep This," an ad for the never-released $700 *New Funk Sampling Series*. It also included "Bonus Groovez" featuring songs from Clinton, NPG bassist Larry Graham, and solos excerpted from *The Undertaker* by harmonicist Jimmy Watson and Hornhead Kathy Jensen. It's a nice memento, but of what?

Live at the Aladdin Las Vegas (2003)

Although nowhere near a full concert and short on *Rainbow Children* material, this specially staged performance two weeks after the *One Nite Alone* tour works, at least musically. Much of the credit goes to the unsung band, which includes Renato Neto, Rhonda Smith, and John Blackwell, and the intrusion of only one guest number: Nikka Costa on "Push and Pull." The song selection stays away from the hits, includes an otherwise unavailable song ("U Want Me"), and manages to overcome the grade school software manipulation that passes for postproduction visuals. The concert intro includes sound-check clips of "The Rainbow Children" and "Nagoya," and a performance of "The Ride" is offered post-credits.

Live at the Aladdin Las Vegas was released on August 19, 2003, on NPG Records. A portion of the show was streamed on the NPG Music Club on April 18, 2003, and sometime during the summer of 2003, the four-song promo single *Live at the Aladdin Las Vegas—Sampler* was released. The video was directed by Sanaa Hamri, a Moroccan who went on to direct *Sisterhood of the Traveling Pants 2*.

This was the last original-material DVD release during Prince's lifetime.

Studio Home Videos

"Gett Off" (1991)

"Gett Off" was released as VHS and Laserdisc maxi-single on September 10, 1991. The five-track, thirty-minute collection features the title track and four related videos. The collection has not been released on DVD.

"Sexy M.F." (1992)

Released on June 16, 1992, the single-track "Sexy M.F." features the five-minute, twenty-eight second, seven-inch version as part of an eight-minute, fifty-one-second mini-saga. It didn't make *The Hits Video Collection* but has been on the YouTube channel.

Always a man of the moment, Prince as Symbol decided to release a CD-ROM game, *Interactive*, to celebrate his birthday in 1994. The game broke no new gaming ground upon its release, but did feature unreleased Symbol songs and otherwise unavailable alternate versions, including an instrumental, karaoke version of "Kiss." *(Author's collection)*

The Hits Video Collection (1993)

The 1993 companion to *The Hits/The B-Sides* gathers fifteen videos from 1979's solo version of "I Wanna Be Your Lover" through 1993's "Peach." The collection was released on VHS, Laserdisc, and DVD on September 14, 1993.

Interactive (1994)

Freed from Warner Bros.'s constraints, Prince released the CD-ROM game *Interactive* on his thirty-sixth birthday. The object of the game was to go through a symbol-shaped building collecting puzzle pieces and solving challenges. A bit awkward when it was released, a digital equivalent of *Glam Slam Ulysses*, its charms are now perplexing. The game includes dozens of song clips, four videos, and six songs. The title song appears in an edited two-minute, fifty-three-second version. "Kiss" appears in an exclusive extended four-minute, twenty-five-second "Instrumental" version and "Loose!" in a forty-seven-second edit, both for the karaoke room. "Race" appears three times: as drums (great version), vocals, and samples. A three-minute, forty-eight-second edit of "Endorphimachine" is the "prize" once you solve the game. I love the song, but it was a lot of work for little reward.

Broadcasts and TV Shows

Parade Live Cobo Arena, Detroit, Michigan, June 7, 1986

For the third year in a row, Prince celebrated his birthday with a special concert. In 1986, he went on the road to celebrate at Detroit's Cobo Arena. This Hit and Run show was filmed for Japanese and UK TV and broadcast as *Parade Live*. The performance is astounding: fifteen electrifying, sweat-drenched songs performed by a band that can turn the corner on a dime. Highlights include "Mutiny," "Life Can Be So Nice," and a leather-clad Prince soaking in the love on Jerry Lee Lewis's "Whole Lotta Shakin'." The only things wrong with *Parade Live* are that it's an incomplete show and it's never been commercially released.

Estadio Santa María del Mar, La Coruña, Spain, July 29, 1990

The Nude tour doesn't get much love. It smells like a money grab and the Not band—Not The Revolution, Not the NPG—isn't remembered fondly. But early shows don't sound that bad in retrospect, and they do offer live versions of "The Future," "Batdance," and "Partyman." This stripped-down ninety-minute show was broadcast live on Spanish TV and then never again. Why in the first place, and why never again? It's unclear. A Spanish radio broadcast from July 22 at Madrid's Estadio Vicente Calderón is a longer, superior show, highlighted by a "Question of U" medley that burns.

Tokyo Dome, Tokyo, Japan, August 31, 1990

Although it's only a month and fifteen shows later, the Nude tour had clearly run its course. The set is similar to the Spanish shows, but the thrills aren't there. The concert was broadcast live on radio and weeks later on Japan's TV Asahi.

Prince's YouTube Channel has featured the languid "A Question of U" video from this show.

Estadio Maracanã, Rio de Janeiro, Brazil, January 19, 1991

Although only a few months later, Prince is clearly reenergized, and it's reflected in a powerful and loose performance. Some of the loose might be that this is the NPG's first major public performance after a low-key Paisley Park show earlier in the month. The set is sparked by "Something Funky This House Comes" and "Horny Pony," songs recorded in Tokyo around the time of the previous broadcast. The set-closing twenty-eight-minute "Baby I'm a Star" medley pulls out all the stops, including Prince doing his best James Brown collapse. The ninety-minute show was broadcast live in fifty-five countries as part of Rock in Rio II and later on Brazil's I-Sat. Prince was reportedly paid $500,000 for the show. Other headliners included Guns N' Roses, George Michael, and INXS. The festival was marred by excessive heat and violence.

The Ryde Dyvine, 1992

The Ryde Dyvine is a forty-five-minute pseudo-concert featuring "reporting" from Prince girlfriend Troy Beyer mixed with performances by The Crayons, Carmen Electra, George Clinton, Rosie Gaines, and Mavis Staples and an eighteen-minute Prince set. Prince's section was recorded on December 17, 1992, at Paisley Park. The show was broadcast on ABC's *In Concert* on December 19, 1992. As usual, it drags when Prince isn't onstage, and he's not on for a lot of the night. Highlights are The Crayons's (aka MPLS) performance of the title song and a rare presentation of "The Sacrifice of Victor," complete with *Parade*-era stage moves.

The Beautiful Experience, 1994

Prince spent a good portion of the mid-1990s creating concert narratives featuring girlfriends. *The Beautiful Experience* stars Nona Gaye as a Web surfer who gets ripped off by Symbol's website, The Dawn, only to fall asleep and end up inside the computer with the songs. It's an entry/barrier narrative like *Interactive* and *The Undertaker* that probably has Jungian overtones that won't be discussed here. The live set, "Days of Wild," "The Jam," "Shhh," and "Now," recorded at "A Beautiful Experience" at Paisley Park on February 13, 1994, is the highlight.

The Beautiful Experience aired in the United Kingdom on Sky One on April 3, 1994. It was also shown in the United Kingdom at 12:55 a.m. on

Channel 4 on Boxing Day 1994 before the film *Mr. Vampire*, a surprisingly good vampire/marital arts comedy.

Love 4 One Another, 1996

Prince makes one last dip into the woman-encountering-Prince story well, this time sending Corrie Dana from Texas to Paisley Park. While the Symbol songs are top-notch, including "The Jam" and "Gold," the cinematography and editing blur the line between studio and live enough that it's ultimately an exercise in frustration. Although Sonny burns on "Rock 'N' Roll Is Alive!," it's worth tracking down unofficial releases from of the time to watch the performances rather than sit through the live material here, recorded at Paisley Park in the fall of 1995. VH1 coproduced the TV special and aired it on January 27, 1996. This was Prince's last released attempt at a long-form narrative.

Emancipation, Paisley Park, November 12, 1996

An eight-song, twenty-five-minute *Emancipation* concert was recorded at Paisley Park for broadcast on MTV, VH1, and BET. It's highly choreographed and tight but not very inspiring. It doesn't say freedom as much as it says televised commercial. And it barely does that, offering only four *Emancipation* tunes.

Art of Musicology, 2004

Prince and the NPG performed a ten-song set at New York's Webster Hall on April 20, 2004. Seven tracks, including the full-band "Musicology" and "Dear Mr. Man," were included in this special that aired on April 28 on VH-1 and four other cable music stations. Part of a *Musicology* media blitz, the show highlight is the five-song acoustic set. The show closed with an interview by program host Sway Calloway.

31

Strays of the World

Maxi-Singles

Prince supplemented seven-inch singles with twelve-inch singles and maxi-singles in both promotional and commercial formats. Prince's twelve-inch releases typically contain the single A-side remixed backed by an extended non-LP B-side.

Prince's first twelve-inch was the 1978 US "Disco Mix" promo of "Just as Long as We're Together" and "Soft and Wet." His first commercial twelve-inch was the UK "Sexy Dancer (Long Version)" in 1980. His first commercial US twelve-inch didn't show up until 1982's "Let's Work (Dance Remix)." The most extreme twelve-inch was 1985's "America," which featured a twenty-one-minute, forty-six-second A-side backed by an "extended version" of B-side "Girl" that more than doubled the original length.

Although related, maxi-singles are different from twelve-inch singles. Maxi-singles expand or offer multiple versions of the single A-side and often include much non-LP material. Although often called EPs (extended plays), they're technically different, as EPs contain at least four stand-alone songs. The closest Prince came to a real EP is the legally blocked six-track *Deliverance*.

This chapter surveys Prince's fifteen maxi-singles.

Scandalous!

Released on December 1, 1989, the core of this self-indulgent release is a three-part "Scandalous Sex Suite" reworking of the title song as a romantic interlude with co-vocalist and then current paramour actress Kim Basinger. "The Rapture" perks up a bit with a blistering guitar solo, but "The Crime" in this groan-filled suite is Eric Leeds's easy-listening "sexophone." Basinger's "The Passion" moan here was sampled in "Peach."

The most intriguing track is the otherwise unavailable "Sex," a seven-minute dance track sung in a Camille-like voice in the guise of yet another character: Endorphin from Venus. The album(s) version of "When 2 in Love" shows up as the final track just in case you missed the point. The Japanese

The December 1989 release of the fourth *Batman* single and Prince's first true maxi-single, the five-track "Scandalous!," featured a whole lot of Kim Basinger moaning and a gem of an anti-free love B-side, "Sex." The Japanese version expanded to near album length with three versions of "Partyman" and "Feel U Up (Short Stroke)."

(Author's collection)

CD adds four "Partyman" twelve-inch tracks for an LP-like fifty-one-minute running time.

"New Power Generation"

The trio of singles beginning with "New Power Generation" are Prince's most conceptually complete maxi-singles. Each centers around a tweak of the title track that anchors alterations and variations that gradually evolve from straightforward remixes to authentic variations. The common element for the three releases is freshly minted New Power Generation, first appearing on backing vocals here.

The core track here is the New Jack "N.P.G. (Funky Weapon Remix)," a combination of the two versions of "New Power Generation" from the seven-inch single and the *Graffiti Bridge* sound track. This is punchier than the originals and, like those, features Morris Day on drums. This track breaks into the fast-paced siren-reliant "T.C.'s Rap" and an expansion of T. C. Ellis's "NPG Pt. II" rap that further developed as the title track of Ellis's solo LP.

The disc slows with Tony M.'s rap "Brother with a Purpose" (or with a porpoise if he came back as a dolphin) before hitting the riff-heavy "Get Off." "Get Off" shares little with the "N.P.G" title track and only a homophone with "Gett

Off." It could have been a stand-alone single. "The Lubricated Lady" is essentially a "Get Off" remix, and "Loveleft, Loveright" shares a groove but is a stand-alone keys-heavy dance track.

"Gett Off"

"Gett Off," the first Prince and the NPG release, is a bone-crunching dance number featuring Family Stone–style vocals and Eric Leeds's wailing flute. Lyrically, it's a delightfully awkward mixture of tough and goofy sexual posturing. The result is so over the top that it's hard not to take it as tongue in cheek (or tongue in little box with mirror inside). It borrows heavily from "Glam Slam '91," released for radio in January 1991 to promote the Glam Slam nightclub.

The song was the result of a challenge that Warner Bros. studio executive Lenny Waronker put to Prince, telling him that *Diamonds and Pearls* lacked a track for black radio. Prince recorded "Gett Off" on May 10, 1991, and quickly submitted it. An EP release was arranged ("Cream," "Money Don't Matter 2 Night," and "Horny Pony") and then canceled. Prince wanted the track released immediately, so he pressed his own vinyl twelve-inch and sent out the "Damn Near 10 Minutes" mix to radio and clubs on his thirty-third birthday. This resulted in the single release and the song's inclusion on the subsequent LP at the expense of "Horny Pony."

The "Gett Off" single was officially released on July 29, 1991, reaching number six on the R&B charts, number twenty-one on the pop charts, and number one on dance/club charts. The seven-track US maxi-single followed on August 12.

Commercial and promo releases in the United States and the United Kingdom offer a dozen "Gett Off" variations. The best is the promo "Extended Remix," aka "Purple Pump Mix." But the maxi-single highlights are "Gett Off"'s cousins although not "Gett Off's Cousin," which is unreleased. "Violet the Organ Grinder" is a funky, almost dirge-like work that hints at darker motives. It should have been a single. "Gangster Glam" features Prince's finest George Benson homage, while "Clockin' the Jizz (Instrumental)" picks up on the jazz groove.

"Cream"

"Cream" is the third and final maxi-single offering a kaleidoscopic, inside-out view of a song rather than multiple, more introverted remixes. It's not about what the song is but rather what it can do and, further, not as much about the power of the individual songs as the pleasure of the movement through the entire project.

The nine-song maxi-single, released on November 4, 1991, is light on "Cream" and heavy on variations. "Cream" features in the album and "N.P.G. Mix" versions, but these tracks and the variations are greater here than on other maxi-singles, with the final "Ethereal Mix" by Dave Friedlander catchy, compelling, and all but unrecognizable.

Unusually, the strongest maxi-single songs are the work of outside remixers. Keith Cohen's "Do You Dance (KC's Remix)" turns in a raucous Sly Stone tribute featuring Javetta Steele. Junior Vasquez takes that tune a step further with a bouncy, almost Jamaican interpretation: "Housebangers." "2 the Wire (Creamy Instrumental)" marvelously plays up the original song's nod to T Rex, and "Q in Doubt (Instrumental)" moves toward the worthy "Clockin' the Jizz" jazz interpretation of the previous maxi-single. "Get Some Solo" is brief and sweet. And, as always, the weakest track features Tony M., rapping as if he doesn't like English, on "Things Have Gotta Change (Tony M. Rap)."

"My Name Is Prince"

If I believed in guilty pleasures (like early Prince, I believe in pleasures, not guilt), "My Name Is Prince" would be at the top of my Prince list. It's arrogant, profane, and musically simple, and it makes me feel like I'm betraying a number of moral ideals to like it. I love it—at least until Tony M. shows up.

But, for all that, this is one of the most disappointing maxi-singles.

Released on October 22, 1992, the US maxi-single features four versions of the song, but none surpass or even contribute much to the original version. The strongest is Keith Cohen's "12" Club Mix," which seems to incorporate the core keyboards from "Do Your Dance (KC's Remix)." The disc also includes the only release of "Sexy M.F. (12" Remix)," a fuller mix than the original.

"7"

"7" is an infectious, sing-along anthem pairing a funky backbeat with an unforgettable guitar lick, topped by angelic, layered vocals and lyrics that portend deep religious importance. It should hold a bigger place in the Prince oeuvre, but it never seems to get the love.

Released as a US single on November 17, 1992, the same day as "Damn U," "7" is the slimmest of maxi-singles, featuring an album version and edit along with three remixes and the US debut of "2 Whom It May Concern." The highlight remix is "Acoustic," which brings forward the acoustic guitar and plays with the background vocal levels. The US promo maxi-single adds two additional versions: "Mix 5 Long Version" and "Mix 5 Edit."

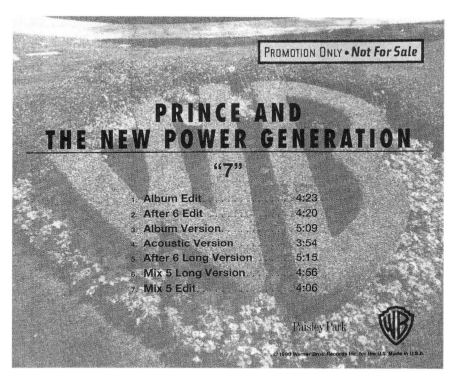

PROMOTION ONLY • *Not For Sale*

PRINCE AND
THE NEW POWER GENERATION

"7"

1. Album Edit 4:23
2. After 6 Edit 4:20
3. Album Version 5:09
4. Acoustic Version 3:54
5. After 6 Long Version 5:15
6. Mix 5 Long Version 4:56
7. Mix 5 Edit 4:06

Paisley Park

© 1990 Warner Bros. Records Inc. for the U.S. Made in U.S.A.

The US "7" promo CD was one of numerous Prince promo releases featuring otherwise unavailable mixes and edits, in this case the "Mix 5 Long Version" and "Mix 5 Edit." It's unclear if Prince released additional mixes simply because he was Prince and he could, or if he was hoping the remixes would light up the clubs, which rarely happened. Either way, fans benefit from more versions.   *(Author's collection)*

The Beautiful Experience

Most dictionaries now define "mind-boggling" as "the number of variations of Prince's 'The Most Beautiful Girl in the World.'" That number hovers around twenty. Why? Because Warner Bros. allowed Prince to independently release "TMBGITW," but only that song, so he got as much mileage out of it as possible. And why did they let him release it? Because they thought they were giving him enough rope to hang himself, but he ended up using the rope to lasso a number three US hit, a number two R&B, and his only UK number one.

The single release of "TMBGITW" on February 9, 1994, was not only the first disc on the independent NPG Records but also Symbol's first release. This basic version of "TMBGITW" is saccharine, almost embarrassing, in its gooey lyrics, bland instrumentation, and unintentionally humorous spoken-word interlude. It feels calculated and hollow. However, the seven-track *The Beautiful Experience*, released on May 17, is engaging and adventuresome. The more successful variations are "Beautiful," an appealing almost-techno version, and "Staxowax," which betrays a tad too much time listening to Salt-N-Pepa. The Ricky Peterson–coproduced "Mustang Mix" was released as a stand-alone single. Hornheadz member Brian Gallagher and Leeds feature on different easy-listening sax and flute versions here and on promo discs that turn the song's insipid factor up to saccharine.

"Letitgo"

Not to be confused with Idina Menzel's chilly anthem, "Letitgo" was released as a maxi-single on September 27, 1994. It's a catchy tune that reached number

Prince as Symbol released "The Most Beautiful Girl in the World" as an independent single in 1994 and milked it for all it was worth, eventually releasing around twenty variants. In addition to an edit of the original version, which was a US number three and a UK number one smash, "Staxowax" and "Mustang Mix" were released as US singles.   *(Courtesy Jeff Munson)*

thirty-one on the *Billboard* singles chart but one lost in a multiyear string of mid-tempo light R&B singles. It sometimes seems as if Prince created the song only to actively ignore it. He recorded the song after the name change but released it as Prince on the disowned "posthumous" LP *Come*. He never performed the song on TV and gave up on it live after two years, often unable to find a comfortable register below the studio song's foregrounded falsetto. And, perhaps most uncharacteristically, he wasn't involved in any of the single's seven versions. The most interesting mixes are the two "Sherm Stick" edits by the Pharcyde's J. Swift, both instrument-heavy breakdowns featuring loops from "The Ballad of Dorothy Parker."

"Space"

This is why maxi-singles were invented. The four remixes expand, explain, reinvent, and reimagine the already appealing second track from *Come*. The standout is the "Universal Love Remix," which shares a chorus with the original song but little else (although it unashamedly shares a vibe with TLC's "Waterfalls"). "Acoustic Remix" isn't guitar-and-vocal "unplugged" but rather a different vocal take paired with an up-in-the-mix acoustic guitar. Great stuff.

The Hate Experience

Symbol dropped "I Hate U" as his first retail Warner Bros. single in early September 1995. A week later, he released the four-track *The Hate Experience* maxi-single, a companion to the previous year's *The Beautiful Experience* and the lead new single off *The Gold Experience*, the first Symbol LP. The tight "7" Edit" shines, cutting the excess of the included LP version. The "Quiet Night Mix by Eric Leeds" is throwaway light jazz. The most remarkable track is "Extended Remix." This sheds most of the main lyrics and (maybe) unintentionally transforms into one of Prince's funniest tracks, an extended dig supposedly at former flame Carmen Electra. The spoken/sung melodramatic memories, recalling "Another Lonely Christmas," include both a *Forrest Gump* reference and the unfortunate attempt to rhyme "myself" and "wealth." "I Hate U" was Prince's last new release single to hit the top forty, and only five more would enter the top 100.

1999: The New Master

At the end of *Anchorman 2: The Legend Continues*, Prince appears with his ragtag crew of Larry Graham, Rosie Gaines, and Doug E. Fresh to battle media groups that failed to adapt to evolving audience tastes. Okay, that didn't happen, but it would have been much more entertaining and less confusing than this seven-track collection of old-school (preschool?) hip-hop tricks served up over rerecorded versions of a classic as *1999: The New Master*.

In late 1998, Warner Bros. rereleased "1999" to encourage people to sufficiently party. Although there was no commercial single, the song hit number forty on the *Billboard* Hot 100, bettering the 1982 single release by four slots.

Since Symbol didn't own the "1999" master, he rerecorded the song and released it on February 2, 1999, on NPG Records. But he released it as Prince and The Revolution (while also crediting the NPG), even though it contained no members of The Revolution (who didn't play on the original track anyway) and he played all the instruments. On top of all that, the flimsy cardboard sleeve is about three-quarters of an inch taller than any other CD holder, inflicting aesthetic havoc on my CD shelves.

The seven tracks here capture all the regrettable slickness and late-to-the-party gimmickry that plagued the contemporaneous *Rave Un2 the Joy Fantastic* but with the additional hindrance of Doug E. Fresh's hip-in-1988 rhymes. The most interesting bit here is the spoken-word piece by actress Rosario Dawson, miming some Jehovah's Witness beliefs about Christmas over the introduction to "Little Red Corvette."

The rerecorded single failed to chart, but the recording hit number 150 on the *Billboard* 200 album chart.

The best thing I can say about this recording is that I'll never have to listen to it again.

"The Greatest Romance Ever Sold"

Don't call it a "comeback," but after nearly three years without releasing new material on a physical single since "The Holy River" in January 1997, Symbol dropped "The Greatest Romance Ever Sold" on October 5, 1999. The song is an agreeable mid-tempo betrayal ballad, a standout on the weak *Rave Un2 the Joy Fantastic*. As with the album, the emphasis on the maxi-single, released on November 23, is on guest artists.

The maxi-single features eight variations, and promos add four more. The most interesting version arrives when hip-hop house producer Jason Nevins (Florida Line) offers up some straight-on old-school disco with "Jason Nevins Extended Remix." Grab your whistle and hit the dance floor!

"The Greatest Romance Ever Sold" is the last maxi-single physically released in the United States.

"Dance 4 Me"

"Dance 4 Me" is the only single from *MPLSound*. The minimal dance tune was released in the United States on September 29 on iTunes in a David Alexander "Icon Remix." A brief video is circulating showing Alexander working on the tune. On December 9, 2011, Purple Music, a Swiss record label headed by deejay Jamie Lewis, released a Swiss-only CD and twelve-inch maxi-single. It featured the single version and five remixes.

"Rock and Roll Love Affair"

Recorded in late 2011/early 2012 at Paisley Park with Ida Nielsen on bass and John Blackwell on drums, "Rock and Roll Love Affair" was released digitally and physically by Purple Music in Europe on November 22, 2012. An odd choice for dance remixes, the song echoes the light country pop of "The One U Wanna C" and explicitly quotes the "Take Me with U" melody. Jamie Lewis's four maxi-single remixes are more busy and self-absorbed than interesting. "Remix 7" and "Reloaded Instrumental Remix" streamed in 2013, and a new version, now titled "Rocknroll Loveaffair," appeared on *Hitnrun Phase Two*.

The Breakfast Experience

"Breakfast Can Wait" was released as a digital single on September 3, 2103, followed on October 24 by *The Breakfast Experience*, the final "Experience" released during Prince's lifetime. Bolstered by the single sleeve featuring comedian David Chappelle dressed as Prince serving pancakes, the slow jam hit number thirty-eight on the US adult R&B chart. The EP features the single version, which also showed up on *Art Official Age*, and four mostly forgettable remixes by current studio pal Joshua Welton.

32

Eye Am 2 Funky and U Can't Handle My Groove

Late 2000s LPs

On March 24, 2009, Prince simultaneously unveiled Lotusflow3r.com and released three LPs, his own *Lotusflow3r* and *MPLSound*, and protégé Bria Valente's *Elixir*. Five days later, the albums were available exclusively at Target in the United States in an $11.98 package. This deal allowed Prince to collect his money (reportedly $500,000) up front rather than wait for the vagary of actual sales. With so much music available at such a low price, the album quickly reached number two on the top 200 and number one on the R&B charts. This is the second time Prince released more than one album on the same day, following the 2004 release of *Musicology*, *The Chocolate Invasion*, and *The Slaughterhouse*, but the first time via CDs.

There was no tour support, but Prince hit the TV circuit and performed several notable concerts throughout the year. From March 25 to 27, he appeared on three consecutive episodes of *Late Night with Jay Leno* and returned on May 28 for Leno's penultimate show. In April, he showed up on *The Ellen DeGeneres Show* with "Crimson and Clover" and was featured on a two-part *Tavis Smiley* interview.

Prince's live performances in 2009 were infrequent but impactful and carefully curated. After a few late-night shows at 77 Beverly Park, Prince engaged in a series of four mini-residencies. The first took place at the Nokia Live Center in Los Angeles at 7:00, 9:30, and midnight on March 28, 2009. The first show was funk, the second rock, and the last jazz. On July 18 in Montreux, he paired up a jazz and rock show, and on August 13 in Monaco, he offered a pop show and rock show. On October 11, he offered two shows at Paris's Beaux-Arts temple the Grand Palais, then followed the next evening with an epic two-hour, forty-five-minute show at La Cigale. On October 24, he was back home at Paisley Park for "The Last Jam of 2009," his first show at home in more than five years.

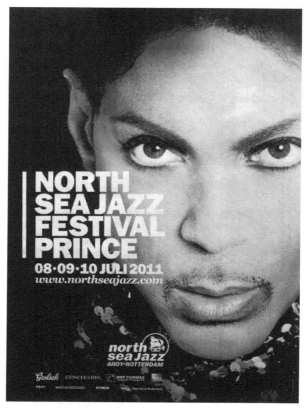

Prince shied away from the festival circuit in the United States, although he played Coachella in 2008, but increasingly embraced European multi-artist programs, especially jazz festivals.

(Courtesy Ric Dube)

Lotusflow3r (2009)

Lotusflow3r is the stronger of the 2009 releases. While *Purple Rain* brought comparisons to Jimi Hendrix, mainly because they were both black guys who knew their way around a guitar, *Lotusflow3r* legitimately bears more than a passing fancy to the trippy tunes on *Axis: Bold As Love*.

Although not a compilation of previously released material, *Lotusflow3r* pulls together tracks recorded over the previous five years. The album has its roots in November 2004 when Prince reunited Michael B. and Sonny T. for the New Power Trio. "3121" came out of that session, as did five tracks here: "From the Lotus . . . ," ". . . Back 2 the Lotus," "Colonized Mind," "Love Like Jazz," and "Wall of Berlin." According to Michael B., the trio recorded about a dozen tracks in three and a half hours. The presence of Tamar on "4ever" and "Colonized

Mind" and the NPG Music Club stream of "Feel Better, Feel Good, Feel Wonderful" all point toward 2006 recordings for these tracks. The Dunhams are on the 2006 "4ever," plus "Boom," "Dreamer," and "$," probably both from 2008, as are the Prince-only "Crimson and Clover" and "77 Beverly Park."

Lotusflow3r doesn't get the love it deserves. While there are some heavy thoughts here about social justice ("Colonized Mind" and "Dreamer"), it's the heavy music that's the point. "Dreamer" apes "Spanish Castle Magic," but it's more homage than theft. The cover of Tommy James's "Crimson and Clover" is hard rock homage, featuring an uncredited lick from the 1960s garage anthem "Wild Thing." All the heaviness isn't just rock. The jazz-oriented numbers veer from trippy heavy ("From the Lotus . . . ," ". . . Back 2 the Lotus," "Boom," and "Colonized Mind") to almost fluffy ("Love Like Jazz," "$," and "77 Beverly Park"). "4ever" is an old-school ballad, "Feel Better, Feel Good, Feel Wonderful" is an old-school dance track, and "Wall of Berlin" is just goofy.

The download LP replaced "Crimson and Clover" with the mid-tempo rocker "The Morning After," likely a copyright issue.

There were no singles from *Lotusflow3r* and no tour for these discs. The tracks were largely neglected.

"Crimson and Clover" debuted in New York in October 2008 and was played about fifty times through 2015. "Dreamer" has a similar history, debuting on *The Tonight Show* on March 26, played about fifty times through 2015. "Colonized Mind" was played about fifteen times, enjoying a good run on the 3rdEyeGirl tours. Another five songs were played infrequently and "From the Lotus . . . ," "4ever," "77 Beverly Park," "Wall of Berlin," and ". . . Back 2 the Lotus" never.

MPLSound (2009)

If *Lotusflow3r* is the rock disc, then *MPLSound* is the dance disc. It's also the weaker product, mechanical and distant, almost sterile. As much as you can feel the warmth of the quasi-psychedelic energy of the first disc, here you can feel the light breeze of a CPU cooling fan gently processing Pro Tools algorithms.

Little is known about *MPLSound*'s recording, although it's all Prince (save Q-Tip's rap on "Chocolate Box") and is assumed to have taken place in 2008. "U're Gonna C Me" is a rerecording of the *One Nite Alone...* track. It's fitting that these cold albums would share a track.

Unlike its companion, this LP spawned two singles. The studio version of "Dance 4 Me" was released on August 31, and a promo edit of "U're Gonna C Me" was released in France in October 2009. It failed to chart.

There are two solid tunes here: the Funkadelic shuffle of "Ol' Skool Company," even if the shout-outs are a bit hackneyed, and the frantic naysaying of "No More Candy 4 U." The rest of the tracks are at best generic, with nothing much to recommend the dance ("(There'll Never B) Another Like Me" and "Dance 4 Me"), easy-listening (the Kirsten Scott Thomas tribute "Better with Time"), and soul ("Here") tracks other than their genres. And then there's "Chocolate Box": tweaked, tuned, and tired, it's aggressively annoying.

Even more than *Lotusflow3r*, *MPLSound* was looked-over live. And, even if the album isn't strong, this is unfortunate, as songs often find a second life live. "Ol' Skool Company" was played an epic twelve times in 2009 and 2010, and it was downhill from there to "Here," "Valentina," and "Better with Time," which were never performed live.

It's unclear if *Lotusflow3r* and *MPLSound* were ever anything more to Prince than a chance to pay the bills.

20Ten (2010)

Like *Planet Earth*, Prince decided that the best way to get *20Ten* out to the public was on the front of newspapers. July 10, 2010, saw the LP distributed with newspapers in Belgium and the United Kingdom, and July 22 saw German and French print distribution. Prince discussed global distribution with Warner Bros., and there were French radio reports in the fall of 2010 of a *20Ten* Deluxe, but it never came to pass. The album was not otherwise distributed. *20Ten* is the Prince album that was never really released.

Prince kicked off 2010 by releasing his worst track ever: "Purple and Gold." Released on January 21 on Vikings.com, it's a tribute to the Minnesota Vikings, his hometown football team. While American football and faith go hand in hand, it's an uneasy union here that makes "Wedding Feast" seem erudite. Other uncollected studio tracks available online in 2010 include "Cause and Effect," "Hot Summer," and "Rich Friends."

It is assumed that *20Ten* was recorded after Prince's return to Paisley Park in the fall of 2009. The album is all Prince except for Shelby J., Liv Warfield, and Elisa Dease on background vocals on seven of the ten tracks and Maceo, Greg Boyer, and Ray Monteiro on "Compassion."

The album doesn't have much to recommend it, although repeated listening breeds familiarity if not contempt. It's as if Prince stepped back into 1982 as the guy who just figured out how to sound like Prince—all form, no function. The highlight, as it were, is the "hidden" track, "Laydown," a whip-smart dance track, while "Beginning Endlessly" at least shows some urgency. Most of the other tracks are derivative, with echoes of past glories haunting every synthesizer riff and quirky drum pattern. "Act of God" is a third-rate Mavis Staple throwaway, and "Sea of Everything" is a slow jazz-like number done better numerous times. The musical bankruptcy is no more apparent than on "Everybody Loves Me." It's his most annoying track, sounding like nothing so much as a guy who got excited when he found a copy of the unreleased 1982 track "Turn It Up" (which finally appeared in 2019).

Prince embarked on a series of brief tours after distributing *20Ten*, his first extended forays since 2004's *Musicology* Live 2004ever tour. The July conclusion of the Prince 20Ten tour marked the end for Cora and Josh Dunham, replaced by John Blackwell on drums and Ida Nielsen on bass. Along with Morris Hayes, Cassandra O'Neal on keyboards, and the vocalists above, this was his band through 2012.

Of note is the July 23, 2010, aftershow at New Morning in Paris. It was a show for the ages: thirty-three songs, almost four hours long and packed with rare gems, such as the debut of "Purple Music," which was released in studio form in 2019 on *1999 Super Deluxe*.

On December 15, 2010, Prince opened the Welcome 2 tours, which included the United States, Euro 2011, Canada, and Australia before concluding in Chicago in September 2012. Not surprisingly, Prince tread lightly on *20Ten* tracks, with only three ever receiving more than ten performances: "Act of God," "Laydown," and "Future Soul Song." "Lavaux," "Walk in Sand," and "Sea of Everything" were never played live.

At this point, fans were starting to wonder why Prince was bothering to release albums in which he clearly had little to no investment. It seems that Prince asked himself the same question and didn't release a new LP for more than four years.

33

Everybody Loves Me

Prince Songs Performed by Other Artists

Prince gave at least fifty songs to other performers that he never released during his lifetime. Most of these songs seem gifted to friends and associates, but some, such as "You're My Love," were simply work for hire. Some artists here, such as Mazarati and Taja Sevelle, are at the border between "associated artist" and protégé, sort of like being "just good friends" or a "girlfriend."

This chapter does include songs performed by Prince released after his death but doesn't include Prince's songs for The Time, the NPG, Madhouse, and so on.

Sue Ann: "Make It through the Storm"

"Make It through the Storm" is the first song Prince placed with another artist that he never released on his own. He wrote the music for "Make It through the Storm" to accompany Chris Moon's lyrics, but Moon was uncredited on the 1981 B-side to Sue Ann's "Let Me Let You Rock Me."

Sueann Carwell was Prince's first protégé. He saw her singing with Sonny T.'s Enterprise in 1978 and decided he'd make her a star. She had trouble following Prince's guide-vocal demos, as would future protégés, but they laid down songs in the summer of 1978. Warner Bros. turned down these recordings, but their manager Owen Husney worked a Warner Bros. deal for Carwell with another producer. Prince felt betrayed, and they had a confrontation at a 1981 First Avenue show. Prince called her in early 1982, and Enterprise opened the March 7, 1982, Met Center show. Carwell joined the aftershow to sing "Still Waiting."

Stevie Nicks: "Stand Back"

Stevie Nicks heard "Little Red Corvette" on the radio and wrote "Stand Back" later that night. While recording the song, she called Prince and recounted her experience. He showed up, played the synthesizers, and she gave him co-songwriting credit on the 1983 top five US hit. In 2011, Nicks revealed that Prince offered her a chance to write the lyrics for "Purple Rain," but she turned him down.

Sheena Easton recorded four Prince songs and hit number one on the *Billboard* US Hot Dance/Club Play charts in 1985 with "Sugar Walls." She also made the US top forty twice accompanying Prince, on the spectacular "U Got the Look" and the decidedly less spectacular "Arms of Orion," released in Europe as a three-track, three-inch CD single.
(Author's collection)

Sheena Easton: "Sugar Walls"

Sheena Easton had enjoyed seven top ten hits when she let engineer David Leonard know she liked *1999* and wanted to sex up her image. Prince wrote "Sugar Walls" for her, which soon moved her from the Pop's Nice List to number two on the Parents Music Resource Center's "Filthy Fifteen," directly behind "Darling Nikki." Prince wrote the song as Alexander Nevermind and played on and produced the track, which he does for the majority of songs in this chapter. In spite of and because of the controversy, the song reached number nine.

The Bangles: "Manic Monday"

"Christopher" gave "Manic Monday" to the Bangles after meeting singer Susannah Hoffs on a plane in February 1985. He also offered "Jealous Girl," but The Hookers reject was again rejected. "Manic Monday," released December 1985, reached number two, kept from the top spot by "Kiss." Prince joined the Bangles on guitar on October 20, 1986, in Hollywood and performed the song live a few times but never took vocals. Prince's version is on 2019's *Originals*.

Mazarati

Mazarati's 1986 Paisley Park album featured one song written, played, and coproduced by Prince, the lead single "100 MPH" (his guide-vocal version was released in 2019), and two with lyrics rewritten by Prince and music by Brown Mark: "Strawberry Lover" and "I Guess It's All Over." But the big takeaway here was literally a takeaway, as Prince reclaimed "Kiss" after he heard Mazarati's version. Their backing vocals still grace Prince's classic track.

Kenny Rogers: "You're My Love"

Prince was so hot in 1986 that everyone wanted a piece of him, even popular country artists. Rogers's management asked for a song and was given "You're My Love," a 1982 solo track that Prince recorded again in 1986 with Clare Fischer. Released on *They Don't Make Them Like They Used To*, it's a generic ballad that doesn't say either Prince or Kenny Rogers. And it literally didn't say Prince since this was his first time using the Joey Coco name. It is available on *Originals*.

Sheena Easton: "Eternity"

One month before the July 1987 "U Got the Look" single, Easton released her own Prince tune, "Eternity," from *No Sound but a Heart*. Prince is credited with writing the tune, but his production credit went to David Leonard. He also provided the instrumentation, this time as Rocker Happyfeller on keyboards and Freddie "The Phantom" on guitar. The album was not released in the United States until 1999.

Taja Sevelle

Minneapolis native Taja Sevelle was one of the first signees to Paisley Park. She was also one of the first artists farmed out to another producer: Chico Bennet. Sevelle's 1987 debut LP featured two Prince compositions: "Wouldn't You Love to Love Me" and "If I Could Get Your Attention." The former had been kicking around since 1976 and was left unreleased with Sue Ann Carwell; Prince released his version in 2019. The latter was recorded by Jill Jones and Mayte and left on the shelf before Prince released his own version on Tidal in November 2015. Sevelle went on to found the highly successful Detroit-based nonprofit Urban Farming.

The Three O'Clock: "Neon Telephone"

The Paisley Underground was a loose confederation of mid-1980s Los Angeles pop-psychedelic bands. The most successful band was the Bangles, although they glossed their roots for a shot at fame. The Three O'Clock was brought into Prince's realm after he saw a video for their song "Her Head's Revolving." The band released one disappointing album at Paisley Park, *Vermillion*, which included the Prince song "Neon Telephone." The band recorded the track with no Prince input. They broke up soon after the album failed critically and commercially.

Sheena Easton: *The Lover in Me*

Ah, those double-entendre titles. Prince gave Easton "101" and "Cool Love" for her November 1988 album *The Lover in Me*. Both feature Prince as Joey Coco writing, producing, and playing the tracks. "101" was released as a single, hitting number two on the dance charts. Easton also recorded "Jaguar," then Prince regifted the song to Mavis Staples.

Madonna: "Love Song"

Prince and Madonna cowrote, produced, and performed "Love Song" on 1989's *Like a Prayer*. According to Madonna, unlike other Prince collaborations, they worked together at the same time and developed the song organically—it was more than just a long-distance collaboration. The result is rather languid. Prince also contributed guitar on the title track, "Act of Contrition," and "Keep It Together." It's assumed that the relationship frayed in late 1988 after Madonna called the *Graffiti Bridge* script a "piece of shit."

Patti LaBelle: *Be Yourself*

Patti LaBelle is the second LaBelle member to work with Prince; Nona Hendryx was the first. Prince gave LaBelle "Yo Mister" and "Love 89," cowritten with Sheena Easton, for 1989's *Be Yourself*. Prince performed and produced the songs and features prominently on "Love 89." Both echo "200 Balloons" and suffer from Prince's late 1980s overproduction.

Kahoru Kohiruimaki: *Time the Motion*

Kahoru Kohiruimaki's manager Seijiro Udo promoted the *Lovesexy* tour in Japan. Uso asked Prince for some songs and was offered two Levi Seacer Jr. collaborations: "Mind Bells" and "Bliss." Prince is prominent in the background on the released versions, the singer simply adding her vocals to the tracks "Mind Bells" in Japanese and "Bliss" in English. How "Bliss" is substantially different from "Sex" is a mystery.

Kid Creole and the Cocoanuts: "The Sex of It"

Kid Creole and the Cocoanuts is the most successful Latin disco/New Wave big-band style band ever. And they might be the only one. The group enjoyed critical fame but little commercial success in the early 1980s, a parallel path to Prince circa *Dirty Mind*. Prince gave Kid Creole (August Darnell) "The Sex of It" in 1989 for *Private Waters in the Great Divide* after meeting up on the *Lovesexy* tour in Europe. Prince wrote the song, plays the instruments, and coproduced with David Z. "The Sex of It" was released as a single and charted on the black and dance charts. Prince recorded the song in July 1987, and it's essentially a Madhouse song with vocals. It's wonderful. He played it once, at the September 5, 1987, Rupert's gig. Circulating August rehearsals for the show feature Prince spending about thirty minutes teaching the song to his band. "The Sex of It" is one of the more noteworthy songs Prince relinquished.

Mica Paris: "If I Love U 2 Nite"

British soul singer Mica Paris released "If I Love U 2 Nite" on her 1990/1991 *Contribution*. Her version contained no Prince input. Paris would go on to an illustrious career as an actress and presenter, crossing the Prince path again in January 2003 with her two-part BBC radio broadcast *Purple Reign—The Prince Story*, which featured a noncritical, interview-based look at Prince's career.

Javetta Steele: *Here It Is*

Javetta Steele of The Steeles released *Here It Is* in 1991 in France. It included "And How," a 1986 Prince song rewritten in 1991 by David Z. and Levi Seacer Jr., and the Prince/David Z./Seacer "Skip 2 My U My Darling," perhaps the most precocious Prince song title. Prince had no other involvement with these tracks. When the disc was globally released in 1993, these songs were replaced by "Hold Me," a Paisley Park–produced, NPG-backed track that was also offered to

Mayte, and "Open Book." The latter was produced by Paisley Park and cowritten by Prince, Seacer, and Martika, intended for the latter's *Martika's Kitchen.*

T. C. Ellis: *True Confessions*

One imagines Paisley Park Records of the early 1990s like an airport, with multiple planes endlessly circling the airport, waiting for air traffic control's permission to land. Rapper T. C. Ellis received permission to land *True Confessions* on May 28, 1991. The Paisley Park release included three Prince songs: "Miss Thang," written, performed, and produced by Prince; the brief, old "Girl O' My Dreams," written by Prince but otherwise a Seacer product; and a cover, "Bambi (Rap)," which is difficult to judge more as funny or embarrassing. Albums like this are why Paisley Park Records would be out of business within three years.

Martika: *Martika's Kitchen*

Marta "Martika" Marrero had a number one single in 1989 with "Toy Soldiers" from her self-titled debut. In November 1990, she saw *Graffiti Bridge*, was enthralled, and let Prince know. Within a month, he sent her four songs that ended up on her 1991 follow-up *Martika's Kitchen*. Prince produced the four tracks as Paisley Park and provided instrumentation. He wrote the title song alone and cowrote "Spirit," "Don't Say U Love Me," and "Love . . . Thy Will Be Done." The latter was a number ten hit in the United States. The NPG recorded the song in 1994, but it was left off *Exodus*. Prince started playing it in 1995 and played it about forty times through 2016. It was released on *Originals* in 2019. An exhausted Martika quit the music industry soon after this album.

Celine Dion: "With This Tear"

Prince gave Dion "With This Tear" as a present. He recorded it in early 1992, but Dion rerecorded it with Clare Fischer for her self-titled 1992 album. The song was intended for Javetta Steele, and Prince recorded a version in 2001 with Milenia. Dion's biggest influence on Prince is *A New Day . . .* , her 2003–2007 residency in Las Vegas that influenced his residency model.

Loïs Lane: *Precious*

Loïs Lane's self-titled debut hit number one in the Netherlands in 1989 and spawned a hit single: "It's the First Time." The group was invited to open twenty-six dates on 1990's European Nude tour. Prince promised them tracks and delivered "Qualified," cowritten with Kirk Johnson. He also let them record "Sex." He provided instrumentation for those tracks and "I Oh I" and "Crying," all of which were produced by Johnson in early 1992.

Louie Louie: *Let's Get Started*

Louis "Louie" Cordero enjoyed moderate success as a rap artist in the early 1990s but is best known for appearing in Madonna's "Borderline" video. Prince gave him the decent "Get Blue," co-composed with Levi Seacer, and "Dance unto the Rhythm," a song finished by producer Michael Koppelman that sounds like a C+C Music Factory parody. But that's better than the rejected song "Hey, Louie Louie," cowritten with Tony M. and Seacer, which sounds like MC Hammer lite—some rough going here.

Monie Love: *In a Word or 2*

British rapper Monie Love's debut album *Down to Earth* hit number twenty-six on the US black charts in 1990. Prince wrote songs with Love in early 1992, five of which ended up on *Carmen Electra* and two here: the title song and "Born to B.R.E.E.D." Prince played on and produced both songs, and the latter, also written with Levi Seacer, hit number one on the US dance charts.

The Steeles: "Well Done"

"Well Done" from The Steeles's 1993 *Heaven Help Us* is one of the secret gems of Prince giveaway songs. Cowritten with David Z. and Seacer, the gospel tune shares a jumping urgency with Mavis Staples's "House in Order." Ricky Peterson produced both tracks. The Steeles, without Prince, performed the song at the September 1993 Begley Warehouse show, but it didn't appear in *The Sacrifice of Victor*.

George Clinton: *Hey Man . . . Smell My Finger*

Hey Man… Smell My Finger (1993) is legendary performer George Clinton's second and final Paisley Park LP. *The Cinderella Theory* (1989) had no Prince input, but Prince added instruments and remixed five excellent versions of the single "Tweakin'." For the second LP, Prince cowrote, coproduced, and played on "The Big Pump," a monotonous song revived from 1990. He also sang background on the superior "Get Satisfied" and played it three times live in 1993. Prince covered

"Martial Law" from the album and included "Hollywood" on *1-800-NEW-FUNK* but was not involved in recording either song.

Tevin Campbell: *I'm Ready*

Tevin Campbell recorded Prince's "Round and Round" for *Graffiti Bridge* and included a "Soul Edit Mix" on his 1991 debut *T.E.V.I.N.* Prince played on, produced, and wrote four songs on 1993's *I'm Ready* as Paisley Park. "Paris 1798430" is a speedier "Sign 'o' the Times" update, "The Halls of Desire" would fit in on *Come*, and "Uncle Sam" is mid-tempo black-power patriotism. Prince reclaimed "Shhh" for *The Gold Experience*.

Rosie Gaines: "My Tender Heart"

It's difficult not to feel sorry for Rosie Gaines. Harassed on the tour bus, stuck behind lesser talents such as Carmen Electra, it took about six years for her "Prince" album to be released. But it wasn't on Paisley Park Records, which no longer existed, and the 1995 release contained minimal Prince input. Raw deal. Gaines worked on a solo album in 1990 during the *Diamonds and Pearls* sessions that also yielded her main vocal numbers: "Daddy Pop" and "Walk Don't Walk." "My Tender Heart," cowritten with Prince, appeared on 1995's CD *Closer Than Close*, then on a twentieth-anniversary digital release, also as "My Tender Love (My Tender Heart Demo)." Prince sang background on both. Both LPs also featured versions of "I Want U," credited to the duo but little more than a rewrite of the Marvin Gaye song, originally intended for the Pointer Sisters. Prince also appeared on the Bob Marley cover "Turn Your Lights Down Low," a disappointing mess.

Fonky Bald Heads: "Rowdy Mac"

The Fonky Bald Heads are Kirk Johnson's early 2000s band featuring Mike Scott and Kip Blackshire. Prince and Johnson cowrote "Rowdy Mac," a busy "make some noise!" groove with Blackshire on vocals that showed up on the band's 2001 *The Self Titled Album*. The band opened some 2001 Hit N' Run shows and played the song.

No Doubt: "Waiting Room"

In 1999, No Doubt singer Gwen Stefani recorded vocals for Symbol's "So Far, So Pleased," which appeared on *Rave Un2 the Joy Fantastic*. "Waiting Room" went the other way, with Prince rewriting, coproducing, and appearing prominently on the 2001 *Rock Steady* song. The vocals are beautiful, and the song is another hidden gem.

Rosie Gaines: "In the Socket"

"In the Socket" was recorded in June 1991 for a 1994 album, *Concrete Jungle*, which was released in 2005 as *Try Me*. The song was felt dated in 1991, and it didn't improve by 2005.

George Clinton: "Paradigm"

A solid Prince and Clinton collaboration, this *Hey Man . . . Smell My Finger* outtake has a slow, open groove that points toward both a Tony M.–less "Sexy M.F." and "Same Page Different Book." Clinton released "Paradigm" on CD-R at shows in 2001, then on 2005's *Sneak Peek* EP and *How Late Do U Have 2BB4UR Absent?* Essential.

Shelby J.: "North Carolina"

Prince cowrote, played on, and produced background singer Shelby J.'s first single: "North Carolina." Although the song was released December 2012, she sang the song during Prince shows a few times in 2009. A single version with remixes was first sold at an August 22, 2013, show billed as "Shelby J. & Liv Warfield with the New Power Generation featuring NPG Hornz with special guests." The tune is lightweight funk supporting Shelby's autobiographical black-power lyrics.

Janelle Monáe: "Givin Em What They Love"

Prince wrote lyrics and played on "Givin Em What They Love," the lead track on Monáe's 2013 *The Electric Lady*. It's smooth and trippy and the first song here where you feel Prince is lucky to be a part of it rather than the other way around. Prince had the film (*Hidden Figures*) and recording star open for him a few times, and he joined her for this song on December 29, 2013, at the Mohegan Sun Arena in Connecticut.

Liv Warfield: *The Unexpected*

As with Rosie Gaines, Liv Warfield worked with Prince for many years but didn't end up with much Prince to show for it. Prince plays on and the duo cowrote

"Your Show," a surprising extended jazz number with tinges of the extended portion of "Come." Prince also gave her "The Unexpected," which he released with 3rdEyeGirl as "Wow."

Prince also cowrote or gave away these songs, all of which are worth hunting down:

- Ren Woods: "I Don't Wanna Stop," *Azz Izz* (1982)
- Deborah Allen: "Telepathy," as Joey Coco, *Telepathy* (1987)
- Nona Hendryx: "Baby Go-Go," as Joey Coco, *Female Trouble* (1987)
- Dale: "So Strong," *Riot in English* (1988)
- Paula Abdul: "U," as Paisley Park, *Spellbound* (1991)
- Patti LaBelle: "I Hear Your Voice," with Rosie Gaines and Francis Jules, *Burnin'* (1991)
- El DeBarge: "Tip O' My Tongue," with Kirk Johnson as Paisley Park, *The Storm* (1992)
- Howard Hewett: "Allegiance," *Allegiance* (1992)
- Candy Dulfer: "Sunday Afternoon," *Sax-a-Go-Go* (1993)
- Dale Bozzio: "Take Me to Your Leader," with Bozzio, *Make Love Not War* (2010)

34

The Second Coming

Unreleased Projects

Prince is almost as well known for what he hasn't done as for what he's done. A touchstone of his mythology is the Vault, Prince's private stash of unreleased material. Unfortunately, the Vault was neglected and degrading, so much so that estate managers in 2017 moved it to a secure California location.

Unreleased project information thrived through multiple channels, such as missives from Prince, blurbs on actual releases, interviews with associates, and memorabilia auctions. Sometimes it's only an offhanded title mention, such as *Heart*, a 1994 acoustic album, or *New World*, a 1995 techno album, but sometimes it's more.

This chapter surveys Prince's major unreleased projects. Songs and videos from some projects are familiar to longtime fans, while some circulate only among elite collectors. Others are lost or were never produced. There are probably many more projects buried in the Vault.

The Rebels

After recording *Prince* solo in early 1979, Prince gathered his band at Mountain Ears Sound Studios in Boulder, Colorado, from July 10 to 21 to record as The Rebels. Unlike later side projects, The Rebels encouraged creative input other than Prince's. Dez Dickerson contributed three songs ("Too Long," "Disco Away," and an instrumental), and Andre Cymone wrote two ("Thrill You or Kill You" and an instrumental) and sang another ("Hard to Get"). Gayle Chapman sang three songs but didn't write anything. For Prince tunes, "Turn Me On" remains unreleased, but "You" showed up as Paula Abdul's "U," and "If I Love You Tonight" was recorded by Mica Paris and Mayte. Bobby Z. and Matt Fink rounded out the band. Prince dropped the project with no explanation, but it's likely he didn't enjoy not being in total control. Worth searching out.

The Second Coming

Devo video director Chuck Statler filmed the March 7, 1982, *Controversy* show at the Met Center in Bloomington, Minnesota. During editing of the planned concert movie, Prince decided to add a narrative and release *The Second Coming* theatrically. Once he saw a rough cut, edited in part by Steve Rivkin, Bobby Z.'s brother, Prince scrapped the project. Prince took possession of the footage in 2007 when he finally paid Statler for his work. In an echo of Prince hero Joni Mitchell's "Big Yellow Taxi," the Met Center was later torn down and paved over, used as overflow parking for the Mall of America.

The Flesh

Prince hit the studio on December 28, 1985, playing guitar and piano with a new band: The Flesh. With Sheila E., her guitarist Levi Seacer Jr., and Eric Leeds, the quartet recorded eight jazz/funk instrumentals during the Four-Hour Paisley Jam. Six tracks remain unreleased, but "Madrid" was recycled for Leeds's "Andorra," and "12 Keys" prefigures "The Question of U." Two days later, they laid down an additional four tracks: "U Gotta Shake Something" and its doppelganger "Damn," "Most Finest Whiskey," and "Voodoo Who." Leeds also overdubbed sax on "A Couple of Miles," the December 26 Miles Davis tribute.

After an epic (for mid-1980s Prince) five-day break, the quartet returned to the studio on January 5, 1986, joined by Lisa Coleman, Wendy Melvoin, and Wendy's brother Jonathan. The fabled Seven-Hour Everybody's Jam produced six songs: "Groove in C Minor," "Slow Groove in G Major," "Groove in G Flat Minor," "Junk Music," "Up from Below," and "Y'All Want Some More?" On January 22, Prince and Leeds pulled together The Flesh's EP *Junk Music*. The A-side presented a nineteen-minute, thirty-seven-second edit of the sixty-three-minute "Junk Music," featuring Prince on drums. The B-side included "Up from Below," "Y'all Want Some More," and "A Couple of Miles." Prince pressed copies of the EP, but Warner Bros. had no interest in another project with *Parade* on the horizon. "Junk Music" would end up as incidental music in *Under the Cherry Moon*.

Dream Factory

Dream Factory recording started as Prince moved into his Galpin Boulevard house with its state-of-the-art twenty-four-track studio in March 1986. It endured three configurations from April to July as a Revolution album but was abandoned when Wendy, Lisa, and Brown Mark all wanted to quit the band in late July.

Nine *Dream Factory* songs have never been released by Prince. Given the state of the band, it's not surprising that Wendy's "Interlude," Lisa's "Visions" and "A Place in Heaven," and their shared vocal "It's a Wonderful Day" remain on the cutting room floor, although the latter pops up in *Under the Cherry Moon*. "Big Tall Wall" and "And That Says What" also remain in the Vault. Mavis Staples released "Train." The hard-rocking "Witness 4 the Prosecution" would seem at home on *Sign 'o' the Times* and the whirly "All My Dreams" on *Parade*. A tenth song, a 1982 version of "Teacher, Teacher," was released on *1999 Super Deluxe*.

In 2017, Susannah Melvoin shared her original *Dream Factory* artwork, revealing that one configuration was credited to The Flesh. This project spilled into the next two unreleased 1986 projects—*Camille* and *Crystal Ball*—before culminating in *Sign 'o' the Times*.

Camille

Camille is an eight-track album Prince recorded in the fall of 1986 as the pseudonymous title character. The release was to be credited to Camille, he or she of highly distorted vocals. All *Camille* songs have been released in some form, although "Rebirth of the Flesh," the album's best song, was released only as a 1988 rehearsal in 2001 through the NPG Music Club.

It's unclear why *Camille* was scrapped, but it seems likely that the dozen songs worked and reworked in the second half of November changed Prince's thinking about the overall project. Warner Bros. assigned *Camille* a catalog number. It would have been the first release featuring the Paisley Park label. In late 2016, a vinyl *Camille* belonging to mid-1980s Prince employee Karen Krattinger was auctioned as part of a nineteen-record lot. The lot sold for $29,645.

Crystal Ball

Crystal Ball began as a Camille release, although it doesn't maintain the vocal conceit. The three-disc set was compiled on November 30, 1986, and soon after rejected by Warner Bros., which felt that the twenty-two-track album was too long. *Crystal Ball* largely ended up as *Sign 'o' the Times*, which used fifteen tracks, adding "U Got the Look." All songs have been released in some form except "The Ball," which appears altered as "Eye Know."

Hard Life

Hard Life is a thirteen-minute movie "misdirected" by Prince, made to accompany Madhouse *16*. It's a stagy romp featuring Matt Fink's parents that offers footage of Madhouse pimping like Sun Ra wannabes and the incongruity of Cat and Prince's dad playing pool.

Rave unto the Joy Fantastic

Prince started working on *Rave unto the Joy Fantastic* in June 1988 but dropped it in early 1989 for *Batman*. He returned to the project a decade later, keeping only the reworked title song. The album went through three configurations. Prince eventually released most of the songs on his own or through protégés, but "The Voice Inside," "Stimulation," "Big House," "We Got the Power," and "Am I without U?" remain unreleased. Both "God Is Alive" and "If I Had a Harem" were played on the *Lovesexy* tour, and the latter is on *Lovesexy Live* as "Blues in C (If I Had a Harem)."

The Dawn

At least four projects share *The Dawn* moniker. Little is known about the 1986 musical or the 1989 movie. "The Holy River" (1997) cassette single (aka cassingle) claims that "Welcome 2 the Dawn (Acoustic Version)" is "from the 4thcoming experience *the dawn*." *the dawn* may have morphed into *The Truth*, which is how the song was released.

Sources indicate that 1994's *The Dawn* was an album of forty songs, seven of which remain unreleased and noncirculating: "Strawberries," "Dream," "Laurianne," "Dance of Desperation," "I Wanna Be Held 2 Night," "Emotional Crucifixion," and "Slave 2 the Funk." A fifty-seven-track fan-made *The Dawn* was released in 2008. It reimagines the 1991–1994 era and creates new versions of songs through imaginative mixing and editing. For many, it is the go-to Prince album of the early 1990s. The *Village Voice* ran an appreciation of *The Dawn* in their 2016 Prince commemorative issue.

Live and *The Live Experience*

After neglecting the audio live market for more than fifteen years, Prince warmed to the idea in 1994. In the summer of 1994, he planned "Live," a single

News of forthcoming projects, both real and imagined, arrived in many different forms. "The Holy River" single included "Welcome 2 The Dawn (Acoustic Version)," announced as from the forthcoming *The Dawn* LP. The acoustic track found its way to *The Truth*, but we never lived to see *The Dawn*. A Borders Books and Music store promo cassette of "The Holy River" also included "The Most Beautiful Girl in the World (Mustang Mix)" … but not "Mustang Mix '96," also rumored for inclusion on *The Dawn*.

(Author's collection)

including the then unreleased "Come," "Endorphinmachine," and "Hide the Bone." By January 1995, he was looking toward the past, with a multidisc set including performances from 1987's *Sign 'o' the Times* through 1993's *Act II*. That summer, he was preparing *The Live Experience*, culled mainly from his June 8, 1995, birthday show at Glam Slam Miami. Prince finally released a live single in 1997, *NYC*, featuring "Jam of the Year" and "Face Down." His first live LP wouldn't arrive until 2002's *One Nite Alone… Live!* sets.

Playtime by Versace

The existence of *Playtime by Versace* (1995) was revealed in 2017 when a mock-up CD appeared in an auction from the collection of Prince's mid-1990s art director Michael Van Huffel. The handmade package was a gift for Gianni Versace and his daughter Donatella. The CD included eleven songs. Two of the songs—"Playtime" and "Stone"—have never been released, "I'll Never B Another Fool" appears here exclusively with Prince vocals, and "Poor Goo," "Van Gogh," and "18 & Over" differ from their released versions. Donatella used an exclusive eleven-minute, now unavailable Prince mix in the summer of 2016. *Playtime* sold for $3,675 in the fall of 2017.

In addition to not releasing his own work, Prince didn't release a lot of work by and with associates. Madhouse gave a couple tries at a third album, Madhouse 24. The first go-around ended up as Eric Leeds's *Times Squared*, and the second, pictured here, remains unreleased, save for "17" from *1-800-NEW-FUNK*.   (*Courtesy Jeff Munson*)

Prince: The Vault—Volumes I, II, and III

Prince announced in a December 22, 1995, press release that he was severing ties with Warner Bros. To fulfill his contract, he would release *The Vault—Volumes I, II, and III*. It's believed *The Vault* would come from the two albums Prince had been working on—*Chaos and Disorder* and *The Vault… Old Friends 4 Sale*—although the third volume is unknown.

Happy Tears

Happy Tears was a multimedia collaboration between Symbol and Mayte to celebrate her pregnancy. The November 1996 release was to include a CD, a storybook, and a read-along cassette. The project was abandoned after the death of their child. The project's "She Gave Her Angels" appeared on *Crystal Ball*, and the updated "Starfish and Coffee" from the *Muppets Tonight* appearance would have been included.

Beautiful Strange

The *Beautiful Strange* album (1998) was set to accompany the video of the same name. The only songs recorded were the title song, which appeared in the video and on *Rave Un2 the Joy Fantastic*, and the cover song "Twisted." In 2002, Prince was seen on tour with a notebook titled "Beautiful Strange" that included the "Twisted" lyrics. It's unknown if he intended to resume the project or if it was just an old notebook.

Roadhouse Garden

Prince announced on September 30, 1998, that he'd work again with The Revolution and a week later announced *Roadhouse Garden*. It's unclear if he intended to work with Wendy and Lisa again; it's probable that if he did, he didn't want to pay them, and it's possible that he wanted to but that his freshly minted Jehovah's Witness faith and Wendy and Lisa's sexual orientation proved too much of an obstacle.

Rumors say that this resumes *Dream Factory*, but Matt Fink claims that the almost completed 1986 album was *Roadhouse Garden*, not *Dream Factory*. Besides revisiting unreleased songs, Prince also planned to assemble new songs "using parts from many tunes." Eight songs have been associated with the project. The title song, "Our Destiny," and "Wonderful Ass" were released in 2017. "Splash" and live versions of "In a Large Room with No Light" and "Empty Room" have been released online. "Witness 4 the Prosecution" and "All My Dreams" are still unreleased.

New Funk Sampling Series

Prince was sampled by everyone from Tupac to Nine Inch Nails to Kanye West. On March 28, 1999, on Love4OneAnother.com, he announced plans to release a samples collection. The seven-disc *New Funk Sampling Series* offered royalty-free access to 700 samples for $700. The seven discs were "Bass," "The Human Voice," "Guitar," "Keyboards," "Loops & Percussion," "Sound FX," and "Orchestral." Samples ranged from the seventeen-second "Bass Loop 001—Come" to the five-second "Voice Sample (Bob George)" saying "The New Power Generation has just taken control" to many tracks that register less than one second, such as "Voice Sample (Female—Dead Like Elvis)." The set was never released but was leaked.

Crystal Ball II

During the 2000 A Celebration, Prince offered Paisley Park visitors the opportunity to vote on his next album. Choices included *Roadhouse Garden*, a live LP, a rock LP, a covers LP, *When 2 R in Love: The Ballads of Prince*, a new studio album, *Madrid 2 Chicago* (a "smooth jazz album"), and *Crystal Ball II*. For the latter, fans were given twenty-two title choices, and seventeen tracks were declared the winners.

While the earlier *Crystal Ball* focused on songs from the mid-1980s and 1990s, *II* broadly splits into solo tracks from 1980 to 1982 and Revolution tracks. The first category includes "American Jam," "Strange Way," "Girl O' My Dreams," "Lust U Always," "Xtraloveable" (since rerecorded for *Hitnrun Phase Two*), "Turn It Up," and "U're All Eye Want," the latter two since released on *1999 Super Deluxe*. The second category includes "Adonis & Bathsheba," "Everybody Want What They Don't Got," "Evolsidog," "Kiss—Xtended Version (Never released b4)," and "Others Here with Us," plus the now released "Electric Intercourse," "Katrina's Paper Dolls," and "Love and Sex." "3 Nigs Watchin' a Kung Fu Movie," a Sheila E. outtake, and 1991's "Eye Wonder" are outliers. "Wonderful Ass," also released in 2017, and the year 1999 track "What Should B Souled" were also on the collection.

The five reject tracks were the early songs "She's Just a Baby," "If It'll Make U Happy" (on *1999 Super Deluxe*), "Come Elektra Tuesday," "Girl," and "Gotta Stop (Messin' About)." Maybe he forgot the last one was on *The Hits/The B-Sides*. It's unclear if "Girl" is the original Time track or the B-side.

When 2 R in Love: The Ballads of Prince

Prince held a press conference on May 16, 2000, announcing he was free of his publishing contract and would start using his name again. He mentioned a retrospective ballads album that he couldn't get Warner Bros. to agree to. The collection, including "Do Me, Baby," "Insatiable," "Scandalous," and "Adore," was a thumbs-down during 2000 fan voting.

High

As announced on NPGOnlineLtd.com, *High* was almost ready to go on August 8, 2000, when Prince received a version from his engineer Femi Jiya. The ten-track album, which reached the point of advanced artwork, was scrapped as the first post-Symbol album in favor of *The Rainbow Children*. All songs were eventually released, and only "My Medallion" and "When Will We B Paid" didn't appear on either *The Slaughterhouse* or *The Chocolate Invasion*.

A Celebration

Prince wanted to give WB some competition in the CD market by rerecording and/or releasing his old hits. On the May 15, 2001, he announced *A Celebration*, a twenty-track album that would do just that. It's unknown if the old songs were rerecorded, and it's difficult to figure the identity of the promised four new tracks, as he was producing so much new material at the time.

Kevin Smith Film

Director Kevin Smith wanted "TMBGITW" in *Jay and Silent Bob Strike Back*. Although Prince liked Smith's *Dogma*, about religious hypocrisy, he declined. Smith ended up with The Time's "Jungle Love" and an invitation to record the 2001 Paisley Park Celebration. Originally a more ambitious project, Smith's footage, including fan discussions with Prince, ended up in *Rainbow Children* promotional material. Smith shared his Prince experiences in two *An Evening with Kevin Smith* videos, perhaps the most biting public ridicule unleased on Prince. Smith apologized for his public reckoning in an April 27, 2016, memorial video.

NPG Music Club Albums 2002

Madrid 2 Chicago was A Celebration voting option before it was announced in the *One Nite Alone* tour book as an exclusive CD to the NPG Music Club. Members would also receive the CDs *Xenophobia*, *Last December*, and *The Very Best of Symbol*. The NPG Music Club released "Madrid 2 Chicago" and "Breathe" on NPG Music Club Edition #12 on January 17, 2002, as from the forthcoming album, but the album never came forth. *Xenophobia* was released sans title song in 2003 as *Xpectation*. Nothing is known about *Last December* or *The Very Best of Symbol*, which would have entailed working with Warner Bros. for tracks, rerecording the Warner Bros. tracks, or limiting the collection to the three non–Warner Bros. Symbol LPs of original material.

Xenophobia

The Paisley Park gathering on June 21–28, 2002, was called Xenophobia Celebration and actually discouraged rather than celebrated xenophobia. The seven shows were quickly bootlegged, and Prince responded with an NPG Music

Club post in July that seemed to indicate that a seven-disc set of the shows, *Xenophobia*, was forthcoming. An NPG Records spokesperson clarified that a three-CD set was to be produced, probably the *One Nite Alone* sets, released on November 24.

The Chocolate Invasion

On October 15, 2003, Prince announced the seven-disc collection *The Chocolate Invasion*. On November 13, a manufacturing bug delayed the unrealized project. *One Nite Alone…* and *The War* were already available on CD. *The Chocolate Invasion*, *The Slaughterhouse*, *C-Note*, and *Xpectation* were made available online over the next sixteen months. The ten-track *Glam Slam Club Mix* was released on January 17, 2002, as part of the final NPG Ahdio Show.

Welcome 2 America

Prince's Welcome 2 tours stretched from America's December 2010 debut through Australia's May 2012 finale. Somewhere in the middle, Prince had plans for a 20Ten follow-up: *Welcome 2 America*. Instead, it would be four years until his next LP releases. While an exact track list has not been found, only the associated songs "Born 2 Die" and "Running Game (Son of a Slave Owner)" remain unreleased or uncirculating.

Purple Rain Thirtieth-Anniversary Edition

Prince kissed and made up with Warner Bros. on April 18, 2014, gaining control of his back catalog and promising a 2015 *Purple Rain* Thirtieth-Anniversary Edition. It was never released, but the 2015 *Purple Rain* remaster was used in the 2017 *Deluxe Edition* set.

35

U See My Way Back Home

The Final LPs, 2014–2019

The post-*20Ten* Welcome 2 tours comprised about eighty-five rote shows stretching from December 2010 to September 2012. Sometime in September, Prince headed home to plot his next move. He trusted bassist Ida Nielsen, whom he found on MySpace in 2010, but needed to break out of the rut of endlessly playing the same hits in the same way live and cranking out the same indistinguishable, inoffensive R&B LPs. He first turned to Hannah Ford Welton, whom he also found online.

Prince liked what he heard when Nielsen and Welton jammed and gave Hannah a test drive behind the kit on "Stratus" at a September 26 Chicago House of Blues aftershow. He perhaps liked even more what he heard when he talked with Hannah's husband, keyboardist Joshua Welton. By October 23, both Weltons joined Prince on *Jimmy Kimmel Live!* performing "Rock and Roll Love Affair." Relying on the couple, Prince then recruited a new guitarist, Canadian Donna Grantis, who first jammed with the band in November 2012. This led not only to the creation of Prince's third official backing band, 3rdEyeGirl, but also to his first work with an outside producer, Josh Welton, and the foundation for his last four studio albums.

Grantis and 3rdEyeGirl made their live debut on January 18, 2013, the "Surprise" night of Prince's three-night, six-show residency at the Dakota Jazz Club and Restaurant in Minneapolis. Over the next twenty-one months, Prince and 3rdEyeGirl rolled out two tours: 2013's thirty-four-date North American Live Out Loud tour and 2014's thirteen-date European Hit N Run II. The latter was Prince's last official group tour.

In addition, Prince, usually with the 3rdEyeGirl and occasionally with NPG, played more than fifty one-off shows during this time, including three spectacular nights at the Montreux Jazz Festival in July 2013. The3rdEyeGirl shows were some of the most unfussy—and fun—shows of Prince's career. This live phase closed with a September 30, 2014, Paisley Park *Plectrumelectrum/Art Official Age* release party that was available as a Yahoo! Live video stream, followed by a November 1 appearance on *Saturday Night Live.*

Released the same day as the 3rdEyeGirl collaboration *Plectrumelectrum*, 2014's *Art Official Age* is the first Prince album with a co-producer, Joshua Welton. Unlike other studio-bound projects that were clearly excuses to create new product, such as the steely *20Ten*, Prince seemed fully invested in this venture.   *(Author's collection)*

In the studio, Prince and 3rdEyeGirl music and video started streaming on March 13, 2013, on Vimeo.com, with the appearance of "Plectrumelectrum." Prince's collaboration with one Welton, Hannah, led to the rocking *Plectrumelectrum* LP. His collaboration with the other Welton, Joshua, led to the electronic/dance LP *Art Official Age*.

Released a few days earlier in Europe, *Plectrumelectrum* and *Art Official Age* were released on CD on September 30, 2014. They were Prince's first US releases in more than five years. Perhaps more amazingly, they were NPG Records albums officially licensed and distributed by Warner Bros. It was the first Warner Bros. release of genuine new Prince material in eighteen years since *Chaos and Disorder*.

Plectrumelectrum (2014)

Plectrumelectrum recording seems to have started soon after Grantis's November 2012 audition. The name 3rdEyeGirl first mysteriously appeared on a streamed

New Year's rehearsal of "Bambi." Throughout 2013 and 2014, Prince and 3rdEye-Girl rehearsal, live, and studio material appeared through various online venues. Band members claim to have worked on more than 200 songs during the period.

Perhaps what's most striking about *Plectrumelectrum* is that it's Prince's most democratic album and the first in which he's truly a member of the band. Aside from live discs, this is the first album with a full-fledged band on every track—and only thirty-six albums into his career. He also gives Hannah Ford Welton lead vocals on three songs. Unlike on the disastrous *Rave Un2 the Joy Fantastic* or the 2015 albums, these vocals are integral, not just guest spots punched in later. The democracy ends at the songwriting. Although the group is credited with writing all the songs, Prince composed them all except Grantis's title track and the cover "Anotherlove." The latter is the weakest song with Prince vocals (although not a weak song), a mid-LP lull hooked up with the mid-tempo, overly pensive "Tictactoe."

Plectrumelectrum is just fun music. It's always engaging, and it never gets too serious or taxing. The top songs here all sort of sound like something else, but at least it's not the fifteenth reworking of "Damn U." The guitar crunch of the instrumental title track recalls Led Zeppelin's "The Ocean," while the hard New Wave pop of "Fixurlifeup" echoes the Cars's "Just What I Needed." "Marz" is just hard New Wave pop. "Funknroll" (available remixed on *Art Official Age*), "Pretzelbodylogic," and "Wow" are all rocking fist pumpers—sing along at your own risk. "Boytrouble," featuring raps by Lizzo and Sophia Eris, is a quirky, jerky tune, the nod toward traditional R&B along with "Stopthistrain." The three songs with Hannah Ford Welton's leads are the weakest: "Aintturninround," "Whitecaps," and "Stopthistrain." Especially on the latter, the vocals just aren't there.

Plectrumelectrum hit number eight on the US top 200 charts and number one on the top rock albums charts. Reflecting the intended demographic, it failed to chart on the top R&B charts. Two singles are associated with the album. The LP version of "Fixurlifeup" was released through multiple digital platforms on May 13, 2013. It failed to chart. The LP version of "Pretzelbodylogic" was available as a digital single on February 3, 2014. It also failed to chart. Long after the LP release, a Josh Welton remix, "Pretzelbodylogic Reloaded," was released on Tidal in the fall of 2015.

Prince didn't tour *Plectrumelectrum* as much as issue the album as a culmination of touring. The Hit N Run Part II tour ended on June 7, 2014, in Vienna. After that, Prince played a half dozen 2014 US shows, with only the July 4 New Orleans Essence Fest performance a major public affair. About twenty-five Hit N Run and Paisley Park shows followed in 2015. The last 3rdEyeGirl gigs were a pair of shows at the Warner Theater in Washington, DC, on June 14. By the fall, Kirk Johnson was reinstalled on drums.

The title song, "Fixurlifeup," "Funknroll," and "Pretzelbodylogic" were all played regularly; "Marz," "Anotherlove," and "Wow" were all played once; and

2015 also saw two Prince LP releases, *Hitnrun Phase One* in September and *Hitnrun Phase Two* in December. Although Joshua Welton isn't credited as co-producer on *Phase One*, his presence is felt as the album continues the more studio-oriented sound of *Art Official Age*, a connection referenced as the CD's center hole forms a third eye for a cartoon Prince.   *(Author's collection)*

"Aintturninround," "Whitecaps," "Boytrouble," "Stopthistrain," and "Tictactoe" never hit the stage.

Art Official Age (2014)

3rdEyeGirl appears on one *Art Official Age* track, the "Funknroll" remix, but the ambitious LP is more of a Prince and Joshua Welton collaboration. In fact, the big revelation here is that, for the first time, Prince offers coproduction credit for an entire album. Prince working with a producer on a Warner Bros. record? Will wonders never cease?

Art Official Age is at turns bombastic and insular, deceptively rich and fulfilling. Its closest comparison in terms of narrative reach is *The Rainbow Children*. Aside from the frantic, multifaceted opener "Art Official Cage" and the pop rocker "Funknroll," both highlights, and the amazingly lazy "The Gold Standard," the only clunker, this is a peaceful, contemplative R&B album. Unlike Prince's recent pop-culture scolding, this work accepts responsibility for the necessary change. Prince highlights this on the sleeve notes, calling this a work of "spiritual healing" and in the "third eye" concept in general. It works.

Art Official Age hit number five on the US Hot 200 charts and number one on the R&B hip-hop charts. It failed to make the top rock album charts.

The album was preceded by three singles. The LP version of "Breakfast Can Wait" was released digitally on September 3, 2013, with *The Breakfast Experience* EP following on October 24, 2013. The song reached number twenty-six on the US adult R&B charts. LP versions of "Breakdown" and "Clouds" failed to chart.

"Breakdown" was played live about a dozen times, but most other tracks were played only once or twice if at all.

Hitnrun Phase One (2015)

Prince largely kept quiet in 2015, with two notable exceptions, both pointing toward an increasing interest in social justice. On May 9, he released "Baltimore," a song written in response to the death of Freddie Gray while in Baltimore police custody on April 19 and the subsequent riots. Prince followed this the next day with a "Rally 4 Peace" concert, which directed some proceeds to local charities. Any support of Gray and his family at this time was controversial in some circles, understood as an explicit lack of support for local police. This is one of the few times that Prince publicly took a divisive stand.

The other 2015 high-profile gig was on June 13 at an African American Music Appreciation Month celebration at the White House. Prince, 3rdEyeGirl, and Stevie Wonder entertained President Barack Obama and First Lady Michelle Obama and a roomful of dignitaries. This featured in a 2018 UK Channel 4 documentary.

Hitnrun Phase One is Prince's more "experimental," dance-oriented 2015 release. While there's one classic and a few key tunes, the album is marred by a stream of guests and a songwriting mentality that tends to confuse things happening with interesting things happening.

Much of *Phase One* was recorded in early 2015, but the songs stretch as far back as 1992 in the case of "1000 X's & O's." Prince and Josh Weldon receive cowriting and production credit, and the duo also created all the sounds, save for a few horn fills and vocals and Donna Grantis's guitar solo on "Ain't About to Stop."

The album has one classic track, the shifty, muddy "The X's Face," or one almost classic track since the killer melody and rhythm don't go anywhere and can't even sustain the brief two minutes, thirty-eight seconds of the song before going off on some tangent about bananas. The other "X" song, "1000 X's & O's," is the other decent tune here, although it could use cleaner production. "This Could B Us" survives as a remixed dreamy ballad from *Art Official Age*. The rest of the album? Knob-twisting sound and fury and an incessant parade of guest vocalists, *Rave Un2 the Joy Fantastic*'s superficial appeal updated for 2015.

Hitnrun Phase One was first made available as a Tidal stream on September 7, 2015, and a week later was obtainable as a download or a physical CD. The Tidal stream was the new LP accompanied by the availability of a major portion of Prince's back catalog, including many NPG Music Club exclusives.

The album reached number seventy on the Hot 200 and number seven on the R&B/hip-hop charts and spawned three singles. The Zooey Deschanel single "Fallinlove2nite" was released on March 17, 2014. It's the second retail single credited to Prince and another person (after "U Make My Sun Shine" with Angie Stone). The three-minute, fifty-two-second version of "Hardrocklover," without albums segues, was released in the United States on July 7, 2015. The album version of "This Could B Us" was released on August 28, 2015. It was the only song that charted, hitting number nineteen on the adult R&B songs chart.

There was no *Hitnrun* tour, although the magical Paisley Park shows in the fall of 2015 incorporated parts of these new songs into longer jams. The most played song was "1000 X's & O's," first played at the O2 in London on August 31, 2007, and then several times in late 2015 and early 2016.

Hitnrun Phase Two (2015)

Hitnrun Phase Two was released December 12, 2015, on Tidal as part of a bundle with *Phase One*. Three days later, it became available individually on iTunes. As a physical CD, it was sold at the January 21, 2016, Paisley Park show before appearing online in April. The album was the last released by Prince during his lifetime. It failed to hit the top 200 but lodged at number forty-three on the R&B/hip-hop charts.

Unlike *Phase One*, which was mainly new on arrival, six of the twelve *Phase Two* tracks had been released online although some in alternate forms. The earliest already available track, "Xtraloveable," a rerecording of an unreleased 1982 track, was released on November 23, 2011, and the most recent, "Baltimore," on May 9, 2015. Two others, a live "Big City" (June 23, 2013) and "Revelation" (September 30, 2014), had been released in edited form.

Phase Two revisits *1999* and *Parade* horn/funk tendencies in some interesting ways. And the production is a highlight—there's actually some space between the instruments on tunes like "Baltimore"—and no Joshua Welton to be heard.

The stars of the show are the horn sections. The Hornheadz power half the songs, and the large-format NPG Hornz hold court on four songs. Prince has used horns before but never to this extent. Beyond the horns, Ida Nielsen is on bass on "Rocknroll Loveaffair," "Screwdriver," and "Big City" and John Blackwell on drums on all but "Stare" and "Groovy Potential."

Album highlights include the "Rocknroll Loveaffair," a catchy if familiar single; the protest track "Baltimore" and its spiritual companion "Black Muse"; and the expansive "Groovy Potential," which does some interesting things in the drum mix. The three quieter songs, "Look at Me, Look at U," the jazzy "When She Comes," and "Revelation," all prove interesting, while in the other direction, "Screwdriver" continues the "Fury" and "Guitar" compact rocker tradition. The only slight drag is the closer "Big City," featuring tour stalwarts Shelby J., Elisa Dease, and Liv Warfield joined by jazz vocalist Ledisi. It's a tad too cartoonish.

The album featured four singles. "Xtraloveable" (as "Extraloveable") was released digitally in November 2011 without horns. It failed to chart. An edit of "Rock and Roll Love Affair" was released for radio in the United States on September 17, 2012, where it reached number twenty-two on the adult contemporary chart. The album version of "Screwdriver" was released on February 4, 2013. The next day, a "Remix," featuring 3rdEyeGirl, was released on 3rdEyeGirl.com. "Baltimore" was released as above.

There was no *Phase Two* tour, but tracks were played live as far back as 2010. Every song except "Groovy Potential," which was never played live, was performed during the 2016 solo shows. This seems to show that Prince considered this album as worthy new material.

4ever (2016)

Released on November 22, 2016, seven months after Prince's death, *4Ever* was a 2016 holiday cash-in. It's the fourth pre–name change compilation, and few rarities surface among the forty tracks spread over two discs. But it does include some beautiful Herb Ritts photographs.

The new track "Moonbeam Levels" is a dreamy but minor track from the *1999* sessions. It would have been out of place on that album. Often mistitled "A Better Place to Die" on bootlegs, the song was performed live three times: once in 1983 and twice in August 2013 during Prince's piano set.

"Batdance (Edit)" marks the first time any *Batman*-era singles have been collected. *4Ever* also includes the first commercial compilation of eight single edits and remixes: "Let's Work," "Little Red Corvette," "Girls & Boys," "Alphabet St.," "Glam Slam," and "Nothing Compares 2 U," "Gett Off (Single Remix)," and "7." "Mountains" and "Sexy M.F." appear on a compilation for the first time without extra sound effects. It also marked the first compilation of the single versions of "Let's Go Crazy" and "Take Me with U," both soon rereleased on the 2017 *Purple Rain* reissue.

The compilation reached number thirty-five on the *Billboard* top 200 and number three on the R&B albums chart, resting on both charts for about six months. There were no singles.

Purple Rain Deluxe Expanded Edition (2017)

After *4Ever*, the estate and Warner Bros. got down to business with *Purple Rain Deluxe*. *Deluxe* was released on June 23, 2017, in a two-CD format and *Expanded Edition* in a four-disc format. The two-disc edition includes a 2015 remaster of the original sound track (brighter but not tremendously different) and a disc of rare material "From the Vault & Previously Unreleased." The four-disc set also includes "Single Edits & B-Sides" and the DVD of the 1985 VHS release *Prince and the Revolution: Live*. The 2015 remaster of the original album was also reissued on 180-gram vinyl.

The eleven tracks on "From the Vault and Previously Unreleased" are a mix of songs that had been widely circulating unofficially in some form and a few that were rumored but noncirculating. Although credited to Prince and The Revolution, they're Prince recordings unless otherwise noted.

The highlight "new" track is "Love and Sex," a full-on rager that sounds like "America" got real angry. The song was voted by fans for inclusion on the never-released *Crystal Ball Volume II*. The slight "Katrina's Paper Dolls" and The slow-paced "Wonderful Ass" suffered a similar fate. "Velvet Kitty Cat" is cute but doesn't add much to the legacy.

Among the previously released tracks, "Computer Blue" makes its full-length debut with the inclusion of "Hallway Speech," and *Graffiti Bridge*'s "We Can Funk" gets more primordial with "We Can F**k" (a much superior version). Prince's studio version of "The Dance Electric," gifted to Andre Cymone in 1985, finally surfaces. The sparse "Electric Intercourse" gets its studio release, while "Our Destiny/Roadhouse Garden," highlights of the June 7, 1984, First Avenue show, are oddly conjoined in their debuts. "Possessed" and "Father's Song," both *Purple Rain* tour mainstays, also see their studio debuts.

Only "Love and Sex," "Wonderful Ass," "Velvet Kitty Cat," and "Katrina's Paper Dolls" were never performed live.

This isn't exactly the collection that a hard-core fan would produce, but it's a good start.

Anthology: 1995–2010 (2018)

Anthology: 1995–2010 is a digital collection of thirty-seven previously released tracks that draws from 1995's *The Gold Experience* (six songs) through 20Ten ("Future Soul Song"). It was released on NPG Records on multiple platforms on August 17, 2018, through a new deal with Sony's Legacy Recordings, along with twenty-three original content albums from which the tracks are culled (although there's nothing from either *The Vault* or *Girl 6*). The collection is an essential introduction to the period for those who weren't paying attention, while the experienced ear can enjoy a different way of listening to these familiar, second-tier hits that all appear for the first time on a Prince studio compilation.

Piano & a Microphone 1983 (2018)

Piano & a Microphone 1983 is the fourth posthumous LP release and the first to feature entirely unreleased material. Clocking in at under thirty-five minutes, the nine-track piano rehearsal, recorded at the Kiowa Trail Home Studio, circulated among fans since the late 1980s, albeit in cringe-worthy quality.

Prince released five of these tracks in finished form ("17 Days," "A Case of You," "Strange Relationship," "International Lover," and "Purple Rain"), and none of these versions add much insight into his creative process. The year 1983 weighs heavily on both "Wednesday," a slight, Jill Jones–associated *Purple Rain* outtake, and "Cold Coffee and Cocaine," which finds Prince in Jamie Starr humble-brag mode. "Why the Butterflies" (aka "Mama") is perhaps the least structured and most ethereal of any released Prince song (shades of "God"), while "Mary Don't You Weep" is well structured and long enduring, a Civil War–era Negro spiritual that also provided lyrical inspiration for Simon and Garfunkel's "Bridge over Troubled Water."

The album peaked at number eleven on the *Billboard* top 200. There was no radio single, but a three-minute, fourteen second, seven-inch version of "17 Days (Piano Version)," backed with "1999" (single edit), was attached to the cover of the October 2018 German *Rolling Stone*. "Mary Don't You Weep" was featured in Spike Lee's *BlacKkKlansman*.

While it's great to have this recording in pristine quality, the execution is disappointing. This short set should have been part of a larger collection, such as an early solo rehearsals collection or a live 1983 collection with the complete August 3 show, or a bonus disc on a 2016 Piano & a Microphone set.

Originals (2019)

The first Prince posthumous "concept" album, *Originals*, collects fifteen Prince demo and guide-vocal versions of songs he wrote, recorded, and gave to other artists but never released. All but one song ("Love . . . They Will Be Done") was recorded in the 1980s. The tunes were selected by Prince Estate representative Troy Carter and Jay-Z, whose Tidal service offered digital access on Prince's 2019 birthday, two weeks prior to the June 21 physical releases. The collection attempts to please both serious fans, who already have most of these songs in lesser quality, and casual fans, who might be interested in hearing what radio drive-time classic "Manic Monday" sounded like before the Bangles got hold of it.

All but two of the songs ("Manic Monday" and Kenny Rogers's "You're My Love") were created for offshoot bands and protégés. More than a quarter of the songs were given to Sheila E. ("Noon Rendezvous," "Holly Rock," "The Glamorous Life," and "Dear Michaelangelo"), and another two were deeded to The Time ("Jungle Love" and "Gigolos Get Lonely Too"). Semiautonomous bands Mazarati ("100 MPH") and The Family ("Nothing Compares 2 U") are each represented with one track, and the rest of the set finds Prince channeling his female POV with Vanity 6's "Make-up," Apollonia 6's "Sex Shooter," Jill Jones's "Baby, You're a Trip," Martika's "Love . . . Thy Will Be Done," and Taja Sevelle's "Wouldn't You Love to Love Me?"

This version of "Nothing Compares 2 U" was released as a single in April 2018. Prince had previously released the song as an NPG duet with Rosie Gaines in 1993. Beyond "Nothing Compares 2 U," which was among his dozen most performed songs, "Jungle Rock," "Holly Rock," "The Glamorous Life," and "Love . . . Thy Will Be Done" were played live in complete versions on occasion, the latter two often with female vocalists. "Noon Rendezvous" was played only a handful of times but was a highlight of the 1984 birthday show.

While you can't argue with the quality of the material, from a fan's perspective, *Originals* feels like another stopgap money grab. Hopefully, this is just a prelude to a comprehensive, archival future in which "Make-Up" isn't part of a thematic hodgepodge but is part of a Vanity 6 reissue that includes the original album, single edits, and all of Prince's Hookers and Vanity 6 demos, guides, and other outtakes. That would be a real wet dream.

1999 Super Deluxe

The Prince Estate released its fifth physical posthumous album, *1999 Super Deluxe*, on November 29, 2019, one month after the release of *The Beautiful Ones*, Prince's cowritten memoir, and just five months after *Originals*. The two-CD *Deluxe* includes a 2019 remaster of the original LP and an almost exhaustive collection of eighteen single variants and B-sides, including such previously uncollected rarities as "D.M.S.R. (Edit)" from the Tom Cruise film *Risky Business*, the Australian "Delirious (Edit)," and mono promo-only edits of the title track and "Let's Pretend We're Married." Still, M.I.A. is a "Delirious" mono promo-only edit.

The *Super Deluxe* edition adds two CDs covering twenty-four tracks from the Vault (recorded from November 1981 to January 1983), a CD of the Masonic Hall late show in Detroit (November 30, 1982), and a DVD of the show at the Summit in Houston (December 29, 1982). The DVD is also included with the ten-LP Vinyl *Super Deluxe* edition.

Eleven of the Vault songs are alternate versions of released songs. "Moonbeam Levels" appears here as a 2019 remaster, slightly longer than the *4Ever* version. "Delirious (Full Length)," "Something in the Water (Does Not Compute)," and "International Lover (Take 1) [Live in Studio]" all feature on the original LP. The earlier version of "Let's Pretend We're Married" B-side "Irresistible Bitch" is sparse, angry, and desperate, mixed here with an earlier version of "Partyman" B-side "Feel U Up." "1999" B-side "How Come U Don't Call Me Anymore (Take 2)" is jaw-dropping: warm, ambient, and better than the original. "Possessed (1982 Version)" is more jarring than the *Purple Rain Deluxe* version.

Two songs here first surfaced on *Graffiti Bridge*: "Can't Stop This Feeling I've Got" and "Bold Generation." The former is punchy and punky, propelled by all the energy lacking on the 1990 LP. The latter is a dry run for "New Power Generation," free of New Jack production and thankfully lacking funky weapons.

"Lady Cab Driver/I Wanna Be Your Lover/Little Red Corvette (Tour Demo)" is the real oddity here. Recorded in Lakeland, Florida, in January 1983, Prince archivist Michael Howe says it was designed to give the band an idea of how the medley would be performed live (although a 1983 Lakeland rehearsal has the first and third songs performed in their entirety). The February 1, 1983, Lakeland show bombed, and the medley was quickly dropped.

The thirteen new songs here, about half of which had been circulating among fans since the late 1980s, provide an instructive glimpse as Prince reinvents himself, transitioning from the compact guitar-based pop/New Wave sensibility of *Dirty Mind/Controversy* to the expansive, experimental, and electronic delights of *1999*. The two new-to-fans highlights are "Money Don't Grow on Trees," a breezy pop song reminiscent of "Why You Wanna Treat Me So Bad," and the long-sought-after "Vagina," its demo-feel bright guitar supporting a story about a half boy, half girl.

"Purple Music" is a longtime fan favorite finally available in pristine audio. It's an experimental, ambitious eleven-minute antidrug tune, often called "So High," with echoes of "Movie Star," "All the Critics Love U in New York," and "Controversy," among others. Like "Crystal Ball," it seems like an overture for a larger project, one that also was never completed (or was it?). The song also circulates as a twenty-minute piano rehearsal. Prince played the song regularly on 2016's Piano & a Microphone Tour.

Also well known to fans, "Do Yourself a Favor," is a stretched-out, smooth pop song that was previously released by songwriter Pepe Willie in 1986 as "If You See Me" by 94 East, featuring Prince on guitar.

"You're All I Want," "No Call U," "Turn It Up," and "Yah, You Know" all mine the same Cab Calloway jumpin' jive as "Delirious." Both "You're All I Want," later rerecorded as "U're All I Want," and "Turn It Up," here without the instrumental "Part 2," were included in 2002 *Crystal Ball II* voting and rejected by fans for the never-released LP.

Both "If It'll Make U Happy" and "Don't Let Him Fool Ya" are catchy if somewhat generic R&B workouts. The latter was offered to Bonnie Raitt in 1987. "Teacher, Teacher" is tight and poppy, with a fresh, clean drum sound. It was later reworked with Wendy and Lisa for *Dream Factory*.

"Rearrange" is a funky dance number that musically trends toward "Lady Cab Driver"; lyrically, it's a typical "cool us against uncool them" catalog entry. The instrumental "Colleen" sounds like Prince was experimenting with sounds and rhythms. It uses engineer Peggy McCreary's middle name and was given to her as a birthday present in 1982.

The bottom line is that this is great. *1999 Super Deluxe* is a giant leap ahead of its *Purple Rain* brethren. But we're greedy, and we do want more—we want it all! Fans bemoaned the omission of well-known tracks "Lust U Always," and "Extraloveable," both lost to #MeToo sensibilities and the absence of at least a dozen known outtakes, multiple alternates, and scores of *Originals*-like demo/guide songs for The Time and The Hookers/Vanity 6. If the Vault does contain enough material to release an album a year for a century, may we all live long enough for this additional material to see the dawn.

36

Prince Esta Muerto

Death and Legacy

Prince and 3rdEyeGirl wrapped up the loose two-year Hit N Run II tour with two shows at the Warner Theater in Washington, DC, on June 14, 2015. These were Prince's last scheduled shows with a full band in the United States and the last 3rdEyeGirl shows. He disappeared until a series of six Paisley Park shows in October and November, including a Judith Hill *Back in Time* release party. These funky, expansive shows featured a new band, drummer Kirk Johnson, guitarist Donna Grantis, and newcomer MonoNeon on bass.

The Paisley Park shows were to be followed by a November European tour—Spotlight . . . Prince Piano & and Microphone—starting on November 21 in Vienna. This tour was postponed and then canceled after the November 13 terrorist attacks in Paris that killed 130 people, including eighty-nine at an Eagles of Death Metal show at Le Bataclan. Prince played Le Bataclan three times and in 2002 released a live single recorded there.

On New Year's Day 2016, Prince played his last full-band show. The show, which swapped in Ida Nielsen on bass, was hosted by Chelsea FC owner Roman Abramovich on the tiny Caribbean island of Saint Barthélemy. Three weeks later, he debuted the Piano & a Microphone concept with a two-show Gala Event at Paisley Park. While Prince had played solo keyboard sets during concerts as early as 1982, this marked his first advertised solo show. An eleven-date tour of Australia and New Zealand followed in February.

The North American leg started with two February 28 Oakland theater shows, followed by a March 4 arena date. He played guitar live the last time on March 12 at Chanhassen's Fireside Theater, guesting on "Let the Good Times Roll" as part of a Ray Charles tribute. On March 18, he performed a sampler set following the announcement of his forthcoming biography: *The Beautiful Ones*. He then proceeded to shows in Toronto (March 21) and Montreal (March 25).

Then things took a turn for the worse.

Prince had two April 7 shows scheduled for Atlanta, but both were postponed the same day because of the flu. Reports indicate that he instead spent the day consulting with his Minneapolis doctor about tackling an opioid addiction.

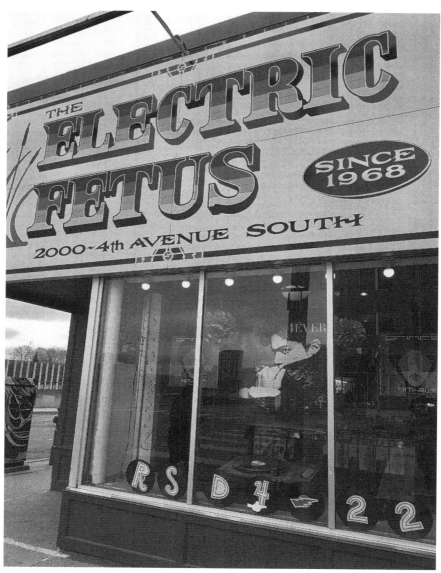

Less than a week before his death Prince purchased six LPs at Minneapolis's Electric Fetus record store to celebrate Record Store Day. Record Store Day 2017 featured six limited-edition Prince late-1980s twelve-inch vinyl re-releases and an exclusive "1999/Little Red Corvette" seven-inch picture disc.

(Courtesy Femke Niehof)

On April 12, he tweeted a Paisley Park photo of a "purple present from Yamaha": a new grand piano. Two days later, he was onstage at Atlanta's Fox Theater making up the postponed shows. A highlight of the first show is "Heroes," a tribute to David Bowie, whose January death had shocked the music world.

After the show, Prince's plane was returning to Minneapolis when it was forced to land in Moline, Illinois, for an "unresponsive passenger." Hill was sitting across a table from Prince when he passed out. She alerted Johnson, and the plane landed. Prince came to on the runway when he received a shot of Narcan, which counteracts opioid overdoses. Prince stayed the night in the hospital, requesting a viewing of *Zootopia* before returning to Minneapolis later that day.

On April 17, he played "Chopsticks" at a Paisley Park dance party, his last live appearance. The next day, "Black Sweat" from Atlanta was Tidal's Purple Pick of the Week and Prince's last release.

On Thursday, April 21, Prince's body was discovered in a Paisley Park elevator. He was declared dead at 10:07 a.m. On June 2, the Midwest Medical Examiner's Office announced that the cause of death was an accidental Fentanyl overdose.

Legal Aftermath

In April 2017, Minneapolis-area authorities unsealed records in the investigation into Prince's death. Authorities were unable to figure out how Prince secured the illegal Fentanyl but discovered Oxycodone prescriptions for Prince in Johnson's name. The records imply that Prince had been addicted to opioid painkillers. No criminal charges have been filed in the case.

Prince left no will, which led to a mad scramble to secure his estate. With no will and no immediate family, Minneapolis-based Bremer Trust was appointed to run Prince's estate. In January 2017, a court put Comerica Bank in charge. Soon after, Comerica installed Spotify's Troy Carter as their Prince point person.

Comerica was in charge while the courts were figuring out Prince's rightful heirs; many stepped forward, some for DNA testing. In May 2017, a Minnesota judge declared Prince's sister Tyka Nelson and his half siblings Sharon Nelson, Norrine Nelson, John R. Nelson, Omarr Baker, and Alfred Jackson as the rightful heirs. Known as the Prince Estate, the group controls Prince's music, his property, and his likeness.

Under Bremer and Comerica administration, the estate partnered with Graceland to open Paisley Park to tours and establish a yearly weeklong celebration. Most important, they negotiated the February 2017 $31 million deal with Universal Music Group to release Prince's post-1995 work. This deal was voided in July 2017 when Universal Music Group realized potential rights conflicted with Warner Bros.'s rights. Sony picked up the rights in 2018 for their Legacy

Recordings label. Carter also signed off on a 2018 UK Channel 4 documentary about Prince's final years.

April 2017 also saw the online release of the *Deliverance*. The six-track EP was assembled by engineer Ian Boxill and released on Rogue Music Alliance. Comerica and Paisley Park Enterprises quickly moved against the release, gaining an injunction on May 22. In April 2019, Boxill was ordered to pay $4 million restitution to the estate. The EP's six songs—"Deliverance," "I Am," "Touch Me," "Sunrise Sunset," "No One Else," and "I Am (Extended)"—are no longer legally available.

Legacy and Celebration

Prince's death brought forth an immediate and enormous outpouring of grief and tributes. Fans flocked to Minneapolis to pay tribute, covering the Paisley Park fence with all manner of purple appreciations. President Barack Obama took to Facebook, stating, "Few artists have influenced the sound and trajectory of popular music more distinctly," and started his day at the US ambassador's house in London by listening to "Purple Rain" and "Delirious." Nostalgic and mournful tweets from celebrities, including Frank Ocean and Justin Timberlake, and everyday people are too numerous to count. There was so much love.

The charts were ablaze with Prince albums. Twenty albums reentered the *Billboard* top 200, with five charting in the top ten, including chart topper *The Very Best of Prince*. The week of May 14 saw Prince with the top twelve and sixteen of the top twenty spots on the *Billboard* catalog album charts. *The Very Best* and *Purple Rain* swapped the top two catalog chart spots through early July.

And, of course, musicians paid tribute through music. Among the more impressive tributes was Bruce Springsteen's "Purple Rain," Pink Floyd's David Gilmour and his interpolation of "Purple Rain" into his signature guitar solo in "Comfortably Numb," and Lin-Manuel Miranda and the cast of *Hamilton*'s "Let's Go Crazy" recitation and dance.

Among televised tributes, Bruno Mars's *Purple Rain*–era impersonation at the 2017 Grammys stands out, as does Madonna's *Billboard* Music Awards performance. The most comprehensive was BET's evening-long tribute, featuring The Roots, Stevie Wonder, Sheila E., and Jennifer Hudson among a score of performers.

The official Prince Tribute Concert took place on October 13, 2016, at the Xcel Energy Center in St. Paul, Minnesota. Stevie Wonder, Chaka Khan, and The Time headlined, backed by different incarnations of the NPG and offset by Mayte's belly dancing.

From 2017 on, competing Prince backing/cover bands toured the United States and Europe. The NPG, playing mostly later Prince songs, included

Besides pizza, Naples, Italy, is perhaps best known for its elaborate Nativity scenes called presepi. Unlike traditional Nativity scenes that include only the Holy Family, the Three Wise Men, and manger animals, Neapolitan presepi also include celebrities and sports stars, especially the recently departed. Prince made his presepi debut in 2016 and is shown here alongside Christmas 2016 departee George Michael. PrinceNativity—Have you had your birth sign today?

(Author's collection)

Johnson and a core band of Morris Hayes, Tommy Barbarella, Sonny Thompson, and Levi Seacer Jr. plus numerous singers and Michael Bland on occasion. The Revolution played a mid-1980s selection of hits, featuring the core *Purple Rain* tour lineup of Wendy and Lisa, Brown Mark, Bobby Z., and Dr. Fink.

Even a year after Prince's death, other tributes continued. In August 2018, cosmetics company Pantone named a deep ultra–purple color Love Symbol #2 after Prince's official symbol's name and further named it their 2018 color of the year. Carolina Panthers quarterback Cam Newton wore *Purple Rain* cleats on the practice field, complete with the era's white ruffles. And Massachusetts's Ipswich Brewery created and marketed an American sour ale called Cranberry Beret.

Prince's autobiography, *The Beautiful Ones*, cowritten and curated by *Paris Review* editor Dan Piepenbring, was released on October 29, 2019. As of late 2019, a Prince Netflix documentary and a "Mamma Mia–style" movie are in the works. Can a Broadway play be far off?

The greatest tribute to Prince will be that future generations hear, enjoy, and are influenced by his musical genius, once again beginning endlessly.

Selected Bibliography

From a February 1976 *Central High Pioneer* article on, Prince has been covered by countless print, video, and online sources. These books, websites, and Internet articles were the most helpful in creating this portrait of Prince.

Books

Azhar, Mobeen. *Prince: Stories from the Purple Underground*. London: Carlton Books, 2016.

Bream, Jon. *Prince: Inside the Purple Reign*. New York: Scribner, 1984.

Draper, Jason. *Prince: Chaos, Disorder, and Revolution*. New York: Backbeat Books, 2011.

———. *Prince: Life & Times*. New York: Chartwell Books, 2016.

Garcia, Mayte. *The Most Beautiful: My Life with Prince*. New York: Hachette Books, 2017.

Greenman, Ben. *Dig If You Will the Picture: Funk, Sex, God, & Genius in the Music of Prince*. New York: Henry Holt and Company, 2017.

Hahn, Alex. *Possessed: The Rise and Fall of Prince*. New York: Billboard Books, 2003.

Hahn, Alex, and Laura Tiebert. *The Rise of Prince: 1958–1988*. Boston: Madcat Press, 2017.

Hill, Dave. *Prince: A Pop Life*. New York: Harmony Books, 1989.

Light, Alan. *Let's Go Crazy: Prince and the Making of* Purple Rain. New York: Atria, 2014.

Morton, Brian. *Prince: A Thief in the Temple*. Edinburgh: Cangate, 2007.

Nilsen, Per. *Dancemusicsexromance. Prince: The First Decade*. London: SAF Publishing, 2003.

———. *Prince: A Documentary*. London: Omnibus Press, 1993/1990.

Nilsen, Per, and jooZt Mattheij with the Uptown Staff. *The Vault: The Definitive Guide to the Musical World of Prince*. Linghem: Uptown, 2004.

Parke, Steve. *Picturing Prince: An Intimate Portrait*. London: Cassell Illustrated, 2017.

Prince and Randee St. Nicholas. *21 Nights*. New York: Atria, 2008.

Ro, Ronin. *Prince: Inside the Music and the Masks*. New York: St. Martin's Griffin, 2016.

Shahidi, Asfhin. *Prince: A Private View*. New York: St. Martin's Press, 2017.

Thorne, Matt. *Prince: The Man and His Music*. Chicago: Bolden, 2016.

Touré. *I Would Die 4 U: Why Prince Became an Icon*. New York: Atria, 2013.

Tudahl, Duane. *Prince and the* Purple Rain *Era Studio Sessions: 1983 and 1984*. Lanham, MD: Rowan & Littlefield, 2018.

Wall, Mick. *Prince: Purple Reign*. London: Orion, 2016.

Walsh, Jim. *Gold Experience: Following Prince in the '90s*. Minneapolis: University of Minnesota Press, 2017.

Websites

https://www.discogs.com—Discogs. Deep, international catalog of all CD/vinyl releases.

en.wikipedia.org—The Free Encyclopedia. Useful starting point for information about Prince and associates.

prince.org—Prince.Org: Online Fan Community. This is the most important site for day-to-day Prince news and discussion.

princeonlinemuseum.com—Prince Online Museum. The historical warehouse for Prince's online presence.

princevault.com—Prince Vault: The Prince and Prince Related Artist Encyclopedia. Based on years of *Uptown* research, this is the most well-researched site for Prince history.

sites.google.com/site/princediscog/home—A Comprehensive Prince Discography. The most user friendly and detailed of countless discography sites.

startribune.com—*Minneapolis Star Tribune*. The best American Prince newspaper coverage https://www.superdeluxeedition.com—Super Deluxe Edition. UK site with deep, exclusive coverage of rock/pop CD/vinyl/DVD reissues.

www.billboard.com—*Billboard*. The go-to for chart information and daily Prince business news.

www.purplemusic.mynetcologne.de/the_time.html—Unofficial Morris Day and The Time website.

www.setlist.fm—The Setlist Wiki. The site for searchable Prince and associates set lists.

www.theguardian.com—*The Guardian*. The best non-US English Prince coverage.

Too numerous to list, this book also relied on individual artist websites and information pages.

Internet Articles

Aswad, Jem. "Prince's Vault Suffered from 'Water Damage, Mold, Degradation,' at Paisley Park, Court Documents Say." *Variety*. November 14, 2017. http://variety.com/2017/biz/news/princes-vault-suffered-from-water-damage-mold-degradation-at-paisley-park-court-documents-say-1202614267.

———. "Sheila E. Looks Back on Prince: Their Collaborations, Engagement & Lifelong Love." *Billboard*. April 26, 2016. https://www.billboard.com/articles/news/7341899/sheila-e-prince-memorial.

Beaumont-Thomas, Ben. "Prince's Sound Engineer, Susan Rogers: 'He Needed to Be the Alpha Male to Get Things Done.'" *The Guardian*. November 9, 2017. https://www.theguardian.com/music/2017/nov/09/princes-sound-engineer-susan-rogers-he-needed-to-be-the-alpha-male-to-get-things-done?CMP=share_btn_fb.

Best, Tony. "Prince Tapped 'Godfather of the Music Video' Chuck Statler to Helm the Ill-Fated Film *The Second Coming*." *Wax Poetics*. April 21, 2016. http://www.waxpoetics.com/blog/features/articles/prince-second-coming-ill-fated-film.

Cole, George. "Interview: Eric Leeds." *The Last Miles*. No date. http://www.thelastmiles.com/interviews-eric-leeds.php.

Dyes, K. Nicola. "The Question of U: Jill Jones Talks 2 Beautiful Nights." *The Beautiful Nights Blog*. February 17, 2013. http://beautifulnightschitown.blogspot.com/2013/02/the-question-of-u-jill-jones-talks-2.html.

Geslani, Michelle. "Rick James Once Threatened to Kick Prince's Scrawny Ass." *Consequence of Sound*. April 4, 2016. https://consequenceofsound.net/2016/04/rick-james-once-threatened-to-kick-princes-scrawny-ass.

Greenwald, David. "Liv Warfield Shares Prince's Lessons and Legacy in Blues Festival Tribute." *Oregon Live: The Oregonian*. July 7, 2016. http://www.oregonlive.com/bluesfest/index.ssf/2016/06/liv_warfield_what_prince_taught_us_blues_festival.html.

Guttman, Dick. "Prince … Launching 'Purple Rain.'" *Huffington Post*. April 22, 2016. https://www.huffingtonpost.com/dick-guttman/prince-the-director-launch_b_9752282.html.

Hann, Michael. "'He Was a Huge Fan': How Prince Became the Patron of the Psychedelic Underground." *The Guardian*. April 24, 2016. https://www

.theguardian.com/music/musicblog/2016/apr/24/he-was-a-huge-fan-how
-prince-became-the-patron-of-the-psychedelic-underground.

Heigl, Alex. "If I Was Your Girlfriend: The Extended History of Madonna and Prince's Relationship." *People.* May 20, 2016. http://people.com/celebrity/ billboard-music-awards-2016-madonna-and-prince-history-of-relation ship.

Hiatt, Brian. "A Final Visit with Prince: Rolling Stone's Lost Cover Story." *Rolling Stone.* May 2, 2016. http://www.rollingstone.com/music/ features/a-final-visit-with-prince-rolling-stones-lost-cover-story-20160502.

Hyman, Dan. "Uncovering Michael Jackson's Bitter Rivalry with Prince." *Esquire.* October 7, 2015. http://www.esquire.com/entertainment/music/ a38630/michael-jackson-mj-biography.

Johnson, Cheryl. "C.J.: Memories 'Billy Jack Bitch,' Prince's 'Biggest Enemy.'" *Minneapolis Star Tribune.* April 24, 2016. http://www.startribune. com/c-j-prince-was-indelibly-interesting/376786671.

Lentz, Andrew. "Hannah Ford: The Princess Ride." *Drum!* No date. http:// drummagazine.com/hannah-ford-the-princess-ride.

Randle, Chris. "Bootleg Prince Album 'The Dawn' Fashioned a Language from the Unsayable." *Village Voice.* April 26, 2016. https://www.villagevoice. com/2016/04/26/bootleg-prince-album-the-dawn-fashioned-a-language- from-the-unsayable.

Rudulph, Heather Wood. "Get That Life: How I Joined Prince's Band 3RDEYE- GIRL." *Cosmopolitan.* February 9, 2015. http://www.cosmopolitan.com/ career/interviews/a36198/get-that-life-donna-grantis-prince-3rdeyegirl.

Shah, Hasit. "Poor Lonely Computer: Prince's Misunderstood Relation- ship with the Internet." *The Record: Music News from NPR.* March 16, 2016. https://www.npr.org/sections/therecord/2016/03/08/469627962/ poor-lonely-computer-princes-misunderstood-relationship-with-the-in- ternet.

Sigelman, Danny. "3rdEyeGirl's Donna Grantis on How Prince Inspired the Sound of Her New Band." *City Pages.* August 4, 2017. http://www. citypages.com/music/3rdeyegirls-donna-grantis-on-how-prince-inspired- the-sound-of-her-new-band/438421973.

Signorini, Renatta. "Ligonier Township Man Who Toured with Prince Calls Him 'Quiet Lion.'" *TribLIVE.* April 21, 2016. http://triblive.com/news/ westmoreland/10347914-74/prince-blistan-musician.

Williams, Elrick. "My Experiences with Prince." *The Africa Channel.* April 21, 2016. http://theafricachannel.com/my-experiences-with-prince.

Index